THE METROPOLITAN OPERA

The Metropolitan Opera

THE FIRST TWENTY-FIVE YEARS

1883-1908

BY

Paul E. Eisler

WITH A FOREWORD
BY
Robert Tuggle
Director of Archives
Metropolitan Opera Association

NORTH RIVER PRESS, INC.
CROTON-ON-HUDSON, NEW YORK

Library of Congress Cataloging in Publication Data

Eisler, Paul E., 1919–1978
  The Metropolitan Opera.

  Bibliography: p.
  Includes index.
  1. Metropolitan Opera (New York, N.Y.)   I. Title.
ML1711.8.N3M426   1984   782.1'09747'1   84-6113
ISBN 0-88427-046-7

*Photographs on pages 14, 37, 81, 130, 167, 187, 190, 202, 226, and 255 are from the Metropolitan Opera
Association Archives and are reproduced by permission.*

Manufactured in the United Sates of America

DEDICATED TO THE MEMORY OF
MY FATHER

Contents

LIST OF ILLUSTRATIONS

Foreword

During 1983–84, the Metropolitan Opera's one hundredth anniversary season, there were banners along Fifth Avenue and exhibitions in five New York City museums, as well as others in Atlanta, Dallas, Detroit and Cleveland. In Washington, D. C., both the Smithsonian Institution and the Library of Congress displayed Metropolitan Opera memorabilia. Back in New York, the Met was honored by breakfast at Tiffany's, a reconstruction at Saks Fifth Avenue of the opera house as it appeared in 1927, Christmas windows at Macy's, and a dinner dance at B. Altman's. There was non-stop treatment by newspapers, magazines and wire services; and countless interviews on radio and television, local, national and international. And books: books on the whole hundred years, the rivalry of the first three seasons, the singers of the Gatti-Casazza era, and the problems dealt with during one recent season. After all this, after the Gala performances, the festivities and celebrations, after the exhaustive attention of the media, and the total immersion of the senses, is there anything new to be said about the Metropolitan Opera and its romantic checkered past? More important still, is there at this point anything one could bear to hear further?

Paul Eisler, in his doctoral thesis for Boston University, hit upon the happy device of investigating the first twenty-five years by referring almost completely to reviews in the *New York Times* and the *Tribune*. Much of this material will be completely new to the twentieth-century reader. Going back to the spring of 1880, Dr. Eisler gives us the most extensive treatment yet to appear of what happened when a group of socially ambitious music lovers decided to build an opera house. In the twentieth century we have seen at Lincoln Center for the Performing Arts just how perilous a venture it may be to put up buildings and attempt to create artistic institutions to match them. In the case of the Chamber Music Society one sees that a gifted board of directors, artistic management, popular support and an ideal building intertwined with seeming inevitability to form a unique musical organization. Moving from Alice Tully Hall next door into the more volatile atmosphere of live drama at the Vivian Beaumont Theatre one finds a well-intended enterprise in which little has gone right.

It is striking to see the day by day involvement of the Met's board of directors in every detail of the construction of the building, choice of a general manager and specifications for the opening season. Often criticized for wanting an opera house as a vehicle for social display, the board should be commended for choosing music rather than yachts, opera rather than race horses, and for doing it in such a way that an institution of permanence resulted.

The financial and artistic problems of the first season in Italian were solved with amazing dispatch by the switch to opera in German for 1884–85 and six subsequent seasons. When things began to succeed with some regularity, reference to acoustics (not just a Lincoln Center phenomenon) and the size and chilliness of the auditorium all but vanish from reviews. However, at the end of the first season, the *New York Times* printed a description of the Metropolitan Opera House that will astonish opera goers who fondly remember the warmth of the old house: "It is hard to discover how the cause of music can be advanced or the establishment of the opera on a sound basis can be effected in the Metropolitan Opera-house....It ought to be a rule...that no house for operatic or theatrical performances which could seat comfortably more than 2,500 people...should ever be erected....But the size of the Metropolitan Opera-house has been its boast and its snare....The voice becomes diluted, its quality changes, and, as the singer forces his tones to make them reach his distant hearers, half the pleasure is lost—and no talk of 'acoustic properties' is a counterbalance of the fact that the proper dimensions have been exceeded...."

It is astonishing to see how quickly some of the great names in operatic history were associated with the Metropolitan Opera: Marcella Sembrich the first year, Lilli Lehmann when the house was only two years old, the de Reszkes when it was eight, both Emma Calvé and Nellie Melba when it was ten, and Enrico Caruso when it was only twenty. There are unfamiliar reviews of them all in Dr. Eisler's book as well as those of many other important names. Significantly, the critics of the period were able to describe voices in a way that decades later still conveys something of the way a particular instrument functioned and sounded. Also, in the treatment of personalities, music journals in the nineteenth and early twentieth centuries spoke out with more candor than would be expected a century later. A description of the young Walter Damrosch enlarges our understanding of his artistic career: "....Mr. Walter Damrosch, after the company's return, will be withdrawn from public sight as a conductor. To some people this will be a serious loss of amusement, for certainly no more amusing sight can be imagined than this youthful Adoni[s] sitting for a quarter of an hour before each rising of the curtain in the conductor's chair and leering at the ladies in the boxes and making the most of his opportunities for demonstrating his personal vanity."

As a by-product of the reviews there is a large body of unfamiliar information about audience and artist behavior at performances. Of the conductor Cleofonte Campanini's first season debut it is reported that "At the close of the first act he received gifts of flowers and a handsome scarf-ring." Apparently, conductors would take bows throughout a performance if at all possible. Of Anton Seidl's debut two seasons later: "Herr Seidl was summoned before the curtain after the first act; his reappearance at the end of the second was injudicious, and prompts the suggestion that a musician of genuine talent needs no aid from self-assertion to establish his claims in this country."

The 1902 gala performance achieved a formality of dress probably never witnessed before or since in New York: "No exceptions were made to the rule requiring evening dress and money was refunded to those who appeared in other attire. A speculator sold a place in the family circle to one man in a sack coat for $8 and returned the money when the purchaser was not permitted to enter. The Janitor of the Opera House, even, wore evening dress and silk hat when, as soon as word was received that the Prince had left the club, he appeared before the entrance and spread from the door to the curb a gorgeous red carpet."

And an account of Caruso's first *Carmen* in French informs us of the young tenor's stage deportment as well as what an artist could expect from an audience in the way of applause: "It was strange that in neither of his entrances in the first two acts was a hand given to welcome him. In the second act, after his flower song, his ingrained Italian impulse to acknowledge applause even in the most affecting situations brought him the tribute of a burst of laughter from the audience."

However, the greatest pleasure in Dr. Eisler's book lies in once again participating in that unique Metropolitan Opera game, choosing the general manager. What have Ernest Gye, Herbert F. Gye, Charles Mapleson, R. E. Hutchinson, Italo Campanini, Col. James Henry Mapleson, Max Strakosch, Carl Rosa, Signor Pollini (of Hamburg) and Anton Schott in common? Why, they were all mentioned in the 1880s either by press, public or board of directors as potential managers of the opera company.

Perhaps one reason for the Metropolitan Opera's longevity is that the pleasures and the disappointments, the challenges and the triumphs, seem infinitely renewable. As these lines are written, we once again await the appointment of a new general manager. When this is done and he assumes his position, he will find that the game continues as press and public alike greet his every move with applause and dismay, usually both at the same time. On its one hundredth and first birthday, the Metropolitan Opera remains endlessly fascinating.

ROBERT TUGGLE, Director of Archives
Metropolitan Opera Association
May, 1984

Acknowledgments

It would be impossible to express sufficient gratitude to all who have rendered invaluable assistance to the author of this document. Countless librarians, officials at various institutions, and archivists have been unfailingly courteous and helpful in this work.

Special thanks are extended to Dr. Robert A. Choate for his interest, encouragement, and help in preparing this dissertation. Dr. Wilbur Fullbright and the late Dr. Howard Murphy have also been most generous in offering counsel in matters of approach and style.

P.E.E.

PUBLISHER'S ACKNOWLEDGMENT

Paul Eisler died on December 12, 1978. He was mourned by hundreds of former students, colleagues, and friends, among them this publisher, who had met him first in the late 1960s.

Paul and I discussed on numerous occasions when and how to publish his history of the first twenty-five years of the Metropolitan Opera. His father had been an assistant conductor and his mother was a singer during the early years of the organization; Paul himself had sung children's parts in Met productions. He had a lifelong interest in, and affection for, the Met. This book was to have been the capstone to his professional career.

With Paul no longer present however, this has not been an easy book to produce. I am deeply grateful to those who have helped make its appearance possible: to Genevieve Vaughn and Margaret Robinson, two skilled and devoted editors; to Jean Taylor, a sensitive designer, and her compositor helper; and finally to Robert Tuggle, Director of Archives at the Met, who read the book in galleys and offered numerous suggestions for correction or improvement.

I think Paul would be pleased by the results.

W.W.C.

Introduction

The Metropolitan Opera occupies a unique position of eminence in an area of expression often considered unsuited to American tastes. The founding and early history of the Metropolitan established many production techniques and patterns of operation which still exist or have exerted sufficient influence to affect current trends in opera, both artistically and administratively. A peculiar analogy exists in the growth of interest and participation in operatic training and careers on the part of major colleges and universities. The teaching faculties of these centers of learning include on their staffs many retired artists who have been connected with the Metropolitan Opera in some capacity and who are indoctrinated with the problems in opera production and with their solutions as carried out at that institution.

For the past century the Metropolitan Opera has been of far greater importance than the various other groups that have spasmodically produced opera in New York City and elsewhere in the United States. A symbol of the ultimate in operatic musical enterprise in this country, it has earned a reputation as one of the major opera houses of the world. The grandeur and scale of the Metropolitan productions, along with its vast financial structure, have been recognized as exceeding those of the other major opera houses. That the Metropolitan has been a private enterprise, whereas most of its major competitors, such as the Vienna State Opera and La Scala in Milan, have been subsidized by the government, has also made its operation worthy of careful study.

For opera companies in rapidly growing cities where symphony orchestras and repertory theatre have been highly successful, thorough study of the unique features and peculiarities of opera production, and of the financial history of specific operatic ventures, can provide the knowledge that is necessary to succeed in organization and operation.

The early history of the Metropolitan Opera reflected the socioeconomic structure of the nineteenth century. The struggle for social position between the newly acquired railroad wealth and the traditional upper class sheds light on the resultant reorganization of society.

The foregoing are some of the considerations that suggested the study undertaken in this book. The purposes of the study were (1) to investigate the history of the Metropolitan Opera from its inception through the first twenty-five years of its existence, (2) to examine the circumstances contributing to its founding, (3) to ascertain factors involved in the relative success or failure of its various managerial regimes during those years, (4) to document the performances and premieres of note and the backgrounds of leading singers and conductors involved therein, and (5) to cite the critical response from the most respected and important reviewers of the period.

The importance of the study lay primarily in the need for determining the causes for the founding of the Metropolitan and the motives of the original subscribers to the corporation, and for accurately documenting these factors. The various changes in administration were the results of pressures that could better be examined in retrospect than by earlier historians such as Krehbiel. It was essential that this material be reevaluated for its significance in the establishing of opera companies at the present time. Critical analysis of now-legendary singers and conductors was necessary. The comparative influence of public opinion and the restricted groups that support an opera house needed evaluation that had never before been documented. Finally, it was considered essential to examine the financial results that could be assembled, in order to judge the effect of certain policies in opera production on the success, both financial and artistic, of the Metropolitan Opera.

Sources of Data.   The sources employed in research for this study included newspapers, interviews, periodicals, books, and private collections of papers. All issues of the two major New York City newspapers, the *New York Times* and the *New York Tribune*, from 1880 to 1908 inclusive, were examined, as well as certain issues of other New York papers. Periodicals cited included *Musical America, Musical Courier, Harper's New Monthly Magazine,* and *Opera News*, the official publication of the Metropolitan Opera-house Company, Ltd. Another collection in the possession of Columbia, comprised of papers, programs, and letters belonging to Anton Seidl, revealed noteworthy facts concerning Seidl and his contemporaries among the outstanding conductors, composers, and singers of the late nineteenth century.

Interviews with persons actually connected with the Metropolitan during the sity, provided new evidence concerning the founding and early condition of the stock of the Metropolitan Opera-house Company, Ltd. Another collection in the possession of Columbia comprised of papers, programs, and letters belonging to Anton Seidl, revealed noteworthy facts concerning Seidl and his contemporaries among the

Interviews with persons actually connected with the Metropolitan during the years under consideration were of great value and provided new insight into the problems and functions of the organization, particularly during the managerial regimes of Grau and Conried. Included among those interviewed were former Metropolitan conductors Artur Bodanzky and Paul Eisler (father of the author of this study); Katherine Moran Douglas and Hermann Weill, who sang for many years at the Metropolitan; and Finley Jay Shepard, grandson of one of the first stockholders of the corporation, Jay Gould.

A number of books, historical, biographical, and autobiographical, were helpful, both for verifying data and for providing information. Krehbiel's *Chapters of Opera* and Kolodin's *The Metropolitan Opera* were both of significant value as chronological guides to the sequence of events, but had certain limitations. Henry Krehbiel was a journalist and critic on the *New York Tribune*, one of New York's two major newspapers during the twenty-five years covered by this study, and his reviews were deemed of great importance to it. The limitations of his book for the present study were due primarily to its inclusion of all opera in New York City. Because of the vast amount of material involved, Krehbiel was not able to provide the needed depth to his treatment of the Metropolitan Opera. The book's 1911 copyright makes it obvious that new evidence has accumulated since that time. Kolodin's book draws heavily on Krehbiel's, and, in addition, tends to be preponderantly anecdotal.

Seltsam's *Metropolitan Opera Annals* and Eaton's *Opera Caravan* provided valuable information as to casts, dates of performances, and premieres. The Seltsam work concerns itself only with performances at the Metropolitan Opera House; the Eaton book is restricted to tour productions.

Delimitations of the Study.   This book was not intended as a complete compilation of casts, conductors, and such details of all performances during this period in the existence of the Metropolitan Opera. This information can be found in Seltsam's and Eaton's books. Quotations from critical response to performances were mainly restricted to reviews in the *New York Times* and *New York Tribune*. News items concerning activities of interested parties and not dealing with musical performance were taken from the *New York Times*, since examination of other newspapers of the period quickly revealed that they contained the same facts or considerably less information. Singers and conductors of minor importance were generally omitted unless they had bearing on policies or careers of greater import.

Financial data were included when possible; complete figures, however, were not available, and frequently the sources of such figures as could be found were not documented. Undocumented figures were included, but noted as undocumented.

No attempt was made to present a history of early opera in America, but rather only to present the necessary background to understand the musical and economic position of opera in America at the time the Metropolitan Opera was founded.

Any one of several events could mark the beginning of the Metropolitan Opera: the decision to found it; its incorporation; the organization of the company; and finally, the initial performance, at which the company assumed tangible reality. For this book, the existence of the Metropolitan was considered to begin with its date of incorporation.

Definition of Terms.   It was deemed preferable to refer to all resident seasons at the Metropolitan Opera House as being performed by the Metropolitan Opera Company. It should be understood, however, that this was done to avoid the confusion that would have resulted from using the various titles given to the performing organizations by their managers. The reluctance on the part of the stockholders to encourage use of the term Metropolitan Opera was created by their fear of further assessments or responsibilities. The opening season was in actuality presented by the

"Abbey Italian Opera Company," which was in turn followed by the "Damrosch German Opera Company." This second company might well have used the term "Metropolitan Opera Company," since Damrosch was paid a salary and produced his opera at the account of the stockholders. After Damrosch's death the directors became even more closely involved when Edmund C. Stanton, who had acted as Secretary of the Board since the opening of the Metropolitan Opera House, was appointed manager. Nevertheless, the company did not carry the term "Metropolitan" in its title. The return of Abbey, this time with Schoeffel and Grau, did not alter the situation, and when Maurice Grau became the sole manager he advertised his company as the "Maurice Grau Opera Company." That Heinrich Conried had spend most of his life as an actor and theatrical manager may have influenced his decision to identify his opera company with the Metropolitan. At any rate his regime marked the first association of the name with a company, being known as the "Conried Metropolitan Opera Company." The decision to refer to all these companies as the "Metropolitan Opera Company," or a similar title including a reference to the building, seemed the most practical solution, particularly when discussing the years when the Academy of Music was operating in competition and also advertising companies with disassociated names, such as the "Royal Italian Opera Company, Ltd."

The period during which opera in German was presented at the Metropolitan, to the exclusion of all other, created another problem in terminology. Both the artists and administrative staffs, as well as the press, used the phrases "opera in German" and "German opera" interchangeably. Both phrases referred to opera written by a composer of any nationality and originally in any language, but now performed in German. By virtue of this terminology, *Rigoletto* and *Faust* were referred to as German opera when performed at the Metropolitan during the period from 1884 to 1891. After opera began to be produced for the most part in the language of its original libretto, German opera came to be interpreted, properly, as being composed by Germanic people and in the German language. After 1891, except in rare instances, this problem of terminology no longer occurred.

Some of the critical reactions to premiere performances of major works have been included because of their value in interpreting the views and reactions of music patrons of the time. However, unless the experience and attitude of the public and press during the era of the productions are taken into account, it is impossible to judge their response without an unconscious application of modern views distorted by the norms of modern tastes and comparisons. An excellent example is provided by the reviews of the first performance of *Die Walküre* produced at the Metropolitan Opera House. This took place during the season of 1884–85 and preceded the production of any other operas in the Ring cycle. It can be assumed that *Die Walküre* engendered a different response from an audience that was essentially unaccustomed to Wagner's more complicated works than would a first performance of the same work today, when mechanical reproduction has brought the lush chromatic sounds of Wagner's music to the attention of all.

Selection of Critical Material. Separating the most essential and pertinent information from the wealth of material involving competitive opera companies proved to be a constant problem. Conceivably this study could have been prepared from an entirely different viewpoint, that of opera in New York City from 1883 through 1908. This, however, was the approach followed by Krehbiel and resulted in a work that provided an overview rather than a study of the Metropolitan Opera in depth. The Krehbiel book, then, becomes prerequisite to any detailed examination of the history of the Metropolitan Opera.

The quotations in this study, in some cases lengthy, were intended to provide the essential material in a primary source. The problem of selecting the most pertinent data from over 13,000 newspaper issues, in addition to books, private collections of papers, and historical references, eliminated any possibility of brevity. The comparisons provided by differing reports are of definitive value in establishing accuracy in the history of as controversial an organization as the Metropolitan Opera has been. Fortunately the newspapers of the time were, for the most part, staffed with men as reliable as W. J. Henderson of the *New York Times*, Henry E. Krehbiel of the *New York Tribune*, Henry T. Finck of the *New York Post*, and August Spanuth of the *New Yorker Staats-Zeitung*. These men provided critiques that were of great value because their evaluations of events, operatic scores, and performers have proved to be reliable and factual. Although their philosophical outlooks and musical tastes frequently differed, their reporting of details connected with important musical events showed remarkable unanimity.

CHAPTER 1

The Founding of the Metropolitan Opera (1883)

American people during the post-Revolutionary period were self-conscious about their nation's youth and especially about its artistic shortcomings. This attitude created an instinctive tendency to embrace the culture currently in vogue on the Continent, including opera, the art form that Mozart had recently injected with new life.

The growing interest of the American city dweller in all forms of entertainment was an established fact, and the period following the turn of the nineteenth century was no exception. An accompanying surge in the population itself greatly increased the volume of the demand. Of paramount importance was the varied population of the cities, whose divergent backgrounds created a constant demand for opera of their own distinct nationality and language.

As New York grew in importance, population, and influence, it also grew as the center of entertainment, a pursuit in which opera figured prominently. However, despite some earlier unsuccessful attempts, it was not until 1854 that New York City finally achieved its first true opera house, when the Academy of Music was erected on the corner of 14th Street and Irving Place. Here was to be the first stronghold of opera in New York City. It had a seating capacity of 4,600 and an immense stage. Nowhere can be found any complaints concerning its physical structure, other than the one which would contribute so strongly to the eventual building of the Metropolitan Opera House—the lack of sufficient boxes.

The Metropolitan Opera emerged from a series of social and cultural pressures of the late 1870s and early 1880s. During these years the Academy of Music encountered revolt by numerous members of society who were not included among its boxholders. Notwithstanding this revolt, the Academy was the most respected of the opera companies in the metropolitan area and presented the most renowned artists. The supporters of the new operatic venture created a complex picture with their various motives; but they achieved a result more or less satisfactory to all involved, although for different reasons. Organizational uncertainties continued for some time—even after incorporation, it was a question of interpretation whether or not the Metropolitan Opera had been established in New York City as a performing company or, instead, merely as a new edifice to house opera.

The original corporation was named "Metropolitan Opera-house Company, Ltd." It did not purport to be an opera company, but was rather an organization owning an opera house and having the goal of bringing to New York City a superior brand of opera performances. Although the title of the corporation did not state so specifically, in essence it was primarily a real estate venture with cultural overtones.[1]

Not until the season of 1903-04 was the phrase "Metropolitan Opera" included in the title of a resident company. At that time the company was known as the "Conried Metropolitan Opera Company," in deference to the then manager, Heinrich Conried.[2]

Social and Cultural Developments

The complex structure of New York society of the time provided the impetus for the establishment of the Metropolitan Opera. The growing interest of the city dweller in entertainment was natural; with the surge in urban life during the 1800s, the demand for both facilities and opportunities for musical production increased rapidly. Of music and society during the two decades before the Metropolitan Opera was founded, the historian Allan Nevins wrote:

> As for music, which an urban society would seem naturally to demand, it was producing only a few eminent organizers and pioneers and they were almost without exception foreign-born. This was the period of Grau, Maretzek and Mapleson (an Englishman) in opera and of Theodore Thomas and Leopold Damrosch in the symphony field; the German saengerbund was to be found scattered from Brooklyn to Topeka, and German opera was about to overthrow the long sovereignty of the Italians in that field. But the native American stock brought forth neither musicians, composers nor musical organizations of distinction.

> The larger American cities were as yet far from standardized in institutions, outlook and manners. Though pulsing with new activities of a kindred sort, they still seemed cast in highly individual molds. New York was of course distinguished among them all by its contrasts of wealth and poverty, splendor and sordidness, philanthropy and vice....So great was the diffusion of riches that a hundred thousand New Yorkers now made some pretense to "fashion." The old Knickerbockers, who combined family culture and wealth in a unique pride of caste, held themselves aloof. There was a much greater body of fashionable folks who made no claim to lineage, but who had some intellectual distinction as well as inherited wealth. They patronized the opera, Wallack's and the classical concerts of Theodore Thomas; they were the figures most sought after at Newport and Long Branch, and they held agreeably democratic receptions at which appeared authors, artists and journalists. But the most picturesque element among the rich were the *parvenus*. It was they who flashed oftenest at the opera in Irving Place or at Pike's Opera House, who had the finest brownstone palaces on the monotonous Fifth Avenue, and who cut the boldest dash at Jerome Park.[3]

In the next paragraph Nevins referred to men of great importance in the early history of the Metropolitan Opera, most familiar among them Cornelius Vanderbilt, William B. Astor, Peter Cooper, and Abiel A. Low.

The interest in opera was part of a general interest in things cultural. The early history of New York theater parallels that of opera, and the public for both types of entertainment seems to have been the same. Many cities organized art museums, and a number had opened before the Metropolitan Opera House was built. Among these were the Corcoran Art Gallery, the Boston Museum of Fine Arts, and the Metropolitan Museum of Art. The last of these received grants of both money and art works from the prominent collector W. T. Blodgett.[4] The Metropolitan Museum opened in 1879 at its present Fifth Avenue location, although original plans had been to house this collection in a special building in the middle of Central Park.[5]

In Europe municipally supported opera houses flourished, frequently with support from court sources. In America the continual changes in opera management and companies provided evidence that opera was then, as now, restricted by lack of government subsidy. For this reason, the growth in individual fortunes provided impetus for the development of opera in America, especially in New York. The desire of these new millionaires to become associated with cultural enterprises funded the expansion of operatic facilities, among them the Metropolitan Opera.

Changing Character of New York City

To gain the proper perspective, it is necessary to understand the New York of this era. Concurrent with the founding of the Metropolitan, New York City was undergoing a metamorphosis. In 1880 the population was about 1,200,000, but the densely populated area extended only to 59th Street. The Brooklyn Bridge was opened in 1883 and the elaborate Vendome Bar became the meeting place of the fashionable throngs from the Metropolitan Opera and the Broadway theaters. To be sure, some elements in New York objected to the cultural shifts taking place at the time. In 1885 an aldermanic resolution banned organ grinders and street pianists. This promoted a bard of the period to pen the following immortal lines:

> I'm fond of classic music, e'en of the Vogner school
> And dearly love to hear it sung by Signor Mike O'Toole
> His runs and his cadenzas in the "Skids are out today"
> Would make a Patti hide her face, an Abbott faint away.[6]

This seems to have been not so much a complaint about Adelina Patti and Emma (Bessie) Abbott, the leading prima donnas of the day, as it was a plea not to let the earthiness of New York City give way entirely to the new cultural "fads" springing up throughout Knickerbocker.

The general uptown movement of the city, the new wealth, and growing concern with cultural achievement all contributed to the founding of the Metropolitan Opera. Up to 1880 the Academy of Music had been the most successful, longest-enduring center of opera in New York. Practically every major singer had appeared there under at least one of the various managements, and performances were consistently reported to be of high caliber. Except for a year's lapse caused by fire damage, the Academy had presented opera continuously since its opening in 1854.[7] The previously mentioned need for additional boxes at the Academy of Music served as a trigger to explode the existing social and economic pressures. A new opera house happened to be among the immediate results. As Mary Ellis Peltz, who was Metropolitan Opera Archivist from 1957 to 1981, stated, "The new fortunes of railroads, banks and real estate stood ready to support the arts."[8]

ESTABLISHMENT OF
THE CORPORATION

Although the chroniclers of the formulative stage of the Metropolitan Opera[9] disagree about the principal facts, all indicate that the shortage of boxes at the Academy of Music was the primary consideration in the discussions of a new facility for opera.

During the years that theater had become established in New York, the city's population of millionaires and quasimillionaires had increased immeasurably. A great percentage of this new wealth lay in railroading fortunes, particularly those amassed by the various Vanderbilts—William H., William K., and the redoubtable Cornelius. Banking and real estate interests contributed other funds to the Metropolitan Opera project.

The increased competition for social positions that this new wealth obviously created brought great pressure upon the Board of Directors of the Academy of Music to provide suitable box space for these would-be patrons and particularly for their wives, who vied actively for social eminence. Such space was not available, and offers as high as $30,000 per box were refused.[10] The New York Transfer Tax Department reported that ownership of an entire box in the newly formed Metropolitan Opera was equivalent to 300 shares of stock in the company.[11] In the papers of incorporation of the Metropolitan Opera-house Company, Ltd. the par value of each share was set at $100. At par, 300 shares provided a total of $30,000, indicating that this figure was the value placed upon an opera box at the time, both at the Academy of Music and at the projected new opera house. As Mary Ellis Peltz observed:

> From the beginning the process of expansion was evident. New York society had outgrown the nine Parterre Boxes available at the Academy of Music, where grand opera had been presented from 1854.[12]

Just before the opening performance at the Metropolitan Opera House, *Harpers News Monthly Magazine* presented a lengthy article that analyzed the moving forces behind the vast project:

> The proximate cause of the building of the Metropolitan Opera-house was demonstration that the volume of boxes in the old Academy of Music was unequal to the wants of society. Beggarly as was the account of these boxes in a commercial sense, and freely as their owners grumbled about their possessions to the reporters with the advent of each successive season, they showed no willingness to part with them to any of the increasing numbers of New Yorkers who were entitled to aspire to the financial and social distinction of an opera-box, yearly reenforced as these were by persons who had made fortunes in other parts of the country. That this aspiration, which was probably more fervent in the breasts of the female members of the

families whose heads competed for boxes than in the breasts of the actual competitors was not a mere desire for the enjoyment of opera seems plain enough....Just
before the project of the new opera-house was undertaken, $30,000 was offered for
one of them.[13]

In spring, 1880, a group of these unsuccessful box-purchasers was represented at a
pivotal meeting with the Board of Directors of the Academy of Music. George Henry
Warren presented their demands to August Belmont, Chairman of the Board, and to
three other members, the Messrs. Lorillard, Von Hoffman, and Dinsmore. The *New
York Times* of April 3, 1880, reported the date of the meeting as the previous
Wednesday, March 31.[14]

> A number of gentlemen of wealth and influence, not especially interested in the
> stock or management of the Academy, have recently had under consideration a proj-
> ect for the construction and establishment of a new and superb opera-house, among
> the number being William H. Vanderbilt, John Jacob Astor, Goelet, Roosevelt and
> Frederick Stevens....The meeting was on Wednesday last, Mr. August Belmont in
> the chair. Among others of the Directory present were Messrs. Lorillard, Van Hoff-
> man, William B. Dinsmore, and other wealthy and influential persons, and Mr.
> George H. Warren appeared to represent the gentlemen who were [considering] the
> building of the new opera-house (*New York Times*, April 3, 1880, p.5).

Irving Kolodin reports that after conferring with other members of the Academy
Board of Directors, August Belmont, on their behalf, offered to add twenty-six boxes
to the nine already existing at the Academy of Music. Warren, on behalf of the new
group, refused this offer.[15] Apparently plans went on as scheduled.

On April 7, the *Times* announced that $600,000 had been subscribed for site-
purchase and a building program. In the article, Warren for the first time divulged
the names of a number of the men involved in the new project.

> The building of a new opera-house, to supplant the present Academy of Music,
> has been under consideration for some time by a number of wealthy gentlemen of
> this city and resulted yesterday in a meeting at which it is stated that the sum of
> $600,000 was subscribed toward the furtherance of the project. It was futher stated
> that this large amount of money had been guaranteed by 60 gentlemen of wealth
> and influence, and that articles of agreement, insuring the immediate execution of
> the work would be signed during the coming week....It is understood that the loca-
> tion of the new building will be in the vicinity of Fifth Avenue and Thirty-seventh
> street, and that the negotiations for the property have been nearly completed.
>
> ....I have not the time now,....neither can I remember the names of the sub-
> scribers but among them are the two Roosevelts, the Iselins, the Goelets, the Astors,
> the three Vanderbilts, the Morgans, myself and others. (*New York Times*, April 7,
> 1880, p.5)

At a meeting the following day in the office of James Roosevelt, further preparations
were made, including the completion of an application to the Secretary of State for
articles of incorporation. This application was signed by George Peabody Wetmore,

George Henry Warren, George G. Haven, Robert Goelet, James A. Roosevelt, and William K. Vanderbilt. Roosevelt stated at that meeting that fifty-five gentlemen had subscribed to sixty boxes at $10,000 each.[16]

On April 11 the *Times* and *Tribune* both reported Roosevelt's receipt of the certificate of incorporation.[17] April 11, 1880, then, can be considered the founding date of the Metropolitan Opera, the founders being the signers of the original application for the right to incorporate.

The initial organizational meeting, typically for the times, was held at a luncheon at Delmonico's on April 28, 1880. The officers elected included: J.N.A. Griswold, president; George Henry Warren, vice-president; Egisto P. Fabbri, treasurer; James A. Roosevelt, chairman of the board; and George Griswold Haven, secretary.[18]

Despite the initial enthusiasm, both financial and social, the ultimate legal fate of these shares in the newly created corporation was unfortunate. In 1918 a report to the managing clerk in the Comptroller's office in New York City noted the corporation's forfeit of rights to do business as early as 1888. In a letter answering an inquiry about the value of the stock, shares of which appeared in the estate of a Mr. Edward B. Smith, the New York attorney Marvyn Scudder stated that it was valueless.

> Value of Stock
> This company was organized under the laws of the State of New York some time ago. It forfeited its right to do business for failure to comply with the laws governing it. It went out of existence in 1888. Since that time its stock has been reported as worthless and we submit it as such at January 7, 1918.
>
>   Approved by
>   M. Scudder[19]

Whereas the stock was described as without value in Scudder's letter, it was nevertheless considered in many estate appraisals to have considerable worth. Apparently, the corporation's failure to comply with the regulations of operation never destroyed the prestige that came with its ownership and the resultant control of box space at the Metropolitan Opera House. Closely held and controlled, the apparently worthless stock maintained value of an arbitrary sort. A letter from the State of New York Comptroller's office in 1916 requested the appraisal of the Metropolitan Opera stock, declaring at the same time:

> ...I would state for your information that our card index shows that this stock has been valued in the following estates.
>
>   Mathew D. C. Borden, May 27, 1912 at 333 ⅓
>   John Jacob Astor, April 15, 1912 at 333 ⅓
>   George S. Bowdoin, Dec. 16, 1913 at 333 ⅓
>   J. P. Morgan, March 31, 1913 at 333 ⅓
>   James B. Haggin, Sept. 12, 1914 at 333 ⅓
>   John E. Parsons, Jan. 16, 1915 at 333 ⅓[20]

Another estate description, that of George S. Bowdoin, a retired partner of J. Pierpont Morgan, listed further examples of the apparent worth of the stock, referring to estates such as those of William C. Whitney, Darius O. Mills, John Jacob Astor, William Bayard Cutting, Cornelius N. Bliss, Mathew Borden and J. Pierpont Morgan.[21] Inquiry of a Mr. Joyce, presumably the Secretary of the Corporation, brought forth the following:

> Mr. Joyce referred us to the Attorney for the Estate who advises he has valued the stock at 250% or $250. per share. He was unable to furnish statements or values of the properties, and we therefore are not in position to state an accurate opinion but consider $250. to be an extremely conservative figure.[22]

During the period of these conflicting reports, John Brown, the business comptroller of the Metropolitan Opera Company, disclosed in a letter that "three shares of stock were sold for One Hundred ($100) Dollars. I know of no other sales of this stock that have taken place in recent years."[23] Marked "personal," the letter also contained figures revealing the financial status of the company.

> ...our Profit and Loss account to date shows a net loss of Three Hundred and Ninety-three Thousand, Eight Hundred and sixty-four Dollars and ninety-eight ($393,864.98) cents, which is more than the entire capital stock.[24]

As for the ultimate value of the stock, it seems safe to assume that the company forfeited its right to do business in 1888, but that an effective value for the stock continued, established and recognized by the families who zealously guarded the privilege of owning a box at the Metropolitan. Since being a shareholder granted this right, the shares of stock remained in families for generations.

THE FOUNDERS
AND THEIR MOTIVES

At the time the Metropolitan Opera came into existence, New York society had already drawn its lines and formulated the arbitrary standards that governed admission to its ranks and retention therein. Ward McAllister, the most celebrated social arbiter of the time, had already drawn the distinction between what he termed the "Nobs," or "Old Families," and the "Swells," or "Newcomers."[25] In 1892 he established what would be known as the "Four Hundred," a list of about 300 names, including bankers, lawyers, brokers, real estate dealers, and railroaders.[26] That several of the founders of the Metropolitan Opera had finally achieved acceptance in the top echelon of society is undoubtedly reflected in McAllister's last category, the railroaders. Although earlier lists of prominent families had included many names connected with the Metropolitan Opera during its infant years, such families as the Vanderbilts, Roosevelts, and Goulds were notably absent. The *Social Register*, not quite as exclusive as the "patriarchs" and "Four Hundred," later included the families of all the subscribers and supporters of both the Metropolitan Opera and Academy of Music with one exception—Jay Gould.[27]

Gould's reputation was tarnished by his financial manipulations; yet his position as one of New York's wealthiest men, however, placed desirable light on his ability to contribute substantially to the funds needed for the venture. Gould's biography discusses his defeat of Vanderbilt's attempted corner of the Erie Railroad stock in 1868, his Missouri and Pacific holdings, Western Union, as well as the New York Elevated Railroad system. He was described as "cold, astute and unscrupulous," without friends and with no diversions save books and gardening. No mention is made of any philanthropic activities or interest in the arts.[28] It may be concluded that the logical reason for his participation in the early development of the Metropolitan Opera stemmed from his desire to achieve social recognition and acceptance, if not for himself, at least for his heirs. The success of his designs is indicated in subsequent lists of society's leaders, which included Helen Miller Gould and George Jay Gould.[29] Helen Miller Gould later married Finley Jay Shepard and spent her life in philanthropic activity, particularly with orphan children.[30]

Gould must be considered an isolated case. The great majority of the contributors to the Metropolitan venture were individuals who possessed worthy reputations as philanthropists in the arts and public welfare. Among them were John Jacob Astor, August Belmont, J. Pierpont Morgan, Cornelius Vanderbilt, and Darius Ogden Mills. Many worthy causes received their generous gifts. The Metropolitan Museum of Art was most prominent; others included the New York Cancer Hospital, St. Luke's Hospital, Vanderbilt University, Lick Observatory, and Mills Hotels.[31] It can be assumed that the contributions made to the Metropolitan Opera by these men were, at least in part, sincere efforts to further the cause of opera in New York.

Another group of contributors seemed to have no direct motive. Their support may have come from close friendships with the most active creators of the Metropolitan Opera. Conceivably, these men were called on to aid, contributing on this basis with no manifest reasons. Most prominent in this category was Pierre Lorillard, the tobacco and snuff magnate. His interests lay in yachting, shooting, and later horse racing. His enormous fortune was utilized philanthropically only twice: for the Metropolitan Opera, and in helping the French Republic finance the Charnay Archeological Expeditions to Central America and Yucatan. (In recognition of this service he was admitted to the Legion of Honor.) Nowhere in his biography is any other record of interest in or subsidy of the arts.[32]

The propounders of the new opera house represented a group made up of both established and newly arrived families. The aggregate presented an enormous degree of wealth, and the venture spread among them was in no way financially prohibitive. It is not possible to say whether the plan was altruistic, philanthropic, or prestige-seeking. All these motives were probably present in some degree. The diversity of the people involved indicated that each person, rather than being stimulated by the same mixture of motives as everyone else, was more likely motivated by a single factor that was applicable in his personal case.

SELECTION OF THE ARCHITECT AND SITE

The Board of Directors invited four architectural firms to submit plans for the new building. At the time this competition was opened in the summer of 1880, the site chosen for the new building was 43rd Street and Madison Avenue. Competitors were allotted three months in which to present their plans to the Board of Directors, and each firm was to receive a stipend of $3,000 for its design.[33] Those asked to submit designs were the firms of G. B. Post, Messrs. Potter and Harrison, G. E. Harvey, and Josiah Cleveland Cady. In October, 1880, under the headline "Plans for New Opera-House," the *Times* described the progress to date:

> The Directors and stockholders of the proposed new opera-house are busily engaged in examining and discussing the plans of the four architects who have been invited to draft designs for the new strucure....Mr. Calvin Goddard of No. 330 East Seventeenth-street, who is Secretary of the Executive Committee, said last evening that all the plans were very much alike in ther general features. The building...will occupy the whole of the block bounded by Vanderbilt and Madison avenues and Forty-third and Forty-fourth streets. The auditorium will seat about 3,000 persons. The chief ornamentation will be bestowed on the interior, although the exterior is designed to be much richer and more imposing than that of the Fourteenth-street edifice.
>
> It is expected that the house will be ready for occupancy in time for the Winter season of 1881–2.(*New York Times*, October 6, 1880, p.8)

Even without the problems that occurred later, the projected date of completion was unduly optimistic. The day following this report brought the announcement of the final design selection, which included seating plans. The newspaper report stressed the obvious importance of Vanderbilt:

> The plans for the new opera-house at Madison Avenue and Forty-third street have at last been adopted. J. Cleveland Cady, of No. 111 Broadway, is the architect. ...The Board of Directors met at Drexel, Morgan & Co.'s office yesterday and adopted designs and specifications for the building, at the same time directing the Executive Committee to conclude the purchase of the land and proceed with the work. E. P. Fabbri is Chairman of the committee....The committee will probably have to await the arrival of Mr. Vanderbilt from Europe before completing the purchase of the land, but they expect to break ground within a short period.(*New York Times*, October 7, 1880, p.8)

The finality of all references to the proposed Madison Avenue site is surprising. Apparently, these influential men had no question in their minds but that concluding the purchase of the land would be a mere formality. A few months later unforeseen complications forced a rapid change in plans. The stockholders, however, asserted that they could have continued at the original site if they had wished to pay the tenants for violations of their leases, which contained a clause forbidding the erection of nonresidential buildings. In view of the financial position of these men, the expense involved must have been huge to preclude their carrying out the original plans. The *Times* article announcing the decision to change the building site described the alternate location, then under negotiation.

> The stockholders of the Metropolitan Opera-house Company have given up the project of building on Vanderbilt Square, adjoining the Grand Central Depot, and were yesterday actively negotiating for the purchase of the block bounded by West Thirty-ninth street, Broadway, West Fortieth-street and Seventh-avenue. The price talked of is $600,000 and the sale was to be consummated yesterday afternoon. The reason why the stockholders did not buy the land adjoining the Grand Central Depot (which they could have had for $300,000, half the price of the Broadway property,) was a discovery of a clause in the leases whereby the erection of any other buildings than residences on the property was prohibited.. ..The block on Broadway...is 245 feet deep with a frontage of 200 feet 6 inches on Seventh-avenue and a triful more on Broadway....
>
> ...The plans for the new opera-house will not be altered by the change of location. ...but the foyer and crush rooms will be larger....The capital stock of the company which was originally $600,000, was increased to $1,050,000 on Feb. 22 last, the certificate of increase being filed on the 1st of March....It is a mistake to suppose that the Vanderbilts own the greater portion of the stock. Of the 10,500 shares, it is said that William H. Vanderbilt holds only 300 shares; William K. Vanderbilt, 300 shares, and Cornelius Vanderbilt, 150 shares....In case the bargain is concluded, the company will take possession on the 1st of May, begin work immediately, and have the opera-house finished by the fall of 1882. (*New York Times*, March 9, 1881, p.5)

It became more apparent than ever that the Metropolitan Opera House venture was considered by many to be primarily a Vanderbilt project; the enumeration of the Vanderbilt shares was in response to such rumors. That three members of the Vanderbilt family were involved contributed to this feeling, and the public sensed the ambition of newly made railroad millionaires. The increase in capital stock indicated that the new opera house was going to cost more than originally planned. Certainly the raise in capitalization was not one to cause serious concern among men of the financial position of the shareholders; it was, however, the first of a series of proposed increases that would assume major proportions relative to the original amount subscribed.

On March 14, 1881, the Board of Directors met and confirmed the purchase of the new site. In round numbers, the price was, as predicted by the *Times*, $600,000. No material change was expected in the cost of erecting the new building, a figure originally set at $430,000.[34] The increase in total cost was $300,000, which was the difference in price of the two sites. The new capitalization, set at $1,050,000, left a surplus of $20,000; no statement, however, mentioned whether the building estimate included all necessary interior equipment.

CONTROVERSY AND PROBLEMS OVER BUILDING

Estimates of the completion date and projected costs proved to be pure fantasy as

time continued, and conditions brought deep concern to those involved in the projected new opera house. During approximately one year, no public notice of any controversy appeared. March, 1882, however, was marked by startling headlines in the
Times. That a report about the venture finally reached the front page indicated the
importance of the announcement. Under the dramatic headline "The Opera-House
Scheme—A Probability That It Will Be Abandoned," a long article described the
problems and decisions that faced the Board of Directors:

> The increased cost of labor and materials makes it too expensive—
> alternatives for the stockholders to consider
>
> It was rumored yesterday that the Metropolitan Opera-house project is to be
> abandoned, and that the company has decided to build an apartment-house instead
> of an opera-house. Mr. James A. Roosevelt, the President of the Metropolitan
> Opera-house Company said last night...that the rumor was not true. In conse-
> quence, however, of the enormous rise in the price of labor and materials it became
> necessary, Mr. Roosevelt said, to revise the first estimate of the cost of the proposed
> opera-house, and the new estimate, which was presented to the Directors at their
> last meeting on the 7th inst., places the cost at a considerable advance on the original
> figures....it was decided to issue a circular to the stockholders, asking them to choose
> one of the three plans, as follows: To sell the land acquired...and divide the loss, if
> any; to hold the land and let it be unimproved until a more favorable time for build-
> ing, or to push forward the work of building, and meet the increased cost by mort-
> gaging the superfluous land at the corners of Broadway and Thirty-ninth and For-
> tieth streets. Only one lot...is needed for the entrance of the opera-house. A meeting
> of the stockholders will be held on the 27th inst., and definite action will then be
> taken on the subject.
>
> The original estimate of the cost, including the purchase of the land, was, Mr.
> Roosevelt said, $1,050,000 and the stock to that amount was subscribed for. After-
> ward it was ascertained that the cost would be increased to about $1,250,000, and
> now, in consequence of the rise of wages and materials, it is necessary to make fur-
> ther increase of about $275,000, making a total of $1,525,000....As to what action is
> likely to be taken, Mr. Roosevelt was unable to give any intimation...."We never ex-
> pected, that it would pay. No opera-house in the world has ever paid as an invest-
> ment, and none ever will pay. It is just a question whether the gentlemen connected
> with the enterprise are willing to spend any more money on it."
>
> ...In conclusion, Mr. Roosevelt said, it is not true that in order to carry on the
> enterprise the price of boxes will have to be raised from $15,000 to $23,000 each.
> ...In case the land is sold it will probably bring more than it cost, but it may not
> bring enough to reimburse the company for the expense of laying the opera-house
> foundations, which has thus far been about $125,000. (*New York Times*, March 14,
> 1882, p.1)

The stockholder's meeting was held on March 27, as proposed, and in accordance
with Mr. Roosevelt's statement, the stockholders were presented with three resolu-
tions. The total number present plus those represented by proxy was fifty-one. The
resolution to continue was passed by an overwhelming vote of 37 to 14 nays. The

figures decided on in the resolution had been revised upon more thorough investigation, and the results were described by Mr. Roosevelt in detail:

> ...he said that...the additional amount required would be $676,000...$476,000 would be needed to complete the opera-house. $100,000 for the stage outfit, properties, and machinery, and $100,000 more for the extras and contingent expenses....to build on the corner lots, a further sum of $200,000 would be required, making in all $876,000, for which the company would have to go in debt. (*New York Times*, March 28, 1882, p.8)

In the refusal of the proponents of the Metropolitan Opera to take refuge in a convenient excuse for discarding the project, the pressures of prestige and social position evidently were strong. The Academy of Music was still presenting reputable casts and repertoire in performances that were well received by opera enthusiasts. After the Metropolitan had been operating for several months, an unidentified Vanderbilt stated his attitude toward the venture. It was revealing, especially in retrospect, that he asserted, "as for himself, he cared little or nothing for music: he went into the scheme strictly for the sake of his family."[35] The Vanderbilt clan was striving very strongly for social recognition during this period, and the newspaper description of Mrs. W. K. Vanderbilt's famed fancy-dress ball and its participants indicated that they had been successful. The guests included representatives of the Astors, DeHavens, Kountzes, Winthrops, Warrens, Belmonts, Goelets, Mills, Sloans, and McAllisters. The list encompassed members of the Academy of Music Board of Directors, as well as the nucleus of Metropolitan Opera supporters. The *New York Times* complimented Mrs. Vanderbilt in its description of the excitement generated by the fancy-dress ball and even on a more personal basis in its comments on her costume.

> The Vanderbilt ball has agitated New York society more than any social event that has occurred here in many years....

> Mrs. Vanderbilt's irreproachable taste was seen to perfection in her costume as a Venetian Princess taken from a picture by Cabanel. (March 27, 1883, pp.1–2)

Such glowing terms as "irreproachable taste" were not used by society editors unless the family was firmly entrenched in the upper strata of the social structure. Surely Mrs. Vanderbilt made it a point to describe her costume in terms of a painting and thus underline the cultural inclinations and interests that pervaded the activities of her family. Two of her sisters, Mrs. Fernando Yznaga and Lady Mandeville, shared her duties as hostess.

THE COMPLETION OF
THE METROPOLITAN OPERA HOUSE

After the March, 1882, decision of the Board of Directors to continue building on the new site, no further evidence surfaced of any problems in the building program. The stockholders met on May 23, 1883, to discuss the completion of the unfinished corners, to draw lots for boxes, and to elect their officers for the ensuing year. In addition to an impressive list of stockholders, a number of the ladies attended, probably as a result of the excited anticipation of the assignment of the boxes. It was announced that the decorators were already at work and had finished a portion of the ceiling. Considerable attention was given to a description of the upholstery, which was to be a "peculiar crimson" tint, manufactured especially for the house, and made of a heavy silk. The contract had been awarded to Cheney Brothers in South Manchester, Connecticut.[36]

Of the seventy-three boxes available, seventy were drawn; stockholders were awarded either a half share in a box or a complete one, depending on their holdings. In a few cases where their investment merited it, stockholders held more than one box. Inconsistent with the constant denials of a preponderance of Vanderbilt money in the venture, five boxes were drawn for that family.

After the drawing, Roosevelt read the report of a special committee, consisting of Messrs. Whitney, Wetmore, Warren, and Iselin, appointed to ascertain the cost of completing the two Broadway corners of the building, on which no work had yet been done. The *Times* summarized the report:

> The amount originally appropriated for the work of building the opera-house will be wholly expended without finishing these corners. The report said that the additional cost of finishing the corners would be $370,000. The advantage in finishing would be that the plans of the corners included the building of reception and supper rooms, which would enable the Directors to rent the house for balls. The Academy of Music during the last year had earned $38,000 in rents acquired from sources outside the opera. Of this amount $30,000 was paid for balls....The addition would raise the indebtedness of the company to $1,000,000.
>
> ...Printed copies of the correspondence which passed between the Directors of the new opera-house and those of the Academy of Music three years ago were distributed. This correspondence referred to a proposed consolidation of the two organizations. (*New York Times*, May 24, 1883, p.1)

Although no copy was found of the correspondence mentioned by the *Times*, it was obvious that no reconstruction of the Academy of Music could possibly have provided box space for the large group that had become associated with the new opera house. Once the small nucleus of the group proposing a new opera house had refused to accept any compromise with the Belmont forces, they were quickly joined by a number of other families. Thereafter the number of patrons involved ruled out further possibility of a sufficient increase in the number of boxes at the Academy of Music. Clearly it was not feasible to enlarge an opera house by the addition of seventy boxes, and so the new venture slowly moved toward completion, although, as has been noted, not without considerable difficulties.

On July 21, 1883, reporters were shown through the new building on what was referred to as a "guided tour." The tour, under the auspices of the Board of Directors, was conducted by Edmund Stanton, Secretary of the Board and later a manager of the Metropolitan Opera. Seating capacity was described as over 3,000, with com-

View of the original Metropolitan Opera House, completed in 1883.

modious boxes. The press was critical of the distance between singers and audience and also of the sinking of the orchestra. In size, the new opera house far exceeded both Covent Garden in London and La Scala in Milan. In what might be considered an early statement in opposition to Victorian splendor, the *New York Times* expressed apprehension that the decorations might be overdone:

> A grave mistake will be made if the methods of adornment are such as to change the light and inspiriting appearance of the place. Too much gold, too much frescoeing, and an excess of costly hangings and upholstery are likely to do this. (July 22, 1883, p.9)

Much of the commentary in the article was complimentary, and considerable architectural detail was provided. Comparison with other opera houses proved to be unavoidable and not always favorable to the new structure.

> Two special features of the Metropolitan Opera-house claim notice. First of these is the fire-proof character of the building. Stone, brick, concrete, iron, and tiles are so combined in its every portion that its destruction by flame appears out of the question. The other point of excellence lies in the means of entrance and egress. The...parquet boxes, balcony, and gallery are all supplied with special doors, lobbies, and stairways, and should an alarm be raised, loss of life from panic would be most unlikely....The Metropolitan Opera-house bears considerable resemblance to Covent Garden, with the difference that, while the masonry of the American building may be a triful less massive, most of the staircases and passageways are considerably broader and higher....The ventilation promises to be very satisfactory. A large fan exhausts the heated air, and a fresh atmosphere is continually forced into the auditorium, the box-holders being particularly well cared for in this respect. ...The expectation...that the Metropolitan Opera-house will be a marked addition to architectural New York is not likely...to be fulfilled....Lacking an imposing entrance, wide doors, a broad stairway, or some charm, the Metropolitan Opera-house, as a structure, will probably be considered rather plain. The idea which has [evidently] controlled its details appears to have been to provide a large, safe and comfortable auditorium for the presentation of Italian opera on a scale of, possibly, too great magnitude. This idea has been adhered to, and while many persons may regret that the Metropolis should not be enriched by a monumental pile of uncommon beauty, the lovers of music, if the acoustics of theatre are perfect, and suitable "attractions" are obtainable, must feel grateful to the liberality of the men who have raised them a new temple of art (*New York Times*, July 22, 1883, p.9).

It was predicted that acoustical success would not be determined until the first act of the opera on opening night, given that a capacity audience was necessary to evaluate a theater's acoustics properly. In forecasting the effectiveness of the fireproofing and safety devices, the *Times* opinion has been substantiated by history, for from its erection to its demolition, the building was the site of neither panic nor fire catastrophe. Many of these safety precautions were copied from Covent Garden, which possessed a similarly fine safety record. *Harper's New Monthly Magazine*, reporting on the new opera-house, noted that the stage area was exceeded in size by only two other opera houses, the Imperial Opera in St. Petersburg and the New Opera in

Paris.[37] *Harper's* was more inclined to praise the building's architecture than the *New York Times* and concluded its description in a complimentary vein:

> The style, in deference, possibly to the purpose of the building, is Italian, and in the Broadway entrance, which is more copiously decorated than any other part, is a correct and academic Italian Rennaissance. This style has more elegance than vigor.
>
> The portico on Broadway is noteworthy not only for the refinement of the detail, which never fails Mr. Cady in whatever style he is working, but for the breadth of the composition.[38]

Henry Krehbiel, at that time the major music critic in New York, provided a fine description of the interior in his comprehensive book, *Chapters of Opera*. The interior was decorated by E. F. Tredwill of Boston and most tastefully done in gold and wine. The decor included two paintings by Francis Maynard, "The Chorus" and "The Ballet." The lighting was provided by gas, but preparations were made for the installation of electricity when it became economically feasible. The total cost, including land, was $1,732,978.21.[39] The *Harper's* article provided the same information.

The success of the venture hinged on two needs—satisfying the social clamor of the stockholders, and providing enough seats for the general public to insure economic success. The *New York Times* listed the seating arrangements: 600 seats with 12 boxes, known as *baignoire* boxes, on the orchestra floor; three tiers of boxes (36 in each tier), totaling 674 seats; balcony seating, 735; "Family Circle" (gallery), 978 seats. This provided an overall seating capacity of 3,045. The *Times* also gave the dimensions of the stage as 90 ft. deep by 106 ft. wide.[40] (Different sources give slightly different figures for seating and dimensions.) The *Harper's* article carried a detailed sketch of the first and second floors superimposed in halves (See Appendix).

In 1958, plans to discard the Metropolitan Opera House prompted Francis Robinson, then assistant manager of the company, to write for *High Fidelity Magazine* an account of the years of existence of the now-demolished building. Robinson provided colorful background material as well as several points not previously on record. The revised capacity of the opera house after its 1953 remodeling showed an increase to 3,614 seats, representing the following divisions: Orchestra (formerly parquet), 1,177; 35 Parterre boxes, 280; Grand Tier 164; Guild and club boxes 124; Dress Circle 516; balcony 647; Family Circle 706.[41] The remodeling also revealed the existence of an acoustical sound chamber:

> The 1953 remodeling also gave the present generation its first look at an amazing detail which earlier it had only heard about, a great egg-shaped sound chamber of masonry under the orchestra pit which through all the years had been making its big contribution to the Metropolitan's celebrated acoustics. Only one other theater in America is known to have such a reverberating shell, the Academy of Music in Philadelphia.[42]

Robinson's article also mentioned a little-known architect, Louis de Coppet Bergh, apparently employed in Cady's office.[43]

Cady was generally known as an expert in the building of churches, primarily of simple Gothic architecture. His accomplishments also numbered the main building of the Museum of Natural History, the now-removed Presbyterian Hospital on 70th Street, and the New York Skin and Cancer Hospital (for which he served as president for many years). Finally, he was responsible for fifteen buildings at Yale and several at Wesleyan, Williams, and Trinity.

Bergh, in contrast, came from a musical family (his father had been the organist at the Little Church Around the Corner). He had studied architecture at the Royal Polytechnicum in Stuttgart and had become a civil engineer. His sister, Lillie d'Angelo Bergh, had studied music in Italy and at the time of the building of the Metropolitan Opera House provided her brother with pictures of opera houses abroad and suggestions for use in his plans. Among these suggestions was one well-known in later Metropolitan Opera experiences, the antechambers with the boxes, patterned after La Scala in Milan. *Opera News* (in an article that preceded Robinson's *High Fidelity* piece) mentioned the exclusion of proscenium boxes at the Metropolitan in order to avoid the rivalry for their possession that had plagued the Academy of Music for many seasons. The fire-prevention features that had drawn so much commendation were attributed to Bergh's research concerning a disastrous fire in the Ringtheater in Vienna. Bergh was further credited, in collaboration with his brother, also an engineer, with the ventilation system of the new building. In fact, it was commented that "for a year everybody shivered." Finally, one of the cherubs that adorned the pilasters carried the features of Bergh's infant son, who died while the opera house was being built.[44]

The well-guarded secret of Bergh's involvement in the plans for the new opera house and their execution would explain Cady's success in winning the architectural contract for the Metropolitan Opera House. His complete lack of background in theatrical construction and his never having been to Europe have both given rise to much conjecture as to why he succeeded in the competition among the four architectural firms. The lack of documentary evidence explaining his success was obvious, but the results tended to counter any questioning of his ability.

In the light of Bergh's contributions and the reactions of newspapers and periodicals to the new building, Cady's complaints about lack of appreciation of his work seem unwarranted. In a letter to the *New York Tribune* dated November 12, 1883, he berated the public for its lack of appreciation for the enormous work and planning that had gone into the Metropolitan Opera House.[45] Yet newspaper accounts, though they contained a degree of criticism, indicated overall acceptance of the project as more than satisfactory.

Between the Board of Directors' guided tour and the opening night, the only reported change of any consequence was in decor and size of some of the boxes. A week after the premiere performance at the Metropolitan Opera House, it was revealed that Henry E. Abbey, manager of the initial season, had added "handsome old-gold draperies" to the proscenium arch and that he planned to remove half of the partitions of eleven of the second-tier boxes. These plans were clearly described in the *Times*:

> They will then become mezzanine boxes, seating four people each, and can be sold for a reasonable price. The space gained in front of them will be filled by a row of chairs of the same size and pattern as those now in the orchestra. These will be called dress circle chairs and will be sold at moderate price, which has not yet been decided upon....A change is also contemplated in the decorations of the boxes, the pale color of which does not show off the brilliant costumes of the ladies to advantage. The back partitions and curtains of the boxes will probably be changed to red. (*New York Times*, October 30, 1883, p.8)

This report explains the origin of the "dress circle" and indicates the stress placed on the concern that the society ladies have a proper showcase at the opera.

ANTICIPATED FAILURE OF ONE OPERA HOUSE

Considerable care, thought, and planning had clearly occupied the three years between the date of incorporation and the opening performance at the Metropolitan Opera House. As it was later obvious, the planners' prime fallacy lay in not realizing that New York simply could not support two opera houses of the caliber and importance of the Academy of Music and the Metropolitan Opera. Fifty years earlier Philip Hone had asked in his diary, upon the opening of another opera house, "Will this splendid and refined amusement be supported in New York? I am doubtful."[46] Even at the time the Metropolitan Opera opened, many anticipated the eventual failure of one or the other organization.

The opening of the new house failed to halt criticism of the venture, and on January 20, 1884, a *New York Times* article mentioned the "futility of two opera-houses in New York City which it cannot support."[47] It should be recalled that Gould and Vanderbilt had been upbraided for forcing the building of the new opera house when

> For $100,000 at the most, the Academy of Music could have been made one of the most attractive, appropriate, and comfortable houses for opera "in the world." (*New York Times*, February 20, 1884, p.5)

In comparison with with the purported $100,000 fee for remodeling the Academy, Krehbiel's figure of slightly over $1,750,000 for the finished Metropolitan Opera House, if accurate, was somewhat less astounding than the $3,000,000 cost stated in the *Times*.[48] Nevertheless, the *Times* still strongly questioned the need for a second opera house in New York City.

The formation of the new corporation and the construction of its opera house resulted from the social competition of the 1880s as well as the rapid expansion of urban life. Applied to opera, these factors led to the creation of the Metropolitan. A reexamination of the names of the prominent people involved suggests that the project might have been a battle between old fortunes and the late-nineteenth-century nouveau riche, a group long since the backbone of American society and wealth. Yet the presence of so many names representing "old money," such as Roosevelt, Astor, Belmont, Lorillard, and Goelet, belies this theory. As is evident from the lists of box-holders in both the Academy of Music and the Metropolitan Opera, "old money" was represented. The only prominent name that might have been construed as nouveau riche was Vanderbilt. The Vanderbilts were certainly new to society; Mrs. Vanderbilt's dress ball might well be termed their debut. Their fortune, nevertheless, had been accumulated almost 100 years earlier.[49] The Astor fortune could not boast much longer existence, and the Astors were considered "old line" by this time. Although Gould qualified as nouveau riche, his position in the list of founders was unique.

Thus indications were that this was a struggle in New York City against control of opera by a small group as exemplified by the Academy of Music boxholders and Board of Directors. Expansion demanded and produced the new opera house, and circumstances dictated the survival of the Metropolitan rather than the Academy of Music. The general uptown relocation of the center of New York City granted a great advantage to a building on 39th street as opposed to one on 14th street. The willingness of the Metropolitan Board of Directors to accept the necessary financial setbacks was another prime factor in the survival of the new opera house.

CHAPTER 2

The Initial Season (1883–1884)

Once the idea of the new opera house was conceived as a reality by the New York public, interest seemed to mount among citizens not directly connected with the venture. Apparently, New York City nurtured sufficient interest in musical productions of all kinds. In January, 1880, the *New York Times* described at considerable length the varied musical fare available to the public, including concerts, lectures, and operatic productions, both comic and serious.

> ...many of the concerts of less merit are not mentioned, but it will be seen that no one need lack musical entertainment in New York. (*New York Times*, January 2, 1880, p.2)

Toronto's opening of a new opera house proved that interest in opera was not restricted to New York. In size, the Toronto building differed considerably from the Metropolitan Opera House; the emphasis on box space in Toronto was not nearly so great as at the Metropolitan.

> The lower floor of the auditorium contains 404 opera-chairs and 152 sofa-seats; the dress circle, 108 opera-chairs and 325 sofa-seats, the upper gallery holds seats for 1000 spectators, the capacity of the house being, therefore, 1,989 seats, not including those in eight private boxes. (*New York Times*, February 10, 1880, p.5)

Mapleson, in the meantime, was bringing some degree of permanence to Italian opera in New York. He had finished a highly successful tour in the western United States and was opening on March 1 at the Academy of Music. In the approaching season, the *Times* predicted,

> ...there should be no doubt the Mr. Mapleson will receive every encouragement in his efforts to place Italian opera on a permanent basis in New York. (*New York Times*, February 14, 1880, p.4)

Mapleson's major star at the time was the tenor Italo Campanini. President Hayes' invitation to Campanini to sing a "number of selections" at the White House[1] stimulated interest in opera. The press, in the meantime, offered further encouragement.

> Italian opera is passing out of the list of luxuries, and is becoming one of the neces-
> sities of Mertropolitan life…the public should recognize it as a performance to be en-
> couraged. (*New York Times,* February 29, 1880, p.7)

Traditional abstinence from entertainment during Lent was being challenged:

> …the brilliant appearance of the boxes each night afforded ample proof that the
> Lenten fast is no longer vigorously kept by the class of people that supports Italian
> opera in the American Metropolis. (*New York Times,* March 7, 1880, p.7)

Possibly, the group that was about to launch plans for the new opera house was
greatly encouraged by the review of the March 16 *Carmen* performance at the Academy of Music. (That *Carmen* was of French origin did not remove it from classifi-
cation as Italian opera, since at this time in New York the opera was produced in
Italian with singers versed in Italian operatic tradition.) The audience was not only
magnificently attired, but huge:

> …the boxes blazed with splendor, and all the other seats were occupied, while hun-
> dreds of persons remained standing throughout the evening. (*New York Times,*
> March 16, 1880, p.5)

The vast and resented ticket speculation associated with the Academy of Music
also stimulated enthusiasm for the new house. A letter to the editor of the *Times* upbraided Mapleson for the deplorable conditions. In "protest against the fraudulent
manner in which the sale of seats is conducted at our Academy of Music," the writer
asserted that speculators lived at the finest hotels and carried on their business from
those addresses.[2]

This was the context of public sentiment at the time of decision to build a new
opera house. The lively general interest contrasted directly with the competitive
motives ascribed to the actual promulgators of the new venture, and it unavoidably
led to speculation over the ultimate choice for a manager.

CHOICE OF MANAGER

Several entrepreneurs either were producing or managing opera in New York or
were sufficiently well-known from European opera houses to be included in the speculation. Frequently, a single issue of the *New York Times* would refer to the various
operatic ventures of these men.

Maurice Grau had managed and produced opera in New York as well as in other
major cities for a number of years. For a short period he was to be one of a triumvirate that managed the Metropolitan; he was its sole manager from 1898 to 1903. The
Gye family was prominent at that time, both in New York and internationally. Frederick Gye, the father, spent many years as head of the Royal Opera at Covent Garden; his sons, Ernest and Herbert, managed that opera house and led several com-

panies in America, both on tour and in resident seasons in the New York area. Although all three were frequently mentioned as possible managers of the Metropolitan Opera, none ever achieved that position.

Two other theatrical producers were active in New York when the Metropolitan Opera House Board of Directors was seeking its first impresario. Heinrich Conried, a prominent actor and producer involved primarily with drama and comic opera, eventually became the head of the Metropolitan Opera, but not until a number of managerial regimes had preceded him. Henry E. Abbey, unlike the others, was an American. He had produced opera in many cities in the United States and had managed many noted singers on American concert tours. Colonel Mapleson was far too firmly ensconced at the rival Academy of Music for serious consideration as a possible manager of the Metropolitan Opera House.

Shortly before the formal announcement that a manager had been selected for the new opera house, the *Times* ran an editorial concerned with "opera management." It also dealt another question soon to predominate in operatic circles—whether enough skilled and experienced singers, musicians, conductors, and chorus members were available to staff both companies during simultaneous seasons in New York City. The observation in the *Times* was astute.

> The visible progress of the builders of the new opera house in their work has once more called forth surmise and discussion as to the probable manager of the place. ...They will learn, before long, that neither primadonnas, nor tenors, nor conductors, nor orchestras, nor operatic libraries or wardrobes can be improvised as readily as opposition railroads....
>
> ...What likelihood is there that a sufficient proportion of the few artists now delighting Europe will be induced to visit America and form the complete double or triple company required to interpret the modern repertoire? (*New York Times*, December 18, 1882, p.4)

The editorial also discussed the scarcity of managers and of singers who might be described as "adequate interpreters." The barb hurled at the railroad magnates and at the ease with which they controlled the manipulations of transportation reflected the attitude of the severest critics of Gould and the Vanderbilts. After lauding the managerial abilities of Mapleson and Ernest Gye, the *Times* predicted further difficulties, again calling attention to the inability of the millionaires to cope with them. The *Times* further castigated what it found to be an overbearing attitude on the part of the Metropolitan stockholders:

> ...it is safe to predict that it will require something more than money and the fiat of a millionaire to accomplish all that sanguine but ignorant people fancy can be achieved by their united potency. (*New York Times*, December 18, 1882, p.5)

The Board of Directors announced the appointment of a manager and producer for the opening season on the last day of 1882. The *Times* report was long and involved, discussing not only the appointment, but also the new manager's projected plans for the first season.

In outlining the possibilities and in defending its choice, the Board of Directors released the following information:

> There were two applicants for the office—Henry E. Abbey and Herbert F. Gye, representing the Royal Italian Opera Company, (limited) of London. At the meeting of the Directors held on Thursday...nine out of thirteen Directors were present, and it was resolved by a unanimous vote to give the contract to Mr. Abbey. The final settlement of the contract was referred...to a committee consisting of Messrs. George G. Haven, Adrian Iselin, Robert Goelet, and ex-officio James A. Roosevelt, the President of the Metropolitan Opera-house Company. This committee selected as its advisor Counsel to the Corporation William C. Whitney, and a meeting was held yesterday afternoon...At that meeting all the details were perfected and the contract was formally executed by receiving Mr Abbey's signature....The contract is for one year and is renewable...at the pleasure of both parties....By its terms Mr. Abbey has full control of the stage arrangements, the preparation of costumes, the engagement of singers and orchestra, and the disposition of the building. A member of the committee said...giving the contract to Mr. Abbey, had been governed by various considerations. In the first place, they deemed it advisable to place the opera-house in the hands of a manager who would relieve them of the care of it from one year's end to the other rather than...one who would run it for only a few months. ..."In the second place,...Mr. Abbey has proved himself a very enterprising and trustworthy manager. Mr. Jay Gould, the owner of the Grand Opera House, which is leased by Mr. Abbey, said...that Mr. Abbey has proved the most trustworthy manager he has ever had any dealings with....Col. Mapleson, who is the recognized manager in this country for the Royal Italian Opera Company, has to say the least, not always equaled his promises by his performances. And besides Mr. Mapleson has a five year's lease of the Academy of Music, several years of which are yet unexpired. It should be stated, however, in this connection that Mr. Gye assured us that his company was not bound by Col. Mapleson's contracts." (*New York Times,* December 31, 1882, p.7)

These comments indicated a relationship between the English company and Colonel Mapleson; it appeared to be in the capacity of a parent company supplying artists to an independent subsidiary. Conceivably this could be construed as an attempt by Mapleson to gain some limited control of the competitive opera house. Herbert Gye described his unsuccessful negotiations with the Metropolitan Board of Directors; in his statement he referred to his attempt to work out a "consolation" with the Academy of Music. Gye's statement, while not definitive evidence, certainly did not preclude an attempt by Mapleson to rescue his position with the assistance and influence of the Gye interests.

> Mr. Herbert F. Gye was found last night at the Academy of Music. He did not believe...that the Metropolitan Opera-house Company had awarded the contract for the management of the building to Mr. Abbey. "The negotiations on my part... began about 18 months ago. I was not an applicant to the company; on the contrary, they made an application to me. Mr. Fabbri, one of the Directors, came over to London about the time indicated and asked me if I would undertake the management of the new house. When I came over here last fall...he referred me to Mr.

Roosevelt, who...had been placed in charge of that matter....On Nov. 22 I was invited to appear before the Directors. They then made me a proposition to take the house next Fall if I would furnish the costumes and scenery. I replied that I would have to consult my brother, Ernest Gye, who is in London....As soon as I received his answer I communicated with them...at a subsequent meeting they informed me that they regarded what they had said before not in the nature of a proposition but of a conversation, and they asked me to make a distinct proposition, which I did. This proposition was similar to the one I had understood them to make me, though it differed in details. I offered also to see Mr. Belmont and arrange for a consolation. By this arrangement the Academy was not to be closed, but the two houses were to be run on some such plan as alternate performances. I saw the Directors for the last time a week ago yesterday, and they told me that they would let me hear from them again. If they have gone off and made a contract with Mr. Abbey without letting me know, all I have to say is, they have a very queer method of doing business." (*New York Times*, December 31, 1882, p.7)

Gye's statement established the premise that last-minute attempts were made for a compromise between the rival opera houses. Apparently in refusing the offer, Belmont and the Academy group were under the delusion that Mapleson had sufficient influence, contractual or otherwise, to keep the Metropolitan Opera House from procuring major artists. The connection between Mapleson's organization and the Royal Italian Opera Company in London unquestionably provided the Academy contingent with further assurance that they were in command of the situation. If Herbert Gye's statements were accepted, the Metropolitan Opera must have suffered a severe setback in its public relations. Gye's implications about their business methods did not place the new group in a favorable position to capture the loyalty of the rank-and-file purchasers of opera tickets. Both Gye and Mapleson, on the other hand, pompously rejected any possibility that Abbey would be able to staff his opera house adequately. Their statements bore a remarkable resemblance in attitude:

In regard to the engagement of singers, Mr. Gye said his company had all of the great singers under contract except Mme. Gerster, who, however was about to sign a contract, if she had not already signed it. Mme. Nilsson, he said, was under contract with his company to sign in London next Summer and in this City next Winter.

Col. Mapleson, when asked how Mr. Abbey's contract would affect him, replied:

"Not at all! We have all the great singers: Patti, Albani, Scalchi, and Campanini, and if the public wants to hear them they will have to come to us. It is true that Mr. Abbey will have a fine new house, and that may attract for a while by its novelty, and it may be that people who come here will consider it their duty to go to see that just as people who go to Paris consider it their duty to go to see the stairway of the Grand Opera-house. The manager of that house told me last Summer that it did not make much difference what kind of performance, for the people were bound to go there anyway. But we shall go right along, as before. A company which has been giving opera for 150 years, like the Royal Italian Opera Company, is not to be frightened or driven out of the field by every new and ephemeral enterprise that is started." (*New York Times*, December 31, 1882, p.7)

Henry E. Abbey's comments concerning his projected season at the Metropolitan Opera House obviously did not agree with the claims made by Gye and Mapleson.

He also remarked on his plans to engage personnel not connected with the Academy of Music at that time. His description of his arrangements with the Metropolitan Opera Board of Directors indicated that the directors had revised their plans after approaching Gye. Following his announcement that the season would open on October 22, 1883, Abbey asserted:

By the terms of my contract the Directors of the new opera-house will give me the building with scenery, costumes, properties, music, and every other appliance for the production on a scale of grandeur that has never been equaled in the City of 20 different Italian operas. These will all be prepared under my personal supervision. That there will be ample stage-room for every requirement of grand opera may well be conceived from the fact that the stage is 62 feet in depth and has a width of about 150 feet from wall to wall. The width of the drop curtain will be just 100 feet, the largest in the City, and the opera-house will be one of the largest and finest in the world....

"I have here a cable from Campanini, the greatest of tenors, from Milan, Italy, dated Dec. 30, which reads:

'Will accept your terms for a seven months season to sing 10 times monthly. CAMPANINI'...

"Mme. Christine Nilsson will be my leading prima donna, and my contract with her is made. I have also engaged as another prima donna Mme. Valleria and am negotiating with a third, whose name I cannot now give. By the way, I to-day received the following dispatch from Mme. Nilsson in answer to one to her informing her of the signing of the contract to-day. It reads: 'Mme. Nilsson's congratulations on securing the greatest opera-house in the greatest musical city in the world.'

"When I left Mme. Nilsson in Denver, after making an engagement with her, I said: 'I suppose, Mme. Nilsson, you don't care anything about singing in the new opera-house on the opening night in case I secure it, do you? It will take care of itself on the opening night you know.' Mme. Nilsson looked at me in a peculiar sort of way, and said: 'Mr. Abbey, if I don't sing there on the opening night, I don't sing there at all.' And while this was said in a good-natured sort of way there was a certain look and a peculiar tone that indicated that she meant just what she said...."

"Have you any other people engaged?"

"But one other, and he is a great favorite with New York people. Signor Del Puente has signed a contract with me as my leading baritone. I think myself that that's a very good quartet to start in with—Nilsson, Valleria, Campanini, and Del Puente....

"Negotiations are pending with several of the leading operatic people in Europe for my season, and I shall manage none but established favorites....Mr. Copleston, who is now managing the Nilsson concert tour, will go to Europe next week, with carte blache to engage the best people he can secure. I shall have...a large and efficient chorus and ballet. The latter will be made a feature...."

"Have you secured a conductor?"

"Not certainly. Negotiations now pending…there shall be nothing wanted in this direction, however, but I cannot now name the party who will probably be the conductor….

"The usual programme will be followed….I shall have a season of ten weeks in the Fall and Winter and a five week's season in the Spring….The opera house may then be used for balls, or for other entertainments if I choose as I have absolute and entire control of the house for the single season for which I have secured it….During the season I shall certainly produce German opera and probably both French and English opera also, though of course the latter I cannot speak definitely about…."

Signor Campanini's Terms

…the possibilities of the opening season…were the chief topics of conversation in the lobbies at the Academy of Music last evening….These rumors announced the engagement of Mme. Patti and Mme. Scalchi….[Abbey's] agents also yesterday visited Signor Galassi and made him an offer…which Signor Galassi declined, as the terms of his contract with Col. Mapleson are such as to preclude him from even considering any offer until after March next. It was also asserted that Mr. Abbey had secured the services of Signor Tamagno, who is now singing in Brazil, where he is an established favorite….

Mr. Abbey will pay to Signor Campanini the largest sum ever paid to a tenor in this country, as the terms cabled to him are known to have been $1,000 a night for 10 nights in each of the seven months of his engagement. (*New York Times*, December 31, 1882, p.7)

The willingness of the Metropolitan directors to give Abbey the necessary and costly equipment that had not been offered to Gye strongly underlined their desire to engage Abbey and at the same time to sever any possible connection with Mapleson that might have emerged through employing Gye. Certainly Gould's promotion of Abbey for the position was influential in the decision to grant him the contract.

It subsequently became clear that Gye, Mapleson, and Abbey, were all in error and overconfident in many of their assertions. Christine Nilsson, Sofia Scalchi, Italo Campanini, and Guseppe Del Puente all sang in the opening performance at the Metropolitan. Adelina Patti never appeared at the Metropolitan in a regular season production. Francesco Tamagno finally joined the Metropolitan Opera in the twilight of his career, during the season of 1894–1895 when the company was under the management of Abbey, Schoeffel, and Grau. Abbey's incorrect claims about the size of the Metropolitan Opera House stage, as well as his indication that he would present an English opera, can be seen as the exaggerations of an impresario describing his plans. The cast lists for Abbey's 1883–1884 Metropolitan Opera Company reveal that Campanini sang a total of 57 times rather than the 70 originally outlined. These appearances included 53 opera performances (24 in New York City and 29 on tour), two concerts in New York City, one concert on tour, and a performance of the Rossini *Stabat Mater*.[3] Whether or not this change in plan altered Campanini's position as the highest-paid tenor in the country up to that time depended on whether he was paid by the performance or guaranteed a minimum of $70,000. Since this information was not available, the question cannot be answered at this time. One source stated specifically that he received $56,000 for 22 performances and two concerts at

the Metropolitan Opera and participation in a two-week tour to Boston.⁴ Since none
of the performances in Brooklyn, Philadelphia, Chicago, St. Louis, Cincinnati,
Washington, and Baltimore nor the *Stabat Mater* in Boston were mentioned, these
figures may be of dubious validity. The difference in total performances in New York
was also difficult to pinpoint, since Campanini's participation in five of the tour performances was questionable; the programs were apparently lost, and the performances were not reviewed in detail.

A few weeks before the scheduled opening of the new opera house Campanini arrived in New York City and was interviewed immediately by the press. He asserted
that he was "glad to be back". Discussing some of the roles he would portray during
the season, he mentioned the title role in *Hamlet* by Ambroise Thomas. His remarks
put forth a little known fact about the role:

> Mr. Abbey also promised me that I should sing the title role in Thomas's "Hamlet."
> ...The part was originally written for a tenor, but there was no one at the Paris
> opera able to sing it, so it was transferred for baritone and given to M. Faure. I am
> very fond of the role and have long wished to sing it. (*New York Times*, October 9,
> 1883, p.5)

Campanini never actually sang this role at the Metropolitan and no record exists as
to whether he sang the part elsewhere. Abbey did produce the opera in the opening
season, but the title role was assigned to the baritone Giuseppe Kaschmann.

In the same interview that revealed the possibility of his singing Hamlet, Campanini praised his brother Cleofonte, who, although only twenty-three years old,
was to be Abbey's assistant conductor. With great enthusiasm Italo Campanini
stated, "He is a thorough musician...he has perfect command of the orchestra and
when he raises his baton you can see that there is a man behind it."⁵ His description of
Augusto Vianesi, the new principal conductor, was glowing.

Interspersed with publicity about the singers in the rival companies, the *Times* ran
an interesting article describing an auction sale of seats and boxes for the opening
night at the Metropolitan. Excitement was mounting, and the public was apparently
willing to pay what might be termed exorbitant prices for tickets to the first production at the new opera house. Two names now familiar to Metropolitan Opera patrons made their first appearance in connection with the opera house. George Tyson,
the founder of the ticket agency, Tyson & Company, and Fred Rullman, then a speculator and later the publisher of the official libretti for the Metropolitan Opera, both
bid on opening-night tickets, with Tyson purchasing first choice. As the prices indicated, the event was of foremost importance to the opera audience of the time:

> An auction sale of seats and boxes for the opening night of the Metropolitan Opera
> House took place in Steinway Hall last night. Those offered for sale were all that had
> not been taken by subscription. There were about 220 seats marked off in the dia-
> gram as taken for the season. In addition to these 22 boxes go to stockholders and 7
> were taken in the upper tier....The upset price would be $10 for orchestra seats and
> all bids must be in advance of that. The first offer was $10 and was quickly raised to
> $13. Then George I. Tyson the speculator, offered $20, and Fred Rullman, another
> speculator, offered $21. Mr. Schoeffel, partner of Mr. Abbey in the management of

the Park Theatre, Boston, bid $30. Finally Tyson offered $35 and got the first choice....

> Boxes were next offered. There were two boxes left on the orchestra floor. One went to a Mr. Scott for $150 and the other to a Mr. Stout for $130. The upper tier was then started. There are 36 boxes in this part of the house and 7 were already taken. The first choice of the remaining ones sold to a speculator for $85 and the second choice went to John D. Townsend for $80....The total receipts of the sale, as nearly as they could be figured last night, were $8,260 for which 580 seats and 31 boxes were sold. The total receipts of the opening night will be between $16,000 and $20,000. (*New York Times*, October 13, 1884, p.4)

The following day's *New York Times* carried a two-column article describing the opera house in detail. The interior of the building was minutely described, including the paintings and sculpture; the work contributed by Louis de Coppet Bergh, however, was not mentioned.[6]

A week before the two New York City rival opera houses opened, Colonel Mapleson provided the *New York Times* with the names of some of his singers for the approaching season. Among the sopranos, Adelina Patti, Etelka Gerster, and Eugenie Pappenheim were mentioned as the returning stars; Antonio Galassi, a baritone of some note, led the list of returning male artists.[7] Mapleson also announced three projected new productions, surely of interest to opera patrons:

> ...the promised productions of Weber's "Oberon," of "Norma," "La Gazza Ladra," and other masterpieces of the operatic stage...is most gratifying. (*New York Times*, October 15, 1883, p.4)

Oberon, the most surprising of this group, was not presented and no reason was given for this change in plans.

In the short period remaining before the seasons opened, Mapleson continued to pursue publicity to the fullest extent. Arriving in New York on October 15 with the bulk of his company, he released considerable information about his plans; at the same time he further decried the methods used by his competitor in attempting to lure artists from his organization. Mapleson reassured the public about rumors of a rift with Adelina Patti. He also gave advance notice of his impending legal action to retain the services of Giuseppe del Puente and Emily Lablache, both of whom were announced to sing at the Metropolitan Opera House on the opening night. On the surface at least, he gave indications of relishing the approaching competition and appeared confident that he would emerge the victor in the struggle. Abbey, he asserted, was having his company arrive in small groups in order to derive the maximum publicity from a continuing series of news releases. The *New York Times* account of Mapleson's arrival appeared on the front page.

> Col. J.H. Mapleson, the opera manager, arrived in this city yesterday morning... with Mrs. Mapleson and the following members of his company: Mmes. Etelka Gerster-Gardini and her husband, Dr. Carlo Gardini; Signori Arditi, Bertini, Bettini, Bello, Bieletto, Campodonico, Caracciolo, Cherubini, Felletti, Francesco, Mighetti, Sivori, Veschetti, Vieini, [Vicini?] Zarini; Mme. Eugenie Pappenheim,

Mme. Valerga, Miss Josephine Yorke, and Mlle. Bettini de Sertis and Mlle. Jiram-
bilia, the baliet-dancer. Mme. Lablache, who is announced to appear at both opera
houses, arrived....Signor Galassi and Lombardelli are already in the City. Signor
Vaselli and Monti are coming on the next steamer. All of the chorus and ballet arrived yesterday....

...."Some people said we were not coming but you see we've come. Plenty of us,
too. About 150 on this ship, and a few more to come....

...."The competition which is going to be seen this season between the Academy
and the new house will be a good thing for the public and the press. Hitherto there
has been no standard for comparison...we shall open with "La Sonnambula," with
Mme. Gerster as Amina....The operas announced in the prospectus will be done."...

...."Signor Perugini and Signor Nicolini will arrive later in the season."

"What about Mme. Patti?"

"She will sail on the 2nd. All the stories about difficulties between her and me
rested on very slight foundation. One thing is certain, she will never sing for Gye
again. He used her unpleasantly and she did not like it. She will stand with me
now."

"Then you are going to oppose Covent Garden?"

"Yes; the new opera-house in London on the Thames Embankment will be built
and I shall manage it, and Mlle. Patti will open it."

"What about Mme. Lablache and Signor Del Puente's engagements?"

"They belong to me, and if I can legally compel them to sing in my company I
shall certainly do it. I shall put injunctions on both of them tomorrow morning the
first thing. Mme. Lablache had a contract with me for last season and this. I paid
her $50 on account. She broke the contract last season and I gave her notice for this.
Now she has calmly walked over to the opposition. If I can be protected I mean to
be. Signor Del Puente came and applied to me in London for an engagement and I
made a contract with him. Soon Mr. Abbey came along and offered him better
terms and all kinds of inducements to leave me. He agreed to pay Del Puente's hotel
and carriage bills, and all sorts of things.

...."Mr. Abbey has got all my old chorus singers, and I have a lot of young, fresh
blood...."

Mlle. Forti and Signori Grassi, Fornari, Contini, and Mirabella of Mr. Abbey's
company arrived on the Amreique. [sic] (New York Times, October 15, 1882, p.1)

The arrival of Giovanni Mirabella signalled a disturbance in the Abbey management. The following day it was announced that a controversy was raging as to his
projected debut at the new opera house. This problem, familiar to all operatic managers, was in itself not of major importance. It revealed, however, that Maurice
Grau, later associated with Abbey in an official capacity, was operating behind the

scenes as Abbey's troubleshooter. Grau's word was of importance in dealing with re-
calcitrant artists:

> The first disturber of the harmony that ought to prevail in musical circles is Signor
> Mirabella, the basso....In his contract according to his statement, was inserted a
> clause stating that he should make his debut as Mephistofeles in "Faust." On arriving
> in America he found that Signor Novara was announced to appear in that role on the
> opening night of the new house. This naturally annoyed Signor Mirabella and he
> hastened yesterday to inform Mr. Maurice Grau that he would sing Mephistofeles on
> the opening night or play the d—l by not singing at all. Mr. Grau insinuated that his
> contract did not say that he should sing the part on the first night, but only on his
> own particular first night, and that was going to be some other night. Signor Mira-
> bella failed to connect with the idea....Mr. Grau said yesterday afternoon that as
> Signor Novara had been so long ago promised the part for the opening night, and
> had been so advertised, and as the public and George Tyson and "Fred" Rullman
> had bought seats for the opening night, with the understanding that Signor Novara
> and he only was to deliver the usual popular lecture on the power of gold, he did not
> see how the state of affairs could be well altered. (*New York Times*, October 16,
> 1883, p.5)

Grau's attitude in the matter was emphatically upheld by the results. Mirabella
made his debut on the fifth night of the season as Giorgio in Bellini's *I Puritani*; al-
thought he did sing the part of Mefistofele in Boito's opera of the same name, he did
not appear in a single *Faust* performance during the entire season, either at the Metropolitan Opera House or on tour.

Grau's reference to Tyson and Rullman supports the earlier complaint by an Academy of Music patron, that in New York operatic ventures, ticket speculators were
given preferential treatment. In the light of such complaints, it is surprising that
opera company administrators not only openly admitted the importance of ticket
speculators, but also permitted them to influence the maintenance of casts as announced.

Mapleson's statements about the extra inducements that Abbey was offering
singers had appeared the day before. The *Times* article describing Abbey's difficulties with Mirabella again referred to the high cost of such extras:

> It was whispered in operatic circles yesterday that Mr. Abbey had been initiated
> into the mysteries of operatic expenses by receiving a bill from the Windsor Hotel for
> eight days' entertainment of Mme. Sembrich, her husband and maid. With the nu-
> merous extras it amounted to $485. Mr. Abbey said it was ridiculous, but he did not
> laugh. (*New York Times*, October 16, 1883, p.5)

MAPLESON'S INJUNCTIONS AND RESULTS

Although it took two days for him to move into action, Mapleson kept true to his
word in obtaining an injunction to prevent Mme. Lablache from singing on the
opening night. In the case of Del Puente, Mapleson's moves were slightly different,
but both cases revealed the court's attitude towards the operatic engagements of

singers. Mapleson's initial move regarding Lablache was reported in the *Times* three days before the projected opening night of the Metropolitan Opera House:

> Mr. J.H. Mapleson, yesterday obtained an injunction…in the Superior Court, restraining Mme. Lablache, the distinguished contralto, from singing in public under any other management than Mr. Mapleson's….Yesterday afternoon, after receiving notice of the injunction, Mme. Lablache called upon Mr. Mapleson in his private office in the Academy of Music.…"Mme. Lablache," said Mr. Mapleson, "says she is perfectly willing to obey the law and sing at the Academy. In fact…she says she is willing to sing in both houses but I'm afraid that can't be fixed." (*New York Times*, October 19, 1883, p.8)

As for Del Puente, Mapleson adopted a more generous attitude. Abbey asserted that Del Puente's contract contained a clause permitting his release for payment of a forfeit of 15,000 francs. Mapleson replied that the clause in question only applied if Del Puente did not come to the United States and that it had been inserted to help the singer convince his wife, who did not wish to make the journey, that the trip was necessary. The same *Times* article contained Mapleson's summary of the situation of the moment: "[It's] the chink of the shekels that seems to fill the air just now that attracts these people."[8]

The following day Del Puente appeared in court, having also been served with an injunction. He claimed that he had experienced trouble in having his correspondence with Mapleson translated and for this reason had been the victim of a misunderstanding. The contract he had originally signed with Mapleson had called for $350 a week and $400 a week "in the provinces." The contract he had executed with Abbey was substantially more beneficial to the singer. In essence it read as follows:

> $500 a week for seven months, all his traveling expenses, a carriage to take him to the theatre, six "distinguished seats" at each performance, 12 days for sickness, and the payment by Mr. Abbey of his forfeit to Col. Mapleson. (*New York Times*, October 20, 1883, p.8)

Mr. Rives, attorney for Del Puente and Abbey, paid 15,000 francs in French currency in order to avert any question of accuracy. Mapleson, for no apparent reason, although conceivably to glorify his own image with the New York City public, made a carefully worded concession:

> …he would not interfere with Mr. Abbey's plans by preventing Signor Del Puente from singing at the Metropolitan Opera-house on Monday evening. The Signor would sing, but the Colonel would yet reserve his legal rights. (*New York Times*, October 20, 1883, p.8)

Argument in the case of Colonel Mapleson against Mme. Lablache was adjourned until Monday. The next indication of further activity in the injunctions appeared one week later. The statement of Haley Fiske, Mapleson's attorney, revealed that Mapleson had also instituted suit against an assistant stage manager and in that instance had successfully convinced the offender to return to the Academy of Music.

...Favor enough had been shown Signor Del Puente by Col. Mapleson in allowing him to sing, despite the injunction, at the opening of the Metropolitan Opera-house....

It was stated by Mr. Fiske that William Parry, against whom Col. Mapleson recently began a suit to restrain him from working at the Metropolitan Opera-house, has gone to work at the Academy of Music as assistant stage manager, under the contract he was charged with having violated. (*New York Times*, October 27, 1883, p.8)

Apparently Del Puente or Abbey felt it was best to abide by the injunction, since Del Puente was replaced in the second performance of *Faust* at a matinee on October 27. On November 5 the court finally handed down a decision on the injunction against Mme. Lablache, and that evening she and Del Puente both appeared in the third production of the Gounod opera. The decision was clear and opened the possibilities for pirating to a far greater extent. The *New York Times* editorialized in its report, using Jay Gould as an example.

Judge *O'Gorman* has decided that Col *Mapleson* is not entitled to an injunction against Mme. *Lablache* because that accomplished contralto, suffering from an embarrassment of contracts, has chosen to keep her contract with Mr. Abbey rather than her contract with himself. The contract, says Judge *O'Gorman*, provides its own penalty for a failure to keep it, and the remedy of Col. *Mapleson* is to recover the penalty from the peccant contralto if he can....

...a mandamus to compel everybody to sing for Col. *Mapleson* and an injunction to prevent anybody from singing for Mr. *Abbey*, would no doubt, have met Col. Mapleson's views of exact justice and of the true interests of italian opera.

Unfortunately, operatic managers work in the shade, while stock gamblers are illuminated with the gladsome light of jurisprudence....Mr. *Abbey* seems to have rather the advantage if the operatic controversy should be adjourned to the courts. Among his patrons are all the eminent stock gamblers, who now for the first time in their lives find themselves in the position of "innocent stockholders." Mr. Gould, for example, who is the foremost living expert in the use of the injunction, and who would be likelier than any other person to put the mandamus on a business basis, could put Mr. *Abbey* up to more new and startling uses of these ancient legal weapons, than Col. *Mapleson* ever heard of...the refusal of Judge *O'Gorman* to help on the good cause with an injunction bodes ill for the future of the lyric drama in this Metropolis. (*New York Times*, November, 5, 1883, p.4)

The court's decision on the injunctions seemed to favor Abbey. The attitude of the press toward his new venture, however, was still pervaded with considerable resentment, due primarily to the scorn directed at many of the Metropolitan Opera House shareholders. The two weeks before attacking Gould in the article above, the *Times* had commented on the makeup of the stockholders in both the Academy and the Metropolitan, and the general tone of the article made it clear that the Metropolitan Opera group was the primary target. The attack was essentially on moral grounds:

...together with the list of stockholders in the old Academy of Music, this list probably includes all of the combined "wealth and fashion" of the City. The investment
of each stockholder in the new opera house is understood to be not far from $20,000,
some boxes of the old Academy have cost their several owners as much as that.

There appear to be 102 of the stockholders and boxholders together, of whom five
only hold boxes in both houses. A generation ago, if it had been conceivable that
there were a hundred men in the community who could afford an investment in an
operabox, the great majority of them would no doubt have been merchants. It is
worth inquiring how the fortunes have been made in our day that will bear so great
a tax.

Hereditary fortunes, now invested in land...are fourteen in number, represented
by eighteen boxes....Twenty-one of them are bankers...not speculators.....Five,
and possibly more, are lawyers....Twenty-one...are merchants and manufacturers.
Eight...acquired fortunes directly in the business of transportation—that is to say,
by building up or managing systems of transportation and receiving profits from the
public in its capacity of shipper or passenger, and not in its capacity of "lamb,"
although several of them have been largely increased by successful appeals to the
public in this latter character. The remaining twenty-five...have been almost indis-
guisedly acquired by "fortunate investments" in Wall Street, which have been very
much in the nature of fortunate investments in a faro bank, except in those numerous cases in which the fortunate operator has occupied the position of dealer and enjoyed the advantage of a previous knowledge of what cards were to appear. In these
cases to call the possessor of a fortune thus acquired a gambler would be a grave injustice—to a gambler.

About one-fourth of the properties of which the operaboxes are evidence have thus
been amassed without the rendering of any equivalent to society; such as is rendered
by the legitimate operations of commerce, manufactures, and by professional
labors.

Two morals seem to be powerfully suggested by this examination. One is that...it
is impossible to make people attach any notion of sanctity to values created by gambling on the Stock Exchange. Another is that, in the words of the late Artemus
Ward, our ancestors knew more than we do, if they were not quite so honest. (*New
York Times*, October 21, 1883, p.8)

The following day was scheduled for the opening performances at both opera
houses. On this occasion the *New York Times* editorial expressed neither preference
nor support for either enterprise; rather it set the stage for what would be a bitter
struggle for survival for both organizations. The Academy was described as "relying
on its ancient prestige and its fresh reinforcements," whereas the Metropolitan was
characterized as "rich in the charms of novelty, and piquing the curiosity of the
town." The editorial summed up the competition:

It remains to be seen how the great public will divide itself between the down-town
Academy and the west side Opera-house. There must be heartburning and jealousies
engendered in this keen competition, but an impartial people will regard the struggle with that calm curiosity which can characterize only those who are left free to
cast in their lot with either house, reserving their commiseration for that which fails.
(*New York Times*, October 22, 1883, p.4)

The *Times'* reporting of the results of the injunction battle and its comments on the stockholders made it quite obvious that the sentiment of those watching from the outside were allied with Col. Mapleson and the Academy of Music. Since Abbey was not attacked personally, he does not seem to have been the object of ill-feeling; rather, antagonism was directed at the group who had petulantly insisted on building and opening the new opera house.

ROSTER AND REPERTOIRE FOR THE METROPOLITAN OPERA HOUSE

Henry E. Abbey (1846–1896), the manager of the first season at the new opera house, was an experienced impresario of theater, concert stage, and opera. Contrary to later Metropolitan custom, he was American born. He came from Akron, Ohio, where his father had been a successful watchmaker. Early in life he rejected any thought of going into his father's business. He made his initial connection with the theater by becoming a ticket seller in a local establishment; after two years, he became the lessee of that establishment. Shortly thereafter he bought a company appearing at the Cleveland Academy of Music. This was in 1869 and the troupe was owned by John Ellsler. They were involved in a production called *London Assurance*. The following year Abbey toured with his first opera company, the Suzan Galton Opera Troupe. During the next few years he managed tours with various stars of the day. In 1876 he formed a partnership and close friendship with John B. Schoeffel, who many years later was his associate at the Metropolitan Opera House. Together they operated the Academy of Music in Buffalo. After a year they moved their center of operation to New York City, where they took over management of the Park Theatre. During the following twenty years Abbey was involved in many ventures, some highly successful and others dismal failures. One of the major artists to appear under his management during these years was the actor Edward A. Sothern.

In 1880 Abbey journeyed to Europe in one of the most important episodes in his career. He signed Sarah Bernhardt, at that time enjoying the height of her career, for appearances in the United States. It was a bold venture and it was highly successful. Bernhardt played 164 performances; the proceeds were $200,000, which was divided equally between the artist and her managers. The managers in this case were Abbey, Schoeffel, and Maurice Grau, who had now joined them and would frequently appear in managerial ventures with both. The Bernhardt tour established Abbey's reputation and must have contributed to the decision to grant him the contract for the opening season at the Metropolitan Opera House. Probably Abbey's greatest contribution to American entertainment was his success in presenting artists of world renown in cities other than New York, notwithstanding the enormous investment necessary for tours of this sort.[9] Grau's position during Abbey's first season at the Metropolitan was apparently that of business manager.[10]

As opening night approached, it became more and more obvious that Henry Abbey had expended great effort and expense in assembling his company—he was able to offer the more attractive fare.

From the Academy and Mapleson he had persuaded four outstanding stars, Emily Lablache, Italo Campanini, Giuseppe Del Puente, and Franco Novara, to join him. Campanini had by this time established a fine reputation, particularly in America. He had made his debut in Bologna in 1871 as Lohengrin. After studying with Francesco Lamperti, he appeared at La Scala in Milan in *Faust* and thus achieved European eminence. He came to America in 1873 and joined Mapleson's company with which he remained until the opening of the Metropolitan Opera House. After starting at eighty cents a night, he had risen to demand a salary of $1,000 a night under Mapleson at the Academy. As mentioned previously, he commanded this same salary with Abbey during the first season but with many more performances, resulting in a total of $56,000. Comparison with Del Puente's salary of $500 per week indicates the enormity of these fees. At the time of his first season at the Metropolitan he was only thirty-seven years old.[11]

Del Puente, a reputable baritone of Spanish birth, had for several years been a highly respected member of Mapleson's company. He was versatile and his repertoire included both heavy dramatic roles and the lighter *buffo* parts in the comic operas of Mozart, Rossini, and Donizetti. His most notable success had been in *Carmen*, an opera in which he had toured the United States with Minnie Hauk and Campanini.[12]

Franco Novara was one of a number of singers at this period who had discovered it worthwhile to change an Anglo-Saxon name (in this case Frank Nash). By this time he had achieved a good reputation, as was evidenced in the opening-night controversy with Mirabella. Performance programs bore witness to his familiarity with a large repertoire of standard bass parts, and his value to any company was without question.

The reviews, reputation, and usual roles of Emily Lablache, the contralto who achieved so much notoriety during the "injunction" episode, do not mark her as an outstanding artist. Chronicles of the Metropolitan Opera seasons as well as those of the Academy of Music show that she was often used as a late replacement in a major role; for this purpose she was of great use to a manager. Flora in *La Traviata*, Marthe in *Faust*, and Mercedes in *Carmen* were roles normally relegated to her, but on occasion she sang such parts as Laura in *La Gioconda*, and even Donna Anna in *Don Giovanni*.[13]

As his leading prima donna, Abbey had secured Christine Nilsson, who although past her prime, was a highly renowned singer and from all indications an excellent artist. She was born in Sweden in 1843, the same year as Adelina Patti, and after several years of study, made her debut in Paris on October 27, 1864, as Violetta in *La Traviata*. She sang with great success in France and England before coming to America in 1870, where she was received with a "perfect ovation."[14] She sang occasionally in the United States until 1881. She then apparently retired, only to reappear at the Metropolitan Opera House on opening night in her most celebrated portrayal, Marguerite in *Faust*.

Christine Nilsson as Valentine in Les Huguenots.

Most notable among the reputable singers Abbey brought to the Metropolitan for this first season was Marcella Sembrich. At that time a rising young star, she later became an immortal name in the list of prima donnas who have appeared at the Metropolitan. Sembrich was born in Polish Galicia in 1858, and thus was only twenty-five when the new opera house opened. Despite her youth she had already received the accolades of critics, singers, and musicians throughout Europe. She had finished her musical tutelage under Franz Liszt and made her debut as a singer in Athens. From 1878 to 1880 she was at the Dresden Court Opera and later triumphed in St. Petersburg and London.[15] As will be discussed later in greater detail, she was an accomplished musician who first amazed a New York City audience with her versatility and artistry during a benefit concert at the Metropolitan Opera House. Her career at the Metropolitan was one of the longest registered and was dotted with great historic moments, including portraying Gilda at Caruso's debut in *Rigoletto* twenty years after the Metropolitan Opera House opened.[16]

Sofia Scalchi was engaged as the leading contralto with the new company. At thirty-three she was already a recognized leader in the operatic world. Scalchi had made her deput as Ulrica in *Un Ballo in Maschera* in Mantua, Italy, at sixteen. At the time of her New York appearances she had already achieved great success both in London and in Rio de Janeiro. Her voice was described as "of delicious quality and unusual range, every note in its compass of two and a half octaves being of a wonderfully soft yet penetrating tone, and of great power."[17] More than ten years later one of New York City's leading music critics praised her continuing success, writing that "her assurance and artistic authority never desert her."[18]

Abbey's other principal singers were artists who, if not as well recognized as those already mentioned, had completed several successful international engagements. The tenors included Roberto Stagno, who shared with Campanini the major tenor assignments. Giuseppe Kaschmann shared the leading baritone roles with Del Puente, except for one performance of *Rigoletto* in which Luigi Guadagnini portrayed the title role; in all subsequent performances of this opera Del Puente assumed the part. Guadagnini's only performance on the tour was in *Le Prophète* in Cincinnati. Achile Augier and Giovanni Mirabella divided the bass assignments with Novara. Among Abbey's female singers, the most notable were the soprano Emmy Fursch-Madi and the mezzo Zelia Trebelli. Trebelli received her greatest opportunities that year in all the performances of *Carmen*, both at the Metropolitan Opera House and on the tour. Her name, like Novara's, had undergone metamorphosis in tribute to current tastes. The original Gilbert she had reversed, dropping the G, and Italianized.

For proper comparison of Abbey's roster with the competition, the major artists at the Academy of Music should be considered. To match the combination of Nilsson and Sembrich, Mapleson was fortunate to have Adelina Patti and Etelka Gerster. Patti had enjoyed monumental success since her debut in 1859 and Mme. Gerster was a young singer of considerable reputation. She drew well at the box office and her welcome by the public was "only slightly less effusive" than Patti's.[19]

With tenors, Mapleson was not so well equipped as Abbey. Campanini's removal to the new company had left him without his most enthusiastically received tenor, and he had not been able to replace him with any of equal caliber. Ernest Nicolini, later better known as Patti's husband, was young at twenty-eight and never achieved much recognition. The other tenors with the Academy were described by Henry Krehbiel as of little consequence.[20] Antonio Galassi was Mapleson's principal baritone, and Enrico Cherubini his leading basso.

The competitive establishments seemed to have little choice among conductors. Abbey had engaged Augusto Vianesi as his principal conductor and Cleofonte Campanini, the tenor's brother, to assist him. Vianesi was an established musical director, as was Mapleson's conductor, Luigi Arditi. Among Vianesi's many accomplishments was conducting the Covent Garden premiere of Lohengrin in 1875, for which he had been highly complimented.[21] Arditi, always Patti's favorite conductor, had led the first performance in England of *Der Fliegende Holländer*.[22] Campanini, although he had not had much experience, received modest praise on his first appearance at the eighth performance of the Metropolitan season.

As Artistic Director of Abbey's company, Vianesi conducted forty-eight performances; Campanini directed only twelve. Ten concerts were also presented, eight under Vianesi's sole direction and two in which the two conductors shared the duties. It would be natural to assume that Campanini's engagement was connected with his brother's position as leading tenor with the company. His performances and reviews during the year, however, provided no evidence of any inefficiency. Although he did not return to the Metropolitan Opera House in later seasons, he appeared with the Manhattan Opera Company for several years. By that time he was a leading conductor no longer relegated to second performances or last-minute substitutions. Vianesi returned to the Metropolitan Opera House in 1891, when he shared the podium with Anton Seidl and Louis Saar. During that season he conducted the greatest share of the performances, since Seidl restricted himself to Wagner and Saar received received relatively few assignments.

Not much is known of the administrative staff during Abbey's initial season at the Metropolitan. Grau, as mentioned, served as business manager. The only other position definitely announced was that of superintendent. As early as May, 1883, Mapleson lost a valuable member of his staff to the new opera house. This fact was briefly mentioned in a *Times* article describing the drawing held for boxes.

> ...it was made known that Mr. A. A. Arment had been appointed superintendent of the new house. Mr. Arment has hitherto been subscription agent for Col. Mapleson, and was, in fact, his right-hand man! (*New York Times*, May 24, 1883, p.1)

A comparison of the two rosters suggests that Abbey's group of artists enjoyed the sounder reputation, notwithstanding the presence of Patti at the Academy of Music. The repertoires of both houses were equally dull, in that they offered little to arouse fervent interests in the public. The only novelty scheduled was the projected American premiere of *La Gioconda* at the Metropolitan Opera House. The Academy offerings included *La Sonnambula, Rigoletto, Norma, Faust, Linda di Chamounix,*

La Gazza Ladra, Marta, La Traviata, Aida, L'Elisir d'Amore, Crispino e la Com-are, and *Les Huguenots* (in Italian). Abbey's fare at the Metropolitan constituted a similar list of old favorites: *Faust, Lucia di Lammermoor, Il Trovatore, I Puritani, Mignon, La Traviata, Lohengrin* (in Italian), *La Sonnambula, Rigoletto, Robert Le Diable, Il Barbiere di Siviglia, Don Giovanni, Mefistofele, Carmen,* (in Italian) and the previously mentioned novelty, *La Gioconda.* In the spring season, Abbey added *Hamlet, Marta, Les Huguenots* (all in Italian), and *Le Prophète. Roméo et Juliette,* although promised on three different occasions during the Metropolitan season, was not produced, owing to the repeated indisposition of Marcella Sembrich. One performance was given in Philadelphia during the final week of the spring tour and Sembrich did appear that time as Juliette.[23]

PERFORMANCES OF MAJOR
IMPORTANCE DURING THE INITIAL SEASON

The opening year at the Metropolitan Opera house was divided into two parts, a regular season and a spring season. The regular season started on October 22 and closed on January 13. From December 25 through January 8, the Metropolitan troupe journeyed to Boston and Brooklyn. After the close of the first season in New York on January 13, the company embarked on a tour that took them to Philadelphia, Chicago, St. Louis, Cincinnati, Washington, Baltimore, and Boston. On March 10 they reopened at the Metropolitan Opera House, remaining there until April 12, when they again traveled to Philadelphia. The season finally closed with a benefit concert for Abbey, held on April 21 at the Metropolitan Opera House.

Opening Night—Faust

On the night of October 22, 1883, the two opera houses began their respective seasons. Although both offered operas that had been heard in New York City, excitement was high enough to provide each company with a capacity audience.

Colonel Mapleson's Academy of Music opened with Bellini's *La Sonnambula,* an opera even then exceedingly familiar to New York audiences. The audience included representatives of the Astors, Belmonts, Dinsmores, and other illustrious families, people who termed themselves the "old guard" of New York City society. Ironically, J. N. A. Griswold, the first president of the Metropolitan Opera House Company, Ltd., was present as a boxholder at the Academy.[24] He had since been succeeded in his position with the Metropolitan by James Roosevelt. The *New York Times* reviewed the performance and was enthusiastic about both the audience and the quality of the production. Arditi was praised as an "industrious and skillful conductor," and Gerster, the Amina, was "greeted with prolonged cheers." The chorus was commended for excellent work and the orchestra was described as "as large and well arranged as ever." The tenor and basso were complimented as well. Most enthusiastic of all were the general comments about the audience and the performance as a whole.

It was such an audience as has rarely been seen in the old Fourteenth street opera
house except upon occasions of more than usual interest, and it was liberal with its
applause...the performance...was one of real artistic merit....

The season at the Academy of Music has opened [a]uspiciously! (*New York Times*,
October 23, 1883, p.5)

The competition and jealousy between the two groups were influential in bringing
as many opera patrons as possible to the two simultaneous openings—references to
subsequent performances do not reveal any evening when both opera houses played
to a capacity audiece.

Opening night at the Metropolitan Opera House merited front-page treatment in
the New York papers. The *Times* filled three columns, dividing its report into four
sections. The first was devoted to the physical plant of the new opera house, including a minute description of the decor. The second section involved itself with a
review of the performance, while the third was a resumé of some of the most important people present. The final part, in the form of a personal experience by someone
who had obtained a balcony seat, was a sarcastic attack on the poor visual and acoustic conditions in the balcony and family circle. The verdict was that except in the first
two rows of these sections, sight lines were unsatisfactory and voices and orchestra
impossible to hear.

The cast was comprised of Abbey's leading singers, except for the minor role of
Marthe, sung by Louise Lablache, the young, inexperienced daughter of the contralto who was under preventative injunction. Faust was assigned to Campanini, Valentin to Del Puente, Mephistopheles to Novara, and Wagner to Ludovico Contini. The
major female roles were portrayed by Abbey's most reputable singers: Nilsson was
the Marguerite and Scalchi sang Siébel. Although the *Times* review of the performance was not completely favorable, it was inclined toward limited praise.

The performance of "Faust" with which the Metropolitan Opera-house was inaugurated...may be considered from two standpoints. Viewed in respect of its impressiveness upon the public, it was somewhat disappointing. Considered as a lyric and
dramatic representation, it contained much that was admirable and little to which
serious exception could be taken...The first two acts of "Faust" were sung with little
or no applause, but for the encore which followed Mme. Scalchi's "Le pariate
d'amor" and the hearty plaudits which came after Mme. Nilsson's "Jewel Song," the
third act would have passed off almost as quietly....The scenery was very beautiful
and the costumes very rich, varied, and accurate....Signor Vianesi's band last night
distinguished itself by a performance which has never been excelled for precision
and nicety of shading. The defective acoustics of the house robbed the tone of some
of its brilliancy, but this can be remedied by the conductor on further acquaintance
with the auditorium he is to fill....The singers who appeared in "Faust" are well
known...Signor Novara, in fact, was a most inefficient Mephisto. A devil who cannot secure an encore for the "Song of the Golden Calf" must be accounted a very
poor devil indeed. Mlle. Louise Lablache was a feeble representative of Marta. The
chorus was numberous and proficient, but the volume and quality of tone it produced was not in keeping with its appearance. At midnight the performance was not
nearly ended. (*New York Times*, October 23, 1883, p.1)

In light of his final sentence, it seems obvious that the critic did not feel he could stay to hear the final trio and still meet the deadline for his morning edition. By commenting so briefly on the singers, he underscored the fact that they had been heard many times in the same opera at the Academy of Music.

The *New York Tribune* reviewer gave considerable more space to the singers' merits.

> The fears which had been generally felt that Signor Campanini would not show a complete amendment of the faults which were so conspicuous during his last season at the Academy of Music were unfortunately realized. Occasionally the old-time sweetness and again occasionally the old-time manly ring were apparent in his notes but they were always weighed down by the evidences of labor, and the brilliancy of the upper tones with which he used to fire an audience into uncontrollable enthusiasm, was gone....

> Of Mme. Nilsson's Margherita there is little to be said that has not been said over and over again....All that Mme. Nilsson sings, as all that she does, is so imbued with a current of sympathy that there is no resisting her whether she be reproducing the ideal of the author or giving instead her own conception of the character. We would not that Goethe's sweet child should do as Nilsson does, but we should not that Nilsson should do otherwise.

> Mme. Nilsson's triumph came in the Jewel Song, where it was expected for it is the golden [link] with which last year she established the connection between her concert room and the memorable night at the Academy when she first sang her way to the hearts of the people. After she had sung it last night the last film of ice that had held the public in decorous check was melted, and an avalanche of plaudits overwhelmed the fair singer. Bouquets rained from the boxes and baskets of flowers were piled over the footlights....Signor Campanini was also remembered in profuse flowers and other marks of kind appreciation; and Mme. Scalchi, who did the most artistic singing of the evening, was not forgotten though her guerdon's were not commensurate with her merits. For Mlle. Louise Lablache, who took the place of her mother who was under the ban of the law, and did her work cleverly, and for Signor Del Puente and Novara, we have time only to chronicle a performance of work of the high degree of merit to which they in part have accustomed us.

> Of the mechanical parts of the performance nothing is to be said except words of praise. The pictures were beautiful, all of them. Nothing was shirked, and the highest skill and most delicate ingenuity seemed combined in constructing scenes of fascinating beauty and almost perfect illusion. (*New York Times*, October 23, 1883, p.5)

The orchestra has been described as being comprised of fifty members from the *Teatro Fenice* in Venice, thirteen from the Leipzig Opera House, five from London (presumably Covent Garden), fifteen from the San Carlo in Naples, and one from the Brussels opera. Their wages were reported to range from $100 to $150 a month.[25]

The members of New York society who chose the Metropolitan Opera House opening were at least as impressive as those who attended the competing Academy of Music opening. Prominent names at the Metropolitan included Vanderbilt, Whitney, Roosevelt, Field, Morgan, and Gould. It was reported that "The Goulds and the Vanderbilts and people of that ilk perfumed the air with the odor of crisp green-backs. The tiers of boxes looked like cases in a m[e]nagerie of monopolists."[26] Mrs. Paran Stevens, née Reed, noted as a "woman with marked social ambition," resolved her opening-night conflict equitably. "Unable to decide where the greater glory lay, Mrs. Stevens divided the evening between the boxes of both houses."[27]

Sembrich's Debut in Lucia

This momentous debut occurred on the second night of the new company's season, October 24, 1883. Combined with the successful opening with *Faust*, Sembrich's performance launched the Abbey company on what promised to be a most auspicious, dazzling season. That subsequent presentations soon became perfunctory was unfortunate; these few early outstanding moments however, sufficed to doom the Academy of Music.

In retrospect, great credit must be given to both New York audiences and critics for their immediate recognition of the artistry of Marcella Sembrich. Her many years as the brilliant prima donna at the top of the Metropolitan roster certainly verified the enthusiastic public acceptance of her work and proved its astute judgment in operatic matters.

The cast for this *Lucia* performance provided excellent support for Mme. Sembrich's introduction to New York opera patrons. Companini sang Edgar, one of his best roles, and the new baritone Giuseppe Kaschmann appeared as Sir Henry Ashton. The conductor was Vianesi. This time both major New York newspapers reported enthusiastically on the debutante's performance. In the opinion of the *New York Times*,

> No singer ever won the recognition of a New York audience more easily than Mme. Sembrich did. The very first note she uttered seemed to establish her in the favor of her hearers, and before the curtain had been lowered upon the first act the new prima donna's triumph was complete...her execution is absolutely faultless, and she sings with a facility of expression and a perfection that are alike most gratifying to the sensitive listener. (*New York Times*, October 25, 1883, p.5)

The *New York Tribune* was not outdone in laudatory terms:

> Mme. Sembrich is a lovely singer—lovely of person, of address, of voice; and her artistic acquirements, in the limited field in which Donizetti's opera called them into activity, at least, are of the highest rank. Her style is exquisite, and plainly the outgrowth of a throroughly musical nature....She carries her voice wonderfully well throughout a wide register, and from her lowest note to her highest there is the same quality of tone. It is a voice of fine texture, too; it has a velvety softness, yet is brilliant; and though not magnetic in the same degree as the voices of other singers still before the public, it has a fine sympathetic vein. It wakens echoes of Mme. Patti's organ, but has a warmer lifeblood in it. (*New York Tribune*, October, 25, 1883, p.5)

In view of the *Tribune's* reference to Patti, the reception for Sembrich must have been particularly deeply felt among the Mapleson forces.

Mignon *Conducted by Campanini*

At a matinee on November 3, Vianesi relinquished the baton to Cleofonte Campanini for the younger conductor's New York City debut. Ironically, his renowned older brother was not on the stage that day. The cast for the performance duplicated that of the season's first *Mignon* on October 31. Campanini was well received as a conductor; a number of years later when he was with Oscar Hammerstein, Krehbiel described him as "then a modest *maestro di cembalo* trying his 'prentice hand at conducting; now the redoubtable leader of Mr. Hammerstein's forces at the Manhattan."[28]

The *New York Times* correspondent was gratified by the performance, reporting as follows:

> The performance...was smooth and commendable, and Mme. Nilsson, Signor Del Puente, Mme. Valleria, and Mme. Scalchi were warmly applauded....

> ...A pleasant feature...was the first appearance in this country of Signor Cleofonte Campanini, brother of the distinguished tenor, as conductor. The young musician received a cordial welcome when he appeared in the place hitherto occupied by Signor Vianesi, and in conducting the performance of Ambroise Thomas's graceful and ingenious music he displayed both intelligence and experience. At the close of the first act he received gifts of flowers and a handsome scarf-ring. (*New York Times*, November 4, 1883, p.8)

American Premiere of La Gioconda

On December 20, 1883, *La Gioconda* received its first American performance in a carefully prepared presentation of excellent caliber. Since this was to be the sole novelty of the season, it unquestionably received minute attention in rehearsals. Christine Nilsson was the Gioconda of the evening, and Enzo was sung by Roberto Stagno. Del Puente, Novara, and Scalchi were the other principal members of the cast. Emmy Fursch-Madi was assigned the role of Laura. Vianesi was the conductor of the relatively new opera, which had received its world premiere in Milan in 1876. The New York papers devoted considerable space to both the opera and its performance. The *New York Times* reported in great detail.

> As represented originally, it was but partially successful; as revised and improved, it has attained a measure of popularity greater even than "I Promessi Sposi," the opera by which Ponchielli first became celebrated in his native land. The libretto...from the pen of Arrigo Boito...bears a certain relationship in plot to Victor Hugo's "Angelo, le Tyran de Padoue,"...the ground is shifted from Padua to more picturesque Venice....

> ...The music...may be characterized as occupying a sort of half-way ground between Verdi's latest manner and the moderate productions of Wagner....The *leit*

motiv, in a mild form, is occasionally resorted to; an almost excessive tendency to modulation is noticeable throughout the score, and the orchestration is full, sonorous, and occasionally brilliant....

The general representation of "La Gioconda" was more commendable for evenness than for the startling effectiveness of any one personation. A cast enlisting the services of Mme. Christine Nilsson, Mme. Scalchi, Mme. Fursch-Madi and Signori Stagno, Del Puente, and Novara could scarcely fail to give satisfaction...Mme. Nilsson, who will undoubtedly "grow into" La Gioconda, is not yet at her best in the part....The role, in fact, is intended for a prima donna *drammatica* and Mme. Nilsson does not belong to that order of songstresses....Mme. Fursch-Madi's performance of Laura was not very animated, but vocally, very telling. Mme. Scalchi lent the never failing charm of her voice to the plaintive measures of La Cieca, and she was heartily applauded. The part of Enzo is a thankless one, but a tenor with a more agreeable voice than Signor Stagno's could accomplish more with it....Signor Del Puente portrayed Barnaba in brighter colors than was expected, but supplied a good performance, vocally and dramatically. Signor Novara was a competent Alvise....the orchestra was in splendid form, the chorus tolerably steady, and the stage attire beautiful and appropriate. Through defective stage management, however, the vessel in the second act was not fired, nor did it sink. In the same act the boy's voices in the sailors' chorus were dispensed with, and a contrast was lost. Parsimony could scarcely have suggested their elimination, and we trust they will be heard when "La Gioconda" is given for the second time. The opera was listened to by a numerous audience, and the applause was generous and frequent. (*New York Times*, December 21, 1883, p.4)

The *New York Tribune* agreed in essence with the *Times*, although it was less kind to Stagno and more appreciative of Nilsson.

The opera was given in a surprisingly brilliant manager...Signor Novara was the only one of the principals who did not reach the plane where his abilities usually move....Of Signor Stagno's Enzo we can only say that it had as little character as his impersonations generally, and his singing throughout was marked by the vicious traits that have characterized his work this season....Mme. Nilsson has in Gioconda a part that enables her to display her strong tragic powers in an admirable light. She did not slight it in any respect and kept the audience in a state of almost painful excitement by the vivid manner in which she depicted the sufferings of the street singer. Mme. Fursch-Madi, Mme. Scalchi and Signor Del Puente all added to their reputations as sterling artists. (*New York Tribune*, December 21, 1883, p.5)

Zelia Trebelli as Carmen

Zelia Trebelli had the distinction of being the first artist to portray the role of Carmen at the Metropolitan Opera House. Although she had a strong reputation in Europe, she was by this time forty-five years old.[29]

This initial performance of *Carmen* at the Metropolitan Opera House on January 9, 1884, was under the direction of the youthful Campanini. Besides Trebelli, the cast included Campanini as Don José, Del Puente as Escamillo, Augier as Zuniga, and Alwina Valleria as Micaela. The *Tribune* hailed Del Puente and Valleria for their singing, and Campanini, on this occasion, mainly for his acting. The stage management was noted unfavorably.

> That Mme. Trebelli would sing the music of the part with fine artistic finish was a foregone conclusion; that she subjected the dramatic elements of it to original and intelligent study, she made plain early in the performance.
>
> In realizing her conception, however, she did not always give the highest degree of satisfaction....Her aim seems to be to make Carmen a beautiful demon, and she leaves no room for either the light heartedness of the gypsy girl or the capacity which she has for tender attachment. Now Carmen does love Don Jose—for a little while; otherwise her seduction of him is wanton wickedness....The hardness which Mme. Trebelli gives the character fits it admirably after the scene in which she learns her fate from the cards and so grimly and characteristically accepts it....But it needs lightness and grace in earlier moments. Signor Campanini was in bad voice, but acted with telling fervor....Signor Del Puente was the Escamillo of old....The vocal success of the opera was Mme. Valleria, who sang beautifully throughout and did her best to save a performance which was almost fatally hurt by poor singing and acting in the subordinate parts and wretched stage management. The opera was handsomely set. (*New York Tribune*, January 10, 1884, p.4)

In the *Times* a far more analytical critique of Mme. Trebelli's portrayal was coupled with a considerably less enthusiastic review of the performance in general.

> The representation of "Carmen" at the Metropolitan Opera-house last evening rather disappointed expectation, and but for Signor Campanini's portrayal of Don Jose, would not have stirred the pulses of the audience....Many representations at the Metropolitan, which would have produced a favorable impression in another establishment have failed to please because of the size and chilliness of the auditorium. Last night's rendering of Bizet's pretty and effective work would undoubtedly have fared better had it been given elsewhere. It was not, however, a brilliant achievement....Signor Del Puente's voice scarcely filled the Metropolitan as it did the Academy; and the labors of the chorus and orchestra, though earnest, were in many instances misdirected, and [productive] of unfinished and unimpressive results. ...Mme. Trebelli...was not exactly successful. It was impossible not to compare her delineation of Carmen with Mme. Hauk's, for it was undoubtedly modeled on the *creation*—in the Italian version—of the German-American songstress. Mme. Hauk, who seldom distinguished herself in other roles—unquestionably presented a very vivid and real picture of Jose's mistress. It was vulgar in tone, but it was powerful and lifelike. Carmen, as sketched by the librettist, is vulgar—that is to say, as vulgar as an operatic personage can be. Mme. Hauk's portrayal was repulsive to just this extent; it was also magnetic, and consequently, telling. Mme. Trebelli's Carmen is intelligent and inoffensive, but nothing more. Last night the singer was disagreeably self-conscious, and much of the music was sung straight to the audience. This *ad captandum* may be borne with in comic opera, but in a performance in which a dramatic story is unrolled...the actor should give no sign of knowledge that an assemblage is gathered before him. Vocally Mme. Trebelli's personation was respectable. She was in good form and the highest and lowest tones of her organ sounded well, even in the vast auditorium. Her execution was musicianly, but her style—histrionically as well as lyrically—was decidedly hard...we can understand that her

steady services as an artist should have endeared her to the London public, but find it less easy to discover the grounds upon which her great reputation in England has rested...the achievements of the orchestra rarely rose above mediocrity. The scenery and dresses were fresh and beautiful. (*New York Times*, January 10, 1884, p.4)

Scalchi in Le Prophète

Sofia Scalchi, who portrayed Fidès in the first Metropolitan performance of Meyerbeer's *Le Prophète*, was one of the few singers in Abbey's initial season who consistently received fine reviews. The opera had not been heard in New York in many years, having last been presented at the Astor Palace Opera House in 1849, only four years after its Paris premiere. In the short time since the season began, Scalchi had established herself an important star of the new company. Her perform- ance in La Gioconda had been commended and the public flocked to the March 21 premiere of *Le Prophète* with great expectations. Stagno, Mirabella, and Valleria sang the other major roles. The role of Fidès is powerful, dramatic, and demanding, and Scalchi's reception indicated that she was equal to the challenge. The *New York Tribune* praised her in the following words:

> In Mme. Scalchi the patrons of opera have learned to recognize a singer who never causes them a serious disappointment....The flaws were few and were more than overbalanced by Mme. Scalchi's exhibition of dramatic power in the climax of the opera. (*New York Tribune*, March 22, 1884, p.5)

In its lengthy report on the revival, the *New York Times* singled Scalchi out for lavish praise. The orchestra and chorus were castigated for another poor showing and some individuals were pointed out as an example of poor audience decorum.

> Its strongest feature was Mme. Scalchi's performance of Fides. The range of the music of the role often made severe demands upon the contralto's high tones, which, by comparison with her lower register, are thin and weak, but whenever the pure contralto notes were to be sung, her voice rolled forth with a perfect wealth of reso- nance. In the trying cathedral scene, with John, Mme. Scalchi acted with consider- able fervor, and the effect wrought at this stage of events, as well as in most of her numbers, and especially in the *a due* passages with Berta, was of the happiest kind. ...The chorus was sluggish, and the orchestra efficient but entirely devoid of ambi- tion as to shading and accent. Signor Vianesi ought to send his musicians to a few Philharmonic concerts, where they could learn what briskness, brilliancy, and power may be attained by talent and toil. The scenery was new and beautiful. ...Last night the youthful tenants of one of the first tier boxes rendered themselves so offensive in this respect that an unkown gentleman, rising from his seat in the par- quet just before Signor Stagno reached the last bars of the second act, loudly re- quested the delinquents to be quiet, "that we may hear the opera." General applause followed the rebuke, and the nuisance was abated at once. (*New York Times*, March 22, 1884, p.5)

Final Benefit Concert for Abbey

The benefit concert for Abbey on April 21, 1884, was important because it turned out to be an evening primarily devoted to displaying the varied talents of Marcella Sembrich. The willingness of the singers to take part in a benefit for their manager was not unusual; earlier in the season, Mapleson's company at the Academy of Music had tendered him a similar honor and gratuity.[30] The artists who participated at the benefit for Abbey included Campanini, Capoul, Corsini, Del Puente, Grazzi, Kaschmann, Mirabella, and Novara, as well as Mesdames Fursch-Madi, Goldini, Nilsson, Sembrich, and Trebelli. The chorus, ballet, and orchestra assisted, and as an added feature Henry Irving and Ellen Terry, with the support of their entire company, presented the "Trial Scene" from *The Merchant of Venice*. The musical part of the program opened with the overture from *William Tell*, followed by selections from Act II of Donizetti's *Lucrezia Borgia*, the entire second act of *Il Barbiere di Siviglia*, a scene from *Aida*, and the adagio and finale from the Violin Concerto No. 7 by the Belgian virtuoso Charles-Auguste Beriot, with Sembrich as soloist. After intermission, the program resumed with the overture and chorus from Meyerbeer's *Dinorah*, Gounod's "Ave Maria," Act IV from *Les Huguenots*, the scene from *The Merchant of Venice* and, finally, a *ballet divertissement* entitled "Farewell," arranged by Vianesi from music of Edoardo Mascheroni.[31] The program must have been terribly long and taxing but the reception brought forth encores.

Sembrich's part in the program was incredible. She first appeared in the excerpt from *Il Barbiere di Siviglia*. During the lesson scene she sang the Air and Variations by Heinrich Proch and the Russian national anthem. She next appeared as the violin soloist with the orchestra in the de Beriot concerto. When she returned for an encore, it was as a piano soloist, playing the Chopin Waltz in C-sharp minor, Op. 64, no. 2. For a second encore she sang an aria from *La Sonnambula*. In the second half of the program, Sembrich returned, this time to play a violin obbligato for her fellow prima donna Nilsson, who sang the Bach-Gounod "Ave Maria." Sembrich's numbers revealed the true musicianship and versatility of this great diva. When she arrived in America, she was known to be an accomplished musician. The stories that rapidly circulated about her abilities as an instrumentalist were amply justified on this occasion. Quite probably this was the first time any one audience had been exposed to her incredible versatility.

> The testimonial benefit to Mr. Henry E. Abbey at the Metropolitan Opera-house last night was attended by a large and brilliant audience, among which were many persons of note in theatrical, musical, literary, and financial circles....Mme. Sembrich carried off a large share of the evening's honors. Her singing of Proch's air and variations in the lesson scene of "Il Barbiere" was admirable for smoothness and ease of execution. She was twice interrupted by applause in the staccato passage and made to return to the beginning. Subsequently she made her first appearance as a violinist, playing the adagio and finale from De Beriot's seventh concerto. Her playing was a surprise. She possesses a delightfully clear and sweet tone, her stopping is accurate, and her bowing strong. Above all, she plays with the sentiment of an artist. A storm of applause followed her performance, and for an encore she played on the

piano, Chopin's waltz in C-sharp minor, proving herself to be also an accomplished pianist. Again recalled, she came before the curtain, sang once more, and retired laden with flowers. She appeared with her violin once more, when she played the obbligato to the Bach-Gounod "Ave Maria," which was sung beautifully by Mme. Nilsson....Mr. Abbey was, unfortunately, ill and unable to answer the loud calls for him. No estimate of the receipts could be obtained last night, but the figures will shortly be given in detail. (*New York Times*, April 22, 1884, p.4)

Abbey realized $16,000 from the evening[32]—concrete evidence of the loyalty of New York audiences, as well as singers and administrative personnel

RESULTS OF THE SEASON

Though Mapleson at the Academy of Music was suffering severe financial and artistic setbacks, his situation was not so difficult as that of Henry Abbey at the Metropolitan Opera House. The pressure of launching a new enterprise was strong and Abbey did not find his task easy. Although they staunchly denied it, Abbey and his associate John Schoeffel, in their efforts to obtain stars to compete with the established Academy company, had been forced to pay salaries that were completely unreasonable in terms of the receipts that were projected at the current box-office prices. This was obvious in the case of Campanini and Del Puente, for Abbey made no attempt to deny Mapleson's statements at the time of the court proceedings against Del Puente and Lablache. In February, Ernest Gye, then becoming involved in an apparent change in managers for the next season, commented in much the same vein that Mapleson had earlier:

New artists would have to be engaged, and this, under existing circumstances, was no small matter. Mr. Abbey...had totally demoralized the European opera market. He had offered and given such salaries that artists could be engaged for America only at prices almost ruinous. (*New York Times*, February 16, 1884, p.5)

An article bearing the headline "Mr. Abbey's Profits" appeared on the same page of the *New York Times;* it referred to a rumor that the firm of Abbey and Schoeffel, which operated theatrical enterprises in Boston, London, and on tour (Henry Irving Company), was about to fail. Shortly prior to this, the newspapers had carried considerable discussion of an additional assessment on the stockholders of the Metropolitan Opera House Company, Ltd. This assessment in all probability generated the rumor about Abbey's solvency. Schoeffel apparently felt differently concerning the origin of the rumor:

Boston, Feb. 15—Mr. Schoeffel emphatically denies the story from Minneapolis of the failure of Abbey and Schoeffel. He said tonight that the firm of Abbey and Schoeffel would pay 100 cents on the dollar on every just claim presented to them. They had made too much money the past year to fail unless they were rascals. The

Grand Opera House, New York, the Irving tour, the Park Theatre here, and the Lyceum Theatre, in London, had paid them a net profit of about $200,000, and to
think of failure in face of such a fact was absurd....As to Col. Mapleson's charges
that Mr. Abbey paid his singers ruinously high salaries, Mr. Schoeffel denied it for
his firm....The Opera House was hired, not owned by Mr. Abbey, and whether the
owners of the building declared heavy dividends or levied heavy assessments Messrs.
Abbey and Schoeffel expressed the opinion that the circulation of the report, was a
trick of Col. Mapleson's to injure a rival opera company. (*New York Times*,
February 16, 1884, p.5)

Evidence strongly refuted Mr. Schoeffel's statement, especially since both Campanini's and Del Puente's salaries had been published. Besides having to pay the
singers, both companies had already found that New York did not have enough
opera patrons to allow survival of two organizations simultaneously producing Italian opera.

Deficit for First Season

Unfortunately there were no definite figures made public at the time as to the exact loss which Abbey incurred during his first season at the Metropolitan Opera
House. Years later Schoeffel wrote to Henry Krehbiel that the deficit was $600,000.[33]
Regardless of how this is applied, whether to performances solely at the Metropolitan
or to include the tours, it was a staggering figure.[34] The only protection Abbey had
was a clause in his original contract that assured him of reimbursement up to $60,000
should there be a loss of that magnitude. On February 14, 1884, Abbey's exact terms
were finally made public by a member of the Metropolitan's Board of Directors, who
stated, "We agreed to give Mr. Abbey the house rent free for all operatic performances and to pay him $1,000 a night for the 60 nights of the Fall and Spring
seasons."[35] The addition of $16,000 realized from the benefit still left Abbey with a
loss in excess of half a million dollars.

Although Schoeffel's figure was apparently based on Abbey's Day Book and auditor's accounts, now in the Metropolitan Archives, the question still exists whether the
reputed loss was an exaggeration. At a Board of Director's meeting in January held to
discuss the mortgage, it was asserted that "Mr. Abbey has lost $53,000 thus far."[36] If
this statement is believed, then it would appear impossible for Abbey to reach
Schoeffel's figure of $600,000 at the end of the season, since by January more than
half of the year's performances at the Metropolitan Opera-house had already been
presented.

The actual figure will probably never be known. Early in the season, however, it
must have become apparent to Abbey that the results would be disastrous for him.
His first public admission of his intention to terminate his connections with the new
opera-house came in February. When the stockholders released this information,
one of them issued a ludicrous comment concerning their "liberal" treatment of him:

> Mr. Abbey has notified the Directors...that he does not want the opera-house for another year. He says there is not enough money in it for him. Of course we have never pried into his business affairs, and we have never asked him how much he has lost or how much he has made out of the opera-house....I do not see, however, under the very liberal treatment he has received at the hands of the Directors, how he could have lost much in the opera-house. (*New York Times*, February 14, 1884, p.5)

Two days later in an article concerning Patti's and Mapleson's plans, the *Times* dealt with Abbey's problems in greater detail:

> The Metropolitan Opera-house season has been financially a disastrous failure. Why it has been so is very easily seen. The house, when filled to its capacity, holds $10,000. The weekly expenses are $35,000. There are four performances weekly in the season, and if the house were full at each one the total receipts would give a profit of $5,000 per week. But the house is never full, and never can be, because there is such a large part of it in which no one can see or hear....It is confidently asserted by persons familiar with the operatic business that there was no week during the Fall season when the expenses of the house were taken in, and in all but two or three the receipts were very far below the expenditures. This kind of calculation, moreover, leaves out all account of the enourmous outlay for costumes and properties, and scenery before the opening of the season. The cost of lighting and heating the house ran far ahead of Abbey's expectations and every cent of it came out of his pocket. ...Naturally he turned to the stockholders to assist him in his difficulties. ...First...that if they would assist him in paying up his losses for the present season he would take the house with a moderate guarantee for the next season. This was declined. Then Mr. Abbey said that if the stockholders would make good his entire deficit for this year he would take the house and run it next year without a dollar's expense to them. This proposition was also declined. The stockholders felt that in taking care of their indebtedness on the building, they had their hands quite full. (*New York Times*, February 16, 1884, p.5)

Little has been said of the tours that Abbey undertook between the fall and spring seasons at the new opera house. Frequently the two rival companies played the same city on the same night and this must have taken its toll in additional losses to both. Abbey's company was traveling with a number of large pageant operas such as *Le Prophète* and *Les Huguenots*, which greatly increased the expense. His chorus was larger, his orchestra was larger, and his travel far more extensive than Mapleson's, so it was not remarkable that he sustained monumental losses. If four performances per week in New York cost $35,000, it certainly must have cost him equally as much to tour, even though he usually presented six to seven productions a week when away from New York. The attendance at tour performances of both companies was poor, although on isolated occasions they drew surpisingly large audiences on the same evening.[37]

The ticket speculators continued to create ill-feeling among the patrons of opera. No evidence suggests that the two opera managers were making any efforts to curtail or control their activities. These manipulations took place while the companies were on tour as well as at home, as evidenced by the following report in the *New York Times* shortly before both rival companies were appearing in Chicago:

It is asserted that there is hardly a barkeeper of a first class saloon in the city who has not got his pockets full of seats for Patti and Nilsson nights. He has not purchased them for his own private speculation, but they have been placed in his hands by others, who will reap the profits, which will be large, and pay him well for his trouble. (*New York Times*, January 19, 1884, p.1)

Since the tour did nothing but place Abbey deeper in debt, he had no alternative but to retire from the Metropolitan Opera House management, and this he indicated as early as February of 1884. Although many of the participants, including Abbey, Mapleson, the Board of Directors, and the stockholders issued affirmations and denials, a number of factors contributed to the financial collapse of the Abbey Italian Opera Company at the Metropolitan. An editorial in the *New York Times* captured the significant factors.

It seems to be settled that Mr. Abbey will not devote himself for another year to "impressing" all the famous singers in the world for the gratification of the stockholders in the Metropolitan Opera-house....Mr. Abbey heroically retires simply because he has lost enough money....

...Mr. *Abbey* has done the thing handsomely and made his ending after the high Roman fashion. Never was opera given in New York, nor for that matter anywhere else, with so prodigal a disregard for expense. The stages of Europe were rifled, not merely to adorn the stage of the Metropolitan Opera-house, but to sequestrate singers from the researches of Col. *Mapleson*, and to keep them corraled under pay and in sumptuous quarters at hotels where they dined with all their music in them. ...A ruined Abbey is a picturesque spectacle....

Most certainly the stockholders of the Metropolitan Opera-house cannot complain of Mr. *Abbey* as certainly Mr. *Abbey* cannot complain of them. He has given them opera handsomely, and they have paid for it very handsomely. They put at his disposal a very costly house, and gave him what people unfamiliar with Italian opera would regard as a very liberal subsidy besides, and most of them seem to acquiesce in the proposition that they must pay for their whistle....

It is altogether unlikely that a season at the Metropolitan Opera-house will ever show a balance upon the right side of the account. Such a result would be contrary to all precedent. The complaints of the building itself are for the most part complaints of a difficulty inherent in the scheme, and not of the manner in which the scheme has been executed. The truth is that the problem of providing over three thousand good seats—that is to say, seats in which all the occupants can hear well and see well—in a theatre of which three tiers are given up to less than seven hundred people is an insoluble problem. The Metropolitan Opera House is probably the last attempt that will be made at its solution. (*New York Times*, February 14, 1884, p.4)

The key element of the description of the "liberal subsidy" lay in the phrase "what people unfamiliar with Italian opera would regard as...." Other than the one stockholder quoted earlier, it is doubtful that anyone felt that the stockholders had been liberal with Abbey. The reduction in the capacity of the house by the use of choice, expensive areas for a plethora of boxes was obvious. The competition from a company as well established as Mapleson's, an artist of the renown and ability of Adelina Patti, and a manager as experienced as Col. Mapleson were additional factors making Abbey's task impossible. Finally, whether or not Abbey drove salaries completely out of the range of possibility was of minimal importance, for the very nature of the competition would have had a terrific impact on the demands of artists anyway.

The Metropolitan Opera House Board of Directors, in acquiescing to "pay for their whistle," were referring to additional assessments. These became necessary both to obtain a new manager and to keep the building solvent. A change was inevitable if they were to succeed in keeping opera performances on the Metropolitan stage.

Basically Abbey had shown himself to be a capable manager and certainly one who was familiar with the technical problems of opera. His tastes were lavish, but it was inconceivable that the group fostering the new opera house would have entered into a contract with anyone not proven to have these lavish tastes. By the expensive facilities, the Board had shown that they, too, were interested in producing opera on the grandest of scales.

Lilli Lehmann, the world-renowned prima donna who came to the Metropolitan during the next era, described the luxurious appointments of the establishment in these well-chosen words:

> The origin of this luxurious abode of art reminds one of a tale from the *Thousand and One Nights*, luxurious, because the Italian opera season had dedicated it two years previously with the stars Patti, Nilsson, Albani, and others, and it had swallowed up frightful sums of money (partly returned in profits indeed) because, aside from the immense salaries, every costume, every shoe and stocking was provided for it by Worth of Paris.[38]

Lilli Lehmann referred to a group of artists who belonged not only to the Metropolitan but also to its competitor. That such expenses were "partly returned in profits" was dubious, but her description of the salaries and wardrobe materials* indicated that nothing was spared to make this the most glamorous and elegant opera house of all.

---

*Editor's note: Lehmann's statement about Worth of Paris has often been repeated, but programs for the first season state that costumes "were manufactured at Venice by D. Ascoli."

CHAPTER 3

The Introduction of German Opera

Early during the initial season at the Metropolitan Opera House it became obvious that the situation was complicated and that almost insurmountable difficulties faced the stockholders, as well as the manager, Henry Abbey. At the conclusion of Abbey's first fall season a long article in the *New York Times* reviewed the efforts of both Abbey's and Mapleson's companies. In essence, it preferred the performances at the Academy of Music but was not unduly harsh with the Metropolitan efforts. In fact, in certain areas of production, notably scenic and choral, the comments favored Abbey. In the opinion of the *Times*, Mapleson emerged victorious in the competition, but owed his success more to the presence of Adelina Patti in his company than to any other one feature. The basic point of the *Times* article was that the founding of a new opera house in New York City was unnecessary:

> ...Mr. Mapleson was fortunate to secure the foremost in the person of Mme. Patti. In a decade hence how many of us will recollect the vastness of the Metropolitan Opera House or the fashionable throngs at the Academy of Music? But who will forget that he or she has listened to Mme. Patti?...

> ...Accomplished and earnest as Signor Vianesi has shown himself to be, his labors have only cast new lustre upon Signor Arditi's. All that Signor Vianesi has accomplished with a more numerous band and chorus and all that he has done at a prodigious and visible outlay of physical energy, has been brought about in the quietest way by Signor Arditi....

> ...New York cannot support two opera houses—indeed, its audiences, as a rule, afford but scant encouragement to one establishment of the kind—and the work performed at the Metropolitan has not been of such a character as to make the impartial observer swerve from his allegiance to the older house. The struggle has simply cost two managers a vast expenditure of money and done nothing for art that might not have been as well done in the old familiar way. (*New York Times*, January 20, 1884, p.4)

Five days earlier, the Metropolitan Board of Directors had held the first of a long series of meetings focusing on the problems of meeting the mortgage, redecorating the house, correcting accoustical problems, and finding a new manager. The directors expended considerable effort to create an aura of tranquility and to show a minimum of concern for the problem of obtaining a new impresario.

> Nothing has been done, and, in spite of the fact that the voices of two or three persons talking at once were audible half-way across Thirty-ninth street...the meeting was very harmonious...there was going to be a very fine season of opera at the Metropolitan Opera House next season. The Directors and Secretary, however, did not know how this season was going to be provided....The question of clearing off the six-hundred-thousand-dollar mortgage on the building came up, but reached no definite settlement. The question of who should be the impresario next season did not come up formally. No applications have been put before the board. The whole matter was yesterday referred to the Amusement Committee....The question of financial support for the impresario was not considered, and it was s[t]outly asserted that it did not need any consideration....It was announced with eagerness and pride that several boxes had been transformed, on account of their holders' deaths, at a premium of 50 percent. The price of a box was $15,000; it is now $22,500. The question of the management for next season has been deferred until a later meeting. (*New York Times*, January 15, 1884, p.8)

THE ASSESSMENT FOR MORTGAGE CLEARANCE

The assessment needed to meet the mortgage and to complete payment for unexpectedly high building expense was handled by the directors of the Metropolitan Opera with a minimum of complications. In mid-February the directors met to deal with two problems: the method of meeting a deficit of $240,000 and the need for a new manager. The newspaper report on the meeting provided this information concerning plans for meeting the deficiency:

> ...the subject which just now perplexes them (the directors) is how to meet a deficit of over $200,000 in the accounts of the house, and to redecorate and finish certain portions of it before the opening of the next season....
>
> ...a resolution was passed directing the Secretary to send to each stockholder a copy of the financial exhibit of the company, and an invitation to take $3,500 additional stock, by doing which the amount of $245,000 would be raised, and this amount, it was estimated, would pay all outstanding accounts, and provide for recarpeting the corridors, redecorating the auditorium, foyer and reception room, providing screens in the vestibules, and furniture for the ball-room....
>
> James A. Roosevelt, the President of the Opera-house Company...said the...statement was correct and had been sent to all the stockholders. The deficiency did not represent a debt entirely, but included an estimate for improvements in the building....
>
> "...Under the charter of the Opera-house Company, the stockholders own their boxes but the Directors are authorized to assess them a certain amount, which is left wholly discretionary with the board for admission to the house. We assessed the stockholders $1,800 for 60 nights, $1,000 to be paid at the beginning of the Fall season, which has been collected, and $600 to be paid at the beginning of the Spring

season, which is yet to be called for. That is at the rate of $30 per night for a box, and
I have had no trouble in renting my box for $60 a night...when I have not wanted to
use it myself.

"...Two plans were suggested...in January for raising the money to pay the debts
and make the changes, one was...by placing a second mortgage on the house, and
the other was for the stockholders to subscribe for $3,500 worth of additional stock.
...Of the 70 stockholders, 46 have already signified their intention of taking the extra
stock, and I know of only four who have positively declined to do so...."

Henry Clews, one of the most active stockholders...said..."if a boxholder finds the
luxury of opera too expensive, all he has got to do is sell out and pocket a profit.
There are plenty of persons who want to come in, and any one of them will readily
pay $22,500 for a box." (*New York Times*, February 14, 1883, p.5)

As to whether the Metropolitan Opera House actually had a waiting list of potential investors, the combined list of stockholders of the two opera houses probably included "all of the combined 'wealth and fashion' of the City."[1] The statement by
Clews might well be interpreted as loyalty or as a scornful remark directed toward
the unwilling. The stockholders who declined the assessment may have done so with
the goal of a combination with the Academy of Music. In the quest for a manager,
this alternative received nominal support. An editorial in the same issue of the *Times*
named business conditions as underlying the resistance both to the last $600 of the
original assessment and to the proposed new assessment. The editorial also paid
tribute to Abbey's gallantry and lavish presentations.

A few of them (the stockholders) have anonymously expressed discontent at the
final installment of the assessment, who would no doubt have maintained an aspect
of sweet serenity if there had been a "boom" during the Winter instead of a depres-
sion in the stock market....

It is altogether unlikely that a season at the Metropolitan Opera-house will ever
show a balance upon the right side of the account. Such a result would be contrary to
all precedent. The complaints of the building itself are for the most part complaints
of a difficulty inherent in the scheme....The truth is that the problem of providing
over three thousand good seats—...in which all the occupants can hear well and see
well—in a theatre of which three tiers are given up to less than seven hundred people
is an insoluble problem. The Metropolitan Opera-house is probably the last attempt
that will be made at its solution. (*New YorkTimes*, February 14, 1884, p.4)

Less than a week later, stockholder opposition to the assessment was reported.
Evidently not enough of them objected to cause a change in plans, and so the needed
funds were apparently forthcoming:

> The Rumors Which Fly Around But Are Brought Up
> Somewhat Short

> The opera-rumor mill...declares that the stockholders of the Academy of Music
> are jubilant over the signs of weakness in the enemy's camp....Rumor further
> declares that there is much feeling among the stockholders of the Metropolitan
> Opera-house relative to the recent assessment of $3,500 each. (*New York Times*,
> February 20, 1884, p.5)

As can be observed from the controversies that followed in the quest for a new impresario and with the continuing efforts by a minority to effect a combination with
the Academy of Music, the unanimity among the Metropolitan Opera House stockholders had been shattered early in the venture. The first display of ill-feeling among
this group was evident in a *New York Times* editorial concerning remarks made by
Cyrus W. Field, one of the early stockholders of the Metropolitan.

Hogs and Opera Boxes

> Our esteemed contemporary...Mr. *Cyrus W. Field*, demands through the influ-
> ential and widely circulated journal the ownership of which he acknowledged in
> court the other day, that the American hog shall be excluded from the opera....It
> will at once be observed that our esteemed contemporary speaks in a parable; and
> does not mean the four-footed swine, but ill-regulated bipeds who prefer their own
> noise to that made upon the stage. It seems it is the box-holders who annoy our
> esteemed contemporary in what ought to be his "quiet seat above the thunder," to
> which the confused noises of the poor and lowly in the parquet come but as a faint
> and far-off murmur....You can no more hinder a man from conversing in his own
> opera-box than you can hinder him from snoring in his own pew....
>
> ...But perhaps the best thing he can do is to protect his ears by buying a box on
> each side of his own and stocking it with deaf-mutes of cleanly appearance and dig-
> nified deportment. We should strongly dissuade him from introducing into the
> opera-house the practice of audible expressions of the opinions held by one box-
> holder touching another box-holder. (November 28, 1883, p.4)

The list of original boxholders revealed Field's neighbor on the left to be J. Pierpont Morgan, while the box on his right was one of those omitted at the original
drawing. Beyond at least token resistance to their assessment, then, the Metropolitan
Opera House directors were faced with internal strife among the stockholders. This
compounded the difficulties of the task ahead of them as they prepared for the coming season.

The Search For A New Impresario

When it was finally definitely established on February 14, 1884, that Abbey would
not renew his lease on the Metropolitan Opera House, the Board of Directors gave
little evidence of concern in finding a replacement for him. Their attitude seemed
best reflected by the statement in the *New York Times* that "impresarios are as thick
as mosquitoes on Sandy Hook and the Metropolitan Opera-house will not go begging
for a lessee."[2] At this point, the directors were far more concerned with the assess-

ment to meet their deficit and redecorate and finish the building interior. The ensuing complications were involved with many decisions, one of them the ultimate result of negotiations between Mapleson and the directors of the Academy of Music. The possibilities open to the Metropolitan stockholders were numerous and complex. They included the possibility of a merger with the Academy of Music, the reengagement of Abbey on a fixed salary, or the negotiation with any number of prospective impresarios and would-be impresarios.

The adverse publicity given the new opera house acted as a distinct deterrent in negotiations, both with prospective managers and with the Academy of Music. In any case, the pride of the contending supporters precluded a successful merger with the Academy of Music, even if it had been economically or artistically feasible. When Abbey announced his offer to manage the opera house on a salary in lieu of a guarantee, the same newspaper release reported that four other people had already approached the Metropolitan directors. The lengthy newspaper account covered the various possibilities thoroughly and provided an excellent resumé of the immediate situation after Abbey's announcement of his forthcoming departure:

> In the meantime four other persons...had made movements toward securing the house. These were Mr. Charles Mapleson, Mr. R. E. Hutchinson, husband of Mme. Alwina Valleria: Signor Campanini, and Mr. Ernest Gye. Mr. Charles Mapleson has had his eye on several propositions to the Directors, none of which were satisfactory to them. Mr. Hutchinson and Signor Campanini also made offers. Mr. Gye, who refused to make any definite movements as long as Mr. Abbey had not signified his intention of giving up the place, was quietly awaiting his time. Mr. Abbey urged the case of Signor Campanini. Mr. Charles Mapleson advocated the cause of Mr. Gye when he found that his own wishes could not be gratified. Of the four...Mr. Gye has the best prospect of securing the house. It has been frequently reported that Mr. Maurice Grau was an applicant. This is flatly denied by those who know Mr. Grau. They say he knows altogether too much about operatic management to want the Metropolitan. Moreover he has been in the house during the present season and has seen what an enormously expensive place it is.

> While the Directors were dickering with Mr. Abbey they asked his consent to their communicating with Mr. Gye. The consent was given, and negotiations were opened. Mr. Gye replied through his agent in this city, that before making any offer he would have to know just what the expense was going to be. The cost of running the house and the intentions of the stockholders in the way of assistance must be made plain to him. He further stated that a great difficulty in his way was the fact that he had no artists engaged under contracts which would permit him to bring them to America. New artists would have to be engaged, and this, under existing circumstances, was no small matter. Mr. Abbey, he said, had totally demoralized the European operatic market. He had offered and given such salaries that artists could be engaged for America only at prices almost ruinous. All these things must be considered by the stockholders here in dealing with Mr. Gye. A conference was held between certain Directors of the opera-house and Mr. Gye's representative about the middle of the week. Mr. Gye's agent was instructed to cable to his principal to come to America and settle the whole matter. This was immediately done. Mr. Ernest Gye is at present on the continent looking out for operatic attractions for London,

and his brother, Mr. Herbert Gye, will, in all probability, respond to the message, and come to America within a short time....

...It is exceedingly doubtful whether an experienced impresario like Mr. Gye will consent to take the house unless important changes are made in the auditorium. Another matter which has been frequently discussed by the newspapers is the possible consolidation of the Academy of Music and the opera-house. No one, however, has been able to point out any satisfactory basis on which this could be accomplished. A prominent stockholder in the Academy put the whole matter in a nutshell recently....

"...They have all the good boxes in the house and they have paid more than $15,000 each for them....There are left only the bagnoir boxes and the third tier. Do you think we are going to oblige them by taking those inferior boxes?...But suppose, for the sake of argument, that we would do so and they would consent to a new allottment. How much is the additional number of stockholders' boxes going to take out of the manager's profits and what impresario is going to take the house on those conditions? It has even been suggested that we might...share boxes with them. But...the dissatisfaction on the first night of a new opera would be so great as to create a split at once. I do not...see any plan by which the two houses can be consolidated. Moreover, no such matter has come up for negotiation, and it is not likely to. Col. Mapleson has another year's right to the Academy. If we consolidate, how are we going to keep our contract with him? The whole thing is absurd on its face."

...[Col. Mapleson stated that] he will not give up the battle by any manner of means, but will give next Winter another season of Italian opera, and he will go on giving it until he is "laid beneath the sod." (*New York Times*, February 16, 1884, p.5)

Since this was the same issue of the *Times* that had carried Schoeffel's denial of Abbey's "ruinously high salaries," it was questionable whether this rumor had been started by Mapleson to harm Abbey, as Schoeffel had asserted. Gye's refusal to enter into negotiations until Abbey had formally retired indicates sincerity on his part. It also suggests that Abbey had, indeed, created a difficult situation for opera impresarios wanting to engage singers for New York.

Abbey's support of Campanini probably resulted from his close association with the tenor and a possible desire to exert influence in the second season at the Metropolitan. Campanini continued to show an interest in producing opera, and four years later he formed his own company with his brother as an associate. Charles Mapleson, the son of the manager of the competitive Academy of Music, was unquestionably seeking to gain control of the Metropolitan Opera House for his father, who was having difficulties with the Academy of Music Board of Directors. The old associations with Gye and the Royal Italian Opera Company were strong enough that the younger Mapleson supported Gye's application as an alternative to his own case. That Maurice Grau was mentioned reflects the opinion held by many that he would have been a successful manager at the Metropolitan. In 1891 Grau did officially become part of the managerial structure of the Metropolitan, when he operated the company with Abbey and Schoeffel, and he was sole manager for five years after Abbey's death. Only after the Metropolitan had enjoyed several successful seasons of opera in German did Grau return to the Metropolitan. Surely his association with Abbey during the initial season left him with grave doubts over the advisability of managing the newly created enterprise.

The possibility of merger between the two organizations came up frequently. The stockholder quoted in the *Times* (above) was indeed perceptive in presenting the obstacles to consolidation presented by the pride of the patrons supporting the two opera houses.

The members of the Board of Directors who continued to hope that Abbey would reconsider his position and operate the house another season were brought to reality about two months later. At that time it was announced that a Mr. Michael Gunn had been relieved of his post with Abbey's Lyceum Theatre operation in London. The reason given was that "as Mr. Abbey intends to personally apply himself to this business for the next season he will do away with Mr. Gunn's assistance, and will save that portion of the receipts."[3] During this period indications pointed more and more toward Gye's concluding an agreement to become the new impresario at the Metropolitan Opera House. Early in March an important report in the *New York Times* described in detail the probable arrangements with Gye and revealed Gye's suggestion that it might be feasible to alternate German opera with Italian. Wagner's recent death must have focused attention on his works and on German opera in general. Not long afterward, New York supported a series of operatic concerts of Wagnerian excerpts and manifested great interest in the Wagnerian repertoire. Gye, who spent considerable time on the continent and was thoroughly involved with operatic production, must have sensed the trend toward German opera sooner than many less knowledgeable managers. The *Times* report also indicated that the Metropolitan stockholders had begun to realize that they would have to modify their demands if they were to succeed in convincing an impresario to take over their opera house.

> The long mooted question of the management of the Metropolitan Opera-house will in all probability be settled today, although the public is not likely to know anything about it until tomorrow....negotiations between Mr. Gye and the Metropolitan Directors have been steadily going forward and are now virtually settled....

> The great difficulty in the way of a speedy arrangement has been the demands of the stockholders of the opera-house. They began by submitting to Mr. Gye a list of artists whom they wished to have engaged for the season. They soon ascertained, however, that such a course of procedure was out of the question as Mr. Gye informed them that the knowledge of such an arrangement would cause the artists wanted to demand enormous salaries. Mr. Gye subsequently submitted to them several different lists of singers who might possibly be engaged. The stockholders expressed themselves as satisfied with any one of the lists laid before them....

> The impresario wanted to bring over a German company to give opera on alternate nights with the Italian organization. The stockholders of the Metropolitan would not consent to such an arrangement. It would in fact be impracticable. German opera cannot be given at the same prices as Italian, and to have opera one night

at $5 a seat and the next night at $3 was considered to be out of the question....The Directors of the Metropolitan Opera-house have for some unaccountable reason chosen to be remarkably reticent in regard to their arrangements for the coming season, but the fact is that they are quite prepared to receive Mr. Gye with open arms and are simply awaiting the result of today's meeting of the Covent Garden Board in London. It is expected that immediately after the meeting Mr. Gye will send a contract to be signed by the Directors of the opera-house. (*New York Times*, March 6, 1884, p.5)

Although only a small minority was involved, the pressure still existed to consolidate the two houses, and this conflict of goals could easily have been responsible for the "reticence" on the part of the Board of Directors. Or, since Abbey's season was not to finish until April 20, some directors may have hoped that the financial results would improve or that Abbey would try another season in spite of the disastrous results of the first one. Regarding a merger, it was obvious that neither board of directors felt impelled to make the first overture. The Board of Directors of the Academy of Music held a meeting on April 28, at which Belmont retired; the resumé of this meeting indicated that they, too, were having managerial problems and were not satisfied with Mapleson's efforts. Entertaining no doubts that he would reappear at the Academy, Mapleson announced that Scalchi would be with him the following season. She lost no time severing her bonds with Abbey and appeared at the Academy of Music about a week after Abbey closed the Metropolitan.[4]

The April 28 meeting at which Belmont announced his retirement also disclosed the name of the leader of the faction interested in consolidation with the Metropolitan. He was a candidate for the Board of Directors on a ticket with other stockholders favoring a merger with the second opera house:

> The annual meeting of the Board of Directors of the Academy of Music was held last night. It had been rumored beforehand that a strenuous effort was to be made to consolidate the Academy and the Metropolitan Opera-house. Mr. J. Coleman Drayton was said to be at the head of a ticket which represented this movement, and it was also understood that a decided opposition to Col. Mapleson as an impresario would be made known....
>
> ...The question of consolidating the two houses was not before the meeting at all, though several Directors stated afterward that the sentiment of the board was against it. The management of the house for next year was not discussed, consequently no feeling of opposition to Col. Mapleson was exhibited, even if it was entertained by some of those present. Col. Mapleson has a contract for the coming season, and he expects to carry it out. (*New York Times*, April 2, 1884, p.4)

The Academy of Music, then, was also guilty of considerable reticence in its managerial manipulations. It would seem logical to assume that they also were waiting to see what the competition would do. Grau, Charles Mapleson, and Hutchinson had now disappeared from the group of prospective managers. Campanini chose the day of Belmont's resignation to remove himself as a possibility. He stated that he would produce ballet in America in the coming season and then embark on a concert tour with a "popular prima donna." Campanini did not rule out future managerial enterprises, and his closing remark was, "I want to feel the novel sensation of being my own manager, and I can't help thinking I shall be a success."[5]

The situation at the Metropolitan, meanwhile, was rapidly approaching an impasse. As usual, the gossip-mongers were able to predict many of the ramifications before they were published. Frankly titled "Gossip In The Opera Foyer," a *New York Times* article stated that "Mme. Scalchi would sing at the Academy of Music during the Spring season." The rumors also touched on the dealings with Gye and Abbey.

> The question of who shall manage the Metropolitan Opera-house next season is not yet settled, but is likely to be by the end of the week. Mr. Gye's contract…is now in the hands of the Directors of the house….Anyone who is fond of collecting rumors can…gather more than he can carry away with him….One was heard last night to the effect that the Directors were wholly dissatisfied with the contract sent over by Mr. Gye and would not sign it under any circumstances….
>
> Another rumor stated that Mr. Abbey would be the manager of the house under a salary….Mr. Abbey's smile appeared to signify that when he had secured enough of operatic management he was conscious of the fact. Something definite will probably be known…by the end of the week. (March 27, 1884, p.4)

In essence the rumors were correct; two days later, however, when the announcement was made, the contract turned out to be a letter, and the dissatisfaction most expressed was on the part of Gye, who questioned the demands placed on him by the stockholders' proposal. Publicly, the directors held back the information that Gye's so-called contract was a letter. When the news was released, they had already sent him a counterproposal. The directors exuded their usual confidence that Gye would accept their terms. The press, however, repeated the rumor that the directors were still considering Abbey's proposition of being a salaried manager:

> Who is to be the manager of the Metropolitan Opera-house next season is still an unsettled question. The contract which, it was stated a short time ago, had been sent here by Mr. Gye for the Directors to consider proved to be no contract at all. It was a lengthy communication from Mr. Gye, in which he set forth certain objections to the proposition made him by the Directors….The Directors have spent some time in making up their minds and have proceeded with a secrecy and caution which would be remarkable were it not that nearly all of the gentlemen have had plenty of experience in Wall-street. They mailed on Wednesday to Mr. Gye a final memorandum of the contract which they would be willing to sign. The details of the document remained buried in the bosom of a transatlantic mailbag, but the Directors say that they have made Mr. Gye a liberal offer….A gentleman well acquainted with their movements said last evening: "There is hardly any doubt whatever that the contract will meet with Mr. Gye's approval and that he will sign it. The Directors propose to have good opera in the house next season, even if they have to run it themselves. It is safe to say,however, that Mr. Gye will accept their terms."
>
> A rumor was floating about the foyer last evening that the Directors had begun to

consider the advisability of paying Mr. Abbey a salary to manage the house for their next season, but the report proved to be wholly groundless. (*New York Times*, March 29, 1884, p.5)

An interview with Adelina Patti on her return from singing in San Francisco also provided gossips with material for conjecture. Abbey was making overtures to her to sing at his benefit; at the same time she seemed certain that German opera would come to New York. In the light of her apparently cordial relationship with Col. Mapleson, it was strange to find her expressing regrets that she had not been able to be with Abbey during the recent season:

> I received a delightful telegram from Mr. Henry E. Abbey asking me to sing at his benefit....I was sorry I could not sing for him this season. He is so kind and gentlemanly....You are to have Wagner music in New-York, are you not? I love it, but I dare not sing it. It strains the voice; but I do sing a little of it now and then. I know it all and play it on the piano. It is good. (*New York Times*, April 9, 1884, p.5)

On April 11 the *New York Times* published an editorial dealing primarily with the forthcoming benefit for Abbey and urging the directors to consider Abbey's offer.

> No definite arrangements have yet been completed, but Mr. Abbey has made a proposition to the Directors that they shall make good the losses he has incurred during the season just past, in return for which he will undertake the management next season upon terms which, it is understood, are more favorable than are likely to be offered from any other quarter. The offer seems to be a reasonable one, and in the interests of the opera-going public it is to be hoped that the Directors will give it careful consideration. (April 11, 1884, p.4)

MAPLESON'S CONFLICT WITH THE ACADEMY BOARD OF DIRECTORS

On April 20 a major conflict between Col. Mapleson and the Board of Directors of the Academy was exposed. Mapleson had been given credit at a New York bank. Guaranteed by the directors of the Academy, it was apparently for his use when he needed funds advanced for running expenses. The guarantee, totaling $30,000, was only a secured loan that under any conditions he was to repay. When Mapleson returned from San Francisco he let it be known that his company had played to huge audiences and that the tour had been a great success. He had drawn $22,000 on his loan fund, however, and refused to repay it, claiming that he did not have the money. He did admit that he had exaggerated the tour receipts, indicating that this was normal procedure for an operatic manager. Far more important, the directors of the Academy charged Mapleson with secret negotiations with the Metropolitan Opera House directorship:

Another charge made against him [Mapleson] was that he had been negotiating with the Directors of the Metropolitan Opera-house, with a view to breaking his contract with the Academy people, which had still a year to run, and managing the new house next season, taking with him Patti and his other artists, and leaving the Academy with neither impresario nor company. (*New York Times*, April 30, 1884, p.5)

This accusation unleashed a series of affirmations and denials that occupied the press for weeks. About the accusation, which was connected with the merger scheme led by Drayton at the time of Belmont's retirement, a director of the Academy commented,

> There was a prospect of that kind on foot, but it was managed exclusively by stockholders who also have an interest in the Metropolitan Opera-house, and it was nipped in the bud....The plan was by means of proxies to secure votes enough to elect a Board of Directors who would carry out the scheme, and for a time it looked as though it might succeed....He [Mapleson] was to be told...that an offer for him for the management would be considered by the Directors of that house, and the Academy would have been devoted to other uses than that of Italian opera....The sense of the meeting was overwhelmingly opposed to any scheme of shutting up the Academy as the house of opera, and the whole movement was confined to the few men who hold stock in both houses and find it a rather expensive luxury....all the meeting did on the subject was to show its disapproval of the entire scheme by giving Mr. Drayton but 88 votes for Director, while all the others received 178. (*New York Times*, April 30, 1884, p.5)

Mapleson, on his part, accused the Academy Board of entering into a secret agreement with Gye and also upbraided the "24 millionaires" who were objecting to his use of the loan fund. When questioned about secret negotiations with the Metropolitan he replied,

> It is utterly false. I am in the market now, however, and if the Metropolitan folks want me they had better speak quickly....I shall have an opera in New-York next season somewhere....I can't be treated this way, you know. (*New York Times*, April 30, 1884, p.5)

He further asserted that any possible consolidation was the business of the directors "but I shall think they are fools if they don't consolidate." A Metropolitan director made the concluding comment in this round, couched, in accordance with diplomatic behavior, in simple words:

> ...while Col. Mapleson's name has often been discussed in connection with the management next season, he has never been made an offer for the house, and no negotiations had ever been opened with him. We shall not decide upon Mr. Gye's proposal for several days. (*New York Times*, April 30, 1884, p.5)

The explanations of no one were allowed to remain unquestioned for long. The following day the *New York Times* reported on the sheriff's visit to the Academy about possible selling of some of Mapleson's scenery and equipment to satisfy the loan-fund judgment obtained by the stockholders. The end of the report gave further details on the negotiations alluded to in the charge against Mapleson, and carried comments by a director of the Academy, an Academy stockholder, Col. Mapleson, and the Metropolitan directors.

It was asserted yesterday by one gentleman interested, who is in a position to know the inside facts of the quarrel, that the charge that the Colonel is negotiating for the Metropolitan Opera-house is true. "I know for a certainty," said the gentleman, "that Col. Mapleson was offered a guarantee of $2,000 a night if he would take the Metropolitan next season, and that he has been considering the proposition for some time. I don't blame the Metropolitan people for wanting to get Mapleson, for he carries with him Patti and several other great artists, but the manner in which the plan has been worked seems to me scarcely fair. Mapleson is bound by his contract to give opera in the Academy next year, and his only chance of being able to accept the offer of the Metropolitan people was for him to get into some kind of trouble with his friends at the Academy and make it appear they had wronged him and themselves broken the contract....Whether, as he calculates, the action of the stockholders will be held a valid excuse for him to break his contract and go over to the other house is another question. I believe that he can be held to his contract just the same as though nothing of the kind had occurred, and he will find that if he does not give us opera at the Academy he will be prevented from giving it anywhere else. That question will have to be decided after he shows his hand, which, of course, will not be until after the meeting of the Metropolitan people, which, I believe, was purposely delayed till after the Academy meeting, in order to give time for this trouble between Mapleson and the stockholders to culminate. I believe that Mapleson has already been secured by the other house, and that the Gye letter has been clothed in mystery to throw the Academy men off their guard. The whole truth will be known after the Metropolitan meeting."

Another stockholder of the Academy said that a number of the stockholders had been approached by a number of the Metropolitan Directors and asked if a proposition to consolidate the two houses would be considered if made formally. They were assured that such a proposition would receive respectful consideration, but whether it would be adopted or not was another question.

"...I want you to deny that," said the Colonel, quickly. "I have had no negotiations with the other house. I mean to stick to the Academy if they leave me anything to give opera with....I shall look about elsewhere, but I'm waiting now to see what the Directors will do today...."

Directors of the Metropolitan Opera-house deny that any offer has been made to Col. Mapleson. "If he leaves the Academy...he will be free for us to treat with, if we feel so disposed; but up to the present time, we have made no advance toward him and he has opened no negotiations with us. Do we want to consolidate with the Academy? Well, that subject has been canvassed a good deal by the stockholders of the two houses, but no formal proposition has ever been made by either. If one ever is made, it must come from the Academy. It will never come from us." (*New York Times*, May 1, 1884, p.2)

It is difficult to conceive that the unnamed director of the Academy invented his entire description of the purported Metropolitan offer to Mapleson. Furthermore, the addition of Patti to the Metropolitan roster would certainly have justified the increase in guarantee (as opposed to the guarantee given to Abbey during the first season). The director in question may well have been one of the group having interests in both houses and thus in a position to know of such a concrete offer. Regardless of conjecture, the Metropolitan director's remarks summed up the attitude of both groups. Mapleson, notwithstanding his earlier comment that he would be looking around, now indicated that at least for the moment he had determined to stay with the Academy of Music and exercise his right to another year there as specified in his contract.

The following day brought another report of a meeting of the Academy of Music directors, primarily concerned with the loan situation. Again, the possible merger was discussed.

> The last subject that came up for discussion, and the one over which most time was spent, was the question of consolidating the fortunes of the Academy and those of the Metropolitan Opera-house. A resolution preceded by several whereases and authorizing the appointment of a committee of three to confer with a similar committee of Metropolitan Directors as to the feasibility of consolidation was actually framed by someone and read to the meeting...but it was said the meeting failed to take decisive action. (*New York Times*, May 2, 1884, p.1)

Mapleson's wry comments were perceptive and pertinent:

> "After the Franco-Prussian war was over the French got to fighting among themselves. The Germans smoked their cigars and looked on through their glasses and saw better fighting than was done during the war. That's what the Metropolitan people are doing now. They are seeing the demolition of the Academy by the Academy people...."

> [Question] "If your friends look for you at the other house next season will they be disappointed?"

> "I think they will. I believe it's all settled with the Gyes." (*New York Times*, May 2, 1884, p.1)

The following day a party "connected with the Metropolitan Opera-house," admitted that the Metropolitan directors were simply waiting to see what action the directors of the Academy would take. His statements took a great deal for granted about the Metropolitan's having a impresario ready for the calling.

> A gentleman connected with the Metropolitan Opera-house said: "We are in a position to secure a manager whenever we wish to and have made up our minds simply to content ourselves with the situation and rest upon our oars. Last year we made some propositions to the Academy people touching the consolidation of the interests of the two houses, but these were not successful, and since then we have done

nothing. True,...certain persons...in both houses...believe that the true interests of
each point to a consolidation, and these persons have made it perfectly well understood to the Academy Directors that whenever their board sees fit to appoint a committee to confer with us regarding consolidation they will be met by us in a similar
spirit. This is just the way that matter stands now." (*New York Times*, May 3, 1884,
p.1)

Mapleson also commented on the situation, except that this time it was he who appeared to be in collusion with Gye:

He [Mapleson] said that Mr. Gye, representing the Royal Italian Opera Company,
which had a lien on some of the properties, had cabled to his legal agent here to
assert his claim to the property, and that action would prevent the promised Sheriff's
sale. (*New York Times*, May 3, 1884, p.1)

Three days passed before the indomitable Mapleson found opportunity to make a
new accusation against the Academy Board of Directors. At the May 6 Board meeting another long report was given on the problems in the sheriff's sale to cover Mapleson's use of the guaranteed loan fund. Since the directors did not appear to be willing
to modify their stand on the repayment of the loan, plans continued for them to force
payment by an auction sale of Mapleson's operatic equipment. It was apparent,
however, that the Academy Board was also taking considerable time to enforce its injunction, and it would be safe to assume that they were also hoping for an amicable
solution to the entire set of problems. At this juncture Mapleson chose to use their
own argument against them and accuse them of forcing him out of his rental agreement for the forthcoming year:

Now I'll tell you what I think is the design behind this matter. I have a lease of the
Academy for another year, and they are trying, I think, to force me to give it up, but
I am not going to do it. (*New York Times*, May 6, 1884, p.2)

At this point, the directors of the Academy reversed their attitude. Although they
had vehemently denied previous reports that they were willing to send a committee
to the opposing group, they adopted a resolution to this effect and thus admitted that
consolidation was at least a live option:

The Academy of Music Directors held a meeting...yesterday afternoon to consider
the subject of a consolidation of interests with the Metropolitan Opera-house. The
announcement made on Friday morning last...that at the meeting of the Academy
Directors on the previous afternoon a resolution was offered providing for the appointment of a committee to confer with the Metropolitan Directors...had been emphatically...denied by the Directors, but the resolution was adopted, and the committee was appointed....No plan of consolidation was broached, however, and no
course of action was decided on, nor was a time fixed for the next conference. On the
part of the Metropolitan Opera-house it was said that it was in a position to close
with Mr. Gye at any time, but that nothing would be done until it was known
whether an arrangement for a consolidation could or could not be made. On the

part of the Academy it was conceded that only one presentation of opera was practicable in New-York.

> The meeting of the Academy Directors yesterday afternoon was called to receive the report of its committee, and to draft a plan of consolidation. The pros and cons of the matter were discussed at length, and a strong sentiment was developed in favor of a combination of interests instead of a consolidation. The committee was finally instructed to hold a further conference with the Metropolitan people, and the meeting, without taking any definite action, adjourned. (*New York Times*, May 7, 1884, p.5)

The following day it appeared as if the Academy had decided that a peaceful resolution of the battle with Mapleson would be expedient. Reportedly, the directors launched discussion about possible changes and improvements at the Academy in line with Mapleson's earlier suggestions. As a result of this reversal of attitude, Mapleson abandoned his plans to leave that day for Europe.[6]

The attempts to reach an accord about consolidation continued. Again, however, two facets of pride were obvious. Each group wanted the other to make the offer; and the Academy partisans were unwilling to desert the older building. The newspaper report, though clear and frank, was not optimistic.

> Another conference of the Academy of Music and Metropolitan Opera-house committees was held yesterday afternoon....The question of consolidation was again discussed...but no definite course of action was determined on. All admitted it would be cheaper and better...to have but one opera next season, and the gentlemen representing each house expressed a desire to have the others make some proposition...but both sides alike were reluctant to take the initiative....The Academy people want to make some arrangement that will not necessitate the abandonment of their house, while the Metropolitan people are willing to make very advantageous terms if the Academy will go to the Metropolitan. The meeting adjourned after each side had asked the other to formulate a proposition. (*New York Times*, May 9, 1884, p.2)

In the meanwhile Mapleson was faced with the result of his conflict with the Academy. The Academy Board of Directors, apparently having decided that they held the controlling hand, refused to give Mapleson any guarantee whatsoever for the coming season. Possibly, the conferences with the Metropolitan representatives had presented them with a feeling of false security, for they made it perfectly clear that they were giving Mapleson only two alternatives; these the *New York Times* described under the headline, "Col. Mapleson Given Hobson's Choice":

> ...so far as Col. Mapleson was concerned, he had been given the option to throw up his contract with the board and give up the house or to give opera next season without any guarantee, as he was bound to do by the terms of his agreement. The guarantee business...was exhausted. (*New York Times*, May 13, 1884, p.1)

ACTIVITIES OF
GRAU AND STRAKOSCH

Although the Metropolitan Board of Directors had repeatedly asserted that their negotiations with Gye were on the verge of completion, they were involved in machinations with at least one other possible impresario, and perhaps two. Beyond question, Nilsson and Patti had proven themselves to be the greatest box-office attractions among existing prima donnas. Along with Campanini, they were the artists who brought the greatest prestige to an opera house, at least in the United States. Naturally, then, the Board became enamored with the idea of having both the prima donnas grace their opera house in the same season, perhaps even appearing in the same performances. Since Nilsson had been, and still appeared to be, controlled by Abbey, and Patti by Mapleson, a neutral impresario logically seemed the most feasible person to maneuver to bring them to the Metropolitan together. The *New York Times* revealed that this plan was underway on May 13, the same day that Mapleson received his "Hobson's Choice" ultimatum.

> The Directors of the Metropolitan Opera-house...have not been idle, and one of their moves...is worth mentioning in print. The scheme involved the engagement for the new house of both Mme. Patti and Mme. Nilsson...an estimate was asked of a well-known impresario of the outlay required to found an Italian "stock company" of the highest order...the weekly cost for four performances, to include all expenses...was put down at $15,000. The manager who supplied the figures was then requested to discard the two "stock prima donnas"...and ascertain whether Mmes. Patti and Nilsson could be engaged in their stead....Mme. Patti...promptly declared that she would be most happy to sing with Mme. Nilsson...the impresario and ambassador hastened to Mme. Nilsson and inquired whether she saw any obstacle to singing under the same management with Mme. Patti. Mme. Nilsson's keen eye detected none...the ambassador...was tendered $100,000 subsidy toward 60 representations, with the understanding that Mmes. Patti and Nilsson should appear on alternate nights. The ambassador, calculating that the salaries of the two prima donnas for the term named would be $210,000...declined the offer. It is believed that the proposal met with a similar fate at the hands of other and much more venturesome spirits. (*New York Times*, May 13, 1884, p.14)

The "ambassador" in question may have been either Grau or Max Strakosch; both were active enough and well enough established in the New York opera scene to make the proposals to both Patti and Nilsson. Strakosch was already in the process of negotiating with Nilsson for a concert tour. Grau was then assembling a company to support a Mme. Theo, a prima donna whom he planned to present during the coming season. He was also sufficiently well-acquainted with the Metropolitan Board of Directors to command their confidence. But since Grau's attitude was reflected in his references to the Metropolitan as a "colossal lemon-colored temple of music," Strakosch seems to have been the more likely choice. Furthermore, Strakosch had departed for Europe.

Mr. Maurice Strakosch departed for Europe hurriedly and mysteriously on Saturday last. It is known that he entered into arrangements with Mme. Christine Nilsson for a farewell tour which will extend over two years, and it is surmised that his hasty leave-taking of the United States is not unconnected with possible managerial relations with the Metropolitan Opera-house next season. (*New York Times*, May 29, 1884, p.4)

It seems safe to assume that the Metropolitan Board was more concerned about the negotiations with Gye than appeared on the surface. Their many months' nonchalance since Abbey's decision not to continue may largely have been due to their non-operatic experiences—where their positions were influential enough to preclude any defiance by their associates. That they now were becoming involved with other possible managers does not necessarily imply any worry about the future of their opera house. During their previous search for a first-season manager the way they had conducted business with Abbey and Gye had done little to enhance their reputation as ethical businessmen.

COLLAPSE OF NEGOTIATIONS WITH GYE

The *Times* that mentioned Strakosch's departure for Europe commented on the status of the Metropolitan's dealings with Gye. Pessimistic about Mapleson's plans at the Academy, the article offered little hope that Gye would come to the Metropolitan. The newspaper's reasons proved to be most accurate:

The Directors of the Metropolitan appear to awaken slowly to the urgent need of determining...a course of action for the Autumn. It is already too late for Mr. Gye even to secure the services of the leading artists of his London company, and the impresario of the uptown-house will have to recruit his forces in Italy—where there is still, happily, an abundance of capable performers—instead of depending upon the singers now delighting France and England. The fact that Mr. Mapleson is likely... to make Chicago and the West his headquarters, and limit his New-York representations to a brief series...is also calculated to spur the stockholders of the Metropolitan to renewed activity. That Mr. Gye will not be the manager of the Metropolitan Opera-house next fall may be regarded as a certainty. Had he hoped to come to terms for a series of New-York performances he would never have allowed his present company to disperse at the close of the London season....On May 3, indeed, Mr. Gye had pretty well abandoned his intention of coming to the United States, and a letter to a friend in this city, under that date, ended with the following words: "America is still asking us to go there. They have offered us $1,400 per night, positive payment, with theatre, lighting, heating, etc., but we have not accepted." (*New York Times*, May 29, 1884, p.4)

A month elapsed with no further press report on the proposition to Gye; in fact, no evidence indicates any activity in the Metropolitan's managerial dilemma. Surprisingly enough, the next news release dealt with new negotiations with Gye, who, contrary to the earlier prediction, had not completely withdrawn from the scene. The Metropolitan Board of Directors was by now sufficiently concerned to have a representative dealing with Gye in London, eliminating the delays caused by correspond-ence. The *Times* announced on June 29 that it had received a cable from George L. Rives, the Metropolitan's London emissary to Gye. At this point Gye, rather than the Metropolitan Board, appeared to be dictating terms.

> A cable dispatch from London...says that Mr. George L. Rives, who is represent-ing the Directors of the New-York Metropolitan Opera-house in London, and Mr. Ernest Gye, who represents the Royal Italian Opera Company, (limited) came to a verbal agreement on Friday night. Mr. Gye is to have the option of leasing the Met-ropolitan Opera-house, in case he is able to engage a sufficient number of efficient artists for next season. The contract will be signed tomorrow, after the details have been settled. It is said that Mr. Gye is indisposed to undertake this enterprise unless he can obtain a thoroughly efficient troupe....Within a fortnight he will know for a certainty. He says he would rather defer coming to America than come with an in-different troupe. (*New York Times*, June 29, 1884, p.6)

On July 3 a cable received at the Metropolitan Opera House announced that "the for-mal contract between Mr. Gye and the Directors had been drafted in accordance with the views of both parties, and that it only awaited their signature."[7]

In the meanwhile the Academy directors were still engaged in verbal battle with Mapleson, who had indicated that he would present a series of concerts at the Acad-emy of Music during the forthcoming season. One director was quoted as saying, "He is not bound to give Patti, but he must give Italian opera after some fashion."[8] The same director, queried about the likelihood of a combination with the Metropolitan Opera House, eliminated this possibility, stressing the contrasting financial sta-bilities of the two opera houses:

> The Metropolitan people have made us offers, but they have not been accepted. Ours, you know, is a free house; it has no mortgage; it is an unencumbered property. This being the case, it is not likely that we will go up town and combine with a house that is fairly covered up with mortgages. (*New York Times*, July 8, 1884, p.8)

The next day the *Times* announced the forthcoming signing and speculated on the artists who might participate in Gye's forthcoming season. In complimenting Gye's ability the article paid tribute to the quality of Abbey's first-season company.

> A cable dispatch was yesterday received from London by the Directors of the Met-ropolitan Opera-house, announcing that the arrangements with Mr. Gye were com-pleted, and that the contract for the coming season would be signed on Friday of this week....It is pretty sure...that Mme. Sembrich will revisit these shores....It may be asserted without fear of contradiction that Mme. Patti will not be heard at the Met-ropolitan....Mme. Nilsson's engagement may be effected within a few days. ...Although it is difficult to see in what respect Mr. Gye's artists will outshine Mr. Abbey's in point of individual brilliancy, there is a likelihood that his company will be better balanced, and a certainty that it will be more skillfully handled. (*New York Times*, July 9, 1884, p.4)

This time the announcement was borne out by the actual signing—three days later the *New York Times* announced that Edmund C. Stanton, the Secretary of the Board, had received a cable confirming the binding of the parties. In this contract Gye agreed to give a season of Italian opera at the Metropolitan, in accordance with "arrangements already set forth." The contract had been mailed to New York immediately after it was signed.[9]

Gye's predictions about possible difficulties with artists who felt themselves in a strong position were immediately substantiated. Nilsson, who was in London the next day, announced that Gye had offered her $2,000 a night and her expenses to and from America and that she had declined the proposition. Her comment was, "if Mme. Patti is worth $4,000 a night, Christine Nilsson is worth $3,000."[10]

The possibility of the directors of the Metropolitan convincing Gye to take over their opera house may have prompted Abbey and Schoeffel to inject a note of discouragement directed at Gye. Unquestionably, Abbey was bitter over his treatment at the directors' hands, and it was certain that he did not have their welfare at heart. Within a few days of Gye's tentative agreement to take over the Metropolitan, an interview with Schoeffel provided the public, and Gye, with concrete figures vastly more discouraging than any previously published. Schoeffel was asked whether the loss on the previous opera season had been very heavy. His reply was direct and exceedingly gloomy:

> Well, from $5,000 to $10,000 a week during the whole season. In the first place, Mr. Abbey had to deposit $50,000 as a guarantee for Mme. Nilsson and $20,000 for Mme. Sembrich. That was tied up all season. Then we ran into an expensive company. We opened to $14,860, and that was the only paying house we had. "Don Giovanni" was one of the most costly operas we gave and drew the least money. We played that opera one night to only $700.72 and yet we had to pay Mme. Nilsson alone for that night $1,300, about $600 more than the entire receipts. We played to a great many $800, $900, and $1,000 houses which, of course, did not anywhere reach our expenses. Mr. Abbey's credit was good, the people had faith in his honesty and integrity, or he never could have pulled through. (*New York Times*, July 14, 1884, p.4)

The next day an Associated Press dispatch from London indicated that Gye was rapidly trying to assemble a company to fulfill his agreement with the Metropolitan. The dispatch announced that his salary would be £600 weekly and that he had engaged Emma Albani, his wife, for £300 nightly. In addition to Albani, Gye indicated that he had engaged two other prominent singers, Emmy Fursch-Madi and Zelia Trebelli, and that he was "negotiating to secure Mme. Nilsson."[11]

A few days later the *Times* qualified Gye's arrangements as "almost completed," both those with Albani, Fursch-Madi, and Trebelli and those with a number of other singers, notably Sr. Galassi, Sr. Monti, and Armand Castlemary. In addition to a progress report on Gye's negotiations with Nilsson, the report responded to Schoeffel's statements, specifically concerning the receipts for various *Don Giovanni* performances. Meanwhile, Mapleson, although receiving less publicity, was moving along rapidly in his efforts to secure a company for the Academy of Music.

> Mr. Gye makes daily progress in organizing his company for the American season. Thus far he has almost completed arrangements with Mme. Albani, Mme. Fursch-Madi, Mlle. Trebelli, Signori Galassi and Monti, Mr. Castlemary....Mme. Nilsson, however, demands $3,000 for each performance, and Mr. Gye hesitates to increase his expenses by so large an amount. He will in due course, however, realize the necessity of yielding....Meanwhile Mr. Mapleson is not idle....Besides Mmes. Patti and Scalchi, Mr. Mapleson is more than likely to secure Mme. Gerster....A statement recently appeared in connection with the receipts of the Metropolitan House last season in which mention was made that on one occasion, "Don Giovanni" drew but $700....It will not be amiss to place on record that the receipts of the first performance of "Don Giovanni" last season at the Metropolitan were $6,492.75—in addition to the $1,000 guaranteed the impresario—that the receipts of the second performance (a matinee) were $3,306, and that the receipts of the third were $5,048.75, also exclusive of the guarantee. Thus almost $17,000 were paid out for the three representations of "Don Giovanni" supplied at the outset of the season. The first two nights of "Gli Ugonetti" [sic] brought, with the guarantee, close upon $14,000 into the treasury. (*New York Times*, July 20, 1884, p.6)

Schoeffel and Abbey never replied to the above "correction" of Schoeffel's statements. Presumably they had selected isolated tour performances to provide their figures. *Don Giovanni* had been produced twelve times during the first year, five times at the Metropolitan and seven times on tour. Since the casts were uniformly satisfactory, the *Times* reporter may have been castigating Abbey for too many performances of the same opera. It was noted that the receipts for the first three performances were excellent; there was no refutation of Schoeffel's low figures for certain productions of the opera. That New York was extraordinarily "star"-conscious was emphasized by the prediction that Gye would "realize the necessity of yielding" to Nilsson.

A detailed description of the contract between Gye and the directors makes it obvious that Gye had been able to extract far better terms from the directors than had Abbey. Possibly, then, he at least entertained the hope of succeeding to fulfill the terms of the contract.

> The contract...bore the signatures of Lord Latham and Mr. Ernest Gye...and Mr. G. L. Rives name was appended to it on behalf of the stockholders of the Metropolitan...Mr. Gye is to supply 52 consecutive performances, including matinees, during a period of thirteen weeks, commencing between Nov. 10 and Nov. 20, and to have the use of the house, lighted and heated, and that of the costumes and scenery for the season. The stockholders of the Metropolitan further agree to provide the scenery for two new operas to be designated by Mr. Gye, and to pay him as a subsidy close upon $1,700 for each of the 52 representations. Mr. Gye is to have the right to rent the Metropolitan for Sunday concerts, but the control of the establishment, except on the regular opera nights, is to rest with the stockholders. The latter have reserved themselves the privilege of canceling the contract should the list of artists Mr. Gye submits prove unsatisfactory. It is expected that the names of Mr. Gye's performers will reach the stockholders and engross their critical consideration today. (*New York Times*, July 22, 1884, p.4)

Two days later the *New York Times* stated the shocking news that Gye "had thrown up the contract because he has not been able to engage the requisite artists."[12] Gye's withdrawal was denied at the end of the same news release, but with the denial it was admitted that either of the parties could abrogate the contract. The news release also offered some solace to those concerned:

> Stephen H. Olin, a partner of George Rives...said yesterday that he had heard nothing from Mr. Rives as to the falling through of the contract. It was, however, stipulated that either of the contracting parties had the right to withdraw from the agreement up to the end of this month....it was understood that Mr. Gye was making his preparations for a brilliant season of opera.

> Mr. R. Wilson, a stockholder...knew little about it. "In all events," said Mr. Wilson, "the Metropolitan Opera-house will be the opera house of the country in the future. I am yet in hopes that Mr. Gye will have charge of the place in the Fall. He may have given it up now but perhaps he will decide to try it after further consideration." Mr. Wilson did not know what the Directors or stockholders would do under the circumstances. He still believed there would be an operatic season. (*New York Times*, July 24, 1884, p.4)

Forty-eight hours later a stockholder was asked whether Gye would be offered "extra inducements." He replied to the effect that this would not be necessary, since the problem generated from Gye's difficulties in obtaining the artists he desired. Asked whether Nilsson's $3,000 was the problem, the unnamed stockholder replied:

> "I think so but I cannot speak positively....However, I hope...that Mr. Gye will yet be able to make suitable arrangements to carry out the contract."

> No other action had been taken as the music committee were all away.

> Mr. Stanton, the Secretary of the company, said that he could add nothing...except that there would certainly be opera at the Metropolitan the next season in any event. (*New York Times*, July 26, 1884, p.4)

On the same page of the newspaper a report from London again denied that Gye had withdrawn from the agreement. This report seemed to contradict the stockholder quoted above and hinted that perhaps Gye was indeed looking for an increase in the offer:

> Mr. Gye has not withdrawn as yet his negotiations with reference to the Metropolitan Opera-house in New-York. But the tenors whom he had intended to engage demand such high terms that it is necessary for Mr. Gye, if he concluded an arrangement, to receive a modification of the agreement which had been previously adopted....If the terms are modified Mr. Gye will engage the tenors....Otherwise he will withdraw and the whole matter will fall through. (*New York Times*, July 26, 1884, p.4)

The following day the *New York Times* carried a special item from its own correspondent, bearing the dateline London, July 26. The correspondent had interviewed Mapleson, who was in London, and ascertained that the latter not only had signed Patti for a season in London but also Francesco Tamagno, the celebrated tenor who would later create the role of Otello upon Verdi's request. Mapleson stated that he considered his contract with the Academy to have been broken by that Board of Directors and that since Gye had failed in the matter with the Metropolitan, there was no manager other than himself who could supply a satisfactory company including Patti, Tamagno, Scalchi, and no doubt, Nilsson. With this comment he openly stated that he was available and considered himself to be a candidate for the post of impresario at the Metropolitan. As almost always during this period, the statement was immediately contradicted. The correspondent in London refuted Mapleson's assertion.

> I can authoritatively contradict the statement that Mr. Gye abandoned the contract for the Metropolitan Opera House on account of his inability to procure artists. It all depends on Mme. Nilsson for final settlement. She has agreed to accept $2,400 per night, but demanded that a guarantee of $30,000 should be deposited by noon on Monday last. This Mr. Gye could not furnish. Herbert Gye said to me last night that it was impossible to provide artists at the rates demanded; but he does not admit that the negotiations with the Metropolitan Opera House are finally concluded. (*New York Times*, July 27, 1884, p.6)

Once more the same issue of the paper carried two reports on the confusing issue of Gye's position. The other article included a statement by James A. Roosevelt, President of the Metropolitan Board of Directors.

> "On Wednesday I thought the contract with Mr. Gye was entirely off, but at present it looks as if the matter may be satisfactorily arranged after all. The trouble arose over the tenor, Massini, who demanded $30,000—per month....Mr. Rives...is at present on the Continent, but he will return to London on Monday, and then the negotiations will be terminated, one way or the other. We shall probably hear from him by Tuesday or Wednesday." (*New York Times*, July 27, 1884, p.4)

On August 2 it was announced that Mapleson had opened negotiations for a ten-day lease on the Philadelphia Academy of Music, to commence on January 12.[13] This removed all doubt as to whether Mapleson planned to be in America during the following winter, but it did not establish where he intended to maintain his company. Again, another report was found in the same issue of the newspaper. In this report Roosevelt confirmed the end of the Metropolitan's involvement with Gye. Roosevelt's statement was prefaced by the newspaper's own comment that no one knew who would be the manager or whether there would actually be a season of opera at the Metropolitan. The reporter also questioned Roosevelt about Mapleson.

> Mr. James A. Roosevelt...said yesterday: "I regard the negotiations with Mr. Gye as entirely at an end. We have done nothing as yet toward getting any one to fill Mr. Gye's place, nor do I know what we shall do."

"Is there any likelihood of your opening negotiations with Col. Mapleson?"

"I do not think so, though I can't tell what may be done by our representatives across the water."

"You will certainly have opera at the Metropolitan in any event?"

"Well, I cannot speak positively about that either."

London, Aug. 1
    As Mr. Gye has given up all thoughts of assuming the management of the Metropolitan Opera House in New-York, Mr. Reeves, [sic] the agent of the Opera House Company, is seeking another impresario. It is unlikely that he will succeed in finding one. (New York Times, August 2, 1884, p.8)

The next day the Times described the possible choices that the Metropolitan Board of Directors had open to them, but first it discussed the hypothesis that Gye may have been seeking revenge for what he considered to have been shabby treatment the previous year when the Metropolitan apparently had signed Abbey for the post of manager after promising Gye that they would await his proposition.

Evil-minded but not ill-informed persons even go so far as to say that Mr. Gye never even proposed to visit America, and only dallied with the offer of the Metropolitan long enough to make it difficult, if not impossible for its Directorate to come to terms with any one else....Mr. Gye had some grounds for resentment at not having been sought when the house was first opened to the public....The Directorate of the Metropolitan must not be taxed with a want of liberality, for they agreed to give Mr. Gye about $90,000 as a subsidy for 52 representations. The total subsidy allotted to the Grand Opera House in Paris, for 250 representations, is only $100,000 and the... list of obligations to which the French manager has to subscribe contains 2,000 clauses, or twenty times as many as an impresario in this country would be willing to read through....But they are to be blamed for their judicious action that has placed them in their present predicament. Their representative in Europe is hard at work....He may finally persuade Mr. Gye to bring over an inexpensive company....He may intrust to Mr. Maurice Strakosch, who is supposed to have a sort of provisional contract with Mme. Nilsson, the task of forming a company....He may come to an agreement with Signor Pollini, of Hamburg, an experienced director of Italian and German opera....He may arrange for a series of representations of German opera and these, [at] popular prices, might draw passable audiences, at the sacrifice of the fashionable reputation of the house. He may persuade Mr. Carl Rosa to bring over his company....And finally he may enter into some contract with Mr. Mapleson by which that shrewd gentleman, who by his contract with the Academy of Music, has the right but is not bound to give performances there, but is debarred from giving representations elsewhere, would contrive to assign his company to Mr. John Doe...and allow Mr. John Doe...to conduct the season at the Metropolitan. The fact that the Directors of the Academy have disregarded recent messages from Mr. Mapleson may impel that gentleman to abandon all thought of supplying operatic performances in Irving-place, and consider a proposition from the uptown establishment. Should Mr. Mapleson's company not be secured for the Metropolitan, the outlook for a really brilliant season uptown is more than dubious. (New York Times, August 3, 1884, p.6)

Regardless of the alternatives listed above, the Board of Directors must have been visibly shaken by the collapse of the negotiations with Gye. That Gye never intended to come to this country is possible; but he was in a severe financial crisis, and the reasons given by him were probably accurate. Abbey's record would not encourage anyone to gamble by entering the project with limited means. When Rives returned to the United States in early September he reported that Gye was a "financial wreck," again suggesting that lack of funds was the prime deterrent to Gye's projected management of the Metropolitan.[14] The Metropolitan showed no interest in Carl Rosa, Max Strakosch, Signor Pollini, or Mapleson. Rather, they turned abruptly to the other alternative, German opera.

THE CHANGE TO GERMAN OPERA

Less than a week after the arrangement with Gye fell through, German opera was discussed on the front page of the *New York Times*. Although it cannot be proved, surely this article must have encouraged the directors to consider proposals for opera in German at the Metropolitan. It also had a few final words on the ultimate fate of the attempts to bring Gye to New York:

> It appears now that the real reason for the breaking off of the negotiations between the Metropolitan Opera House Directors and Mr. Gye was not so much the latter's inability to obtain tenors as the financial embarrassment of the Royal Italian Opera Company, (limited,) with which Mr. Gye has been so long identified as manager, and which has since been placed in the hands of a Receiver. It was reported last night that the Metropolitan Opera House directory is considering the feasibility of giving German opera instead of Italian....It is asserted that the services of Mme. Nilsson may be secured...together with those of one or two other eminent artists. ...With these singers, backed by a strong company of German artists, a very acceptable presentation of German opera can be given, and the practicability [of] organizing such a company is what the Metropolitan Directors are said to be devoting their attention to. (*New York Times*, August 9, 1884, p.1)

In numerous statements and circumstances indicating an interest in German opera, the evidence pointed more strongly to a declining interest in Italian opera, suggesting that German opera was considered more as an alternative than as a deliberate choice. It was certain, however, that the German population in the New York area had increased. "New York–Brooklyn was the greatest center of immigrants in the world—as many Germans as Hamburg....Four out of every five residents of greater New York were foreigners or of foreign parentage....Germans and Irish predominated."[15]

In reviewing one of the spring, 1884, series of Wagner concerts held at the Metropolitan Opera House, the *Times* critic had pointed out the decline in interest in Italian opera, describing the "slow boredom for Italian opera which was approaching."[16] A few days before, the artists who were to take part in the series of Wagner programs had presented a concert for the members of the Liederkranz

Society. Here the crowd was huge, and the selections were from some of Wagner's heaviest works.

> The concert...was crowded to suffocation and the program consisted chiefly of numbers from "Götterdämmerung," "Die Meistersinger," and "Tannhäuser," interpreted by Mme. Materna and Herren Winkelmann, Scaria, and Heinrich. (*New York Times*, April 21, 1884, p.4)

A month later Nilsson appeared in a Wagner concert devoted to less monumental works; this event also attracted a capacity audience. The *Times* reviewer indicated that Nilsson was in all probability the drawing power. His comments also indicated that the public must have felt the lack of Wagner's more complicated scores.

> ...last evening, a Swedish songstress, educated mainly by French teachers, and identified with Italian opera for almost twenty years, attracted the largest and most enthusiastic audience gathered there since the present series of Wagner concerts was entered upon....She did not sing the bright and tuneful measures in which "Götterdämmerung" abounds, nor did she make known her familiarity with the fluent progressions and symmetrical themes of "Tristan and Isolde"—which for years was kept from the stage by the obstinacy with which Wagner's singers forgot one act as fast as they memorized another—nor did she seek to develop the latent beauties of "Parsifal."...The spacious auditorium was filled in every part, and as Mme. Nilsson has been concerned in this concert only, it is fair to assume that the Swedish prima donna was the magnet that drew the unusually numerous assemblage. (*New York Times*, May 10, 1884, p.4)

The ultimate decision to turn to opera in German may also have been prompted by the desire of the Metropolitan directors to avoid direct competition with the Academy of Music. Henry Finck, a music critic of wide reputation, noted a few years later in a memorial to Anton Seidl, the foremost Wagnerian conductor of the time:

> Some of the newspapers had been persistently clamoring for Wagner in the original and for other German operas. The suggestion was accordingly made that German opera should be given a trial, as that would not conflict so directly with the Italian opera at the Academy.[17]

Late in July, a few days before Gye's coming to the Metropolitan was ruled out, the stockholders may have read of the enthusiasm of German music-lovers. A *Times* report describing the dedication ceremonies for a statue of Beethoven in Central Park gave promise that German opera might well attract some patrons from neighboring towns and cities.

> The trains from all over the state that rolled into the Metropolitan railroad stations yesterday morning bore hundreds of sturdy German citizens, whose broad chests and capacious diaphragms indicated unabounded capacity for basso-profundo and lager beer. (*New York Times*, July 22, 1884, p.8)

In the great influx of Germans during the nineteenth century the largest number 38.9 percent (in 1880), settled in the east-north-central states; the second-largest portion, 30 percent, located in the middle-Atlantic area.[18]

> German emigration reached its first crest in the southwest and west in the middle of the 1850's, its second in central Germany towards the end of the 1850's, and its third in the east in the 1870's and 1880's....
>
> ...From 1820 to 1930 nine-tenths of the Germans who departed overseas went to the United States, nearly 6,000,000 in all.[19]

All these factors combined to indicate to the Board of Directors that an experiment in German opera—and opera in German—would be justified. The continual problems of the previous months in trying to obtain responsible management for the Metropolitan's second season simply forced serious consideration of this bold move.

ARRANGEMENTS WITH DR. LEOPOLD DAMROSCH

At the end of the second week in August, 1884, it became known that the Metropolitan Opera House Board of Directors had entered into preliminary negotiations with Dr. Leopold Damrosch, conductor and founder of the New York Symphony Society. A highly respected and responsible musician, Damrosch had been one of the many talented students of Franz Liszt.

In his autobiography, Damrosch's son Walter credited two members of the Roosevelt family with having been most influential in the consideration of his father for the post of manager.

> Their [Metropolitan Opera-house Board of Directors] president was James Roosevelt, an uncle of Hillborn Roosevelt who was then president of the New York Symphony Society and who was a staunch and devoted friend of my father's. He suggested to his uncle that my father be appointed as Director and that a season of opera in German be inaugurated, as Italian opera was evidently on the wane and Wagner, especially, on the ascendant.[20]

On August 14 the *New York Times* first released the name of Damrosch in connection with the coming season of opera. When the news was released Damrosch had already departed for Europe on his mission:

> It transpires now that the Metropolitan Opera House Directors, after the failure of the negotiations with Mr. Gye, did really open communications with Col. Mapleson, but after an examination of his contract with the Academy of Music they decided its nature...preclude[d] the possibility of their entering into an arrangement with him...the Directors turned their eyes toward German opera as the only alternative. Negotiations were opened with Dr. Leopold Damrosch of this city, and these resulted finally in the selection of Dr. Damrosch as the Musical Director of the

Leopold Damrosch.

Metropolitan Opera House, and his hurried departure for Europe yesterday...to engage a company....Under this arrangement the Directory will assume the risk of running the house, and Dr. Damrosch will simply act as Musical Director. While abroad he will visit Bayreuth and other musical centres of Germany, and will select his company from the best artists available. It is proposed to rely more on the general strength of the company than on the attraction of stars, and thus to leave these to look to the European capitals for the high prices they demand. (*New York Times*, August 14, 1884, p.4)

Previous dealings between Damrosch and the Board were not published. Three days later, however, a *New York Times* editorial not only lauded the selection of Damrosch but also castigated the Metropolitan directors for not considering an earlier proposal from him. No evidence of this previous meeting was found, but in all probability the *Times* reference was accurate:

Although *Dr. Damrosch* met the Directors of the Metropolitan some months ago and submitted to them a project...which would have been far more advantageous for them...than the agreement entered into later...no action was taken upon it, and the choice of *Dr. Damrosch* as musical director for the stockholders of the Metropolitan was practically the victory of a "dark Horse." This appointment made at the last minute was...a judicious one....It was decided to have German opera—or, rather, Italian opera with German words...and this question being settled, the selection of *Dr. Damrosch* was the happiest that could be made....

...*Dr. Damrosch* is by far the best suited for the work he has undertaken. He is not only a virtuoso and a composer, but a conductor of considerable magnetism, if somewhat too nervous at times; a man of imagination and refinement, and an operatic leader who has had experience under *Liszt* at Weimar, and still greater practice at Breslau, where for four years he conducted the performances at the Opera House. ...Although he belongs to the advanced school of German musicians, there is reason to believe that he does not sympathize with the wild theories of the ultra-Wagnerites. If his plans are successful, the frequentees of the Metropolitan...may occasionally be refreshed with a draught of Rossini, and even with a sip of Auber....

...*Dr. Damrosch* too may be depended on to organize an efficient company, thanks to the catholici[s]m of taste...which is rather uncommon among Germans of the period....It is not out of place to note that had *Dr. Damrosch's* first proposals been acted upon, three or four months ago, contracts then pending with several artists of moment would have been signed immediately....

...If the Directors of the Metropolitan like...opera in German they will attend the representations and make it "fashionable" for other people to do so. There is in this city quite as large a "floating public" for good German opera...while *Dr. Damrosch* will be heard from in a fortnight, it will be quite three months before the matter of the prosperity of German opera at the Metropolitan is finally disposed of by the experience of the initial nights. (*New York Times*, August 17, 1884, p.6)

Rives finally arrived back in this country on September 5. His predictions for the coming season were gloomy; he considered English opera to be the coming attraction.

Mr. George L. Rives, one of the Directors of the Metropolitan Opera House, who went abroad on a mission for that corporation,...is reported to have said that he believed Italian opera to be dead both in Europe and America and that the coming attraction is English opera. Artists have come to regard America as the place to make fortunes and consequently demand [exorbitant] salaries....[Rives] fears Dr. Damrosch's mission will not be very successful, because German artists demand as much money as Italian artists. Abbey's course at the Metropolitan last year has, he thinks, ruined the prospects of opera in New-York, and therefore there is not likely to be any opera here this winter. (*New York Times*, September 6, 1884, p.5)

Critics, managers, and members of the general public had variously condemned the practices and boredom associated with Italian opera. However, all the discussion that Italian opera was dying out did not necessarily indicate general agreement that it would be replaced by German opera. On September 6 a noted tenor added his views, asserting that Wagner's music was harmful to the singing voice:

London, Sept 5—Mr. Sims Reeves, the famous tenor...declared that Italian opera was dying out....German opera he thought was unlikely to replace the Italian. Wagner's music, he asserted, would do more harm to a voice in two years than other music in ten years. The only ones of Wagner's operas which were suitable for production and likely to keep the stage were "Lohengrin," and "The Flying Dutchman."...Mr. Reeves advises singers to study Mozart. (*New York Times*, September 6, 1884, p.5)

The first word of any action by Damrosch during his European trip appeared on September 7 under the heading, "Topics of Interest Abroad." It was announced that Dr. Damrosch had "engaged Marianne Brandt, Frau Materna, and Herren Schott [and] Kegel [Kogel]...for a season of German opera in New-York."[21] This short report indicated that in a brief period Damrosch had managed to garner the three most revered stars of Wagner productions, in the persons of the first three listed. The *Times* did not feel that the communiqué from Damrosch was encouraging. In Rives it found a source close to the Metropolitan directors that audibly shared its concern:

The prospects of opera in this city for the coming season appear to be enveloped in the haze of uncertainty. So far as the Metropolitan Opera House is concerned...the Directors...turned their eyes to German opera as a last resort....a brief cablegram was received a few days ago by the Directors from Dr. Damrosch, saying that his mission was progressing satisfactorily, but as the message gave no particulars...it did not create a very hopeful feeling. On the contrary, a gentleman connected with the company said that he feared that the telegram was little more than an expression of the doctor's enthusiasm.

[Rives's statement] "As to the prospects of German opera I know nothing, for the arrangement with Dr. Damrosch was made while I was still abroad. But I am not hopeful of the success of the experiment. In the first place, I do not think that German opera can be produced at much, if any less expense than Italian opera....I had occasion while abroad to inquire into the chances of engaging a celebrated German artist. I found that she was getting a salary of about $6,500 a month and besides that, she was extremely reluctant to leave her home....And besides, the expense of mounting German operas at the Metropolitan would be very great. Excepting the "Lohengrin" sets there is no scenery at all in the Metropolitan for the production of German opera. The scenery for "Tristan and Isolde," for example, is very elaborate and very expensive. If the company did not have to incur the expense of having new scenery made I think that one season of German opera here would prove successful, because nearly everybody would go to see it as a novelty; but I am doubtful if a second season would pay....

"...For the American public I think Col. Mapleson is by all odds the best operatic manager to be found, for nobody knows so well as he the wants and peculiarities of the American people. It is true he has no money, but he unquestionably...has the experience." (*New York Times*, September 9, 1884, p.4)

The artist referred to as receiving the $6,500 salary was almost certainly Amalie Materna, and the fact that she was a high-priced artist was never denied. That Damrosch's cablegram had not given "particulars" was dubious, for the previous day a concise description of the cablegram had been released.

On Thusday last the Directors...received a cable dispatch from Dr. Damrosch at Berlin announcing that he had succeeded far better than he had expected to and had organized not only a complete but also a really brilliant company....Dr. Damrosch only awaited the approval of the Metropolitan Directors to close the contract....

...Mr. Whitney concurred with the other members of his committee in approval of the artists selected and the terms arranged by Dr. Damrosch, and that impresario was immediately advised by cable to close the contract. The full list of artists is not yet obtainable, but among the foremost of them are Frau Materna, Fraulein Brandt, and Herr Schott, who is probably the leading German tenor. For some of the chief parts the doctor is in a position to engage two artists, and has been advised to secure both in each case. (*New York Times*, September 8, 1884, p.8)

Surely this implied a vote of confidence from the Directors. Damrosch apparently considered it as such, for about a week later he listed a number of additional artists as members of the new company. The most prominent among these were Lilli Lehmann, Marie Schröder-Hanfstängl, and Adolph Robinson, a renowned baritone. Much of the newspaper article was devoted to descriptions of the careers of the artists, which were indeed impressive. Of primary interest, however, were the dates, length of the projected season, and tentative repertoire, which although described as incomplete, provided insight into the type of opera season Damrosch envisioned:

...the season at the Metropolitan will open on the 15th of November next—last continuously for about 13 weeks, comprising 50 performances, and end on Monday, Feb. 16 the night before Ash Wednesday....The programme will not be confined by any means to purely German opera, but will include the singing in German of many of the Italian masterpieces. The complete repertoire cannot...be ascertained...but it will certainly embrace the following works: Wagner's "Tannhäuser," "Lohengrin,"

"Rienzi," and "Die Meistersinger," Beethoven's "Fidelio," Mozart's "Don Giovanni," Meyerbeer's "Les Huguenots" and "L'Africaine," Gounod's "Faust," Halevy's "La Juive," Auber's "Masaniello [La Muette de Portici]," and Rossini's "William Tell." (New York Times, September 13, 1884, p.4)

At this juncture all plans proceeded in due course. Since Damrosch remained in Europe until perilously close to the opening date, announcements and items of interest concerning the new company appeared in a somewhat detached but steady series of short press releases. *Aida, Rigoletto, Il Barbiere di Siviglia,* and Marschner's *Hans Heiling* were added to Damrosch's prospectus, and details were released about arrangement of the seating and standing-room facilities at the opera house.[22]

The impression created was that every artist Damrosch engaged was a leading singer or prominent technician at one of the foremost opera houses in Germany. On September 25 the *Times* carried a short list of additional singers hired.[23] Among the singers was Herr Aschenbach-Alvari, first tenor in Weimar, who did not appear at the Metropolitan until a year later and then simply under the name Max Alvary. Previously one Herr Bely had been announced—probably an error on the part of the newspaper, for it developed that Herr Bely was in truth Hermine Bely, a soprano who made her debut as Zerlina in *Don Giovanni* on December 10. The article listing the name Bely, in fact, questioned its own accuracy.[24] Damrosch's departure date for New York was given as October 1 and it was announced that he would be accompanied by various "minor officials."[25]

On October 2 the Metropolitan directors announced changes in decoration, involving more gilding and rose-colored satin, adopted from a plan submitted by Francis Lathrop, one of the original contributors to the interior design of the opera house. Of greater importance in the same announcement was information about a rescaling of prices for seats and admission, and the change in opening date:

> The schedule of prices adopted is as follows: General admission, $1; orchestra chairs, $3; dress circle chairs, $2; chairs in the three front rows of the balcony, $1.50; other balcony chairs, $1; gallery, 50 cents; boxes for four persons, $10; third tier boxes for six, $20; baignoire boxes, $35....Unless otherwise determined...the season will begin on Nov. 17 and will include 38 evenings and 12 matinee performances. (*New York Times*, October 2, 1884, p.4)

The difference in prices between the first three rows of balcony chairs and the rest of the balcony seats was a response to the complaints during the first season that one could not see or hear well beyond the third balcony row.

Damrosch supporters, aware that many might dread the long and heavy qualities of German opera performances, made certain that this was discussed in the press and offered reassurance to the public. Apparently there was also a rumor that the city lacked enough good orchestral players to staff the Academy of Music, the Metropolitan Opera, and the Theodore Thomas Orchestra concerts.

This was refuted as well:

The public is not only promised "German opera," but "opera in German." German opera, as popularly, if not wisely, understood is often considered as typified by the "Trilogy," by "Tristan and Isolde," and by "Parsifal." These elaborate and ponderous compositions have their admirers, but there is no gainsaying that their frequent performance is widely regarded with an apprehension somewhat akin to the feeling that would be roused by the threatened visit of an epidemic. The friends of Dr. Damrosch…are justly anxious that the impression should not gain ground that the audiences at the Metropolitan are to be put upon an exclusively Wagnerian regime. …The orchestra is almost complete, and no one will be surprised to learn that Dr. Damrosch's assistants have had no difficulty to bring together as efficient a body of instrumentalists as can be desired. In no European city is it easier to gather at quick notice three or four thoroughly competent bands than in New-York, and it is certain that Col. Mapleson, Dr. Damrosch, and Mr. Thomas will all be well equipped in respect of instrumental coadjutors. (*New York Times*, October 5, 1884, p.8)

Two days later the *Times* printed the entire roster as listed in a letter from Damrosch. It seems that most of the artists recorded in that letter did, in fact, appear with the Metropolitan during the season. The chorus masters were given as Karl Lund and Herr Reichett. Damrosch's son Walter was not mentioned but since there is no evidence that Reichett ever appeared, he must have been replaced at the last moment by the younger Damrosch. Among the auxiliary forces, A. A. Arment was announced as managing the subscription lists; Arment, it can be recalled, had held this position under Mapleson at the Academy of Music as well as with Abbey during the initial season.

There is a full chorus of 70 members and a large corps de ballet, and three premiere danseuses. The instrumental music will be given by the full orchestra of the Symphony Society. The subscription lists for the season…are now open, under the experienced personal management of A. A. Arment. (*New York Times*, October 7, 1884, p.8)

Damrosch himself made a statement concerning the problems he had encountered in assembling his company. Considerable space was given to the social standing of the artists, probably as an answer to the question of whether his season would be a fashionable one. He announced the possibility of a spring season and also implied a possible tour of leading cities.

About his difficulties, Damrosch stated:

I had to contend not only against the difficulty that all of the artists were under engagements, from which in many cases they could not escape except by the payment of heavy forfeits, but also the equally serious obstacle that they were in receipt of tempting offers from other parties. But I was personally acquainted with most of them, and then, too, the idea of forming a company of German artists to produce grand opera in New-York appealed to them with all the force of novelty, and furthermore touched their national pride. For these reasons they consented to come with me to New-York; in preference to going elsewhere. (*New York Times*, October 11, 1884, p.5)

Other than reports on Mapleson's progress, the press was silent on the opera season for the next sixteen days. On October 17 the *Times* described the new decor in great detail, noting that construction work was completed in direct conflict with Damrosch's last-minute rehearsals.

> Since it was decided that opera in German should be given this Winter at the Metropolitan, there has been the usual lack of energy in meeting the worst faults of the new opera house as a place of resort for fashionable people....The time to accomplish these changes is so short that rehearsals will be held by Dr. Damrosch before all the scaffoldings will have been removed....This Winter the red satin and gold will afford a richer, more tasteful, and far more becoming background for the artistic agonies of Worth and other man-milliners of renown. Better than that; they will set off complexions in a way hitherto unknown to the faithful and long-suffering lady stockholders of the Metropolitan. (*New York Times*, October 27, 1884, p.4)

Damrosch started orchestra rehearsals at the opera house on October 29. That evening the new decorations of the auditorium were presented to a small group of interested stockholders and officials.

> The Metropolitan Opera House was lighted up last evening, for the first time this season, to show the effect of the new decorations....The decorations showed to excellent effect under the gaslight, and they [the guests] particularly admired the decorations of the proscenium arch, which by a row of lights that has been placed above the arch is displayed to great advantage....The first rehearsal of the orchestra took place yesterday under the personal direction of Dr. Damrosch. (*New York Times*, October 30, 1884, p.5)

As for the main part of the company,

> The chorus sailed from Hamburg early last week, and its arrival is daily expected. The principal artists sailed from the same port on Sunday last, and will probably arrive here about the middle of next week. (*New York Times*, October 30, 1884, p.5)

The general tone of the press was most favorable, and the *Times* complimented the opening two weeks' repertoire. The reference to the huge burden of work that fell on Damrosch's shoulders is significant in view of his death a few months later.

> The arrangements for the opening of the operatic season at the Metropolitan Opera House progress rapidly. The orchestra holds daily rehearsals, the chorus, most of the members of which arrived yesterday, will begin work next week, and about Wednesday the singers who are to appear in the early representations...may be looked for. The repertoire for the opening fortnight is already announced, and as the production of the operas in the order set forth may be depended upon, it will at once be seen that the familiarity which breeds contempt will surely not be created by the selections for the first two weeks of the season. On the opening night "Tannhäuser" will be brought forth, "Fidelio" and "The Huguenots" following on Wednesday and Friday of the same week. The second week is to be inaugurated by the representation of "William Tell," and "Lohengrin" and "Der Freischütz" are to

be given on the succeeding opera nights. The production of six grand operas within 14 days will tax the energies of the performers and their conductor, Dr. Damrosch, pretty severely, but there is still time for careful preparation before Nov. 17, when the season begins, and not an instant will be lost....Wagner's noble work (Tannhäuser) will be represented with new and appropriate stage attire, and unusual pains will be taken to endow with all the requisite spectacular effect the pantomimic incidents and mythological pageant prefacing the great love scene between Tannhäuser and the mistress of the Venusberg. The subscription books for the season are to be closed on Saturday next. (*New York Times*, November 2, 1884, p.8)

The artists arrived on November 10 and Damrosch took them to see the opera house that evening. Although the house was only dimly lighted, they were pleased and tried their voices. They found the acoustical effects "thoroughly satisfactory" and Damrosch was delighted and happy at the success that this boded for his enterprise.[26]

As of the day before opening night, the box-office prospects were excellent, and those who had been permitted to attend rehearsals were impressed:

The season of grand opera in German at the Metropolitan Opera House will begin tomorrow evening....Frequent and careful rehearsals have been held under the direction of Dr. Damrosch, and those who have been permitted to hear them express a flattering opinion of the company. The popular interest in the experiment is evidenced by the fact that all of the desirable boxes have been taken for the season, and by noon yesterday every seat in the house, except five or six in the dress circle, had been sold for the opening night. The boxes have been taken up in the same way as last year, all of the prominent stockholders having re-engaged the boxes they then held. (*New York Times*, November 16, 1884, p.2)

The *Times* listed the whole assemblage of boxholders; the old group were all present, even Cyrus Field, who had been greatly offended by the decorum of his neighbors during the previous season. A number of new subscribers had been added to the regular list of boxholders. As a final favorable gesture, the *Times* carried an encouraging, highly complimentary editorial describing the prospects and goals of the forthcoming season.

The approaching season of opera at the Metropolitan Opera House is awaited with no little interest, not merely by German-American lovers of the lyric drama, but by all persons for whom music is a study and a relaxation. More interest, indeed, than is usually evinced...appears to prevail in relation to the performances which Dr. Damrosch and his forces are about to supply at the up-town theatre. Just at present Italian opera...is somewhat under a cloud. Pessimists generally, and ultra-Wagnerites in particular, have long proclaimed that the art of which *Bellini*, *Donizetti*, and *Rossini* are typical exponents was doomed, and that Italian opera, for lack of the life which new composers could breath[e] into it, was on the point of giving up the ghost. Predictions of this sort are simply nonsensical. Anyone acquainted with the history of Italian opera for the last half century is well aware that it undergoes periods of eclipse and return to favor....

In point of fact, such opera as Dr. Damrosch proposes to give is not German opera at all, but opera in German....For the manager and musician of shrewdness and a catholic taste the term signifies the best operas written by German composers, the best operas composed by Italians, with German text....That a series of representations undertaken with such praiseworthy and withal practical ideas will have an excellent influence upon the future of Italian opera, as well as strengthen public admiration for the best music of every description, may be expected. It is only to be hoped that the musical public of New-York will profit by the opportunity to make a careful investigation into the merits of a subject which has hitherto been considerably misunderstood and misrepresented. (*New York Times*, November 16, 1884, p.8)

PROBLEMS BETWEEN MAPLESON AND ACADEMY OF MUSIC DIRECTORS

The operations of the Metropolitan Opera House and the Academy of Music were intrinsically related, and in obtaining artists, competition between them was unavoidable. For these reasons it is necessary to examine the problems that confronted Mapleson, both during the Gye episode and even after the Metropolitan had set its course upon opera in German. Unquestionably Abbey's activities made it more difficult for Gye to assemble a prospective company for the Metropolitan. The problems of the Metropolitan directors in trying to settle on an impresario for their next season, furthermore, reassured the Academy Board of Directors enough to grant them license to be harsher than usual with Mapleson.

Throughout the first season, it was obvious that the antagonism between Mapleson and Abbey, and in turn between singers of the two companies, was purely professional. When the benefit for Abbey was given at the Metropolitan, both Mapleson and Patti contributed generously, and one Theodore Moss gave a magnanimous gift on behalf of Abbey's "brother managers."[27] Sofia Scalchi, who had gone from Mapleson to Abbey, returned to Mapleson with the complaint that she had been "treated in a very shabby manner," and even sued Abbey for back salary that he had withheld because she would not substitute on one particular evening.[28] Emily Lablache had returned to Mapleson after the end of the season with Abbey and would continue there. Mapleson welcomed her back in spite of the decision against him that had resulted from his lawsuit against her.[29] These constant reversals among the singers and managers revealed that much of the conflict was either generated by the press or designed for publicity.

The competition to engage singers was a genuine one, however, and this was the area in which Mapleson and the Metropolitan were constantly involved. When Gye was still trying to sign Nilsson to a contract for his company, she admitted that Mapleson was also making offers to her for the Academy.[30] This open bidding for singers' services created the problem of fees that turned the Metropolitan directors away from Italian opera. No impresario could meet the directors' terms and still secure the best artists.

By September 5 Nilsson had signed a contract with Mapleson "to sing in England and America for $2,400 per night."[31] Four days later the Colonel had concluded arrangements with the tenor Masini, who had been one of Gye's possibilities.[32] The major singers did not capitulate to Mapleson's overtures, however, until the Metropolitan had reached its decision to give the opera in German.

With the removal of any possibility of Mapleson's managing the Metropolitan, the Academy Board of Directors became far less cooperative with him. On September 9, after Damrosch had departed for Europe to engage his company, the *Times* forecast Mapleson's problems over a guarantee.

> The prospect at the Academy of Music...is at any rate no better. Although Col. Mapleson still holds a contract...it is an open secret that they have refused to give him a guarantee....A few weeks ago it was whispered that although Col. Mapleson had failed to get a guarantee from the Directors...he had received assurances of financial assistance from several wealthy, personal friends....it is now said that recent events have had the effect of causing the withdrawal even of those assurances. (*New York Times*, September 9, 1884, p.4)

Clearly the recent events referred to were the removal of competition for Mapleson's services by the Metropolitan's decision to hire Damrosch. A few days later it was reported that Mapleson had written Augustus Brown, president of the Academy of Music Board, and asked that the "usual assessment" be made on the stockholders for a guarantee. He asked for $50,000 and indicated that he could get along with $35,000. Brown informed him that the directors were out of town and that the matter would be put before them at the October meeting. Mapleson's immediate need at that time was for $15,000 for Patti; this was sent to him by Fred Rullman. Concerning the support of private individuals, the *New York Times* had this to offer:

> ...it is said that Pierre Lorillard, William R. Travers, H. N. Smith, August Belmont, and another gentleman as long ago as last Spring signified their willingness to put up $10,000 each to assist Col. Mapleson if he would bring over a first-class company this Fall. To secure such an array of talent as Patti, Nilsson, and Masini it is believed that these gentlemen will not hesitate to make good their offer. (*New York Times*, September 13, 1884, p.4)

On September 18 a report from London gave Mapleson's location as "on the continent" and stated that it was believed "Mme. Patti will appear" at the Academy of Music. The following day, it was announced that the Academy Board of Directors had considered Mapleson's request for a guarantee. Mapleson by this time had placed the blame on the Board for his failure to secure the services of Tamagno.[33] He gave no direct assurance that he had secured Nilsson, but indicated that this was highly possible. In this reference, Mapleson placed his request for an almost immediate subsidy:

> The main object...was to make sure of Mme. Patti. To do this Mr. Mapleson required $16,000 on or before Oct. 9....On Mr. Mapleson's arrival here $14,000 more must be paid into his hands. In other words...Mr. Mapleson demands the same guarantee or subsidy as was...given him, i. e., $30,000...a cable dispatch was sent to Mr. Mapleson setting forth that a guarantee fund of $30,000 was not to be thought of, but that a meeting of the stockholders will be called for Oct. 2 when the question will be settled whether the stockholders are willing to be assessed for the coming season, and, if so, to what extent. (*New York Times*, September 20, 1884, p.4)

As was usually the case with Mapleson, his reply was sharp and placed the burden of the responsibility for the continuation of opera at the Academy on his adversary, in this case, Brown. He asserted that if "Academy people don't give me some encouragement...then, I shall release all my singers during their stay in New-York, and, of course, they will be immediately snapped up by the Metropolitan." After discussing his proposed tour and giving a thirteen-city itinerary, Mapleson spoke of his intended presentation of the American premiere of *Lakmé* with Emma Nevada in the title role. He concluded by referring to the situation with Nilsson and commenting on the condition of Italian opera.

> The contract with Nilsson is still hanging. It will be signed as soon as Col. Mapleson receives favorable word from Mr. Brown. The Colonel is as buoyant and confident as ever. "Talk about Italian opera being dead," he said, "Why, it will never die. The only trouble is it has been performed in such vile manner that the public has lost its patience. This is a most opportune time for a grand revival, and you may tell *The Times* that the Colonel will be on hand to create one. (*New York Times*, September 25, 1884, p.4)

Nilsson suffered a fall from a carriage in London two days later. Reporters found this to be an opportunity to question her about her negotiations with Mapleson. She spoke freely and provided the following details:

> Mme. Nilsson says that nothing has yet been settled in regard to a contract between herself and Col. Mapleson, whom she has not seen for some time. She...had promised him to keep free from other engagements until Oct. 2, to enable him to arrange certain guarantees....It was ascertained this evening that Mme. Nilsson's minimum terms for the coming season are £500 per night, with a guarantee of £5,000 for the season, exclusive of traveling expenses for herself and her suite, comprising three persons. (*New York Times*, September 28, 1884, p.2)

On October 1 the Academy directors met to discuss the imminent stockholders meeting. Toward the projected question of a guarantee for Mapleson, the result was that "the sense of the meeting was decidedly adverse."[34] The results of the stockholders' meeting the next night became the major point in later altercations between Mapleson and the Academy group.

> The stockholders of the Academy of Music...contrary to the general expectation, voted by a large majority to assess themselves to aid Col. Mapleson in the production

of Italian opera at the Academy during the approaching season. The action was a surprise even to the Directors....Mr. Brown...explained the object of the meeting, which he said, was to determine whether the stockholders were willing to levy an assessment on their shares for the purpose of assisting Col. Mapleson. He next submitted, without recommendation, a plan by which the stockholders assess themselves to the extent of $2, $3, and $4 a seat, according to the location for each night of two series of performances, to extend over 40 nights of a Fall and Spring season. The conditions are that either Mme. Patti or Mme. Nilsson shall appear on each of these nights, and that Col. Mapleson shall only be allowed the assessment for representations in which either Mme. Patti or Mme. Nilsson shall take part. The assessment is to be paid to the Executive Committee, and at the close of each week that body will hand over to Col. Mapleson the amount due him for the performances by Mmes. Patti and Nilsson.

...The poll taken on this question resulted in 86 votes being cast in favor of the assessment and only 31 against it....It is estimated that this assessment will produce $30,000.

Stockholders who are not willing to pay the assessment on their seats will be allowed to retain the right of admission to the academy [sic], but will not have the use of their boxes or stalls....It is the general understanding that this season the Colonel will not need any further financial assistance than the assessment voted to him last evening. (New York Times, October 3, 1884, p.1)

It was obvious at this point that Mapleson was not to be treated as liberally as in the past or as generously as his competitor at the Metropolitan. Four days later, Brown received a cablegram from Mapleson asking for a remittance. The *Times* commented, "It is not likely that his request will be complied with."[35]

On October 12 it was reported that of the 200 stockholders, 115 had already agreed to pay the assessment, and that there had been no negative responses up to that date.[36] Mapleson announced that the season would open on November 10 with *Il Barbiere di Siviglia*, featuring Patti as Rosina. In the same report the prices for subscriptions were announced:

The subscription will consist of 20 nights and the prices of boxes will be as follows: For the season—balcony boxes, $500; artists' boxes, $500; proscenium boxes, (to hold six persons) $350; mezzanine boxes, (to hold four persons) $300; seats in the parquette and first three rows of the balcony, $75; other balcony seats, $60. (*New York Times*, October 21, 1884, p.4)

These prices were slightly higher than those set at the Metropolitan, yet the difference was not enough to make the attendance at the Academy prohibitive to the ordinary opera patron.

On October 23, a rumor appeared in print that Patti would not participate in the opera season at the Academy as had been previously announced. The *Times* reported that "Investigation showed that these rumors were, unfortunately, founded upon fact." The primary issue was given as the $16,000, and the Academy directors sent a cablegram to Mapleson stating that the money requested would not be forth-coming.[37] Since Patti did ultimately arrive and the directors did not give Mapleson an advance, it is possible either that Mapleson and Patti had indulged in a joint bluff or that Mapleson was able to secure the money elsewhere. It is remotely possible that Patti agreed to journey to the United States without the advance; this is dubious, however, in view of Patti's general policy of payment in advance.

On October 26 Charles Mapleson, the Colonel's son, granted an interview to the press. After quoting from a letter from his father,

> "I have been singularly lucky in securing Nevada, the next best singer in the world after Patti,"

the younger Mapleson disclosed plans for the projected premiere of *Lakmé* and answered questions about Nilsson's absence from the Academy.

> "The Governor...pays Mlle. Nevada $1,500 a night for every night she sings....After appearing in 'Sonnambula' Mlle. Nevada will sing in 'Lakmé.' The Colonel and Ar-diti were dining with Delibes...on the day when I sailed, getting final instructions from him in regard to the first production of his opera in this country."...

> "Why no Nilsson contract?"

> "The reason is very simple....The fact is that, much as she likes America, Mme. Nilsson likes her home better....She has signed a contract with my father, however, for the season of 1885–6, when, of course, we shall not have Patti. Nilsson will be our bright particular star for that season...

> "...at the Metropolitan Opera House last Spring I took Patti on the stage to pay her compliments to Mme. Nilsson....They both spoke of singing together in the same company, and both seemed to be pleased at the notion they might do this in the future...I don't think the New-York public will ever see those two divas on the same night until both are in much less demand than they are now, and are consequently willing to sing for much less than they get now."

Charles Mapleson also spoke of the fate of Gye's Royal Italian Opera Company.

> ...Mr. Gye has had his operatic fling in London. As a last resort he counted a great deal on the Metropolitan Opera House here, which, with the subvention promised by the stockholder, would, he thought, put him all right again. But this fell through, and I am afraid it is all over with Gye now, as I heard just before leaving London that the old Historical Covent Garden is to be turned into a circus. The Covent Gar-den Royal Italian Opera Company Limited has exploded and I don't believe that it can be repaired. The last thing I heard, however, before leaving London, was that Gye was trying to get 10 gentlemen to invest $3,000 each in a new season at Covent Garden. Whether he has succeeded or not I have no means of knowing yet. (*New York Times*, October 26, 1884, p.3)

Two new operas were announced for the Academy, *Lakmé* and Gounod's *Mireille*.[38] On November 1 it was announced that Mapleson would arrive on November 2 concurrently with Patti.[39] That day's newspaper carried the announcement that the "subscription books for the season were closed yesterday, and the figures they contain are most encouraging."[40] Patti's arrival drew a huge crowd and she announced that this would be her last time in New York. Mapleson took the opportunity to prophesy that Italian opera "will never fall into disfavor as long as love of melody lasts."[41]

The opening of the Academy of Music took place as scheduled, on November 10. The artistic merits of the production were judged excellent, and Patti, was, as usual, lauded as outstanding. In line with the new attitude toward Italian opera, the *Times'* critic had words to say concerning the selection of the opening opera and other matters that affected the gala occasion.

> ...there was no mistaking that the event was a triful less brilliant than an opening performance of bygone days. The reasons for the falling off are numerous and easily divined. Among the most potent may be cited the somewhat overcast horizon of the financial world, the counter-attractions put forth by other theatres, and the lack of drawing power of "Il Barbiere." Against the two hostile influences first referred to a manager finds it difficult to struggle; the simplest way of escaping the unprofitable results of bringing out such works as "Il Barbiere" is to omit them from the repertoire. (*New York Times*, November 11, 1884, p.5)

Since a survey of box-office results for Italian opera over a long period of years would place the Rossini work near the top of the list, the remark about the drawing power of *Il Barbiere* appears to have been merely a further symptom of the popular revolt against Italian opera at the time.

Two days after the opening, Patti was rumored about to cancel her engagement and return to Europe, and Mapleson attacked the directors of the Academy. The question at hand was the interpretation of the agreement to assess the stockholders. Mapleson's statement was in this vein:

> ...the Directors have not come up with their agreement. I understood before I came here that an assessment of $30,000 had been levied on the stockholders...but I have not seen the money. I expected that they would turn that money over to Mme. Patti as a guarantee, but they refuse to do so, and propose instead to dole it out in small parcels....The stockholders have done their part, but the Directors have not. It would look as if some of them at least had formed a society for the total extinction of Italian opera. As the matter stands, we will go as far as our money lasts and then throw up the sponge. (*New York Times*, November 12, 1884, p.2)

In his campaign to enlist public sentiment and support, Mapleson did not hesitate. The following day's paper carried an advertisement that read "Farewell appearance of Adelina Patti."[42] The *Times* published statements from three sources involved in the dispute. The first statement was Mapleson's, the second belonged to a stockholder, and the final words were those of Brown, the president of the Academy Board.

> ...the truth is that the Directors agreed to give me a guarantee of $16,000, in consideration of my bringing over Patti, but now they refuse to keep that agreement. Unless I get the $16,000 I shall withdraw Mme. Patti and finish the season without her. The notice of her withdrawal will be published in all of the papers to-morrow morning.

> After the performance on Monday evening last, Mr. Mapleson was tendered about $700, which was the proportion of the assessment levied on the stockholders due for that night. This was refused by Mr. Mapleson.

> They never agreed to give him $16,000. They carried into effect a resolution adopted by the stockholders to assess themselves so much a seat for each performance in which Mme. Patti or Nilsson appeared, and regulating the manner in which that assessment is to be paid over to Col. Mapleson. (*New York Times*, November 13, 1884, p.4)

The following day Patti's manager, a Signor Lavelli, threatened that

> If it is not paid very soon I shall consider the contract vitiated, and Mme. Patti will certainly retire from Col. Mapleson's management. (*New York Times*, November 14, 1883, p.4)

This was followed by a statement from Mapleson.

> Col. Mapleson...said there was no change in the situation, but something would have to be done very soon, and it was really too bad to be kept in such a state of uncertainty. The Directors of the Academy were as dumb as oysters. It is said that if it comes down to a question of Patti or no Patti, some of the leading stockholders will take the matter in hand and consider the advisability of advancing Col. Mapleson the money he requires. (*New York Times*, November 14, 1883, p.4)

Mapleson's statement made it fairly obvious that he was responsible for the pressure from Patti's manager. Whether the Board of Directors mistrusted Mapleson with the money, or whether they questioned the need of advancing that sum to Patti was not clear, but they arranged another stockholder meeting and invited her to attend and clarify the situation.[43] The next day's paper carried a short report titled, "Col. Mapleson's Tactics," in which it was stated that he planned to appeal from the directors to the Academy stockholders. He further explained that Patti would not return to England until May 2, and then it would be to sing under his management. According to him, his contract with her called for "40 nights in six months" and apparently the opera house or location was not specified therein.[44]

PROSPECTS FOR THE SEASON
OF GERMAN OPERA

As the two opera houses opened their seasons, Mapleson was confronted with an unpleasant situation and poor relationships with the directorate of the Academy of Music. The only factor that gave him any power whatsoever was his control of Patti, whom the Academy stockholders viewed as their most precious commodity. In addition to the problems with the directors, Mapleson was fighting against a strong revolt against Italian opera. Whatever the causes may have been, the press had granted sufficient publicity to its opponents and their objections that Mapleson was placed in the position of having to defend his stand and convince the public that Italian opera was neither dead nor dying. He was strong, however, in the quality of his company. In addition to most of his artists from the previous year, he had several new ones. He also had a number who had enjoyed considerable success under Abbey at the Metropolitan but had either returned to Mapleson or had gone over to his company for the first time.

Damrosch's position was quite different. His relationships with the Metropolitan Board of Directors and stockholders were extremely cordial and he could rely on their support to the utmost. His product, opera in German, was a novelty and also an answer to the clamor of public and press alike. The strong growth in interest in Wagner and the attention focused on his operas as a result of his recent death favored Damrosch's position. The new company was solidly built and numbered among its ranks seasoned, reputable singers from the major opera houses of Germany. Damrosch's own reputation was firmly established and he had enjoyed the favor of the New York public and press for over ten years.

The problem that faced Damrosch dealt with the complaints about the new opera house. These were twofold, the first and foremost being the reputedly poor acoustics and unsatisfactory sight lines. The other problem revolved about the Metropolitan's having been constructed by the boxholders with their own comfort in mind, so that the preponderance of boxes left the opera house economically burdened.

The most effective attack on the acoustics had come in a long letter to the editor of the *New York Times*, entitled "Its Boast and Its Snare" and discussing both the problems mentioned above.

> It is hard to discover how the cause of music can be advanced or the establishment of the opera on a sound basis can be effected in the Metropolitan Opera-house, or that any desirable result could be attained by a fusion of the two opera-houses. The leading idea of the projectors of the Metropolitan Opera-house seems to have been "boxes."...So to questions about such details about the Metropolitan Opera-house as "How can you see or hear?" or "Isn't it too big?" the reply has been, "Look at the boxes."
>
> It ought to be a rule...that no house for operatic or theatrical performances which could seat comfortably more than 2,500 people...should ever be erected....The box

system itself is European; it is defective for the accom[m]odation of a great number; and nowadays, with operatic salaries from five to twenty times as great as they were a generation ago, impossible. The object of boxes in an American theatre is not clear, unless to minister to exclusiveness and fashion....

...But the size of the Metropolitan Opera-house has been its boast and its snare. In order to have boxes...it was necessary to have many tiers and a much greater depth, circumference, and height of auditorium wall, and hence an enormous unoccupied space within the auditorium....The voice becomes diluted, its quality changes, and, as the singer forces his tones to make them reach his distant hearers, half the pleasure is lost—and no talk of "acoustic properties" is a counterbalance of the fact that the proper dimensions have been exceeded....It happens sometimes that age improves auditoriums, like violins; as they respectively dry and grow resonant they improve in hearing. The great width, depth, and height...combine against this being probable for the Metropolitan Opera-house.

In the matter of seeing the stage from the sides of the auditorium, it is almost impossible by any artifice except a ladder to give people in the upper tiers any satisfactory sight of it. There are almost 400 seats...from which the stage is nearly, if not quite, invisible, while from those centre seats in the upper tiers in which the stage is visible it is so remote and so dwarfed, without the aid of glasses as to possess but a languid interest for the average spectator....As thus constituted the opera is a heavy tax on even the wealthy boxowners, and its perpetuity can bring litle pleasure to the average New-Yorker, for if the city can support but one opera it is not desirable that it should be one outside the reach of all but the wealthy.

There is another and a better way to obtain a good and permanent opera, but it is to be regretted that large sums and so much effort have already been expended on a house which brings more regret than delight to the real amateur. (*New York Times*, May 4, 1884, p.4)

To be sure this was a long, involved list of complaints, but certainly it was constructive and not comprised of petty malicious phrases. On the same page of the *Times* a news item described additional problems, centered about production needs. These included poor ventilation and also poor accessibility because the dressing rooms (except for that of the prima donna) were on the second and third floors. One further comment was that there "seems to be no way of getting horses into the house."

Concerning the defective acoustics of the house, the errors in construction which make the upper parts of the auditorium almost valueless, the singular lack of architectural beauty or fitness in the main entrance, and the fiasco of the decoration of the house, many of the artists are outspoken....

One of the most distinguished members of Mr. Abbey's recent opera company avers that the stage arrangements and the accom[m]odations for the artists are such as to interfere seriously with the success of the performances. ...This must have been designed by a novice in theatre building. The scenic arrangements are such that no change can be made without lowering the curtain and losing time. The scenery itself...is in so many places that thirty-five well-paid men instead of a dozen are needed to manage it. The lights are all at the level of the stage or put in the flies, leaving the central portion in semi-darkness, an arrangement which is cited to explain why no really brilliant stage effects were seen there during the past Winter....

...arrangements for the discomfort of the artists are superb and the facilities for catching cold unequaled. (*New York Times*, May 4, 1884, p.4)

The complaints listed above generated mainly from those engaged in the operatic productions; for this reason they were of utmost importance, not only for utilitarian reasons, but also psychological ones, if the company performing at the Metropolitan were to be cooperative and effective. This was written prior to the redecoration of the auditorium, and the new color schemes were deemed to be an improvement. Insofar as moving the scenery was concerned, the Metropolitan Opera House experienced more trouble in later years, when the unions forced the employment of as many as 75 to 100 stagehands. The ventilation and draftiness of the house were apparently never corrected, for complaints persisted until the demolition of the building.[45]

When viewed circumspectly, Damrosch's position was far more secure than Mapleson's and less fraught with critical problems. The crux of the matter lay in the different financial positions of the two men. Mapleson was still gambling with his own money, although he was receiving a minimal subsidy. Damrosch was on a salary and was presenting opera basically at the account of the stockholders of the Metropolitan. His salary was not large, but his contract was such that he could not possibly lose any money of his own.[46]

In essence, Leopold Damrosch, who had migrated to America only twelve years before, had solved the problem confronting the Metropolitan Opera directors. Although he had been known primarily as an operatic conductor while in Europe, his career in America had been largely connected with oratorios and symphonic concerts. His belief in German opera was obviously sincere. That his death a few months later did not halt this movement gave ample proof of its timeliness. Years later at the premiere of his own opera *Cyrano de Bergerac*, Walter Damrosch in a speech from his box attributed to his father the introduction of German opera in this country. Krehbiel commented on the speech as follows:

Possibly the elation of the moment may be pleaded in extenuation for...[Walter] Damrosch' faulty history. As a matter of fact German opera in German had been fighting its way toward recognition for nearly thirty-nine years when Dr. Leopold Damrosch began his memorable experiment at the Metropolitan.[47]

Probably the greatest factor in the decision of the directors of the Metropolitan to present opera in German was their need for an alternative after the fiasco of the initial season. The rise of interest in Wagner's operas, combined with the apathy toward Italian opera, were certainly fortunate circumstances. Finally, the foresight and opportunism of Damrosch solved the problem confronting the Board of Directors and made possible this dramatic shift in policy.

CHAPTER 4

The German Opera Era (1884–1891)

In spite of the late decision to produce opera in German at the Metropolitan, Leopold Damrosch had succeeded in assembling and training a company that gave every indication that it would perform admirably in the second Metropolitan Opera House season. Damrosch had engaged experienced artists, among them Amalie Materna, the most celebrated interpreter of German opera at the time. Damrosch himself had an unimpeachable reputation as a well-schooled, responsible conductor, and his operation in the dual capacity as artistic directer and general manager precluded internal administrative conflict. Damrosch had also directed the rehearsals of all the forces, including orchestra, chorus, and principals, thus permitting the performances to have a cohesiveness that was unusual in operatic endeavor.

Mapleson's company at the Academy of Music had opened a week earlier with Rossini's *Il Barbiere di Siviglia*. Although the newspapers reported a somewhat lackluster attitude, they reviewed the performance favorably. Mapleson's company, with all its attendant difficulties, was a reputable one and still had Patti as its major attraction. The success of the company at the Metropolitan, therefore, hinged upon the projected attraction of German opera, aided by some of the established successes in Italian grand opera, performed, however, in German. As for celebrated artists, Mapleson was in an advantageous position, for not only had he been successful in reengaging most of his leading singers, but he had also garnered several artists who had enjoyed great success with Abbey the year before at the Metropolitan. The most prominent of the group who switched over was the mezzo-soprano Sofia Scalchi, who had been a major box-office attraction under Abbey's management.

THE SEASON OF 1884–1885

During the season of 1884–1885 the Metropolitan company staged fifty-nine performances, two of which were opera concerts. Three opera performances and one concert were conducted by John Lund, three operas were conducted by Walter Damrosch, and the balance of the productions were led by Leopold Damrosch. The repertoire was strongly oriented toward German opera, and of the German operas, the preponderance, suitably, were works of Wagner. Beethoven, Wagner, and Weber accounted for twenty-nine performances, twenty-five of these devoted to Wagner. Three French composers were represented: Auber, Halévy, and Meyerbeer; of the twenty-two performances of French operas, fourteen were Meyerbeer's works in the grand opera tradition appropriate to the skills of a German opera company. The remaining six operas were divided among Mozart, Rossini, and Verdi, Mozart's *Don Giovanni* being here classified as an Italian opera. The intention had unquestionably been for Leopold Damrosch to conduct all presentations of the season, but his sudden illness and unexpected death made it necessary to enlist the services of Walter Damrosch and John Lund.

Although Materna did not make her first appearance until January 5, 1885, she appeared in eighteen performances, as well as in both opera concerts, and she relinquished only one performance in any of her roles, that of Rachel in *La Juive*, to Marianne Brandt on the final performance of the season, a matinee. She had sung the previous night in the last presentation of *Die Walküre*. Marianne Brandt appeared in thirty-five performances and in both opera concerts; Adolph Robinson sang eighteen performances and the two concerts. In a season barely lasting eight weeks these were impressive totals, and it was obvious that Damrosch expected major efforts from his artists, notwithstanding the demanding character of their roles in operas of this type. The lessons learned from Abbey's financial catastrophe the previous year surely contributed to this obviously economical move. Regardless of the motivation, however, it was quite a remarkable feat for the identical cast to present *Die Walküre* not only on a succeeding night and matinee but four times within five days. In fact, the season's seven performances of *Die Walküre* occurred within three weeks of one another. Examination of the repertoire for the season reveals that performances were frequently bunched together (e.g., four performances of *La Prophète* in eight days). The lack of storage space for scenery and the expense of transportation to and from the warehouse may possibly have been a major factor in this unorthodox scheduling.

The reviews of the season were generally excellent. Basically, Leopold Damrosch was given the largest share of the credit for the artistic excellence of the performances. The chorus was well received, and Damrosch's careful and meticulous training of this group was highly praised. The orchestra was treated only in the most laudatory terms, as was the work of the stage director, Hock. The ballet received little mention, a neglect possibly deriving from the minimal use of dance in the operas produced. German artists were also considered not particularly disposed toward ballet; conceivably the ballet corps was less effective than the rest of the company. The singers comprised an admirable collection of major artists from all the leading German opera houses. The principal lyric soprano roles were usually assigned to Marie Schröder-Hanfstängl, who had come from the Imperial Opera House in Berlin.[1] Auguste Kraus, already married to Anton Seidl but not using his name, was the youthful dramatic soprano essaying the less demanding Wagnerian roles such as Elisabeth in *Tannhäuser* and Elsa in *Lohengrin*. Materna assumed the role of Elisabeth after her arrival, and in addition she portrayed such dramatic parts as Valentin in *Les Huguenots*, Rachel in *La Juive*, and Brünnhilde in all the performances of *Die Walküre*. Marianne Brandt took all major mezzo-soprano and contralto roles, as she had at the Imperial Opera in Berlin. She also ventured into the dramatic soprano repertoire as Leonora in *Fidelio*, a role for which she had become famous in Berlin.[2]

Damrosch's male roster was equally well supplied. Anton Schott and Anton Udvardy shared the responsibilities as leading tenor, but Schott dominated the scene. Acknowledged for many years as the outstanding tenor in Germany, he had created the title role in Berlioz's *Benvenuto Cellini*.[3] Udvardy, from Budapest, received favorable reviews during the season and appeared in *Les Huguenots*, *Der Freischütz*, *Don Giovanni*, *Fidelio*, *Guillaume Tell*, *Rigoletto*, and *La Juive*. Adolph Robinson dominated the baritone roles, although Alois Blum frequently sang major roles in the repetitions. Krehbiel asserted that the single performance of *Rigoletto* given during the season was "to gratify the ambition of Herr Robinson to be seen and heard as the Jester, and of Mme. Schröder-Hanfstängl to sing the music of Gilda."[4] Josef Kogel assumed the bass roles, with Josef Staudigl appearing in parts that usually required a bass-baritone voice.

Opening Night—Tannhäuser

The first season of German opera at the Metropolitan Opera House was launched on November 17, 1884. It was an auspicious debut for Damrosch's company and the performance was hailed by critical acclaim. *Tannhäuser* was a fortunate choice, since it was considered less complicated than works from Wagner's period of deep involvement with leitmotive and more complicated mythological plots. It had also received far fewer performances in the United States than had *Lohengrin*, and it represented no great departure from the operas of Meyerbeer and Weber, which had been cordially received for a number of years. Finally, Abbey had not produced it the year before, and for this reason it might be considered a novelty.

The *New York Times*, which had granted rather brief treatment to the Academy of Music opening the previous week, heaped lavish praise on the performance.

> The choice of Wagner's works was, indeed, proof in itself that the occasion was not to be placed upon the same footing as ordinary operatic representations....It would have been an easy task to have adhered to routine practice by presenting the leading artists, one by one. Faithful to his opinions, however,...[Dr. Damrosch] preferred arranging his repertoire with a closer regard to the novelty and interest of its elements....["Tannhäuser"] is less hackneyed than "Lohengrin," less flimsy than "Rienzi," and less involved than anything the German composer wrote during the last years of his life. It contains, in truth, much that is wearisome, but portions...are delightfully melodious, some of the numbers...are equal in massive grandeur to anything found in Meyerbeer's most elaborate musical pageants, and in the portion of the work allotted to the orchestra is a long symphony, tedious perhaps at certain stages...but abounding in melodic and harmonious passages of ravishing loveliness. (*New York Times*, November 18, 1882, p.5)

The *Times* also lost no time in emphasizing that the favorable outlook for serious opera was evident from the outset:

> ...Dr. Damrosch evinced judgment in bringing it forth as a fit prelude to a season which promises to be notable and successful, not merely through the appearance of efficient performers, but mainly through a varied, interesting, and important repertoire. The representation last evening was admirable in many respects. The orchestra was simply perfect in point of expressiveness and technical precision, the chorus, but for an occasional inaccuracy of intonation in the first scene, could lay claim to almost as cordial praise, and the singers entrusted with the leading roles worked well together, and in two or three instances produced a decided impression. Herr Adolf Robinson...is one of the best baritones the opera-going public has lately had a chance of listening to. He has a noble voice, which he used with German energy and intelligence and with the skill of a master of Italian *cantabile*, according as occasion suggests, and his acting is full of ease, breadth, and power....Herr Joseph Kögel... proved to be a basso equipped with sonorous tones and a declamatory style quite equal to the exigencies of his role....Fräulein Kraus...is a songstress of experience, whose voice becomes a little reedy when forced, but whose declamation is expressive, and whose acting is highly dramatic....Venus, as portrayed by Fraulein Schlach and the young shepherd, as embodied by Fräulein Stern were respectable delineations. Regarding...Herr Anton Schott...possibly he was overcome by nervousness or overexertion, and possibly the change of climate may have affected him unfavorably. Bearing in mind that the tenor has a European reputation it would be well to suspend judgment upon him until a second hearing offers him an opportunity of making a more pleasant impression than he wrought last night....Let us add that the opera was placed upon the stage with new and magnificent scenery and dresses, that the episodes in which the chorus took an active part had an...animation and reality seldom beheld in performances of Italian opera, that there was frequent and enthusiastic applause, and that Dr. Damrosch, who, of course, conducted the orchestra, was called before the footlights and cheered after the curtain had fallen on the first act. (*New York Times*, November 18, 1884, p.5)

It was obvious that the *Times* review was inspired by a well-rounded performance and that its author was thoroughly impressed by the presentation in all its aspects except Schott's participation. His judgment of the value of the work itself was candid and not one to discourage patrons from attending the German operas.

The *New York Tribune* reviewer took the opportunity to philosophize, and the results were highly complimentary to Damrosch's experiment:

> The season of grand opera in German under the direction of Dr. Damrosch was opened at the Metropolitan Opera House last night under circumstances of the most auspicious character. So far as the externals were concerned all the brilliant features of the opera of the Italian season were repeated, but those who understand the significance of the movement into which the directors of the Opera House have been carried by what seemed to them unfortunate circumstances will realize that a somewhat different state of affairs existed in the artistic regions of the establishment.... Last night's performance was the beginning of an effort to establish grand opera in New York on the lines which obtain in Continental Europe. The highest significance of last night's performance, therefore, consisted in the publication which it gave with reference to these purposes....

The audience surpassed in number that of the memorable opening a year ago. It numbered fully 5,000 people and many hundreds who came were unable to obtain admission. (*New York Times*, November 18, 1884, p.5)

Brandt's Debut in Fidelio

Contrary to its usual practice, the *New York Times* called particular attention to the forthcoming debut of Marianne Brandt in *Fidelio*, to take place November 19 at the second performance of Damrosch's season. Her appearance in this role was quite remarkable, since she was a contralto and sang all the lowest roles in that voice range. Leonora is a dramatic soprano part of the most demanding kind, and the famous aria "*Abscheulicher, wo eilst du hin?*" has unquestionably one of the widest ranges in opera. Enthusiasm and interest were at a higher pitch than during the opening season.

The representation of "Fidelio" at the Metropolitan Opera House this evening will...be interesting...because the work will be the medium of introducing to the public Fräulein Marianne Brandt, the foremost of German contraltos. Fräulein Brandt, like Mme. Materna, was one of Richard Wagner's favorite artists, and her name is inseparably associated with the festal days at Bayreuth. (*New York Times*, November 19, 1884, p.4)

The review of the performance indicated not only that Brandt had lived up to expectations, but also that Schott had vindicated himself for his disappointing opening-night performance. Robinson, Staudigl, and Josef Miller were considered adequate, as was the chorus. The orchestra and Damrosch received the highest praise, as would continue to be the case throughout the season.

...Fräulein Amalia [*sic*] Brandt, a mezzo soprano and contralto, who has long been a favorite with audiences in Germany, effected her first appearance as Leonore, and wrought an immediate and decisive impression. Her voice is brilliant and powerful, her method eclectic, by which we would imply that she has the vigorous enunciation and accent of the German school of song, and no little of the fluency and taste of the Italian, and as an actress she is intelligent, impassioned, and forceful. Three recalls followed the rendering of "Abscheulicher."...Fräulein Kraus' Marzelline was an excellent performance, and particularly interesting as showing her versatility....Herr Schott as Florestan was in much better form than on the occasion of his debut. That he is an artist of experience, and the very reverse of a mere vocalist, was already perceptible on Monday, but overexertion told so severely on his voice that judgment upon his merits had to be suspended. Last night he was heard to much greater advantage, and he sang Florestan's music in the second act with infinite pathos and considerable charm....Herr Robinson...personated Pizarro, and did all that could be done with that thankless character, whose single air is so overwhelmed by the orchestral accompaniment that no singer in the memory of man has managed to make its measures audible. Herr Staudigl was seen as Don Fernando, but the role is so unimportant that another opportunity must be awaited before speaking of the newcomer's voice and talent. Herr Miller was an efficient Rocco, the chorus was numerically strong and reasonably well drilled and Dr. Damrosch's orchestra was perfect. (*New York Times*, November 20, 1884, p.5)

The *New York Tribune* correspondent referred explicitly to Mapleson's considerably less successful presentation of *Fidelio* two years earlier. The *Tribune* was as enthusiastic as the *Times* about Brandt's performance and also complimented Kraus's portrayal of Marzelline:

> ["Fidelio"] has frequently been given...the last time by Mr. Mapleson's [company] in March, 1882, but never, we venture to say, with the excellence of ensemble, the delicacy and the vividness of last night's performance.
>
> The importance of the production was further enhanced by the first appearance of Fräulein Brandt, who enacted the titular role. The artistic stature of this woman is too great to permit a thought of her performance being reviewed in the fugitive minutes which are at our command. We wish...to record only our conviction of the depth of her genius as a dramatic singer, and the gratifying fact that her performance met with the recognition it merited....All the parts when not in brilliant were in good hands. Frau Krause's [*sic*] versatility as an actress was shown by the ease with which she adapted herself to the part of *Marzelline*—a character contrasting strongly with *Elizabeth* and yet proving her to be an artist of high rank. And the same conscientiousness appeared in her singing, which, as on the opening night, was made delightful by the richness, dewy freshness and mellowness of her voice, and her easy style. (*New York Tribune*, November 20, 1884, p.5)

Obviously, public and press were enthusiastic over Brandt's performance.

Materna's First Appearance

During the intervening period before Materna's debut in *Tannhäuser*, the press and public were in full, favorable accord. Reviews were excellent, and the company played to capacity audiences. By January 5, all the operas of the season's repertoire, except for *La Juive* and *Die Walküre*, had been performed several times. *Tannhäuser*, in fact, had been presented five times, with Kraus portraying Elisabeth in four presentations, Schröder-Hanfstängl in one.[5] The excitement over the sixth performance of *Tannhäuser* was purely the culmination of the long anticipation of Materna's first appearance at the Metropolitan. As might have been expected, one critic did not feel that the role was particularly well-suited to her voice:

> The German soprano possesses a voice of uncommon richness and power, her delivery is broad and varied, and her temperament thoroughly artistic...as a vocalist pure and simple Mme. Schröder-Hanfstängl, one of the prima donnas of the same company of which she is a member, is unquestionably her superior. Frau Materna, however, is far better equipped for the lyric drama of the period than any of her German or Italian contemporaries....We do not, however, consider the part of Elisabeth...as the artist's happiest effort....Frau Materna's passion and power must be pent up while she depicts the love, the grief, the piety, and the heart-broken

sorrow of that tender creature....To say that Frau Materna sang her music most ex-
pressively, and gave to every line of the text its significance and to each of the...
situations...its value, is, of course, to do the prima donna common justice....Frau
Materna's voice was in good condition last night, although slightly tremulous.
...After the third act Frau Materna was called before the curtain again and again,
and when she and her associates withdrew from sight each of them was laden with
flowers. (*New York Times*, January 6, 1885, p.5)

New York's other major newspaper was enthusiastic. The reviewer, however, had
several less favorable comments about the performances of the other artists.

The entrance of Amalia Materna on the operatic stage of this country was effected
last night at the Metropolitan Opera House under circumstances which were most
flattering to the lady and most significant in their bearing on the operatic problems
which the Metropolitan management this season engaged with....Amidst the tumult
of applause which greated her entrance into the minstrel's hall in the second act, she
began her song of greeting. In a moment her powerful and ringing voice had quieted
the glad noise, and from then till the end of the act she had the attention of the audience to her artistic creation rather than to her personality. At the close of the act,
however, the listeners gave way to their pleasure to testify their pleasure at her coming, and she had repeatedly to come forward to acknowledge their tributes. Unfortunately, the presentation of the opera, as a whole, was not up to the standard fixed
by Dr. Damrosch's artists earlier in the season. Herr Schott was obviously under the
weather; Herr Koegel could not sing and Herr Miller had a short notice to abandon
the part of Siterolf into less capable hands and himself impersonate the Landgrave.
Herr Schueller sang the part of Walther heretofore cared for by Herr Tiferro to the
manifest improvement of the sextet...because of the greater beauty of his voice,
although his singing lacks breadth. (New York Tribune, January 6, 1885, p.5)

During the week of Materna's debut two other news items indicated that interest
in opera and in its problems was significantly high. Mapleson had taken his troupe to
Boston, as was his custom during the first week of the New Year. On January 2 they
presented *Semiramide* with a cast including Patti and Scalchi. The audience was
reported to be the largest opera audience ever known in Boston, and the box-office
receipts totaled between $10,000 and $12,000.[6]

Later that week Damrosch encountered problems with the male chorus members,
who went on strike. The performance, Auber's *La Muette de Portici*, was presented
without their services. Dr. Damrosch made a pre-curtain speech that "astonished the
audience" and provided details concerning the disagreement. Whether the demands
of the strikers were directly attributable to the large audiences that were attending
opera performances was a valid, if unanswerable question:

...Dr. Damrosch announced that, in consequence of a strike on the part of a small
number of male choristers, the choral forces might prove slightly less effective than
usual....The facts of the case are said to be that 23 members of the male chorus...sent
an unsigned letter to Dr. Damrosch yesterday morning, demanding an increase in
salary. Dr. Damrosch requested that signatures be appended to the letter, but these

were not forthcoming. As the choristers...receive $16, $18, and $20 weekly, accord-
ing to their usefullness, for four representations, as they are paid extra for all performances exceeding four a week, and as the pay is somewhat more liberal than that
habitually allowed this class of performers, it was deemed inexpedient to comply
with the demand....Late last night arrangements had been made to fill up the ranks
with efficient men, in ample time for today's matinee...and it was believed that the
season would progress to a successful termination in spite of the strikers' menaces.
(*New York Times*, January 10, 1885, p.4)

Metropolitan Premiere of Die Walküre

No event during the first season of German opera elicited the excitement and
anticipation that accompanied the Metropolitan premiere production of *Die
Walküre*. Although the premiere had been announced at the beginning of the season,
as the date approached almost every operatic newspaper article referred to its forthcoming presentation. On January 25 a review of *La Juive* mentioned the directors'
decision to reengage Damrosch for the following year. In discussing future plans the
report commented on the coming performance of the second opera of Wagner's *Ring*
cycle.

> The Directors night before last simply confirmed the assurances...that Dr. Dam-
> rosch would once more—and most judiciously—be interested with the artistic direc-
> tion of the representations. There is good ground for believing that Herr Vogel, the
> most distinguished Wagnerian Tenor of the age, and Frau Unger will be members of
> the new troupe; that several of the favorites, including Frau Schröder-Hanfstängl,
> are to be retained, and if "Die Walküre" proves as impressive as it is anticipated it
> may, that the whole Trilogy will be produced in due course. (*New York Times*,
> January 25, 1885, p.6)

The fervor of anticipation continued to mount and four days later a review of *Le
Prophète* included these references to the premiere of *Die Walküre*:

> Although Wagner's ponderous work has already been listened to in this city, (the
> Academy of Music being its place of earliest production and Mme. Pappenheim its
> first heroine in this country) Friday's representation will undoubtedly be the first
> rendering thoroughly worthy of the German reformer's music-drama....Notwith-
> standing the "cuts" which we believe Dr. Damrosch has judiciously made, it is to be
> apprehended that tomorrow's rendering of "Die Walküre" will run well into the
> small hours of the next day. Every seat in the auditorium was bought up a week ago.
> (*New York Times*, January 29, 1885, p.5)

The initial performance of the opera was to take place on Friday, January 30, and
that day's *New York Times* carried a lengthy report of the previous day's dress
rehearsal. It presented an interesting summary of the last-minute problems, as well
as an optimistic outlook on the quality of the significant premiere at hand:

> A final rehearsal of the work took place yesterday, and it occupied six hours. This
> would indicate that tonight's performance would come to a close toward one o'clock

on Saturday morning. Subsequent renderings of "Die Walküre," however, will not require more than four hours…including the hour needed to set the elaborate scenery of the second and third acts. Yesterday's rehearsal does not call for critical notice. Although sundry experiments made during its progress indicated that some questions concerning the…lights and the handling of the accessories were not yet definitely settled…the performance was interesting and valuable as denoting the thorough familiarity of the orchestra with its task and…of the singers with their… roles, and as revealing the appropriateness, massiveness and beauty of the three sets freshly painted for the production of the opera. Whatever delay arose during the rehearsal grew out of the adjustment of details of the minor business of the stage or out of some slight changes in the scenic arrangements; the interpretation of the score was sufficiently smooth to make sure of an excellent representation this evening. The second performance of "Die Walküre" is already announced for tomorrow afternoon, and the third for Monday of next week. (*New York Times*, January 30, 1884, p.4)

Damrosch had obviously assembled his cast for *Die Walküre* with scrupulous care and with particular attention to the successful experience that the singers had enjoyed in previous Wagnerian productions, in Bayreuth as well as other opera houses in Germany. Materna, who was to portray Brünnhilde, had been chosen by Wagner for that part in the first complete *Ring* cycle at Bayreuth in 1876. On first hearing her when she was singing in Vienna, Wagner reportedly stated, "Now I have found my Brünnhilde [*sic*]. I take her with thanks. I am glad to have found her in Vienna."[7] She had already appeared in the United States at Theodore Thomas's festival in 1882, when she was received with great enthusiasm. Schott was to essay the role of Siegmund and his reputation was of the highest order. Auguste Kraus, who had received fine reviews at the Metropolitan since the very beginning of the season, was the Sieglinde, and Staudigl and Kögel assumed the roles of Wotan and Hunding, respectively. Kögel had already appeared in smaller parts at Bayreuth. Brandt, who had followed Materna as the second Kundry at Bayreuth in 1882, demonstrated her willingness to contribute to Damrosch's company in a most self-effacing manner by assuming the role of Fricka, not normally assigned to an artist of her superior international reputation, and the *New York Times* reviewer commented on her graciousness.[8]

Given its importance, the first Metropolitan performance of *Die Walküre* received long, detailed coverage in the major newspapers. The excerpts quoted below, although in themselves lengthy, represent only the most pertinent portions of these reviews. As was usually the case, the *New York Times* critic was more inclined to deal with the performance itself, whereas his counterpart on the *New York Tribune* confined his remarks basically to historical and biographical features. On this occasion, however, the *Times* reviewer accorded a paragraph to analyzing the position of *Die Walküre* in Wagner's works.

…two years after its production at Bayreuth it was sung at the Academy of Music in this city. Without disregarding the good intentions or enterprise of the persons then concerned…it must be said that the performance, interesting and meritorious, was not on a scale of magnitude befitting the importance of the work. Last night's production of "Die Walküre" is to be regarded in fact as the earliest adequate attempt to convey a complete impression of the dramatic, lyric, and spectacular characteristics of Wagner's music-drama. An auditorium crowded to overflowing, an air of expectancy such as one rarely beholds in the playhouse of the period, and the unbroken silence begotten of almost painful attention indicated the deep concern of the musical public in the event....

The music of "Die Walküre," although its flow is almost as unchecked by conventional operatic forms as that of "Tristan und Isolde," is more closely related to "Lohengrin" by its themes and treatment than to the products of the composer's maturer years. The reformer's theories as to leading motives are, however, put into much more frequent practice than in "Lohengrin," and the designation of each personage by a theme, which forshadows the coming or accompanies the appearance of the character, and even recalls his or her existence to the listener in the character's absence from the stage—an idea, by the way which originated with Gluck—is adhered to throughout the score with absolute consistency....it may safely be affirmed that until the listener of the Tetralogy has mastered them all he will not quite realize the eloquence and ingenuity of the composer's lyric narrative. On the other hand, the score is rich in music that appeals with sensuous luxuriance to the most superficial admirer of sweet strains and glorious harmonies....

The representation of "Die Walküre" at the Metropolitan Opera House yesterday was brought to a close half an hour after midnight had struck. Its shortcomings and defects were so few and insignificant that it may be referred to with fairness as a perfect performance. In almost all respects Wagner's music-drama had almost as complete a rendering as when it was brought out at Bayreuth, eight years since, and no public-rehearsal of either the opera or its best known scenes that has ever been listened to in this city is to be at all compared to the one under notice....The largest measure of praise belongs undoubtedly to Dr. Damrosch's orchestra, whose energy never flagged, whose proficiency was unimpeachable, and whose talent and enthusiasm enabled the listener to catch the finest shades of the composer's music, as well as enjoy its most brilliant and powerful tone-pictures. To Dr. Damrosch...is to be ascribed...no small part of its admirable condition, and when it is borne in mind that the conductor's labors extended into every department of an opera house, it will be understood, too, that something more than a share of the praise bestowed upon the musicians falls to his lot. Next in order are to be mentioned the faultless personations of Herr Schott and Frau Materna, and, as standing almost in the same plane, Frau Kraus's delineation of Sieglinde and Fräulein Brandt's Fricka....Frau Materna's Brünnhilde is...a portrayal of world-wide celebrity and her impressive scenes with Siegmund and Wotan last night—scenes in which her deep feeling, expressive tones, and majestic appearance...told quite as strongly as the beauty and volume of her voice, were awaited with a confidence that was fully justified by the event. Herr Schott's Si[e]gmund was an agreeable surprise. A representation combining dignity and picturesqueness of look and bearing and frequent declamatory outbursts of unquestionable force had been looked for, but the delightful cantabile delivery of the love song, and a hundred dainty touches of tenderness in his scenes with Sieglinde, came under the spectator with agreeable freshness. Frau Kraus contributed a refined and highly dramatic sketch of Sieglinde, and when Fräulein Brandt good-naturedly took upon herself the rather thankless duties of Fricka she did so in the certainty that a finished representation of even so thankless a part would not fail of appreciation. Except in the last scene, when Herr Staudigl's voice occasionally gave evidence of fatigue, that skilled artist was quite equal to the task imposed upon Wotan, and Herr Koegel proved himself a competent Hunding. The Walkyries all had comely representatives, but in their final interview with Wotan their shrieks were even more out of tune than Wagner intended. The scenery was quite new and as massive and appropriate as that in use at Beyreuth....The costumes and accessories, too, were in keeping with the lyric quality of the production. Dr. Damrosch and the principal singers were summoned before the curtain at the end of the first act, and, when the opera terminated, its climax was followed by a still more enthusiastic demonstration. (*New York Times*, January 31, 1885, p.5)

The *New York Tribune* reviewer specifically likened the performance to those in Bayreuth and spoke highly of certain facets of the production as well as providing background material of interest:

As was to have been expected from the earnestness, thoroughness and intelligence exhibited in the preparation and the character of the people concerned in the representation, the production of "Die Walküre" at the Metropolitan Opera House last night was the crowning achievement of Dr. Damrosch and his artists. So far as it was possible...the representation followed those at Bayreuth, which must of course be regarded as the model for all time since they were...carried out under the eyes of the poet composer. The scenery and costumes were faithfully copied, except that for...increased picturesqueness draperies took the place of a modern door in Hunding's hut in the first act, a larger expanse of the moonlight background was opened to the view in the transporting love scene which follows the so-called entrance of the spring, and, in the third act, the costumes of the Valkyries were more varied in color. Among the stage people there were also reminders of the first series of festival plays....Frau Kraus, then too young to take a leading part, was, we believe, among the women who greeted with mute sorrow the dead body of the hero, Siegfried, in the last drama of the tetralogy. Fräulein Brandt, self-sacrificing and earnest as usual, was the Fricka of the second act, and in the third act did effective service in throwing a deal of energetic life into the opening scene as one of the Wish-maidens. Her connection with the Bayreuth performances did not begin until three years ago when she alternated in the impersonation of Kundry in "Parsifal."...Bearing these things in mind, therefore, and remembering, besides, that the stage was in the hands of Herr Hock, as experienced and efficient a stage-manager as Germany can boast, and that the whole representation was directed by a zealous devotee of Wagnerian art, it will be evident that the admirers of "Die Walküre" had good cause for the enthusiasm which they exhibited last night....Last night's presentation...was in every respect worthy of the drama, of the music, of the creative artist, and all the interpreters from Dr. Damrosch down....the interpretation of the drama as Wagner conceived it. (*New York Tribune*, January 31, 1885, p.4)

The enthusiasm of the press was shared by the public and at the end of the season it was noted that *Die Walküre* had brought the largest box-office return per performance of any opera in the repertoire during that season, $3,200.[9] The obvious excellence of the production and the interest in Wagner's music were the factors responsible for the artistic and financial success of the first performances of this work.

Death of Leopold Damrosch

On the evening of February 10, 1885, Damrosch was rehearsing the Oratorio Society for its forthcoming performance of the Verdi *Requiem*, to be presented in collaboration with the Symphony Society, of which he also was conductor. Earlier in the evening he had complained of not feeling well, and he seemed to have caught cold the previous day when he had napped in a cold room and awakened with a severe chill. Partway through the rehearsal he "stopped the chorus and orchestra in the middle of a passage, laid down his baton, and prepared to quit the stage."[10] The following day he summoned his son Walter to his bedside and, according to Walter, "went over every note of the score (*Tännhäuser*) with me and assured me that I could conduct that evening."[11] The younger Damrosch directed that performance and also *Die Walküre* on February 12 and *Le Prophète* on February 14.

On February 15 Leopold Damrosch died unexpectedly. The operatic world, especially in New York City, demonstrated its respect and affection for him in a series of remarkable tributes. The initial report in the *New York Times* appeared on page 1, filling one full column in addition to a half column more on the next page. The opening of the article described his collapse at the rehearsal and acknowledged that his illness had not been considered a fatal one. The malady was described as pneumonia, and a specialist had been called in as Damrosch's condition appeared more serious. News of the conductor's death was slow in reaching the public, for the benefit concert scheduled for the evening of the 15th drew a large audience who were unaware of the tragedy:

> A benefit concert for the box office men of the Metropolitan Opera House was advertised for last night. Materna, Brandt, and the full chorus and orchestra expected to participate when the programme was arranged. There was a good sale of seats, and the people ready to purchase admission tickets filled the horse cars that run to the opera house. They were astounded at the black bordered notice of Dr. Damrosch's death posted near the box office window. Young men put their money back into their pockets, and young women talked busily with each other regardless of the formality of an introduction. Most people were simply surprised, but many regular patrons, who have assumed a feeling of familiar acquaintanceship with the hardworking director during the performances this Winter, felt as though they had sustained a personal loss, and expressed sympathy for the bereaved family....It was announced that the final performance of "Tannhäuser" advertised for tonight, would be postponed until Thursday night.
>
> There was fully as much astonishment and a deeper sense of sorrow and grief among the members of the opera company and the orchestra, when they faced a similar notice of their conductor's death just inside the stage entrance. Some of them cried and the others wandered sorrowfully around in search of definite information. Two or three were sent to Dr. Damrosch's house to learn the particulars. (*New York Times*, February 16, 1885, p.5)

The Metropolitan Board of Directors, in addition to being once more faced with the search for a new manager, this time had a scheduled tour to consider. The first performance was planned for Chicago on February 23, so that there was little or no time for a decision.

> The news of Dr. Damrosch's death was such a surprise that the Directors of the Metropolitan Opera House have not yet had time to form any plans as to the future. It was said last night, however, that the dates in the Western cities would certainly be filled....It had been arranged that Walter Damrosch should go with the company and lead the orchestra for the first week in Chicago. (*New York Times*, February 16, 1885, p.5)

The family must have been gratified to note that the manager of the Thalia Theatre interrupted the concert in progress there on the evening of Damrosch's death, and after announcing the news and paying a tribute to the Metropolitan impresario, dismissed the audience. The company of that theater met the following afternoon to discuss suitable action. They decided to offer a high floral tribute and to appear at the funeral in a body, as well as to sing a dirge at the grave.[12]

Damrosch's career was recalled in the press, with particular reference to his close friendships with such illustrious musicians as Liszt, von Bülow, Cornelius, and even Wagner himself. It was pointed out that he had introduced many major works to America, including the music from *Siegfried* and *Götterdämmerung*, as well as Berlioz's *La Damnation de Faust*, and that he had organized the first great music festival in New York City.

Damrosch's reverence for Wagner, his vast accomplishments, and his willingness to defend his positions were stressed in the report of his death.

> At a recent dinner given to Mme. Patti, Dr. Damrosch, alone among the partisans of German music in New-York, accepted an invitation to compliment the songstress by his presence. During the evening a humorous remark reflecting on Wagner brought the musical director of the Metropolitan to his feet, and in a brief but pithy speech he promptly convinced the doubting orator, that the world owed no small debt to the German reformer. In so doing, however, Dr. Damrosch kept in sight what Mme. Patti's song had done for the world, and the earnestness and felicity of his remarks and the liberality of his views will not soon be forgotten, although revealed quite informally in the course of an ordinary social reunion. The tidings of his death, which will bring surprise and sorrow to many persons in many lands, will be fraught with special sadness to those who knew him best. For twenty years Dr. Damrosch, mindful of his responsibilities as a citizen, as well as ambitious to acquire distinction in the world of art, had struggled hard to secure something like a competence. The season now ended was the first, we have reason to believe, that in any way satisfied his material needs, and the arrangements for next year—by a sad irony of fate his new contract with the Metropolitan was only signed by the Directors of that house on Saturday—were such as to promise a continuance of his good fortune. He died just as material success was about to crown a life time of aspiration and toil. Some consolation will doubtless be derived by his family and friends from the thought that he passed away full of honors, and that nothing he could have achieved in the future would have added much to his record as a gifted and sincere artist, and a kindhearted and estimable man. (*New York Times*, February 16, 1885, p.1)

In the same issue the *Times* also published an editorial that, although brief, was highly complimentary to the deceased musician:

> The interests of German opera in this city and country have suffered a severe blow in the death of *Dr. Damrosch*. It will be hard to fill his place. In musical attainment and in the experience which enabled him to direct the work of a large orchestra with such marvelous skill as he has shown at the Metropolitan Opera House during the present season he has not many rivals, and for such as he had search must be made beyond the seas. But to his ripe powers as a conductor he added an equally thorough understanding of the not less difficult business of managing opera. In his double capacity as conductor and manager he has done priceless service to the cause of good musical entertainment in New-York, and he has been cut off in the very fullness of his powers and of his usefullness. (*New York Times*, February 16, 1885, p.4)

Damrosch's funeral was held on February 18 at the Metropolitan Opera House. Musical selections were performed by the Metropolitan Opera House chorus, the Symphony Society, and the Oratorio Society. Selections included Siegfried's Funeral March from *Götterdämmerung*, excerpts from Bach's *St. Matthew's Passion* and Mendelssohn's *St. Paul*. Although earlier announcements indicated that Carl Schurz, the eminent German writer and politician, would deliver the eulogy, the funeral addresses were made by Henry Potter, the Episcopalian assistant bishop of New York, and Henry Ward Beecher. The Metropolitan Opera Board of Directors attended in a body to pay final tribute. The same day it was announced that Walter Damrosch would conduct the tour performances.[13] The Oratorio Society and the Symphony Society ultimately canceled their programs for the balance of the season. As a final mark of respect the directors of the Metropolitan passed a resolution about Damrosch's death (See Appendix).

Problems of Succession

Damrosch's untimely death immediately set opposing forces in motion, concerned both with the policy to be followed and the selection of his immediate successor. The Board of Directors quickly published a statement dictated by the enormity of the financial and artistic success of the first season of German opera:

> We are of the opinion that the interests of the house will be best solved for the present by adhering to the policy sketched out by Dr. Damrosch before that distinguished musician and worthy gentleman passed away. (*New York Times*, February 18, 1885, p.5)

The pressure in this matter was indicated by the appearance of the above statement in a separate article on the same page as the newspaper description of Damrosch's funeral. The actual purpose of the report was to describe the final matinee of the season, to take place three days later. Walter Damrosch's conducting was criticized, the beginning of a series of criticisms that would continue for many years in mounting intensity.

If it were necessary to bring forth the operas that have constituted the season's repertoire, it is likely that Mr. Walter Damrosch would be found somewhat deficient in
authority and experience. (*New York Times*, February 18, 1885, p.5)

The news report also carried incomplete data pertinent to the comparative popularity of the operas presented during the season.

Certain it is, that German opera, or rather opera in German, has this year so to
speak, paid its way. The assessment upon the stockholders...will have been expended by the end of the season, but no greater outlay has been needed. In other words,
the stockholders have simply paid for their seats, like the public at large. The weekly
expenses, averaging $14,000, exclusive of the interest on the cost of the building,
which represents its rental, have been met by the receipts and subsidy which last has
been $1,750 for each evening performance. As no less than 658 persons have occa-
sionally found simultaneous employment at the Metropolitan, the expenditure does
not appear inordinate. Taking the total receipts...and calculating the drawing
power of each opera, it would seem that...opera in German, and not exactly German opera, has proved most attractive. "Die Walküre," it is true, brought more
money into the treasury than any other work, but had it been given as frequently as
"The Prophet," it would probably have been less profitable. German thoroughness,
rather than Wagnerian repertoire, has, in truth, attained the brilliant results
recorded in...the current season. The average amount drawn by each of the operas
was as follows: "Die Walküre," $3,200; "The Prophet," $3,000; "The Huguenots,"
$2,819; "The Jewess," $2,700; "Lohengrin," $2,515; "Tannhäuser," $2,500; "Don
Giovanni," $1,862; "William Tell," $1,602; "Masaniello," $1,519; "Der
Freischütz," $1,829; "Fidelio," $1,276; "Rigoletto," $1,138. These figures stand for
the moneys received at the box office, and are in excess of the subsidy. (*New York
Times*, February 18, 1885, p.5)

Three days later a *Times* editorial evaluated the season at length and commented
on the company's future administrative structure. The remarks were highly complimentary to the Wagnerian performances and to the singers in general. They observed, however, that the German artists were considerably less effective in operas
outside the Wagnerian repertoire, especially those of Rossini, Auber, and Meyerbeer. Materna was described as somewhat of a disappointment; her ineffectual portrayals of such roles as Elisabeth in *Tannhäuser* were referred to specifically, and it
was emphasized that heavier parts such as Brünnhilde in *Die Walküre* suited her
voice and personality far more than the lyrical roles.[14]
The first news item indicating a schism in the ranks of the German opera supporters appeared on the same day as Damrosch's funeral. The tenor Anton Schott
emerged as the proponent of a plan to change the managerial structure and at the
same time obviously remove Materna as well as a number of others from the next season's roster. The urgency and tone of the article indicated strongly that the movement was motivated not only by Schott's own desire to assume artistic management
of the company, but also by a strong fear that Walter Damrosch would be appointed
as his father's successor.

While the funeral of Dr. Damrosch was in progress yesterday a plan of reorganization of the company, with Herr Anton Schott as Director, was placed in the hands
of Secretary Stanton at the request of the Directors. There have been differences in
the company, which Dr. Damrosch was able to hold in check. On one side were
Frauen Materna, Bely, and Schlach, Herren Robinson, Udvardi, Koegel, and Hock
[sic]. The other comprises Herren Schott, Blum, and Staudigl, and Frau Krause
[sic], Fräulein Brandt, and nearly the remainder of unnamed singers, chorus, and
orchestra. Herr Schott some time ago set to work to fortify himself and his friends.
He entered into correspondence with leading musicians in Germany and found
them ready to come here at his bidding. Meantime he was approached by the Academy people, who desired him to organize German opera in their house and direct it.
When the death of Dr. Damrosch came so suddenly he was prepared with his plan at
once when the Metropolitan Directors made this request.

His proposition is to reduce the expenses 30 per cent, and create a musical conductor to relieve the Director and permit him to sing his leading roles. For musical conductor the name of Herr Seidl, one of the greatest of German conductors, is included
in the plan. Herr Seidl is the husband of Frau Krause [sic]. He was a pupil of Wagner, and had earned a reputation equal to Herr Richter's. Assistant, and next to him,
Walter Damrosch is named. The plan proposes to place all the new company under
contract for three years, reserving the privilege to discharge any unsatisfactory persons at the end of one year. It demands that the opera shall be conducted on strict
German principles and thorough discipline, and that Secretary Stanton shall be promoted and have the power of veto. It proposes to use Materna's salary of $12,000 per
month to pay three singers to be secured in Germany, who have a higher reputation
there than she and sing for less money. Among these at least Schroeder-Hanfstaengl
is decided upon. The salaries of singers are cut down in this plan and the standard of
ability raised. Herr Schott preceded this with another proposition, which the Directors rejected. He proposed that the country tour should be given up and opera continued in New-York until May, the proceeds to be given to Dr. Damrosch's family.
He offered to cut his own salary from $5,000 per month to $300 per night until May
if his plan was substituted. The Directors decided on the country tour and appointed
Walter Damrosch to succeed his father. Last evening he visited Herr Schott and
stated that his family's honor was at stake in carrying out the [company's] contracts,
and begged him to help the project all in his power. Herr Schott decided to accede to
the request, although it is questionable if the death of Dr. Damrosch does not legally
do away with any obligation of contracts made with him. Meanwhile, the Academy
people are hoping that the Metropolitan Directors will reject the plan of Herr Schott
for reorganization, so that he can accept their offer and at once proceed to prepare
for next season. (New York Times, February 19, 1885, p.5)

The following day the proposal was again described, this time in an interview
with Schott himself. The tenor spoke of opera in English and also commented on
his alleged dealings with the Academy Directors. The headline for the article was
"Opera To Be Reorganized," and the Times indicated, incorrectly, that acceptance
of the proposal was an accomplished fact.

The plan of reorganization of German opera presented by Herr Anton Schott is
based on the official standard of the court theatres of Germany. Herr Schott in
adapting his plan to American needs has had the warm cooperation of Mr. Stein-

way. The plan proposes to create a General Intendant, who will approve or veto all financial and artistic arrangements, and asks that Secretary Stanton shall be elevated to that position. Next, an Intendant will be created who will be responsible to his superiors for repertoire. There will be strict rules of government for all members of the company. Next in rank will be a conductor, who shall take charge of rehearsals and orchestra, and below him will be the stage manager. These officers will be held personally responsible for any delays in rehearsals or performances. The stage manager must watch the painters, machinist, and inspector of wardrobes, and be familiar with every detail, and thereby save much expense. The painter must be of the German school, such painters being less expensive and familiar with the scenery of Wagnerian operas.

Of the present company the only leading singers which the plan mentions are Herren Lund, Staudigl, Blum, Miller, Frauen [Schröder-] Hanfstaengl, Kraus, and Fräulein Brandt....Herr Schott said yesterday that the morning paper's had mysteriously but correctly anticipated his actions.

"What have you to say regarding your enterprise for next season?" was asked.

"Some lessons have been learned by the first season's attempt," was the reply. "The plans of the present season were not entirely effective. Success was secured, but greater success could have been attained by a more experienced management. We are to look forward to the time when German opera will be as sacred here as in its own home. My own ambition is to present German opera here in the English tongue, and I promise you that we shall yet be able to do so, as our musicians are quick to learn your language. Opera in Germany is still governed by Richard Wagner, and opera there could not exist under any other regime yet created. Only those theatres which have recognized this fact are successful there. One fact Americans must learn at once is that the 'star' system of opera died long ago abroad. That system surrounds its star with weak and cheap support, but our German plan admits of nothing weak, demanding a strong ensemble throughout. We propose to take German opera here as Wagner himself might, and in order to do so have secured Wagner's only pupil Herr Seidl for conductor. Wagner taught him every detail of opera, and particularly the intricacies of his own work. Herr Seidl resided with Wagner for six years at Bayreuth, and is to-day Europe's greatest interpreter of the dead master.

"The succession of operas was not well chosen this season. We should have commenced with 'Lohengrin' rather than 'Tannhäuser,' on account of the dramatic and declamatory style of the latter, which is difficult to understand. We should have followed 'Lohengrin' with 'Rienzi,' and thus prepared the way for 'Tannhäuser.'" Then we could have produced 'Die Walküre' before Christmas and had the same success five weeks sooner. The experiments with 'Fidelio,' 'Don Giovanni,' 'Rigoletto,' 'Tell,' &c were worthless, and cost much time and money. The course adopted, however, was unavoidable in a new enterprise and reflects no discredit on Dr. Damrosch. All German artists usually engage themselves before the 1st of May, and for this season I have avoided the error of last year by which many inferior artists were secured, and have already booked my artists." (*New York Times*, February 20, 1885, p.5)

A number of contradictions appeared between the February 19 report and that of February 20, and it was obvious that this intrigue had been initiated some time before Damrosch's fatal illness. That Schott was in a position to make definite assertions about contracts and plans substantiated the second newspaper report. Kraus's presence in the list of Schott supporters accounted for the success of the tenor's overtures to Seidl. The *Times*'s laudatory opinion of Seidl's ability, interestingly, was not shared by Seidl himself; writing of his own career, Seidl said of Richter: "There is only one artist among conductors and that is Hans Richter."[15]

Schott's nationalistic statements about German discipline and principles were to be expected and were intrinsically no more offensive than many made by Lehmann in her autobiography.[16] His proposal to divide Materna's salary among three singers appeared ludicrous when he added that they enjoyed greater reputations in Germany than Materna. She had been chosen by Wagner himself for Bayreuth and never would have received her initial salary from Damrosch had her reputation not warranted it. The Metropolitan directors, it shuld be recalled, had been insistent that she be engaged as the only "star" of the German company. This had been their only edict to Damrosch.

Stanton had obviously been close to Leopold Damrosch, and time would substantiate this in his work with Walter in engaging the new company. Schott's motive was clear. By proposing Stanton's elevation he hoped to prove his altruism and minimize his own prestige under the new structure. The *Times*'s source for the February 19 article reported that Walter Damrosch was to be engaged as assistant conductor; Schott omitted this detail in his statements the following day. Conceivably, Walter Damrosch's visit to Schott, although solving the tour problem, created a deeper rift between the two factions. Such a rift could easily have resulted from the younger Damrosch's own ambitions toward the Metropolitan management. Schott's proposal to cut his own salary for the extended season from $5,000 per month to $300 per night was elusive. He sang fifteen times during December and made fourteen appearances in January. If this schedule was representative, it was observed that his financial concession was minimal and certainly profitable to him when the personal expenses encountered on a tour were taken into consideration.

Schott's statement concerning the mysterious anticipation of his plan by the *New York Times* indicated either that he had not read that the February 19 information was reported as coming from the Board of Directors, or that he hoped to create confusion by this remark. His suggestions about the order in which Damrosch had presented his operas were possibly valid. Of the four operas he listed as worthless experiments, three featured Anton Udvardy in the leading tenor role. Udvardy was listed as a member of the opposing group, which was aligned with Materna.

The Metropolitan Directors ultimately put many of Schott's suggestions into effect, but his behavior and fraudulent statements in presenting his proposal certainly must have been evident to the directors; he undermined their faith enough to influence their decision to place the leadership of the company in other hands.

The Appointment of Walter Damrosch

The renewal of bitterness between the Academy of Music and the Metropolitan Opera had been evident a few days before. At that time rumors had been circulated that the Metropolitan Board was engaged in a devious scheme with an operator of a dime museum in Boston. This man, named Austin, denied any collaboration:

> "It is true that I have leased the Academy of Music in New-York for two weeks beginning on the 23rd of next March, with the privilege of three weeks longer if I desire it. It has created a great deal of talk in New-York, and some persons said that I was induced to take the house for the purpose of giving it a bad name in the interest of the Metropolitan Opera House managers. Nothing could be further from the facts." (*New York Times*, February 16, 1885, p.3)

What was important was not whether Austin's statement was true or false, but rather that the reappearance of this kind of allegation brought pressure on the officials. In the same dispatch as the interview with Schott, directors of both opera houses made statements. Roosevelt's comments were restricted to his appraisal of the management problem.

> Mr. James A. Roosevelt...of the Metropolitan Opera House, said last evening that nothing had been done yet with regard to the future of the house....The matter had been placed in the hands of the Amusement Committee, of which Mr. Roosevelt is an ex-officio member. A number of applications had been received from persons anxious to manage the next season at the house, and the Directors expected to receive more when the foreign mails came in. (*New York Times*, February 20, 1885, p.5)

LeRoy of the Academy had strong answers to accusations of unethical negotiations with Schott. In the light of LeRoy's remarks, Schott's statements about the Academy's desires for his services appeared exaggerated.

> Mr. Herman R. LeRoy, President of the Board of Directors of the Academy of Music, expressed much annoyance last evening over the statement printed yesterday that the Academy of Music had been in negotiation with Herr Anton Schott, of the Metropolitan Company, in regard to the production of German opera at the Academy. "There is not a word of truth in it," Mr. LeRoy said earnestly. "The article conveys the impression that some of our Directors approached Mr. Schott secretly with the view of getting him away from the other house. That is not so. I do not believe there is a man in our board who would do such a thing. The Metropolitan may be called an opposition house, but we do not carry the rivalry to the extent of trying to get its singers away. So careful indeed are we in this respect that if any one connected with that house should come to us seeking negotiations or engagement our first question would be 'Are you released from the other house, or have you been unable to make an arrangement there,' and unless the relations of that person and the Metropolitan had ceased, or were certainly to cease, we would decline to make an arrangement. The Directors of the other house are my personal friends. Some of them may now think that our Directors, I among them, have been trying to deal

with Mr. Schott or others of their company as the printed statement charges. Men have spoken to me about it to-night. I have said to all, as I say now, that there is not a particle of truth in it."

"Have the Academy Directors thought of going into German opera in another season?"

"No, nor have we as yet considered what to do. Next Winter is a long way off. It will be time enough two or three months from now to begin to lay plans for that. At any rate we have not considered German opera." (*New York Times*, February 20, 1885, p.5)[17]

It was inconceivable that Schott could have had the audacity to invent his statements about the Academy of Music without some basis. In all probability, isolated members of the Academy Board of Directors had secretly approached him with at least an implication that they would be interested in his services. LeRoy was surely unaware of any such approach, and made his discreet denial in good faith. Whatever the case, Damrosch was sufficiently concerned with the entire discussion to write a card to the *New York Times*, reassuring the public that the company would depart in its entirety for the western tour under his direction.

To The Editor of the New York Times:

Certain statements having appeared in the morning paper of this date to the effect that a division had occurred between the artists of the German Opera Company, I take this first opportunity to contradict such rumors, and say that the entire company will start upon the contemplated tour under my direction, and that without exception the artists are willing to carry out, with myself, all the contracts entered into.

Walter J. Damrosch
The Metropolitan Opera House, Thursday, Feb. 19, 1885[18]

The *Times*, in its previously mentioned editorial, deliberately or inadvertently supported the proposal of bringing a major conductor to work with Damrosch, but suggested that Damrosch be in charge. They complimented the operation of the Metropolitan and predicted the successful resolution of the problems. The season of German opera had immeasurably changed the attitude of the *Times* toward the new opera house, and the frequent innuendos cast against the stockholders during the first season were replaced by cordial comments.

There is a strong inclination, we think, to test Mr. Walter Damrosch's mettle, and, if an experienced aid were provided—a sort of lyric prime minister, in fact—it is scarcely to be doubted that the experiment would prove successful. The foundation of a dynasty is not generally accomplished but, in this case, there are grounds for concluding, from what Mr. Walter Damrosch has done thus far, that he is worthy of inheriting his father's celebrity as well as his name. And while it is to be desired that the lamented leader may have a successor worthy of new memory, it is to be wished

that the newcomer may discover a friend and business manager as shrewd, energetic, and faithful as Mr. Morris Reno, who relieved the dead director of many
cares, and whose counsel in critical moments was simply invaluable. The Directors
of the Metropolitan will, of course, be represented as heretofore, by Mr. Edmund C.
Stanton, whose mild but potent sway will in all probability be more absolute even
than it has been until now. With liberality and good will such as were shown by the
stockholders of the Metropolitan during the current year, and with the judgment,
tact, and experience,—the latter acquired by two seasons' close study of the house
and its manager and frequenters—of Mr. Stanton, there is slight cause, we should
say, for fear that the up-town house will not be kept abreast of the demand likely to
be made upon it for lyrical entertainment of the highest order. (*New York Times*,
February 21, 1885, p.4)

No record was found of any official activities by Morris Reno; it can be assumed
that he served Dr. Damrosch much in the same capacity that Grau had assisted Abbey during the initial season. The *Times* later sharply reversed its opinion of Walter
Damrosch; limited opportunity to observe his conducting may be cited in justification of the newspaper's original opinion.

The Board of Directors had by no means made their decision, although the foregoing discussion seems to indicate that it was immediately expected. The tour took
place, embracing stops in Chicago, Cincinnati, and Boston. Damrosch conducted all
performances with the exception of three presentations of *La Juive*, two of *Der
Freischütz*, and a single performance of *Die Walküre*. Forty-two performances were
given, of which five were matinees. Chicago and Boston each enjoyed a single performance of *La Dame Blanche* by Francois Boieldieu, an opera the company had not
previously performed. Also omitted during the regular season but performed on the
tour was Gluck's *Orfeo ed Euridice*, which received a single performance in Boston.
La Muette de Portici was performed, under its alternate title, *Masaniello*. For one
performance of *Tannhäuser* in Boston, Damrosch engaged an American tenor,
Charles R. Adams, who had apparently sung with Materna in Vienna.[19]

While the tour was in progress, the Board of Directors issued a statement explaining their plans for the following year. The *Times*'s description of the projected season
was detailed. Surprisingly, it indicated that Richter would probably occupy the first
conductor's chair.

The plan adopted does not at first sight differ materially from that agreed upon
when Dr. Damrosch lived. In other words, German opera will be given next season
under the artistic directorship of a competent person....During the season of 1885–6
the Opera House will be under the immediate management of the Directors, represented by Mr. Edmund C. Stanton. Mr. Stanton will sail for Europe on May 9, and
in a two-months' stay complete the negotiations now progressing in respect of conductors and a company. Dozens of applications for the position of leader and assistant have, of course, been received from all parts of the world....The chances are
strongly in favor of Herr Hans Richter's assumption of the duties of Dr.
Damrosch....Herr Richter's presence here would create a sort of a revolution in lyric
matters, and if...his sojurn were indefinitely prolonged, music in America would
take a greater stride in advance...than it has taken in the past ten years. Should Herr

Richter be unwilling or unable to accept the offers of the Metropolitan, the conductorship will be given to one of the leading German directors who have signified their willingness to visit America. None of the resident candidates for directorial honors will be chosen. The post of assistant conductor will be reserved for Mr. Walter Damrosch, about whose fitness for the work, there can be no question. Mr. Damrosch's youth is regarded as an obstacle to his assignment to the more trying position, but the obstacle is one that will be only too promptly overcome. (*New York Times*, March 18, 1885, p.5)

Returning singers were also discussed.

It is likely that many of the members of the company lately before the public will be retained for next season. Among those whose return can be depended upon are Fräulein Brandt and Fräulein Slach, together with several other useful artists. Strenuous efforts will be put forth to secure the co-operation of Frau Schroeder-Hanfstaengl, and if Frau Materna can be engaged on reasonable terms—her worth as a songstress of some Wagnerian parts being widely acknowledged, but the smallness of her repertoire and her inability to draw audiences in keeping with her *honoraria* being quite as well established—she, too, will reappear during the Winter months. (*New York Times*, March 18, 1885, p.5)

The coming season's dates and repertoire were noted, as were changes in the boxes.

The season will commence between November 17 and November 20 prox., and include 60 performances, to occur in 13 weeks in this city, 10 final or mid-season representations being given in adjacent places, the repertoire has already been decided upon, and the scenery and dresses will be made ready during the Summer. The new operas of which the production may be counted upon are Wagner's "Rienzi," "Meistersinger," and "Götterdämmerung," and Goldmark's "Queen of Sheba." It is probable that Rubinstein's "Nero" will also be brought out. The only change of importance to be made in the Opera House involves the transformation of the highest row of boxes into balcony seats, and, possibly, the removal of two baignoires to afford additional standing room on the ground floor. (*New York Times*, March 18, 1885, p.5)

Finally, Edmund Stanton's management was given a favorable prognosis.

...Mr. Stanton, whose influence was felt throughout last season, enters upon a new path of duty. Although young in years he has acquired much experience...and, by representing the Board of Directors since the Opera House was opened...he has been able to watch carefully such methods of management as are visible to the naked-eye. As an intelligent and prudent gentleman he will undoubtedly avoid most of the errors committed by his predecessors. Still, he may be destined to make new mistakes, the possibilities of operatic-management in this particular being practically unlimited....It is cheering...that Mr. Stanton enjoys the...best wishes of all persons he has met during his connection with the Metropolitan. The new Opera House swallowed up the fortune of its first manager and brought about the death of its second. The fates should have some kinder lot in store for its third. (*New York Times*, March 18, 1885, p.5)

Essentially the above plan followed Schott's proposal while avoiding his appointment. Although Damrosch did not receive the top position, the faction favorable to him apparently emerged victorious. This was substantiated by the omission from the above article of the artists that Schott had originally listed as the most outstanding. Finally, although Materna was the object of some questions, her dismissal from the company was not mentioned; in fact, her possible return was indicated. Schröder-Hanfstängl and Blum, two of the most prominent artists in Schott's proposal, did not return. Kraus's reappearance was not surprising after her husband received the top post.

Plans were for Damrosch to accompany Stanton on his European journey; there was, however, no record of Stanton's immediate departure. In his autobiography Damrosch explained Stanton's staying behind and also recounted one of his own first accomplishments in his new post as assistant conductor.

> In the spring of 1885 I was to accompany Mr. Stanton...to engage singers for the following season at the Metropolitan Opera House, but as Mr. Stanton's little daughter became ill and subsequently died, I went over alone and have always been quite proud of the four contracts I had ready for Mr. Stanton's signature when he, a month later, arrived in Germany. There was Lilli Lehmann, soprano from the Royal Opera House in Berlin; Emil Fischer, bass from the Royal Opera House in Dresden; Max Alvary, lyric tenor from Weimar, and Anton Seidl, conductor of the Angelo Neumann Wagner Opera Company. These four artists became subsequently the mainstay of the German opera and in America developed to greater and greater power and fame.[20]

Lehmann and Alvary had both been announced for the first season, but something had gone amiss and they had never appeared. Damrosch's statement was accurate about the value to the company of the four artists he mentioned. Lehmann came to the Metropolitan as a singer of lyric parts, but during her stay in America she developed into an outstanding dramatic soprano most revered for her portrayal of the most demanding Wagnerian roles. Her versatility was such that she performed as Rachel in *La Juive*, Brünnhilde in *Götterdämmerung*, and Donna Anna in *Don Giovanni*, all during the same season, 1889–1890. Alvary stayed at the Metropolitan for four seasons, during which he was the leading tenor of the company, although he shared a few roles with Albert Niemann for two seasons. Niemann was in the twilight of his career but was still celebrated for his portrayal of Siegfried in *Götterdämmerung*. Fischer was a member of the German opera troupe through its final performance, at which time he departed with the reappearance of Abbey. He returned as a guest artist during the season of 1906–1907, when the Metropolitan was under the management of Heinrich Conried. Seidl spent eleven consecutive seasons at the Metropolitan, during which time his reputation exceeded that of any conductor before him; his name is still included in the top rank of opera conductors of all times.

Mapleson had achieved his most successful results on his long tour, and when he returned he castigated the German opera experiment in arbitrary fashion and in terms that offended many partisans:

The sauerkraut opera cannot last. Italian opera is the only opera that can depend upon fashionable support. German opera bankrupted the Gyes in London, and closed up Covent Garden, and my "Nibelungen" experiment cost me $30,000 which amount was only one-half of the total loss. (*New York Times*, April 21, 1885, p.1)

The term "sauerkraut" resulted in an equally distasteful return insult, "ashcan," applied to Italian opera by German opera enthusiasts. A brief exchange of these epithets resulted in an editorial in the *New York Times*, which pointedly asserted that there were disadvantages to both types of opera but also inherent beauties that attracted patrons to them.[21]

THE SEASON OF 1885-1886

A period of silence followed this controversy and the newspapers were strangely devoid of any news concerning the future of the Metropolitan Opera. Damrosch had apparently preceded Stanton to Europe, as stated in his autobiography. There seems to have been no mention of either man's departure; a lengthy report, however, was published upon their return in late July. Stanton provided a valuable, detailed description of his plans for the ensuing season. His statement did not substantiate Damrosch's claim of having negotiated the contracts with Alvary, Fischer, Lehmann, and Seidl:

"The difficulty of engaging a first-class company of German singers...can be properly appreciated only by those who have tried it. All the popular artists are attached to...one of the Court opera houses and are held to iron-bound contracts. Many of them are looking forward to pensions which the government provides for them after a certain term of service and which they forfeit...if they break their contracts and come to this country without securing leave of absence....I have secured a company of great strength,...certainly stronger than that of last year, although Dr. Damrosch, considering the short time he had,...did remarkably well.

"I have retained only four of the artists who sang here last season....The four old faces will be those of Marion [*sic*] Brandt, contralto; Auguste Krause and Fräulein Slach, soprano, and Herr Robinson, baritone. Among the first of the new engagements I made was that of Lilli Lehmann, soprano and the leading prima donna of the Imperial Opera House at Berlin....I had a great deal of trouble to secure her.... The Directors of the Opera House, which is a Court theatre, refused to grant her a leave of absence, and finally, as a last resort, she appealed to the Emperor himself, with whom she is a great favorite. His Imperial Majesty listened to her appeal, and an order was issued to the Directors to grant her a year's leave to come to America. Her position in the Imperial Opera House is a life one and but for the gracious intercession of his Majesty she would have been obliged to remain or to sacrifice her brilliant prospects in Germany....Her repertoire is a very extensive one and ranges from light to heavy roles. Among her greatest roles are Brünnhilde in 'Die Walküre;' Tristan in 'Isolde;' [*sic*] 'Carmen;' Marguerite; Sulamith in 'The Queen of Sheba'; Elisabeth in 'Tannhäuser'; and Rachel in 'La Juive.'...

"Frau Kraemer-Weidl...is another soprano, whom I engaged at Mannheim. She is almost as large as Materna, and should be classed, I think, as a dramatic singer....

"Upon the tenors I have secured I pride myself particularly. We were weak in tenors last year....I have secured Herr Anton Stritt from Frankfort; Herr Elois Sylva, from the St. Petersburg Opera House, and Herr Alvary, from Weimar, all of them great popular favorites on the other side....You see I have plenty of tenors, so that if one is indisposed there will be no trouble in filling his place, and the programme for the evening need not be changed....

"I have secured the man who is recognized as the finest basso in Germany, [Emil] Fischer, from Dresden. Herr Fischer held a life position at the Imperial Opera House in Dresden, and the King of Saxony refused to grant him a leave of absence to sing here. He was so anxious to come, however, that he resigned his position, and I suppose left the King plunged into despair....."

"...The chorus this year will be stronger than that of last season, numbering 74 singers all of whom I have engaged in Germany. You see that, numerically speaking, we shall have a very large company to handle. Of its artistic merits I leave our subscribers to judge at the proper time."

"Why did the negotiations for securing Herr Richter as conductor fall through?" asked the reporter.

"I was very anxious to secure Richter, who is undoubtedly the best conductor in Germany, and he was just as anxious to close the engagement and pass a season in New-York. The Directors of the Imperial Opera House in Vienna, however, positively refused to give him a leave of absence. Richter has a very large family, and after serving another year, I believe, he would be entitled to a pension....I couldn't promise him any pension from the Metropolitan Opera House, and so the negotiations were abandoned. In place of Richter I secured Herr Seidl, who is a younger man, and, of course, has not had the experience of Richter. But he is an excellent conductor and stands very high in Germany. He...was an intimate friend and protege of Wagner, with whose music and methods he is thoroughly familiar. He will be assisted by Walter J. Damrosch, of whose ability as a conductor the public have had plenty of opportunity to judge. Herr Seidl will not have so much work to do as Dr. Damrosch did, because much of the doctor's work will fall on my shoulders as director....

"Before the end of our next season the people of whom I have been telling you will be as well known and appreciated here, I am sure, as the Italian singers who have been before the New-York public for years."

Walter J. Damrosch proved a valuable assistant to Mr. Stanton in making his engagements. Mr. Damrosch, while abroad purchased the right to produce "Parsifal," Wagner's last opera. It is not to be done at the Opera House, but Mr. Damrosch will probably make use of it in his oratorio performances. (*New York Times*, July 19, 1885, p.7)

In the same interview Stanton mentioned five "novelties" that he planned for production during the approaching season. These included *Aida, Götterdämmerung,*

Die Meistersinger, Rienzi, and *The Queen of Sheba,* the last by Karl Goldmark. *Aida* did not in fact appear until the season of 1886–1887, and *Götterdämmerung* was first produced a year later than that. Stanton made several explicit remarks about the Goldmark opera, with which he planned to open the season. He was confident that it would "create genuine excitement in New-York," and announced that he had brought sketches of the proposed scenery with him. His colorful description of the sensational sandstorm was calculated to arouse interest in the new production.

> In the last act there is a representation of a sand storm in the desert, which is very effective. I forgot to say that I purchased abroad several new appliances for using the electric light in scenic effects, and the effect of the sand storm is greatly heightened by means of these. (*New York Times,* July 19, 1885, p.7)

The first indication of competition for Stanton appeared in a short news item revealing that Mapleson would still carry on at the Academy of Music. The directors of that house assumed their usual arbitrary attitude:

> Col. Mapleson has signified his desire to have the Academy of Music for the purpose of giving Italian opera during the coming Fall season, and the Directors say he can have the house, but he will have to pay for it. (*New York Times,* August 12, 1885, p.8)

Given the attitude of the Academy directors, Mapleson did not appear to be in a favorable position to compete with Stanton, who had the full cooperation and support of the Metropolitan directory. About two weeks later Stanton revealed final details and a prospectus of the company and its plans. His list of artists was highly accurate; when the season opened all those mentioned were with the company. In citing the repertoire Stanton mentioned five operas as "possibilities," along with a number of certainties. None of the "possibilities" were presented that year, but among those that the manager said would "surely" be given, only *Aida, Gotterdammerung,* and *La Juive* failed to receive performances.

> The prospectus commences with the official declaration that the season is to open on Monday evening, Nov. 23, and to extend over 13 weeks, including 39 subscriptions and 13 matinees. These representations, however, will not be continuous as performances are to be given in Philadelphia between Dec. 19 and Jan. 2; after the latter date the season at the Metropolitan is to begin anew and to progress uninterruptedly until March 6....The principal tenors are, Herr Albert Stritt, Herr Eloi[s] Sylva, and Herr Alvary; the chief baritones are Herren Adolf Robinson, and Alexi; the leading bassos are Herren Emil Fischer and Lehmler....Sopranos, Fräulein Lilli Lehmann, Frau Krause, Frau Kraemer-Wiedl, Fräulein Anna Slach and Fräulein Ida Klein; mezzo-sopranos and contraltos, Fräulein Marianne Brandt and Carrie Goldsticker....The conductors are Herr Anton Seidl and Mr. Walter J. Damrosch and the stage will be under the control of Herr Van Hell and Herr Theodore Habelmann. The general director of the opera...is to be Mr. Edmund C. Stanton, who with the cooperation of Mr. Damrosch has effected the engagement of the artists. (*New York Times,* August 23, 1885, p.6)

The *Times* coverage also revealed the startling change in the attitude toward the masses that had emerged with the departure of Italian opera.

> ...there is abundant indication in Mr. Stanton's manifesto that the company is an organization of marked efficiency. The partisan of the star system will seek in vain for the three or four names habitually associated with notable lyric events, but persons familiar with the German stage will readily concede that among the people secured are some of the very best in Germany, and that the troupe has been so made up as to bring together a well balanced ensemble of genuine excellence....attention is asked to the fact that "opera here differs from opera abroad; in that it is supported by subsidy from individuals instead of from Governments," and the consequent statement made that "the Board of Directors count upon the aid of all music lovers to assist the stockholders in their endeavor to make New-York a musical centre." (*New York Times*, August 23, 1885, p.6)

Two days later a long *New York Times* article described the vast redecorating that had been done at the Academy of Music. The refurbishing had truly been thorough and included painting, complete reupholstering, and replacement of all the chandeliers with new fixtures that provided "steadier and more powerful light" in spite of a decrease in burners. The primary color used in the decor was red, but it was shaded in degrees to produce a "pleasing and harmonious" effect. On the same page another article gloomily forecast the outcome of Mapleson's negotiations to use the Academy:

> The plans of Col. Mapleson in regard to giving a season of Italian opera in this city during the coming Fall and Winter are still shrouded in mystery, and his intimate friends here know as little about them as the general public. Mr. Murphy, Superintendant of the Academy of Music, says that the Colonel is negotiating for that house, but that up to the present time he has failed to accept the terms offered him by the Directors, and that they decline to alter their views to meet his. (*New York Times*, August 25, 1885, p.5)

Although it was generally conceded that the first season of German opera had been extremely successful, both artistically and financially, it quickly became evident that the following season would surpass it. Not only did the roster appear more attractive, but the first week of subscription sales brought a remarkable response:

> Subscription books were opened in the office of the opera house last Monday,...and the result was surprising to Mr. Stanton. Subscriptions came in with a rush and up to yesterday over $12,000 worth of boxes and seats had been engaged for the 39 nights of the season. The rush was totally unexpected and the tickets were not ready for distribution, but the subscribers left their money behind them, and will receive the tickets as soon as they can be made ready. (*New York Times*, August 30, 1885, p.3)

The season at hand brought new competition for the Metropolitan Opera. Theodore Thomas, a revered conductor of the day and the founder of the Chicago Symphony as well as many festivals, launched a new organization to produce American opera. By this term he meant opera in English performed by American casts. He arranged to lease the Academy of Music and to initiate his season on January 4, 1886. Prices were to be about the same as those for the German opera at the Metropolitan; Thomas stated his purpose as endeavoring "to establish a standard for opera in this country."[22] The prospectus listed a rather strange assortment of operas, including *Orpheus and Eurydice, The Merry Wives of Windsor, Lohengrin, Les Huguenots, Faust, Carmen, Lakmé, Oberon,* and *The Marriage of Figaro.* As a novelty, an opera by Hermann Goetz, *The Taming of the Shrew,* was announced, as was the possibility of a work by Anton Rubinstein. A few days later Mapleson announced that he would open on October 26 and that he had agreed to pay rent at the Academy, the amount not being stipulated.[23] He promised a meager six-week season, making it obvious that his influence and capacity had diminished considerably since the Metropolitan's original opening. The report stated that a "friend" thought he would open with *Lakmé*; this was impossible since the American Opera Company had secured exclusive rights to its production in this country.[24] The announcements of rival companies prompted the *New York Times* to issue a strong editorial championing German opera. The final paragraph contained harsh words for those complaining that German opera was destroying them:

> Having to depend on Germany for the classics, on German schools and teaching for the training of our producers and on German performers for the interpretation of our music, "it does seem odd that once or twice annually people should be warned that German art and its color bearers are once more actively engaged in crushing out everybody and everything else, in face of the fact that most hurried examination must prove that there is really nobody or nothing for the enemy's powers of destruction to be exerted against." (*New York Times,* September 27, 1885, p.8)

Apparently the attacks on German opera were fruitless, for a fortnight later the *Times* reported that subscriptions to the Metropolitan on that day were "four times as large as the total sum taken for the season when the initial representation of last year's series was given."[25] The same *Times* issue carried an article announcing that the "Opera by Americans" season would include fifteen weeks with forty evening performances and fifteen matinees. Thomas also indicated that his chorus would number one hundred voices. As before, Mapleson promptly countered with an announcement, this one including two novelties as well as a drastic reduction in prices. The newspapers allotted scant space.

> The repertoire of the past few years is to be drawn upon for most of the operas to be sung, but one genuine novelty is promised in the shape of Massenet's "Manon" of which Mr. Mapleson has secured the sole right of performance in the United States. "Maritana" is also to have its first representation on the Italian stage before the season closes....
>
> ...this year, at least, Italian opera will be within the reach of the least extravagant admirer of a style of music that will move and delight mankind long after reformers, theorists, and partisans shall have passed away. (*New York Times,* October 17, 1885, p.4)

The reduction in price resulted in parquet seats being offered at a subscription rate of $40 for twenty performances. Thus Italian opera, which was accustomed to demand the highest prices, became less expensive than opera in German. The Academy of Music had lost its position as society's showplace for entertainment. On November 2 Mapleson's company opened with *Carmen*, with Minnie Hauk in the title role. The *Times* reviewer said of the performance, "although not up to the highest standard, [it] was a smooth one."[26] Notwithstanding the low prices set before the season opened, Mapleson was obliged to reduce prices further. This move he revealed in a document given to subscribers and patrons, in which he described his act in typical phrases:

> Mr. Mapleson...has the honor to announce that for the remainder of the season, in compliance with continued requests, the prices of seats will be modified to come within the means of the numerous class that gives cheerful patronage to the higher order of music as far as circumstances permit. (*New York Times*, November 15, 1885, p.8)

Metropolitan Debut of Anton Seidl

During the last few weeks before the Metropolitan Opera opened its third season, Stanton changed his opening-night opera from *The Queen of Sheba* to *Lohengrin*. Of the leading male singers, two were new to the company, Albert Stritt and Emil Fischer, while Robinson and both female principals, Marianne Brandt and Auguste Kraus, now using the name Seidl-Kraus, were returning from the previous year. Of major importance was the fact that the first appearance of Anton Seidl, the new conductor, would open the season. Seidl, who was to become one of the most respected conductors in Metropolitan history, even then brought with him a reputation that was uncommon for a thirty-five-year-old man. In 1876 Richter had recommended Seidl to Wagner, stating that "a fine artistic future for him can be predicted."[27] Seidl had demonstrated his extraordinary focus on detail and precise records when he had kept a list of all singers and orchestra members and their attendance during the first rehearsals at Bayreuth in 1875.[28] A telegram to Seidl from Wagner, dated September 25, 1878, reveals Wagner's faith and interest in the young conductor:

> The future offers twelve performances of *Tannhäuser* in Trieste to conduct, telegraph me.[29]

During part of 1882 Wagner had ceased speaking with Angelo Neumann, the German impresario, and communicated through Seidl, who was Neumann's conductor. Wagner and Seidl exchanged a number of cordial letters, and Seidl's wife, Auguste Seidl-Kraus, mentioned a performance of *Tristan* that Wagner had objected to but ultimately approved. Her words were, "Wagner did not wish to allow it but was then rapturous over the success."[30] As his career at the Metropolitan flourished, Seidl received many honors, and eventually he was called back to Bayreuth by Cosima and Siegfried Wagner.[31]

The reviews of the November 23 opening performance of *Lohengrin* concerned themselves greatly with Seidl's performance as conductor. The report in the *New York Times* was highly complimentary though tempered by some criticism of his manner and musical effectiveness as well as of what appeared to be excessive vanity:

> The rendering of the opera was uncommonly impressive as a whole, very striking at some stages of action, and quite free from glaring defects....Herr Stritt...promptly established himself in the good graces of the public. His voice is neither powerful, nor vibrant...but it has the tenor timbre,...of sufficient range, and even quality, and its tones fall pleasantly upon the ear....The new conductor from Munich, Herr Anton Seidl...is a German leader of high repute. Though still a young man his efforts denote...solid attainments, and his familiarity with the score of "Lohengrin" was happily illustrated....Herr Seidl, however, is not exactly a magnetic conductor, nor...gifted with much warmth. It is to be regretted, too, that he should waste so much physical energy while controlling his forces. A little more tranquility would accomplish quite as much. Now and then...Herr Seidl missed some opportunities of bringing out the tonal beauty of certain passages of the score, but he often produced effects of great loveliness and power. The crescendos with which the swan scene and the prayer in the first act terminate, and the crescendo in the processional scene at the close of the second were finely managed, the fortissimos being wrought up by well nigh imperceptible gradations. Herr Seidl was summoned before the curtain after the first act; his reappearance at the end of the second was injudicious, and prompts the suggestion that a musician of genuine talent needs no aid from self-assertion to establish his claims in this country. It only remains to add that "Lohengrin" is placed upon the stage of the Metropolitan with more than past accuracy and magnificence, and that the initial performance of the season was a welcome earnest of the substantial and brilliant representations which may be counted upon during the operatic Winter thus cheerily begun. (*New York Times*, November 24, 1884, p.5)

The *Tribune* was far more generous than the *Times*, and in no way qualified its compliments.

> To Herr Seidl it is proper to pay a deserved tribute...at the outset since the majority of the features which compel us to place it on record as the finest [intepretation] that the opera has ever received in this country were plainly traceable to the new intelligence brought to the...work by the conductor. Herr Seidl in last night's performance opened many pages that had hitherto been closed to the public and even to many musicians. He gave the orchestral language an eloquence that was new and thrilling; he held the forces...both choral and instrumental together with so firm a hand and inspired them with so earnest a desire, that even the short choruses of the first act—the rocks on which every previous representation had struck—were sung musically and with precision. (*New York Tribune*, November 24, 1885, p.4)

Lilli Lehmann's Metropolitan Debut in Carmen

The choice of *Carmen* for Lehmann's first Metropolitan Opera appearance has never been explained; the sensational success of the opera itself must have been the reason, for it was not one of her most successful roles. Krehbiel, many years later, likened her *Carmen* to Trebelli's, as a departure from Hauk's, commenting that Lehmann "stripped the character of the flippancy and playfulness popularly associated with it, and intensified its sinister side."[32] The *New York Times*, in any case, had complimentary remarks about Lehmann's November 25 debut.

> ...Fräulein Lehmann wrought at once a distinctly favorable impression. The new songstress possesses a powerful and ringing voice, of which only the lowest tones are of rather inferior quality, and her phrasing and execution are most admirable. Considered as a vocalist, she is undoubtedly, with the exception of Mme. Schroeder-Hanfstangl, the most finished German songstress that has visited America for many years. Physically, Fräulein Lehmann is comely as to countenance, though severe in expression; her bearing is dignified and graceful, and her every movement denotes an artist of intelligence and experience. The audience was quick to notice Fräulein Lehmann's excellences, and under its enjoyment of her work lay, furthermore, the conviction that in a more dramatic role she would approve herself one of the new performers potent to move critical hearers to enthusiasm. (*New York Times* November 26, 1885, p.4)

Seidl, on the other hand, received one of the very rare poor reviews given him during his tenure at the Metropolitan Opera House.

> The German Conductor, however, has scant knowledge of the tempos and shadings that a musician of more sympathetic temperament would divine if he had not already acquired them at second hand, and it cannot be conceded that the unceasing changes of light and shade and rich contrasts of tone-color in which the French composer's score abound, or the vein of pathos that runs through it, were apprehended and made clear as frequently in last night's representation as was desirable. (*New York Times*, November 26, 1885, p.4)

Shortly after her November 25 debut in *Carmen*, Lehmann sang her first Brunnhilde in *Die Walkure*. Her performance in this role elicited high praise from the reviewers in both major newapapers:

> Fräulein Lehmann interpreted the music allotted to [Brunnhilde] with eloquence and charm; her scene with Wotan was characterized by genuine pathos, and her acting throughout the opera was full of expression and dignity, and unmarred by a trace of affectation. (*New York Times*, December 1, 1885, p.5)

> ...Fräulein Lehmann was a most statuesquely beautiful *Brunnhilde* and her voice glorified the music in which many people insensible to the poetic depth and power of the drama and its musical investment hear only noisy declamation. (*New York Tribune*, December 1, 1885, p.5)

First American Production of The Queen of Sheba

Karl Goldmark's *Queen of Sheba* created a sensation in its first production at the Metropolitan on December 2. Fifteen performances were given, an enormously large

Lilli Lehmann as Brünnhilde in Die Walküre.

figure, considering that the year's performances for the entire repertoire numbered fifty-two. The opera was kept in the repertoire through 1890, and in the 1905–1906 season it received five performances; its reception, however, was not enthusiastic and it has never been restored to the Metropolitan repertoire. The long review in the *New York Times* was particularly interesting in the light of the opera's failure to hold its place in the repertoire.

It was after 12 o'clock when the curtain fell on the final scene, but the vast audience remained to the end, and if there was any sense of weariness expressed...the feeling was rather the outcome of a surfeit of sensuous music and splendid stage costume than of mediocrity or dullness, either on the part of the composer, his interpreters, or his scenic illustrators....While the directors, singers, and scenic artists of the Metropolitan all merit recognition...mention should be made of Mr. Edmund C. Stanton's share—the lion's share...in the matter. If last night's..."Queen of Sheba" was worthy at all points of the oldest opera house in Europe, this result was largely due to the personal and untiring labors of the young and able director....

The music...may be described in a general way as eclectic...the vocal writing inclines rather toward the Italian than toward the German school...it reminds one occasionally of "Aida,"....On the other hand there are few indications of Wagner's influences...[Goldmark] has resisted the temptation of following in Wagner's footsteps, when inspiration fails him, by depending upon ugliness as an offset to occasional felicity of thought, and if there is little that stamps itself upon the memory by novelty or loveliness, there are few or no passages of the score in which uncommon intervals, wild progressions, or painful dissonances fret the ear. Modern theories and practice are especially and delightfully shown in the orchestration. Goldmark...has adopted, of course, the latter-day method of dividing his orchestra into an array of smaller bands, and his writing teems with the shimmering effects produced by muted violins and violin playing in the highest positions, with rough and vigorous progressions standing out against a delicate background of tone, and with strange but not unpleasing chromatic phrases that soar upward and die away, all unfinished in the uppermost regions of sound...."The Queen of Sheba,"...is characterized, as a whole, by depth, clearness, richness, and brilliancy. It is marked, too, by a plentitude of local color. What is accepted as Oriental modes and rhythms abound in it....

...Portions of [Goldmark's] most important contribution to the lyric repertoire are intended to be distinctly effective, and may be taken up separately....In the first act are noticeably a weird and pretty chorus...("Der Freund ist dein.'"); Sulamith's verses which are somewhat vague as to form, but poetical...and daintily accompanied; an exquisitely written narrative of Assad's meeting with his unknown charmer, marked by unusual variety of accent, ending in a finely dramatic crescendo, and exquisitely accompanied by the orchestra; some broad cantabile passages for the baritone; a showy march,...and a beautifully concerted piece after Assad's recognition of the Queen....In the second act are to be cited the Queen of Sheba's first air...[and] an extremely pretty arioso for tenor and soprano, the latter piece being more German than Italian as to themes and handling. In the "temple scene," ...a powerful concerted piece, sung after Assad has again succumbed...some pretty measures for the soprano, and the ingenious use of Hebrew melodies and of the strange blast of the ram's horn used in the synagogue invite consideration....the vivacious ballet music in the third act and the concerted piece with which the act closes, and Assad's lament...in the fourth, should not be omitted from the enumeration of effective parts of the score....

...the representation moved with unbroken smoothness [and] the beautifully finished execution and pure and vibrant voice of Fräulein Lehmann (Sulamith), and the sonorous tones and broad and flowing delivery of Herr Robinson (King Solomon) won the largest measure of approbation....The chorus was in excellent shape, and the orchestra's task was faultlessly executed....No opera has ever been placed upon the stage with anything approaching the gorgeousness and historical accuracy of last night's production; the scenes, the costumes, and the pageants—the latter involving a personnel aggregating 600 persons—offer to the eye a succession of pictures that for dazzling color, correctness, and life-like realism have had no equals within the recollection of the present generation of theatregoers. (*New York Times*, December 3, 1885, p.5)

The *Tribune* commented on the music but also gave more attention to the value of the story as a vehicle for an opera. Both reviewers, it is interesting to note, referred to *Aida*:

In "The Queen of Sheba" are combined more of the elements which go to make up a successful opera than in any new work we have seen since Verdi enriched the stage with "Aida," unless it be "Carmen," which for many reasons must be given a unique position among latter-day creations....

...Thoughtfully considered this book is not one of great worth, but in its handling of the things that give pleasure to the superficial observer it is certainly admirable. ...It presents a dramatic story which is rational, which strongly enlists the interests if not the sympathies of the observers, which is comparatively new to the stage, and which abounds with impossible spectacles that are not only intrinsically brilliant and fascinating, but that occur as necessary adjuncts to the story. Looked at from the ethical side, and considered with reference to the sources whence its elements spring, it must fall under condemnation....

Herr Goldmark's music is highly spiced. He is plainly an eclectic whose first aim was to give the drama an investiture which should be in keeping with its character externally and internally. At times his music rushes along like a lava-stream of passion; every bar pulsates with eager, excited and exciting life. He revels in an instrumental color; the language of his orchestra is as glowing as the poetry attributed to the King whom his operatic story celebrates. Many other composers before him have made use of Oriental cadences and rhythms, but to none have they seemed to come so like native language as to Goldmark. It is romantic music against which the strongest objection that can be urged is, it is so unvaryingly stimulating that it wearies and makes the listener long for a fresher and healthier musical atmosphere. It is tyrannous in its demands upon the voices, but it inspires its singers with the ability to render it. (*New York Tribune*, December 3, 1885, p.4)

The public reaction to the new opera held throughout the season, and the Goldmark work drew large box office receipts at all performances. After the second production the *Times* commented equally favorably, and again alluded to unpleasant aspects of Wagner's works. Speaking of Goldmark in broad terms, the *Times* found his work "characterized by poetic thought, by rare ability to bring forth graceful and elegant themes and clothe them in a garb of uncommon sensuous loveliness, by a wide knowledge of stage effect, and by a happy and continuous avoidance of the Wagnerian ugliness that defaces many of the reformer's most admirable writings.[33]

First American Production of Die Meistersinger

Shortly before Christmas the company journeyed to Philadelphia for a brief series of performances, returning to New York for its reopening on January 4, 1896. Theodore Thomas's new American Opera Company chose the same night for its premiere and presented a little-known opera by Hermann Goetz, *The Taming of the Shrew*. A *Times* editorial the following day supported the American Opera venture.

> It may well happen that out of the opportunities furnished by an American opera company may yet be developed an American type of the lyric drama. (*New York Times*, January 5, 1886, p.4)

While opera was being sung in English at the Academy of Music, the Metropolitan created history on January 4 with its first *Meistersinger* production, sung in German by its German company. Emil Fischer, who had already established a great European reputation in the role, portrayed Hans Sachs. The cast also included Seidl-Kraus as Eva and Stritt as Walther, as well as Brandt (Magdalene), Kemlitz (Beckmesser), and Staudigl (Pogner). The *Times* pointed out the vast difference between this opera and Wagner's other works that had been heard in New York:

> Wagner's music to "Die Meistersinger" is different in many respects from that by which the master is best known....The two leading characteristics of its dissimilarity lie in its very close resemblance to the master's ideal art-work in which the melos is to flow on uninterruptedly, unruffled by anything recalling, even, conventional lyric forms, and, further, in the light and comic character which he has occasionally sought to infuse into it. That leading motives are freely employed throughout the opera need scarcely be mentioned; as an instance for Wagner's fondness for representative progressions or harmonies, attention may be called to the introduction into the passage of "Die Meistersinger" in which a passing allusion is made to the legend of "Tristan und Isolde," of the brief but striking leit-motiv upon which that typical music-drama is mainly constructed. It may almost be said, indeed, that complete enjoyment of the opera is not attainable before familiarity with the most important illustrative and suggestive measures of "Die Meistersinger" has been acquired. Some of these are distinctly beautiful and some are fraught with a strange impressiveness, while the skill and ingeniousness with which all are treated by a harmonist and contrapuntist of exhaustless resource is, for the student, a deep well-spring of edification and delight. The polyphonous finale of the second act is a marvel of order in disorder, or, in other words, a wonderful combination of contrapuntal writing and theatrical effect. The instrumentation, as may be inferred, is most elaborate and sonorous. Whatever verdict posterity may pronounce as to the lasting value of what Wagner has accomplished, his title to supremacy as a producer of instrumental music full of depth, color, and detail is not likely to be contested.

...last night's representation...was extremely smooth, and, save in respect of occasional faulty intonation on the part of some of the singers, well nigh perfect from a technical standpoint....The orchestra's share of the night's proceedings—the lion's share—was carried out in a flawless manner. (*New York Times*, January 5, 1886, p.4)

The *New York Tribune* theorized about Wagner's motivation for composing this opera, unique in his ouevre.

There are two ways of looking at "Die Meistersinger"; it can be weighted with a symbolic character...or it can be taken as an example of pure comedy with no greater significance than that which lies on the surface....If the former course be pursued many stumbling-blocks will be met. The theory is that the purpose of the opera is to celebrate the triumph of the natural poetic impulse, stimulated by communion with nature, over pedantic formulas and in this interpretation *Walther von Stolzing* becomes a prototype of Wagner himself, *Beckmesser* of Wagner's opponents, and *Hans Sachs* of enlightened public opinion which neither despises rules nor is ridden by them. But when this theory is advanced critics will ask in the future...how this can be accepted as the artistic motive of the opera when the hero who triumphs over the supposed evil principle of the play does so not to advance the virtue that stands in opposition to the evil but simply to win a bride! *Walther* nowhere discloses himself as the champion of a free expression of spontaneous, vital art, but only as a young knight who flirts with a young woman during divine service in church, falls in love with her, and learns to his horror that he can win her only by becoming a mastersinger and defeating all comers in a poetic contest on the morrow. He does his best...and [succeeds] aided by *Sachs* and the circumstance that his rival, *Beckmesser*, defeats himself in his anxiety to win the prize by foul means....To give color of reason to the dramatic scheme which the radicals see in the opera, *Beckmesser* should not have been the blundering idiot and foolish knave that Wagner made him, but at the worst a short-sighted, narrow-minded, and perhaps, silly pedant. As he stands in the book he is an ill-natured buffoon, a caricature of the grossest kind, and no corrective idea lies in the fact that a manly young knight who loves a pretty if somewhat forward young woman should have saved her from falling into such a rival's hands by marrying her himself. He would have had the sympathies and votes of the public in such a contest; if he has sung like a crow and *Beckmesser* like Anacreon. (*New York Tribune*, January 5, 1886, p.4)

Evidently, the *Tribune* reviewer had also done some historical research.

For the sake of the opera it is preferable to look upon it as a comedy with none other than the general purposes of high-class dramas of this character. This view will avoid the contradictions which the other comes in conflict with, leave in their full vigor the many dramatic beauties of the work, and disclose the correctness of Wagner's designation of it as a comic opera....As a picture of the social life of a quaint German city three centuries ago its vividness and truthfulness are beyond all praise; it is worthy to stand beside the masterpieces of the world, and has no equal in operatic literature. The food for its satire, too, is most admirably chosen, for no feature of the social life of that period and place is more amiably absurd than the efforts of the handicraftsmen and tradespeople with their prosaic surroundings to keep alive by dint of pedantic formularies the spirit of minstrelsy which had a natural

stimulus in the chivalric life of the troubadours and minnesingers. In his delineation
of the pompous doings of the master singers Wagner is true to the letter. He has vital-
ized the dry record to be found in old Wagenseil's book on Nuremb[e]rg, and intensified the vivid description of a mastersinger's meeting which those curious on the
subject can read in August Hagen's novel "Norica." His study has been marvelously
exact, even the melodies which Wagenseil prints as examples of the favorite
"Weisen" or modes of the mastersingers, have been placed under contribution. The
first phrase of the march melody which accompanies every entry of the mastersingers and plays so important a part in the prelude, is a literal quotation from one of
these, which…was sung to a "poem" beginning in this fantastic fashion: "In the
twenty-seventh of Genesis it is reported how Esau cheated his brother Jacob," a
verse which can safely be accepted by the reader as a specimen of the poetic frenzy
which used to find expression in the old Church of St. Catherine, in Nuremb[e]rg,
on such an annual occasion as Wagner's first act presents to us. (*New York Tribune*,
January 5, 1886, p.4)

Several weeks later it was announced that the American Opera Company would
continue the following season although not necessarily at the Academy of Music.
Although the possibility of renting the Metropolitan on alternate nights was mentioned, this never occurred. Among the chief supporters of the venture were Levi P.
Morton, August Belmont, Andrew Carnegie, and George M. Pullman.[34] On January
29 a letter to the editor of the *Times*, signed "R. C. H.," commented favorably on a
performance of *Faust* and encouraged the inclusion of more of the older operas:

The music of the future (oh, would that it were true!) has had its day or rather
nights, and now why not an inning for music of the past. (*New York Times*, January
29, 1886, p.4)

It was obvious that although German opera was drawing huge audiences, a strong
faction still consistently showed disdain for the heavier works being presented at the
Metropolitan.

First Metropolitan Production of Rienzi

Although the first Metropolitan performance of Wagner's *Rienzi* has been referred
to as the American premiere, the opera had previously been performed in the United
States in 1878 at the Academy of Music by a company featuring Eugenie Pappenheim.[35] Its reception was poor, and it did not reappear until the first Metropolitan production on February 5, 1886. The opera remained in the repertoire,
although spasmodically, through 1890 and has not been revived at the Metropolitan
since. At its Metropolitan premiere it failed to generate much enthusiasm, and the
Times openly admitted that it was inferior to contemporary works.

The character of the music is distinctly Italian as to themes, treatment, and form.
Both the manner and matter of the work differ in every way from all of Wagner's
later compositions. Even "Der Fliegende Hollander," which follows "Rienzi" bears

no likeness whatever to its predecessor. "Rienzi," in truth, is neither original nor suggestive; it is by no means poor in melody, many of its phrases have breadth and eloquence, some of its concerted pieces glow with youthful warmth, and stir the listener to enthusiasm by rhythm and a tonal brilliancy, but compared with the products of Wagner's contemporaries the German reformer's first effort discloses little creative power—at least in the field in which Meyerbeer and Auber have won immortal renown—and its writer's workmanship appear both superficial and unnatural—unnatural if Wagner's theories as to the ideal attributes are accepted—when laid beside the fruits of Wagner's maturity. (New York Times, February 6, 1886, p.5)

The *Times* reviewer, however, pointed out the effective points of the opera and praised the quality of the performance.

On the other hand many portions of "Rienzi" produce by a combustion of lyric, dramatic, and scenic incidents, a very vivid effect. The tuneful and spirited overture, the chorus of messengers of peace, a fine concerted number just before the close of the second act—the impressiveness of which is lessened by the somewhat vulgar though animated dance measures that follow—and Adriano's air in the third act may be alluded to as most worthy the notice of lovers of music....

The performance of "Rienzi" at the Metropolitan last evening is to be reckoned with the very best that have occurred at this house. (New York Times, February 6, 1886, p.5)

The *Tribune* gave more credit to the book than to the music. The newspaper predicted large audiences for the opera, owing to a combination of factors, rather than to the quality of the work or the production:

Its ["Rienzi's"] revival is not in the line of the loftiest endeavors of the Metropolitan management, though we have no doubt it will swell the tide of prosperity which has supported German opera so bouyantly ever since....It will do that because it is a brilliant and imposing spectacle; because its music...appeals to the majority of the public even to-day; because a great many people will attend...out of curiosity, to study the growth of Wagner, to listen to the youthful utterances of one of whom it is known historically that he did not attain to artistic manhood till he rebelled against the state of things under which for a time he sought to work out his artistic salvation. For those who are inclined to apply seriously...a standard of judgment...however, it is safe to predict that the chief pleasure that "Rienzi" will afford will be that given the eye...."Rienzi" is in form an opera of the old style, with all the absurdities against which the mature Wagner fulminated his crushing criticisms, but...in this form it is unworthy of him. Compared with the operas that served as its models... "Rienzi" is unqualifiedly weak, and this in spite of a noble subject; and...a cleverly constructed and suggestive book. (New York Tribune, February 6, 1886, p.4)

Performances and Reactions to the Season

Novelties, it will be recalled, comprised thirty of the fifty-two presentations during the season of 1885–1886. Although performances of each opera often came in groups of rapid succession, operas were more dispersed throughout the year than during the first German opera season.

The tour was undertaken under the direction of Herman Grau, uncle of Maurice Grau. Stanton, although he did not put a stop to the tour, was concerned over its success and its artistic impression. Neither Lehmann, Stritt, nor Brandt went on the spring tour, nor did Seidl, whom Grau replaced with Adolf Neuendorff.[36] Grau also engaged several new singers to substitute for those who did not accompany the tour. These included, among others, Frau Staudigl and Georgine Januschowsky, who was Neuendorff's wife.

In February a *Times* editorial provided a resumé of the changes in the New York operatic scene since the inception of German opera. The editorial strongly supported the elimination of the highly paid prima donna in favor of better balanced performances.

> The conditions of opera have now been so totally changed that a scoffer might say that we had in abundance every requisite for opera except principal singers. This is so far true that the principals are of less importance to opera now than they were up to within a few years, and their proportion of the gross receipts is correspondingly diminished. At the two houses where operatic seasons are now maintained the receipts do not depend, as a few years ago they almost exclusively depended, upon the reputation elsewhere acquired, and here assiduously worked up, of the principal singers. Of both of these houses it may be said that the previous reputation of the principal singers scarcely enters into the attractiveness of the performances, while scarcely one of the singers at either has been such a celebrity as used to be considered the first condition of a successful operatic season.

> ...here are two houses devoting themselves to getting what in journalism are called "beats" upon each other in the production of German operatic novelties, or of revivals which in New-York have all the effect of novelties.

> This is a complete reversal of the old order of things. It remains to be seen whether the new fashion is merely a "fad" or a serious and significant movement....it will probably be admitted by most people whose partisanship has not galloped away with their judgment that there is very much more promise of an operatic school in modern German than in modern Italian opera....At any rate, the tradition of Italian opera seems to be dying out, and no new composer has arisen to revive the glories of *Verdi* and *Rossini*. When such a composer appears his work can scarcely be free from the influence of the more learned and systematic composers of the North. It will suffer a sea change from the tenuities of *Bellini* into something rich and more or less German while retaining the spontaneous grace and charm of its compatriotic forerunners. Until such a composer appears it seems a safe prediction that German opera will possess the field. (*New York Times*, February 7, 1886, p.6)

Three days before the season ended the *Times*, in a highly complimentary summary of the Metropolitan season, printed a number of statistics about the year. Stanton was lauded for the season's artistic success. *Carmen* and *Lohengrin* drew the smallest audiences, whereas *The Queen of Sheba* averaged over $4,000 per performance at the box office. It was estimated that by the end of the season over 40,000 people would have seen it. *Rienzi*, along with *Die Meistersinger*, had averaged slightly less, but the first had 20,000 hearers and the second about 19,000. The regular payroll had ranged from 405 to 700 people. Expenses, not including rent, music, scenery, and costumes, amounted to $60,000 per month. The interpretation of the results was revealing:

> ...the figures...indicate distinctly that semi-spectacular opera, whether by Wagner or Goldmark, is more acceptable to the New-York public than Wagner pure and simple. (*New York Times*, March 3, 1886, p.5)

THE THIRD GERMAN SEASON
(1886-1887)

The roster for the third season showed minimal change in personnel. Elois Sylva, Josef Staudigl, and Anton Stritt were absent from the male list and were replaced by Rudolph von Milde, Albert Niemann, and the returning Anton Schott. Neither Carrie Goldsticker nor Anna Slach returned, and the only new female artist of consequence was Theresa Herbert-Förster, the wife of Victor Herbert, who was at that time a cellist in the Metropolitan Opera House orchestra.

Niemann was by this time fifty-five years old and well past his prime, but his portrayal of Siegmund in *Die Walküre* at Bayreuth in 1876 had given him an enormous reputation. He had been selected by Wagner for this honor.

The season offered four productions of particular interest, while the balance of the performances were operas that had been presented during the two previous seasons. *Aida* was to have its first Metropolitan production and *Tristan und Isolde* its first in America. Two less familiar operas also received their first American presentations: *Das Goldene Kreutz* by Ignaz Brüll, and *Merlin* by Goldmark. The premiere of *Tristan* was looked upon as the most attractive event of the coming season, although after the success of *The Queen of Sheba*, Goldmark's *Merlin*, with its Arthurian background, was also attractive fare.

Niemann's Metropolitan Debut as Siegmund in Die Walküre

Albert Niemann's interpretation of Siegmund was the definitive one, and on November 10 the public thronged to hear him at his first Metropolitan appearance. Although his voice was admittedly tired, his acting and projection of the role were of great interest. The *Times* was lavish in its praise of his performance.

> It is gratifying to say that the newcomer at once revealed himself as an artist of rare intelligence and experience and that the uneasiness felt in some quarters as to the impaired condition of his vocal organs was promptly dispelled, partly through the evidence afforded that the German tenor is still in possession of a pretty robust voice, partly through the remarkable cleverness with which he contrived to reparer des ans l'irreparable outrage....Herr Niemann is a man of tall and commanding ap-

pearance, his manner is stately and impressive...and his looks and bearing suggest that he is continuously alive to the action of the drama....His conception of Siegmund last night was pitched in a rather low key....It was carried out, however, with extreme simplicity, directness, and consistency. Vocally the new tenor gave abundant satisfaction....His love song, half sung, half declaimed, was rendered with most delicate expression and admirable effect; his delivery of the Wagner text...was a delight throughout the opera. He was applauded to the echo...and his debut in America will surely be remembered with pleasure by the singer and his hearers. (*New York Times*, November 11, 1886, p.5)

The *Tribune* reviewer, though less impressed by Niemann's voice, was strongly affected by his magnetism on the stage:

Herr Albert Niemann's entrance on the American stage...contributed a great deal toward a performance of "Die Walküre" which, in spite of much bad stage management and numerous vocal deficiencies...was in some respects the most beautiful and thrilling that Wagner's admired drama has ever had in New-York....Herr Niemann in the first act possessed the stage like an elemental force and filled his colleagues as well as the audience with a glad excitement which culminated after the fall of the curtain in an inspiring demonstration of enthusiasm, but it would be unjust to the artist and unfair to the public after a performance which lasted to a very late hour to attempt to discuss the qualities of Herr Niemann. We have had most admirable interpretations of "Die Walküre" heretofore, though none which on the whole had quite so much dramatic fire as that of last night. In those performances, moreover, ...we had copies, and not bad ones either, of the *Siegmund* who appeared in his proper person yesterday. Whether we consider Herr Niemann's interpretation alone, or view it in comparison with the imitations and predecessors...it is so full of suggestiveness and it adds so many new elements to Wagner's drama...that it challenges at least an effort at a careful and thoughtful study. (*New York Tribune*, November 11, 1886, p.5)

First Metropolitan Production of Aida

Two days after Niemann's debut the Metropolitan presented a lavish production of *Aida*, an occasion resulting in exceptional disagreement between the reviewers of the city's two major newspapers. The *Times* critic disparaged the performance, complimenting only Brandt, who sang Amneris:

It was evident...that different conductorship and, in some instances, different singers must be had if Italian opera, pure and simple, is to be sung with German words at the Metropolitan....the representation as a whole did not cast as rosy a light upon the strength of the company as its preceding achievements have done. Many of the most beautiful and striking passages of the score lost all their effect through the unconscionable dragging of the tempos by Herr Seidl, many distinctly symmetrical and melodious strains were drawn out of shape by a tendency to excessive emphasis on the part of the performers—Herr Robinson being notably guilty...—and in the labor of almost all the artists there was discernible...a want of refinement in feeling and expression, which responded ill to the necessity of light and shade essential to the impressiveness of the music....The most successful personation...was that of Amneris by Fräulein Brandt, whose acting was full of significance and power and whose singing...was at least commendable....Frau Herbert-Förster...revealed...a voice of considerable strength and vibrancy and showed that in a more dramatic role, demanding less lyric and histrionic finesse, she might easily rouse her hearers to enthusiasm....Herr Zobel produced a somewhat indefinite impression. If he was at his best last evening, his emission is extremely defective, and it will be injudicious to entrust him with any trying parts. Herr Robinson...will prove a capital Amonasro when he confines himself to singing Verdi's music, with Verdi's breathing places and Verdi's tempos....Herr Fischer and Herr Sieglitz were both in good form. (*New York Times*, November 13, 1886, p.5)

The *Tribune* reviewer, in contrast, considered the interpretations accurate and impressive. The general tendency of the *Tribune* critic, Henry Krehbiel, to react more enthusiastically to German opera may have indicated that his taste also differed as to the performance of Italian opera; but it was surprising that differences between the two reviewers became evident as seldom as they did.

> ...to describe the stage dress and the costumes which the Metropolitan management have brought together to decorate "Aida" is a task which it would be rash to undertake. They are much richer, as much more varied in color and design than those of the Mapleson *regime* as those were superior in all respects to the flimsy tinsel and tawdry habiliments of the ordinary Italian opera. One feature is particularly noteworthy, namely the fairly consistent effort to accentuate the Egyptian physiognomy of the drama....
>
> It is pleasant to record the fact that the new "Aida" is not merely a show piece. Verdi's music was finely interpeted last night. There is a superficial and conventional passion in Verdi's score to which most German artists seem insensible, but to its broad and genuinely dramatic effects they did full justice on this occasion. Herr Seidl's reading was not essentially different from that to which we are accustomed, and reflected enough sympathy with the work to disprove the insinuation which has frequently been made against him to the effect that his appreciation is limited to Wagner's dramas. Of the individual performers Frau Herbert-Förster, Herr Fischer and Herr Robinson divided the honors evenly....To the new tenor, Herr Zobel, unfortunately we can accord hearty praise only for his appearance. His voice is not in proportion to his stature, and though it rings out effectively at times, it sounds squeezed and thin and cannot be depended upon always for correct intonation. Fräulein Brandt deserved the applause she received more for her acting than her singing. (*New York Tribune*, November 13, 1885, p.5)

First American Production of Das Goldene Kreutz

On November 19, less than two weeks after the season opened, the Metropolitan presented its third novelty and second opera new to the United States. Although Lehmann had created the role of Christine in *Das Goldene Kreutz* in the premiere at the Royal Opera House in Berlin, she relinquished the honor to Seidl-Kraus for this performance of Ignaz Brüll's opera. The opera was received favorably by the critics, but its choice by the Metropolitan management was questioned on the basis of its operettalike character. Both major reviewers mentioned the influence of Lortzing; the reaction was similar to that of many when Rudolf Bing revived *Die Fledermaus*. It was surprising that the favorable reviews of the work on its own terms did not result in productions outside the Metropolitan; however, no record of any other performances was found. The *Times* review was brief but enthusiastic:

> Judging from a single hearing, it does not seem that Herr Brüll is possessed of remarkable creative power; his themes, however, are alternately graceful and spirited, his instrumentation, when the score is intrusted to an orchestra of rather reduced proportions, is thoroughly adapted to the subject in hand....The music to "Das Goldene Kreutz" is, in fact, illustrative and descriptive, accompanying and emphasizing most happily a series of well chosen situations of no deep emotional significance; it must, therefore, be considered and praised rather as a whole than on account of a few detached numbers. (*New York Times*, November 20, 1886, p.4)

The *Tribune* reviewed the performance equally favorably, and noted the influence of German folksong on its musical content.

> It belongs to a species of opera which used to be much cultivated but has fewer examples in Germany each year. It is a clever specimen of the German form of the *opera comique* and it follows closely its model as it was cultivated by Lortzing and other German opera composers fifty years ago.
>
> The music of Brüll's opera is essentially melodious, and fresh and charming, though it would be difficult to point out any strong individual characteristics in it. The German *Volkslied* has exercised a by no means small influence on it, and ever and anon one meets with bits which have a familiar physiognomy though they elude identification. The whole spirit of the piece is cheerful and inspiriting, and it is to be said in praise of the composer that he keeps modestly within the limits of the action. He does not turn on a torrent to float a bit of cork. The performance was bright and fluent, the stage pictures handsome, the costumes fresh and tasteful. The spoken dialogue was cut down to its lowest denominations, and yet the little that was left acted depressingly upon the performance. It is entirely out of place in a house like the Metropolitan. (*New York Tribune*, November 20, 1886, p.4)

American Premiere of Tristan und Isolde

The most significant event of the 1886–1887 season was unquestionably the *Tristan und Isolde* premiere, which took place on December 1. The opera had created a sensation in Bayreuth, and New York audiences awaited its coming with great interest. The Metropolitan cast enlisted all the major singers in the company, including Niemann, Fischer, and Robinson, as well as Lehmann and Brandt in the leading female roles. Seidl was known to have studied the score with Wagner himself, and all these factors combined to make the event most auspicious.

The headline in the *Times* proclaimed sarcastically, "For once Wagnerites have it all their own way," further indicating less boundless enthusiasm for German opera and specifically Wagner than did Krehbiel, who wrote for the *Tribune*. The subhead to the same article stated: "First performance in America of a work not wanted outside of Germany, and not too often there—beginning of the end of the craze for symphonic music in opera." The size of the *Tristan* audience that season, and on countless occasions since, indicated a hasty judgment, to say the least, as was the opinion that the "craze" was nearing its end. The *Times* review gave some credit to Wagner however:

> Viewed as a specimen of the musical...development of a thought or...as an example of orchestration, "Tristan und Isolde" is a matchless achievement. Whatever the idea underlying the music, it is treated with an ingenuity and a technical skill which no living writer can even approximate. Of the instrumentation..quite as much can be said. Its suppleness, richness, depth, and variety of tone-color are such that Beethoven's symphonies and Meyerbeer's marches, performed after portions of Wagner's music, pale their intellectual fire. (*New York Times*, December 2, 1886, p.5)

Nevertheless, it pointed out characteristics of the opera that seemed unsatisfactory.

> Unhappily the genial attributes of the German reformer's work are not, in our judgment, of the type essential to opera, or even...to the music-drama. If thematic development and varied and gorgeous tone-color were the sole end of this art form, the case would be different. In "Tristan und Isolde" this appears to be the assumption, and the outcome is seldom felicitous. Constructed on a comparatively limited number of leading motives, of which a few are lovely and apposite, while many are shapeless, unsuggestive, and wholly arbitrary in their significance, the composer's meaning seldom takes a recognizable and appreciable shape. The two or three themes typical of the love-stricken pair, though fragmentary, are of genuine beauty, and however frequently they reoccur, their impression is invariably vivid and grateful. But the composer's dramatic and lyric creativeness only assumes a well-defined and impressive shape at semi-occasional stages of the action; in the fine and well known *vorspiel*, in which the ebb and flow of passion is symbolized with an unmistakable feeling and skill; in the tremendous love duet in the second act, which is led up to by a crescendo of great emotional strength and intensity, and in the alternately tender and impassioned final measures sung over the body of Tristan. Add to these numbers, if...that irreverent word be permitted [of] a composition which avowedly includes nothing of the sort, some bright and breezy sea-music in the first act,...some harmonious strains heightening the effect of the forest scene in act the second, and some too infrequent melodious bits of accompaniment, and the sum total of striking incidents in the music-drama will be realized. To the student or to the auditor that finds his delight in following the orchestra and ignoring the sung and acted story...no syllable of discouragement can be whispered. That the world is just now prepared to accept symphony for opera is another matter, the probability of which no reasonable being will be inclined to accept. (*New York Times*, December 2, 1886, p.5)

The *Tribune* review, divided into three days, provided a considerable contrast. The first day's report dealt with the audience's reception of the performance, the size of the crowd, and similar matters. The next day's article concerned itself with reviewing the performance, while the third became involved with the psychological aspects of the opera. The final statement of the third review revealed Krehbiel's awe and enthusiasm for Wagner's work and appreciation of the importance of this premiere.

> We are constrained to believe that the significance of this first performance of "Tristan und Isolde" in America is not so trifling nor its probable influence on the future of the lyric drama in this country so small as is imagined by those whose artistic wants are satisfied with the pretty measures of Bellini and Donizetti. Lovers of the musical drama in New-York are neither few in numbers nor lukewarm in their affections. The reception accorded to the work...was not such...as comes from an audience gathered together by curiosity alone. It told of a keen and lofty enjoyment and an undisguised confession of the power of the drama. The applause came after the last note of the orchestral postludes—[a] fact the value and meaning of which we need not explain. It is far from our purpose to argue that only Wagnerian operas are wanted, or even that they should have a majority of representations at the Metropolitan. Musical comedy has its rights as well as musical tragedy and from the agonies of the heroes of the Wagnerian drama it will be a welcome change to the modified sorrow or the happiness of the heroes of other composers or the amiable pleasures of the ballet. But it would not be wise to say that the majority of the patrons of the opera in New-York today are not different in their aesthetic tastes from the rest of the world. (*New York Tribune*, December 2, 1886, p.4)

First American Production of Goldmark's Merlin

On January 3 the Metropolitan produced for the first time its final novelty of the season. Goldmark's prestige had been established with the success of *The Queen of Sheba*, and either his position, or possibly his friendship with Seidl, was apparently strong enough for him to write Seidl and select the cast he desired. Since Damrosch directed the work, it was probably Goldmark's reputation that awarded him this prerogative. Whichever was the case, in a letter to Seidl Goldmark listed Lehmann, Brandt, Robinson, and Fischer for the cast, and these four did appear in the leading roles.[37]

Merlin was not the success that the composer's previous work had been; this was asserted in the reviews of both major papers. The general tone of the two articles is quite similar, and Goldmark was accused of drawing too heavily both on Wagner and on his own earlier work.

> As a dramatic work it is in some respects superior to "The Queen of Sheba." Both subjects being legendary...there is quite as much human interest in the love of Merlin and Viviane as in the infatuation of Assad for Solomon's royal guest, and...far more life and variety in the story of Merlin than in the [earlier] semi-Biblical plot.... That the score of "Merlin" will lift its composer to a higher plane than that...assigned by critical admirers as well as the general public is more doubtful. The somewhat depressing influence of the Hebro-Oriental modes pervading well-nigh every scene in "The Queen of Sheba" is not felt in "Merlin," which abounds in wholesome and spirited music; at the same time there is no denying that the element of local color distinguishing "The Queen of Sheba" is missed in "Merlin," and that nothing original has been contrived to take its place. Moreover "Merlin" is reminis-

cent of its predecessor and, unfortunately, suggestive again and again of the influence of Wagner. The great duet in the second act, admirable and effective though it is, recalls so vividly and persistently the duet in the second act of "Tristan und Isolde" that the listener, while deeply stirred by its passionate intensity, cannot escape the conclusion that at his best Goldmark is not a creative genius. As to its scoring, "Merlin," as may be imagined from the slightest acquaintance with the composer's works, is a masterpiece. The living musician has borrowed from the dead reformer many of his devices and processes, but he has almost consistently kept clear of Wagnerian confusion and ugliness; his themes, if not strikingly new, are graceful and symmetrical, and his harmonies sensuously sweet and fluent when not productive of rich and brilliant tone color. (*New York Times*, January 4, 1887, p.5)

The usual agreement between the critics of the two newspapers is demonstrated by the observations in the *Tribune*.

Herr Goldmark's new music is more likely to call out sweeping criticism than that of "The Queen of Sheba." It is also likely to be treated with more injustice. A critic who arms himself with a score of "Tristan und Isolde," and insists on sending its heavy projection into this score, will have no difficulty in demolishing it. A single shot will suffice. But this style of criticism is shortsighted. Had it always been used in the past neither Verdi nor Gounod would have had a patch left to their artistic backs. There are planets and there are satellites, and the latter are interesting, even beautiful phenomena in spite of their proximity to and dependence on their central luminaries. It is plain enough that frequently Goldmark in this score seems to be floundering out of his natural element. More strikingly than Disraeli in literature, he in music is an Oriental. He has never till now attempted to hide his birthmarks, and now that the opportunity to use Eastern intervals and cadences and those characteristic instrumental combinations...is denied him, he is often at a loss....It would be foolish to deny this...and equally foolish to deny that in his dilemma he forgets to an extent that it is difficult to forgive the difference between mine and thine. His drafts on Wagner are flagrant, going to ideas, to instrumental effects, and to modes of treatment. (*New York Tribune*, January 4, 1887, p.4)

The *Tribune* also drew attention to the resemblance in the second-act duet.

The musical climax of the second act is a love duet...which is plainly constructed after the duet in "Tristan."...He is not happy always in his invention and among his melodies there is a discouraging amount of the commonplace and threadbare....In a word, "Merlin" is not a great work, not even a "Queen of Sheba," but it is worth performing, worth hearing and deserving a respectful treatment at the hands of critic and public. (*New York Tribune*, January 4, 1887, p.4)

Repertoire of Performances during 1886–1887 Season

The season ended on February 26 with a matinee performance of *Rienzi*. This was the first season since the opening of the Metropolitan Opera House to have no tour. No reason was found; however, it might be assumed that Stanton was neither prone to take the company on tour, nor to entrust it to another manager if an interested one was available.

Sixty-one performances were given of fourteen operas. Fifteen were matinees, while the balance were regular subscription performances. Damrosch was assigned nineteen performances, embracing all productions of five operas; the balance Seidl conducted. The operas under Damrosch's direction were *Le Prophète, Das Goldene Kreutz, Faust, Merlin,* and *La Muette de Portici.* All performances of the Brüll opera were followed by a *ballet divertissement* comprised of Viennese waltzes. *Tristan und Isolde* led in number of productions with eight, while *Tannhäuser* followed with six. *Le Prophete, Merlin, Die Meistersinger,* and *Rienzi* were each performed five times. Thirty-one performances were devoted to Wagner's operas. With the exceptions of *Faust* (performed three times within nine days), *Merlin* (four performances in twelve days), *Das Goldene Kreutz* (three productions in eight days), and *La Muette de Portici* (twice in three days), the repertoire was spread more evenly throughout the season than during the first two German seasons at the Metropolitan.

THE FOURTH GERMAN SEASON
(1887–1888)

The roster of artists for the fourth season showed even less change than the previous year's. Schott had departed for what proved to be the last time; all the other major artists were reengaged, however, with Alvary and Niemann sharing the roles previously assigned to Schott. The prospectus called for the initial American productions of two more operas from the Ring—*Siegfried* and *Götterdämmerung*—as well as the first American performances of Weber's *Euryanthe* and Gasparo Spontini's *Fernand Cortez.* Another Metropolitan premiere, Victor Nessler's *Der Trompeter von Säkkingen,* was of minimal importance; the opera received seven performances during this season and three more two years later, whereupon it disappeared from the repertoire of the Metropolitan and competitive companies.

The season opened on November 2. Although it actually terminated with a matinee of *Siegfried* on February 18, one additional performance was given, Brandt's farewell in *Fidelio* on March 17. She was permitted to select this opera as her final vehicle.[38] Because the usual Christmas tour break did not occur, productions at the Metropolitan continued throughout the holiday season. As a result of the omission of the Philadelphia trip, the number of performances at the Metropolitan Opera House rose to sixty-five.

American Premiere of Siegfried

In accordance with the custom the Metropolitan had established, the first scheduled premiere took place early in the season—on this occasion, the fifth performance, November 9. The cast for the premiere of *Siegfried* was comprised of the first echelon of artists. Alvary sang the role of Siegfried and was joined by Brandt as Erda, Lehmann as Brünnhilde, and Seidl-Kraus as the Forest Bird. Like Marianne Brandt's portrayal of Fricka in *Die Walküre* three seasons earlier, the remarkable willingness of Seidl-Kraus to take on a part as small as the Forest Bird indicated a sense of altruism that failed to continue under later regimes at the Metropolitan. Fischer assumed the role of Wotan and von Milde that of Alberich.

The *Times* reviewer emphasized that the opera was rewarding to students of Wagner's works and stressed the need for preparing for the task of listening to its complexities:

...it is necessary to an intelligent hearing of "Siegfried" that one should know the previous dramas of the tetralogy. This is as true of the music as it is of the book, not only because the reappearance of certain characters renders necessary the repetition of leit motifs [from] the foregoing works, but because the music in its entirety bears a distinct relation to that of the other dramas. The four operas of the tetralogy have been likened to the four movements of a symphony, and this is by no means an unhappy comparison. "Siegfried" is the third movement, the scherzo, bubbling over with the vigor, and grace and sweetness of youth and its inevitable dawning of love. The presence of evil in the persons of Mime and Alberich supplies the necessary contrast in the tone pictures which are further supplemented by the representation of Wotan's mournful dignity.

The music of "Siegfried," generally speaking, is beautiful. It is learned and complex and demands some study; and this militates against its success among those who seek musical performances simply as a mode of entertainment. For them Wagner's music, with a meaning in every phrase, is not an enjoyment but a task. And it must be confessed that the Wagnerian music drama is a very serious business, for which one must prepare by intellectual fasting and meditation, not without prayer. There are many who are willing to take this trouble for the sake of reading Wagner in the light of his own beliefs. Such students will find much in "Siegfried" to repay them for their labor and self-sacrifice. (*New York Times*, November 10, 1887, p.4)

The *Tribune* predicted easier popularity for the opera.

..."Siegfried," in spite of defects, is a strangely beautiful and impressive work, which last night, under trying circumstances, challenged the plaudits of an audience that...found all the obstructions of convention...lying between its appreciation and Wagner's work. It ought to become popular and take the place in [this] season... that "Tristan and Isolde" took in the last, as much for the sake of the composition as in...recognition of the splendid interpretation...it received at the hands of the Metropolitan company. Timidity need cause no one to be chary of praise. (*New York Tribune*, November 10, 1887, p.4)

The*Tribune* compared the Metropolitan production favorably with European productions, though asserting that the Metropolitan was less versed in the use of lighting than its foreign competitors.

Few of those...familiar with European performances of "The Ring of the [Nibelungen] since it was withdrawn from the Bayreuth festivals are likely to institute comparisons injurious to the Metropolitan representation. The tetralogy is the loftiest achievement each year of the Court Opera at Dresden, which is ambitious to become a sort of minor Wagnerian Mecca. Now the scenic outfit of "Siegfried" at the Metropolitan Opera House is in some particulars finer than at the Saxon capital while the singers are equally good to say the least. It is only in stage management that the Dresden representations surpass the performance of last night, the most striking discrepancy being in the treatment of light effects—a mechanical detail in which American theatres are many years behind the theatres of Continental Europe. (*New York Tribune*, November 10, 1887, p.4)

First Metropolitan Performance of Der Trompeter von Säkkingen

Victor Nessler's *Trompeter von Säkkingen*, termed a *Volksoper*, was written in 1884 and had achieved rapid popularity. Musically similar to *Das Goldene Kreutz*, it was attractive to German-speaking people, particularly to recent immigrants to the United States, who were still rooted in the culture of their native land. The Metropolitan cast included Fischer, Robinson, and Seidl-Kraus. At the opera's November 23 premiere the *Times* found it delightful and effective.

> Nessler's music is admirably adapted to the story. It is, first of all, melodious in the commonly accepted meaning of that abused word. It would perhaps be more precise to call it tuneful. The measures are light, airy, and graceful, with a captivating rhythmic quality. People who want to be amused by their music and not instructed or made to think, will fall in love with this dainty comic opera—for such it truly is. The opening student song: "Oh, Heidelberg, thou fairest," is delightful in its sentimental melody, and the fanfares of Wagner's trumpet under the windows of the electress, accompanied by the chorus, are passing sweet and full of grace. The opening chorus of the first act is breezy and light and the processional music at the close of the first scene full of merit. (*New York Times*, November 24, 1887, p.4)

Several aspects of the production and performance, however, were considered flawed.

> The music is of the kind that the public ear loves—full of melody and sentimental grace, admirably scored for both the orchestra and the voices. The use of the trumpet…was sadly marred at times last night by abominable playing….Herr Fischer…was admirable and his singing…was one of the features of the evening….Frau Seidl-Kraus was altogether unsatisfactory as Maria, a part which calls for a more extended range of voice and more skill in singing than she possesses….The production of the opera was the most slovenly yet seen at the Metropolitan Opera House. Some of the scenery was passable, but most of it was strongly reminiscent of the Academy in its worst days. But the opera distinctly pleased the audience….The Wagnerites said it was a failure, but they appeared to take it dreadfully to heart, and there was quite as much enthusiasm in the house as on the first night of that noble work "Siegfried." (*New York Times*, November 24, 1887, p.4)

The *Tribune* reviewer was more pleased with the performance and equally attracted to the opera.

> The music is generally fresh and melodious and, especially in the prologue, it touches a chord which is bound to vibrate responsively wherever Germans form a considerable community. It voices the national love for jollity and male chorus music. It is not good dramatic music and is innocent of the devices which opera writers usually employ to stamp their characters with individuality. It is simply

good, tuneful music, now stirring as the chorus sings, now sentimental and charming and pretty when the lovers are voicing their sweet passion. But the opera has one element which splendidly adapts it to the uses of the Metropolitan Opera House. It admits of much opulence of stage attire and picturesque pageantry. The settings...are set forth on such a scale indeed, that they overcome the objection which has heretofore existed to accept a work of small dramatic and musical calibre [on] the Metropolitan stage....

...All the parts in the opera are well filled, and the performance last night moved smoothly. (*New York Tribune*, November 24, 1887, p.4)

American Premiere of Weber's Euryanthe

Although Weber had composed *Euryanthe* in 1832, the opera had never been performed in America before the Metropolitan production. Although the attraction of this opera to non-German audiences might have seemed negligible—certainly it was not an opera that bore the attention of Strakosch, Mapleson, or any of the impresarios of Italian opera or opera in Italian—the tradition of Beethoven and Wagner justified this experiment with a well known but neglected work. The critical reviews, as well as the production itself, held interest more as a historical event than as a contribution to the Metropolitan repertoire. *Euryanthe* was produced during only one other season (1914–1915), when it received five performances under Toscanini. The *Times* review of the December 23, 1887, premiere reflected interest rather than enthusiasm.

Wagnerianism was preceded by Weberism, not followed by it; but retrospect is always instructive. The composer of "Siegfried" has acknowledged his indebtedness to the composer of "Euryanthe," and musical students will find much to interest them in searching for the germs of the Wagner manner in that of Weber. Beethoven is credited with saying that this work was an opera of diminished sevenths, and Chorley found fault with it because it was full of unexpected modulations. These would be deemed strange grounds for fault-finding in the present period of restless harmony. The criticisms of Weber's contemporaries are chiefly interesting now as showing the surprise and uneasiness with which his innovations were regarded then....

The music of "Euryanthe" is, fortunately, a different matter from the libretto. It is surcharged with the grace, beauty, poetry, and vitality of that powerful romantic school of composition of which Weber...must remain the accepted founder....The music is written in Weber's characteristic manner, full of nervous energy and fire. It is music that makes us cease to wonder at the stately, gigantic Beethoven's hailing him as a "devil of a fellow." Dramatic intensity and marvelous wealth of expressiveness are combined with delightful fluency of melody and symmetry of form. Indeed, the perfect manner in which the music fits the dramatic—and undramatic—situations has resisted all attempts at altering the libretto. But it is painting the lily to praise this noble music, of which some of the finest themes have been made familiar through frequent performances of the splendid overture. The tableau vivant, representing the tomb of Emma, was given during the performance of the overture last night. This is in accordance with Weber's own arrangement, but it is a lame and impotent attempt to counteract the weakness of the work and only makes it more manifest. (*New York Times*, December 24, 1887, p.4)

The *Tribune* specifically complimented Seidl for his restoration of the tableau. In addition to commenting favorably on the performance, the *Tribune* also assessed the opera's historical significance.

> The work is...impossible to approach without affection, but appreciation of its beauties is conditioned upon the acceptance of theories touching the purpose and construction of the lyric drama which are only now obtaining validity amongst us. ..."Euryanthe" comes before us...modestly conscious of grievous dramatic defects, and pleading for pardon, even while demanding with appropriate dignity recognition for the soundness and beauty of the principles that underlie its music and the wondrous tenderness, sincerity, and intensity of its expression of passion. When it was first brought forward in Vienna in October, 1823, Castelli, a German poet and librettist, observed that it was some fifty years before its time....

> All that can be done to give coherency to the book has been done by Herr Seidl at the Metropolitan down to the restoration of Weber's strange device of exhibiting a tableau during the large episode in the overture....The picture disclosed by the preliminary rising of the curtain is the interior of the tomb, with Euryanthe in prayer beside Emma's coffin....

> For the performance of the work...we have only words of praise. The loving care and intelligence bestowed in the preparation bore the best of fruit....The spirit of the performance was profoundly tragic, and Fräulein Lehmann's exhibition, both as to conception and execution, made it almost impossible to believe...that she sang the role of the heroine for the first time last night. (*New York Tribune*, December 24, 1887, p.4)

First American Performance of Spontini's Fernand Cortez

Gasparo Spontini's *Fernand Cortez* was performed four times within eight days during the season of 1887–1888, and the opera has never since been heard of at the Metropolitan. It is not clear why *Fernand Cortez* was selected for the Metropolitan repertoire. The newspaper reviews of the January 6 premiere, unanimously unenthusiastic, provided no insight into the choice. The *Times*, however, contended that the work was superior to Spontini's *La Vestale*.

> The opera cannot be said to have made as deep an impression as more recently composed works have done.

> There are on the whole fewer faults of harmony and less piling up of effects in "Cortez" than in "La Vestale," and it is generally conceded to be the better work of the two. Musicians have always admired Spontini's work. Schumann, one of the keenest of critics, declares that he heard this opera for the first time with rapture. Berlioz wrote an adulatory letter to Spontini, praised him warmly in his public writings, and points out to students of instrumentation some of his striking effects in orchestration. The judgment of both these men has been in some measure justified.... There are defects in the work of this Spontini, to praise whom would be a pleasure, because he is a new acquaintance to us....it must be frankly admitted that as an in-

strumental composer he does not rank high. The immense resources of the art of instrumentation were not at his command for he had never been thoroughly disciplined in this important school....Added to...frequent baldness of instrumentation is general hardness and inflexibility of melody which prevents it from being the mastering element in the mass of sounds....

...Spontini's opera, taken as a whole, is not to be regarded in the same light as it was 79 years ago....In his day he was a strong factor in the development of his art. But the tremendous evolution of the opera since the production of "Fernando Cortez" [sic] has demonstrated...that the lyric stage is destined for higher things than Spontini ever dreamed of....The day of recitative strumentato is gone, and it may as well be frankly admitted that the long passages of this antiquated style...in "Fernando Cortez" fell flat last night and were plainly wearisome to the hearers. (New York Times, January 7, 1888, p.5)

The *Tribune* reviewer noted that the enjoyment of outdated works was possible when they were viewed from the light of newer compositions. In this manner the historical interest becomes paramount:

...Spontini, no matter what may be thought of the relation of his music to the taste of to-day, stands as the representative of a principle, and if it were possible for the management to supplement "Ferdinand Cortez" [sic] with "Armide" or "Iphigenia in Aulis" the Metropolitan repertory would admirably exemplify the development of the dramatic idea and its struggle with the simple lyrical in opera composition. We should have been asked to take the steps in reverse order, it is true—Wagner, Weber, Spontini, Gluck—but this fact would only add to the clearness of the historical exposition. The light which significant works throw out falls brightest upon the creations that lie behind them in the pathway of progress. We are this season enjoying "Euryanthe"through the mediation of "Tristan und Isolde."

If we put aside the attractiveness of "Ferdinand Cortez" as a spectacle (and we fancy the resurrection of the mummy is due in the first instance to the picturesqueness of its cerements) the opera will be found to have chiefly an antiquarian interest. With Spontini the people of America have had but little opportunity to become acquainted. Of all of his music we can recall only the overtures to "La Vestale" and "Olympia," and a scene from the second act of the former opera as having figured on local programmes; and only the scene from "La Vestale" performed at the music festival in the 7th Regiment Armory in 1882 contributed anything to our knowledge of Spontini's style as an opera composer. (New York Tribune, January 7, 1888, p.4)

First American Performance of Götterdämmerung

The importance of the January 25 premiere of *Götterdämmerung* commanded the attention of all the newly acquired patrons of the Metropolitan. Its presentation left *Das Rheingold*, due the following season, as the only work of the *Ring* yet to be brought to the Metropolitan audience. The cast, as in all earlier Wagner premieres, was outstanding and included Niemann, Robinson, Fischer, von Milde, Lehmann, Brandt, and Seidl-Kraus. The "Norn" and "Waltraute" scenes were omitted; they were not included in Metropolitan performances until the first "uncut" version of the *Ring* in the season of 1898–1899.

The *Times* correspondent, who had frequently been critical of Wagner's larger works, was impressed by *Götterdämmerung* and admitted that past performances had made it possible for hearers to become accustomed to long, serious passages in these operas. His critical response to the performance itself was highly favorable:

> Musically, "Die Götterdämmerung" is surpassingly rich. This is a result of Wagner's leit motif system. We not only have representations of most of the striking themes introduced in the foregoing work, but new ones constructed with especial reference to the additional characters and emotions of this drama....The use of those introduced in the earlier dramas, it is almost needless to say, is at all times skillful and effective.

> The first two acts of "Die Götterdämmerung" are full of gloomy and tragic music, which in days gone by would have been extremely tiresome. Since we have become accustomed to looking for fitness and meaning in our operatic music we are better able to understand the composer's reasons for writing many pages which, separated from the libretto, would be intolerable....

> The third act from beginning to end is indescribably beautiful. It is hardly too much to say that it surpasses everything else in opera. Yet very little of it is new. It is a marvelous working over of the riches of the earlier works of the tetralogy, here brought together in one mass and poured out in a magnificent stream of matchless melody and harmony....

> ...It must be stated briefly that the evening was one of veritable triumph for Fräulein Lehmann, whose superb acting and singing as Brün[n]hilde has never been surpassed on the operatic stage in this country; for Herr Niemann, whose Siegfried was a noble piece of acting, and for Herr Seidl, who brought out with admirable skill all the beauties of the score. (*New York Times*, January 26, 1888, p.5)

The *Tribune* critic reacted in essentially the same mood, one of great enthusiasm. He spoke of the dramatic intensity, the orchestration, and the magnificence of the music, and particularly emphasized the striking quality of the funeral music.

> The play is full of action, and in the piling up of scenes, musical and dramatic effects it overtops its predecessors in the tetralogy, and forms a fitting climax and end to that wonderful creation. Its chief moment, the murder of "Siegfried," is unquestionably the most impressive scene ever created by Wagner. An element of naivete and a most refreshing melodiousness are brought into the prologue associated with the Rhine daughters. Besides the music, much of which was familiar last night from performances in the concert-room, there is a considerable draft on the exquisite orchestral idyl which makes the second act of the preceding drama so charming, (the so-called "Waldweben") and three purely orchestral numbers which belong to the most beautiful and stupendous music that the tetralogy boasts....

> Ah! that death march! Where in the literature of music shall we look for its like! Let the cold-blooded analyst dissect it, tell of the phrase out of which it is built, and

marvel that "Siegfried's" simple horn call could be metamorphosed into so colossal a hymn as that which marks its climax, one may feel its beauty to the full without getting within this technical sway. Such knowledge, indeed, may add [k]eenness to our appreciation but without it we may recognize music which tells of the death of a demi-god and of his deeds. (*New York Tribune*, January 26, 1888, p.4)

Performances during the Season of 1887–1888

Of the sixty-five performances that comprised the season of 1887–1888, thirty-seven were devoted to Wagnerian opera. The four "novelties" of the season accounted for thirty-three performances. Eighteen of the season's performances were matinees. Damrosch's conducting assignments were reduced to nine; these were all involved with *Faust, La Juive,* and *Le Prophète.* The single novelty outside the German school, *Fernand Cortez,* was retained by Seidl, indicating the beginning of dissatisfaction with Damrosch. It was apparent that the policy under Stanton was to introduce a new production and then repeat it many times; *Siegfried* and *Götterdämmerung* received a combined total of eighteen performances. *Tristan* was reduced to three performances, and *Die Meistersinger* to one. *Lohengrin* continued to enjoy frequent performances; with six repetitions, it received more productions than any other operas not newly introduced during the season.

THE FIFTH GERMAN SEASON
(1888–1889)

In contrast to the four previous seasons of German opera, the fifth season saw a number of significant changes in the roster of artists. Among the tenors, Niemann had retired and Lehmann's husband, Paul Kalisch, had been engaged, as well as a new tenor, Julius Perotti. In her autobiography Lehmann denied any part in Kalisch's coming to the Metropolitan. He had not originally been scheduled to appear, but replaced Alvary as *Tannhäuser* in an emergency. He sang the role again two days later and then did not appear until the final weeks of the season, when he sang Siegfried in *Götterdämmerung* and one performance as Siegmund in *Die Walküre.* Lehmann described the incident as follows:

...Alvary, who was to sing *Tannhäuser* for the first time, acted very strangely at the rehearsal. The manager had to call his attention to the fact that the role should not be taken so lightly, and should not be treated as a joke, but he did not seem even to know his part. At two o'clock on the next afternoon, the manager burst in upon us to entreat Herr Kalisch to sing *Tannhäuser* that night, in the place of Alvary who was ill. My husband, who was not a so-called "stop-gap," defended himself energetically against the unreasonable demand, but, as there was no end to the entreaties and importunities, he finally agreed to save the performance, and to substitute for the invalided Alvary, who, contrary to all professional rules and his own declaration, was amongst the spectators that evening.[39]

Perotti sang a great deal that season and two other tenors, Alois Grienauer and Karl Moran (presumably the husband of Fanny Moran-Olden, a new dramatic soprano), each appeared in isolated performances. Robinson and Fischer were still the leading baritone and bass, respectively. Among the female singers, Brandt had departed, as had Seidl-Kraus. The newcomers of note were Moran-Olden and Katti Bettaque, a lyric soprano. Schröder-Hanfstängl returned after an absence of four years. Seidl and Damrosch remained the only two conductors.

In comparison with previous seasons, the number of new productions was considerably curtailed. The American premiere of *Das Rheingold* was announced, as well as the first performance of the "Paris" version of *Tannhauser*. Other than those, the only other item of outstanding interest was the first American production of the complete *Ring* cycle. The season opened on November 28 and continued without interruption through March 23.

First American Performance of Das Rheingold

The last opera of the *Ring* to come to the Metropolitan was the prelude to the trilogy. The cast for the January 4, 1889, premiere was reputable, if not quite so impressive as those of the Metropolitan premieres of the other three operas of the cycle. Fischer sang Wotan and Alvary assumed the role of Loge. Fricka was portrayed by Moran-Olden, Freia by Bettaque. As usual, Seidl conducted. The critics agreed in judging the opera the least effective of the *Ring*, although the *Times* reporter excused the limitations of *Das Rheingold* because it was an introduction and therefore not able to draw on the wealth of thematic material at the disposal of the later operas. The review appeared a day late because of the length of the performance.

> ..."Das Rheingold" is open to the same objections as the other operas of the tetralogy for its want of vocal beauty. It is much more barren in this respect than its successors....
>
> On the whole we may set down "Das Rheingold" as the poorest of the four Nibelungen dramas. The writer's system made this inevitable. Restricting himself to the use of motives indissolubly allied with the personages and movement of the drama, he limited himself to a small amount of material. The skill with which it is employed is that of a matchless genius; but intellectual appetite is better satisfied by the succeeding dramas of the series. If we adopt the only fair view—that "Das Rheingold" is the first act of the great Nibelungen play—we are bound to admit that this stage of things is defensible. (*New York Times*, January 6, 1889, p.4)

The *Tribune* was less critical, but it commented on particular aspects of the staging of the drama.

> ...Although "Rheingold" is the most trying of the four Nibelung dramas, there were no evidences of weariness at the close of the representation....The circumstance may be accepted as evidence that the people of New-York are likely to give the same generous treatment to the new work that they gave last year to "Siegfried" and "Die

Götterdämmerung." Such treatment will be no more than the drama and all concerned in its representation deserve....The structural peculiarities of the stage of the Opera House compelled the omission of the two veiled transformations from the Walhalla scene to Nibelheim and back again. Instead a new curtain, which opened in the centre and was drawn back in graceful folds, was used. This is unfortunate, for the closing of the curtain distracts attention from the between-scenes music, which is highly descriptive and significant to those who are familiar with Wagner's system of composition. (*New York Tribune*, January 5, 1889, p.6)

First American Production of the "Paris" version of Tannhäuser

The January 30, 1889, performance of *Tannhäuser* in which Paul Kalisch made his Metropolitan debut was the first American viewing of Wagner's revision of the work for French audiences, with their penchant for ballet. Besides Kalisch, the cast included Fischer as the Landgraf, Grienauer as Wolfram, Bettaque as Elizabeth, and Lehmann as Venus. The *Times* review presented the most complete historical background of the revision.

> Wagner's "Tannhäuser," owing to the intercession of a friendly German Princess was performed on March 13 (1861) by order of the Emperor. But the composer was told that a ballet was indispensable. His dramatic mind at once seized upon the opening scene, in the home of Venus, as an opportunity for a choreographic scene of some real meaning. "I was even delighted," he (Wagner) says, "with the task of thus remedying a weakness of my earlier score, and I drew upon an elaborate scheme, according to which the scene or the hill of Venus should be raised to a position of great importance."
>
> But the director insisted on having the ballet in the second act...because the box-holders arrived late, and the ballet was for their special edification. However... Wagner proceeded to work out his own ideas. He, as he says, "went through the score again with the greatest care, wrote the Venus scene entirely new, as well as the ballet that preceded it, and especially endeavored to bring the music of the whole into the most exact accord with the translated text." (*New York Times*, January 31, 1889, p.4)

In the *Tribune*, Krehbiel described the revision's changes in great detail and with vivid clarity.

> ...The overture has been deprived of its final repetition of the Pilgrims' Canticle and the Hoerselberg music leads directly into the bacchanalian orgie in the domains of Venus. The ballet here has been considerably extended and likewise the succeeding duet. For those who sympathize with Wagner's feelings as to the province of a ballet in such a situation (it is not a dance, but an allegory in pantomime with a few attributes which might be spared—the illustration of Jupiter's adventures brought in near the close, for instance) there can be no doubt that the new version marks an improvement over the old; but the second scene, it seemed to us last night, has lost some of its freshness and lovely simplicity from the changes made. (*New York Tribune*, January 31, 1889, p.6)

Krehbiel, who had previously heard Kalisch in concerts with Lehmann, was generous in his praise of the tenor, who as mentioned earlier, had filled in for Alvary at short notice.

Herr Kalisch's manly voice and excellent method have challenged and received our praise heretofore. In the trying part which he essayed (without rehearsal, said the house bill last night) he succeeded in a degree for which few...in the assemblage were prepared. Especially did he gratify all purely musical instincts, for his voice was unswervingly true in pitch....Besides this he acted and sang with fine taste, intelligence and profound earnestness. (*New York Tribune*, January 31, 1889, p.6)

First American Production of the Complete Ring Cycle

During the last three weeks of the season the Metropolitan embarked on one of its most ambitious efforts, producing the complete series of the Wagner *Ring* tetralogy. (Although all four operas were given, however, some internal cuts were made.) The performances were enthusiastically received, and the receipts, which will be discussed later, were rewarding. Two cycles were performed; the first began on March 4. Interspersed among the eight performances were one of *La Juive* and also a single production of *Il Trovatore*. Two extra performances of *Die Götterdämmerung* and one of *Das Rheingold* completed the last thirteen productions of the season.

Repertoire during the Season of 1888-1889

The number of performances continued to creep upward each year, and this season the total was sixty-eight. *Das Rheingold* qualified as the only novelty, but the interest in the *Tannhauser* revision and in the *Ring* cycle provided sufficient impetus to make the season an artistic success. Wagner's works received thirty-five performances, of which twenty-three were operas of the *Ring* cycle. Damrosch conducted fifteen performances of four operas, *Faust*, *Le Prophète*, *La Juive*, and *Il Trovatore*. Of the non-Wagnerian operas, Seidl conducted *Les Huguenots*, *Guillaume Tell*, *Fidelio*, *L'Africaine*, and *Aida*. Eighteen matinees were given, of which six were operas from the *Ring* cycle; the rest of the performances were subscription.

After a two-year interruption the Metropolitan Opera Company embarked on another tour. This time Stanton took the group, which consisted of regular members of the company. Other than one performance of *Fidelio*, the tour consisted entirely of Wagner operas. Forty-two performances were given in five cities. Milwaukee was added to the itinerary for the first time, although only for four performances.

THE SIXTH GERMAN SEASON
(1889–1890)

Regardless of Lehmann's assertion that she had not used her influence in Kalisch's engagement, Alvary was not reengaged. He was notably difficult, which may have been a prime factor; however, the appearance of Theodore Reichmann, a close friend of the Kalisches, and Heinrich Vogl, similarly associated with them, indicated that Lehmann's prestige deliberately or otherwise contributed to the selection of singers for the Metropolitan company. Robinson was released to make room for Reichmann, and Vogl joined Kalisch as a leading tenor. Lehmann's explanation of the Alvary affair, if not convincing, revealed that there were public feelings directed against her for her alleged interference.

> Perotti, the tenor, once upon a time a beginner at Prague, now engaged for Italian parts, and Alvary, who had tremendously increased his demands since his success as Siegfried, were not to be re-engaged. Without a word being said by us or a step taken, Stanton suddenly came to Kalisch with an excellent offer, which the latter accepted only after Stanton had assured him that there was no question that Alvary would be engaged. Nasty articles appeared against me in the papers, but I promptly blunted the point of them by declaring that I would not sing again unless the management refuted the attacks by publishing the truth. This was done by a public statement that Alvary's demands were excessive and that therefore it was impossible to re-engage him. Alvary turned his back on us. I was reluctant for a long time to recognize the possibility of an unworthy thought towards me being the reason for such conduct, and I took Alvary to be ill, but this was not the case; he thought that we were both capable of perfidy, and so he spoiled a beautiful comradeship which grieved me more for his sake than for my own.[40]

Lehmann's statement concerning Alvary lost much of its credibility because of her attack on Perotti, who had in no way received any unfavorable publicity. Her statement that he had been engaged for Italian parts was wholly inaccurate, since he sang the leading tenor roles in *Le Prophète, La Juive, Faust,* and *Die Walküre* while both Kalisch and Alvary were members of the company.

The new members of the female roster included a lyric soprano, Sophie Wiesner, and a contralto with considerable experience, Emmy Sonntag-Uhl.

The only novelty announced for the season was Peter Cornelius's *Der Barbier von Bagdad,* in a revised version by the highly respected conductor Felix Mottl. Cornelius's opera had been less than a success a few years before in Europe, and the revised version was considered to be an improvement. Another performance, although not announced in the prospectus, was also of particular interest. This was a benefit for Lehmann, who chose Bellini's *Norma* as a vehicle to show the diversity of her talent to the New York audiences.

First American Performance of Der Barbier von Bagdad

It was not until January 3 of the 1889–1890 season that Metropolitan audiences had a novelty to attract them. The premiere of Cornelius's *Der Barbier von Bagdad*, in its revision by Mottl, had been scheduled for December; however, Kalisch, who was to appear in the production, became ill, making it necessary to postpone the performance. After the scheduled postponement Seidl was incapacitated, and Damrosch was called upon to direct the performance. The opera, which because of its brevity was followed by a ballet, was well received and its sparkling humor particularly attracted the *Times* reviewer:

> ...Cornelius' music will bear further hearing and, if we are not greatly mistaken, will grow in favor. The score is full of the most characteristic and fluent melody, admirably written and distributed among the various voices and instruments.
>
> The themes are rich in meaning and fairly radiant with individuality. The musical characterization is wonderfully faithful and the musical humor simply delicious. This last quality is so exhuberent [sic] and withal so scholarly refined and delicate that it is far and away above the appreciation of the multitude; but it will be source of constant and widening interest and enjoyment to those who have a fondness for studying their scores....The work is a very difficult one, though it appears to flow along so smoothly, and it was given last evening with admirable effect. Further performances will reveal to us beauties not now perceptible, and the general public will undoubtedly learn to like its quiet humor and occasional bursts of broader merriment. (*New York Times*, January 4, 1890, p.5)

The assessment of the ballet by the *Times* revealed the attitude of the press toward the young wealthy opera patrons.

> The opera was followed by a new Viennese ballet entitled "Die Puppenfee," of which detailed account must be reserved until a future occasion. Suffice it to say at present that it was an agreeable and picturesque novelty quite within the comprehension of the most fashionable brain. (*New York Times*, January 4, 1890, p.5)

The *Tribune* critic was also impressed with the opera and spoke glowingly of Cornelius's attributes as a composer. Damrosch's effort was appreciated far more than the assistant conductor's results.

> ...Cornelius' comic opera, which was a flat failure in one of the intellectual capitals of Europe less than a generation ago, was a success on its first performance in New-York. Yet it is not music for the frivolous, nor a play for those who think that comedies are only made to grin at, and it was performed under many disadvantages, chiefest of these was the illness of Mr. Seidl, who had prepared it with great care and devotion, yet had to place the baton for the first representation in the hands of Mr. Damrosch. Mr. Damrosch is to be congratulated; it is no small matter to conduct a work so difficult as this opera, and though one ensemble came near suffering shipwreck and there were many instances of disagreement between the singers and the

orchestra, Mr. Damrosch deserves words of praise and gratitude for making the performance possible....

It is a superb work, fresh as the morning, brilliant as a jewel, and might furnish texts for a sermon running up to fortiethly [sic]...

It is the product of a mind fertile enough in invention to get along without much descending from the plane of high-class music—music which has a special charm for those capable of appreciating the subtleties and refinements of the harmonies and orchestral effects peculiar to the new romantic school of composers. (*New York Tribune*, January 4, 1890, p.7)

Benefit for Lilli Lehmann

Benefits for managers were commonplace during this period; benefits for singers were less usual. In the case of an artist with the stature of Lilli Lehmann, however, a benefit was considered to be a fitting tribute. Just as Brandt had been permitted to choose the opera for her farewell appearance, Lehmann was given her choice for the production to be presented at her benefit. In *Norma* she apparently felt she could impress the public even beyond her enormous success during the regular season's offerings. The Bellini opera was produced on February 27; Lehmann's supporting cast included Kalisch, Fischer, and Betty Frank, a new contralto. The *Times* reviewer bluntly declared that the opera was of little value except as a display piece for a prima donna:

...the time has gone by when the serious music lovers of this community can be induced to accept "the worn out elementary rhythms" of the Italian stage and its surprising florituri against which even Fetis cried out as dramatic. The old fashioned Italian opera can only maintain its hold as an excuse for exhibitions of vocal technique, and it is pretty safe to say that Lilli Lehmann selected "Norma" for that very purpose....She certainly met with popular success. She demonstrated that her voice possesses far more flexibility and that she had a greater command of the pure ornamentation of singing than any one suspected, and so long it is since this public has heard so excellent an exhibition of this sort that the audience was fairly carried away. (*New York Times*, February 28, 1890, p.5)

The *Tribune* commented that the public had no need to demonstrate its appreciation of Lehmann's art, other than by bringing material reward to the artist. It warned that the custom of benefits for leading singers might become a threat to the public acceptance of German opera.

It was scarcely necessary that a benefit performance should have been arranged for Madame Lehmann to vindicate the significance which she has attained in the operatic activities of the American metropolis....So far as the extra performance of last night enabled the public to testify their appreciation of her merits in an especial manner, and to put that testimony in a form more substantial than joyful noises and ruddied palms, it was, of course, beautiful and gratifying. Still, it is much to be hoped that the custom, which is not without its threats of danger to the permanency of German opera, will not become fixed....

It requires no deep penetration to discover why Madame Lehmann chose "Norma" for her benefit. It enabled her to add another to the many proofs which she has given in the past of her great versatility as a singer. (*New York Tribune*, February 28, 1890, p.7)

Repertoire during Season of 1889–1890

The 1889–1890 season consisted of sixty-eight performances, of which seventeen were matinees. Wagnerian operas, comprising thirty-seven performances, again dominated the repertoire, but not overwhelmingly. Twenty-one of the Wagner productions were presented after February 11, indicating that public dissatisfaction demanded this change in policy. Twenty different operas were performed, the largest variety in any one season up to this time.

Damrosch conducted eighteen performances; although they included one Wagner opera (*Rienzi*), they were primarily comprised of the traditional Italian repertoire. Circumstances gave Damrosch an opportunity to broaden his scope somewhat when Seidl was forced to step aside for the Cornelius opera. Other than that and *Rienzi*, Nessler's light opera *Der Trompeter von Säkkingen* was his only departure from the less attractive segment of the season's offering. Seven operas received five performances each, and no single opera was performed more than five times. *Norma* (the Lehmann benefit) and *Rienzi* were presented only once.

Stanton granted Damrosch permission to take the company to Boston and Chicago; this was the extent of the 1889–1890 tour. Seidl did not participate. Thirty tour performances were given; although fourteen of these were Wagnerian operas, three productions of *Die Meistersinger* represented the only venture into Wagner's mature works. The popularity of German opera on the road was rapidly diminishing, and opera patrons in the tour cities were not attracted by the production of the Italian–French repertoire in German by German singers. Lehmann and Kalisch were the featured artists on the tour, with Reichmann sharing the honors in many performances. Julius Perotti was the alternate tenor. When Lehmann did not sing the leading soprano role Sophie Wiesner and Felice Kaschowska shared the performances.

THE FINAL GERMAN SEASON
(1890–1891)

The final Metropolitan season of German opera showed a number of significant changes in the list of singers. The new group of tenors indicated obvious improvement in quality. Perotti was released and three tenors were added, two of repute, since Kalisch had returned to Europe with Lehmann. The foremost new tenor was

Andreas Dippel, who had come from the Vienna State Opera to start what was to be a notable career at the Metropolitan. (Dippel later became active in the Metropolitan management, but was forced out as a result of pressure exerted by Toscanini through Gatti-Casazza.) The other newly acquired tenor of renown was Heinrich Gudehus, who had sung at Bayreuth.[41] Adolph von Hübbenet was engaged for smaller parts. The female roster had a strange look, as all the leading singers of the previous seasons had departed. The three major artists among the newcomers were Minnie Hauk, Marie Ritter-Götze, and Pauline Schöller-Haag; Hauk was the most celebrated interpreter of Carmen at this point, having created the part in London. The remaining singers of importance were the same: Fischer, Reichmann, and Kemlitz. As in past seasons, Seidl and Damrosch were the only conductors listed.

The season opened on November 26 and ran continuously through March 21. Three novelties were to be presented; all were American premieres of little-known operas. The new productions were *Asrael* by Alberto Franchetti, *Il Vassalo di Szigeth* by Antonio Smareglia, and *Diana von Solange* by Ernest II, Duke of Saxe-Coburg-Gotha.[42] The first performance of *Asrael* took place on opening night.

American Premiere of Asrael

The opening night of the 1890–1891 season interested opera patrons not only for the presentation of a new opera, Alberto Franchetti's *Asrael*, but also for the cast, which included Dippel, Ritter-Götze, and Marie Jahn, all singers yet to be heard in America. As in New York reviews of most operas first heard during this period, the critics of both the *Times* and the *Tribune* noted strong resemblance between *Asrael* and Wagner's works, and certainly a more than passing influence by the Bayreuth reformer. The *Times* was strong in asserting that the similarity brought discredit to Franchetti:

> ...Franchetti is an imitator of Wagner. There can be no doubt about this. In fact, there need be no hesitation in saying that in two instances the imitation exceeds the bonds of toleration and becomes something dangerously like plagiarism. This is the case with the first duet....It is the same with the passage prefatory to Loretta's solo in the third act, when the violins play a figure precisely like that of the "Waldweben," and snatches of pastoral melody for the flute, under the following note in the score: "La brezza fa tremolare le fronde ed increspare le acque del fiume." And a few measures further on Franchetti writes "Spunta la luna" over a passage of sustained high chords for the strings with harp arpeggios, very like to the "spunta la luna" in "Die Walküre."...
>
> The instrumentation is...disappointing. The score is exceedingly difficult, but the orchestration is not rich and it lacks color....
>
> The opera was received with no small favor, but it will have to grow into deep public affection. It is not the kind of work to carry an audience by storm. There is too much thought in it. (*New York Times*, November 27, 1890, p.6)

Since this was an opening night audience, it was not surprising that the opera received some measure of favorable reaction. The *Tribune* review was more satisfying, and although it referred to the opera's lack of originality, the implication of plagiarism was not nearly so strong:

> ...it appeared...that the new opera, whatever shortcomings critical analysis might discover in it, was yet always an engaging, sometimes a fascinating entertainment and...the new singers were excellent artists and comely....

> ...the music...in spite of the fact that it is not strikingly original, is yet full of evidences of a talent far beyond the ordinary and one disposed to most admirable seriousness of purpose. It is based on Wagnerian models,...it is free in form...the orchestra is made the vehicle of expression and the ingenious use is made of typical phrases to convey meanings....on the whole, it is interesting music, rhythmically varied and effectively orchestrated. (*New York Tribune*, November 27, 1890, p.6)

American Premiere of Il Vassallo di Szigeth

The second new production of the season, Antonio Smareglia's *Il Vassallo di Szigeth*, listed a cast of six characters. Four singers of the cast were leading members of the company; Dippel, Reichmann, Schöller-Haag, and Fischer joined with Seidl in giving this premiere the best possible opportunity for success. Indeed the opera was better received than the opening-night novelty, and after the December 12 premiere Smareglia received favorable comment from both major New York reviewers. The *Times* noted evidences that the composer had seriously studied the work of a number of major composers and had profited thereby:

> ...Smareglia's music is interesting, and in many places full of dramatic power. If any one expects to find any of the old-fashioned Italian forms and sunny melody in this work he will be disappointed. The music is sombre in color, like the story, for Smareglia writes in the modern style, with every evidence of a desire to make his music reflect the passions of his characters. It is strong, richly colored, original music, and shows that the composer has studied, not only Wagner, but Boito, Verdi, Gounod, and Massenet intelligently and profitably. (*New York Times*, December 13, 1890, p.4)

The *Tribune* reviewer shared his colleague's reactions to Smareglia's music but was clearly shocked by the libretto. He paid Smareglia a great compliment by ranking him above Boito.

> To sup one's fill of horrors it will only be necessary to attend a representation of the new opera which was brought forward at the Metropolitan Opera House last night. Whether operatic literature can produce a parallel to its exhibition of monumental wickedness we doubt. A small army of moral monstrosities that have chosen the familiar figure of the operatic basso in which to manifest themselves stalk past the mental vision like the ghostly kings in "Macbeth."...

...Like Boito and Franchetti, [Smareglia] owes much to Wagner, but he cuts a better figure in the German masquerade than either of those men, for he is better able to keep to the lines which at the outset he laid down for his guidance. Throughout "Der Vasall" we find persistent use of the most marked rhythms of the Wagner language and melody....to sum it up, he has written a score worthy of much respect, free from platitudes, magnificent in orchestral color, and aristocratic in tone. Between it and the book to which it is wedded there is a tremendous gulf, bridged only by national traits. (*New York Tribune*, December 13, 1890, p.6)

American Premiere of Diana von Solange

The history of the Metropolitan Opera contained no darker moment than was brought on by the January 12, 1891, production of Ernest II's *Diana von Solange*. The press reacted violently, as did the public, who enforced cancellation of the third scheduled performance by petitioning for a substitution. In response to this urgent plea, the management changed the opera to *Fidelio* on January 17. The chroniclers of Metropolitan Opera House performances are unanimous in castigating the management for introducing this work, which was described in the most deprecating terms. As will be discussed later, the public reaction to this work, combined with the derogatory criticisms in the newspapers, helped the directors of the Metropolitan Opera to justify the abrupt change in policy that they instituted at the close of the 1890-1891 season.

The summary manner in which the *Times* dismissed the music as "rubbish" set the tone for the response of the public when the opera was scheduled for repetition:

> There may be many reasons for the productions of "Diana von Solange," but it would be difficult to discover them....

> It was reported before the production of "Diana von Solange" that the music was Donizetti and water. Poor Donizetti! He was drowned. It was all water and as a *Puck* poet said of the fountain of eternal youth, very poor water at that....

> To speak seriously, the work has a tolerably good libretto, but the music is simply rubbish. There is no excuse whatever for the attempt of the Amusement Committee of the Opera House to foist such trash upon the public. There is a marvelous amount of patience in this community, but it is not illimitable, and if the course entered upon this season is pursued, disaster is sure to result.

> The performance last night was very little better than the opera. There were abundant evidences of haste in the preparation, and frequently the principal singers, as well as the chorus, were sadly uncertain in their work. (*New York Times*, January 10, 1891, p.4)

The *Tribune* reviewer spoke much in the same vein, but added an attack on royalty that chose to dabble in the arts and then use its influential position to further the results. His comment about the ballet resembled that in the *Times*, except that the

Times made no implication that the dance music might have been composed by someone other than the duke. The *Tribune* attack was launched in colorful prose:

> The question "Why was it given?" was much oftener asked at the Opera House last night than the usual one on first nights, "What do you think of it?"...If our opera patrons were particularly interested in European royalty and ready, like most European communities, to see beauties "per ordre de Mufti" when there are none, simply because royalty has condescended to play at music-making, there might be some occasion to talk about the music of "Diana von Solange."...The opera which for a mysterious reason which it is of no concern of ours to try to discover, was performed last night has been lying about between thirty and forty years. The Duke...succeeded in having it brought out...in December 1858, and May 1859...and Dresden did him the honor of performing it in January, 1859. It may have been done somewhere in Germany once or twice since, but if so the circumstances [did] not...fix the fact in the memory even of those who set for themselves the task of watching the world's musical activities...
>
> ...It is a royal libretto and has been set to royal music in the style of the immature [V]erdi and the mature Meyerbeer. It fell like hoar-frost on the listeners last night, who were warmed into interest only by a pretty ballet in the third act, the music of which, plainly enough, did not belong to the opera. (*New York Tribune*, January 10, 1891, p.6)

During the week following the premiere of *Diana von Solange* the Metropolitan directors entered into an agreement with Abbey, Schoeffel, and Grau to manage the Metropolitan Opera for the following year and to perform opera in French and Italian.[43] Stanton's reaction was to turn back to Wagner and to attempt to recoup the enormous losses the season had undergone up to that time. Figures indicated that this deficit was directly attributable to the disastrous failure of the three novelties, which had brought in an average of 2,000 patrons per performance, as opposed to approximately 2,700 patrons per performance for Wagner presentations. Starting on January 14 the company presented twenty-eight performances of Wagnerian operas; one concert devoted to Wagner; and only twelve non-Wagnerian opera productions, of which six were devoted either to *Fidelio* or to *Der Barbier von Bagdad*—both operas calculated to attract German opera devotees. A *Tribune* editorial strongly supported Stanton's move, predicting that public reaction would be most favorable and would result in vastly increased attendance.

> Financially Wagner must save this season or it will suffer shipwreck. Mr. Stanton knows that, and it is not a rash prediction to say that the whole unperformed list will be sacrificed from this time forth to the production of Wagner's works. The policy will be voted wise by the directors because it will go further than anything else to save the season; it will be welcomed by the public because of their disappointment with the novelties which a shortsighted policy attempted to foist upon them. (*New York Tribune*, January 20, 1891, p.6)

Final Performances under the Stanton Regime

The last two operas performed under the Stanton management and with the German company were *Tristan und Isolde* and *Die Meistersinger*. The second of these was particularly significant because it was the occasion of Emil Fischer's farewell performance at the Metropolitan.[44] The cast for the March 20 *Tristan* performance was the same as for all the *Tristan* performances during that season and included Heinrich Gudehus as Tristan, Antonia Mielke as Isolde, Juan Luria as Kurvenal, and Fischer as King Mark. Seidl was the conductor. The performance was a gala occasion, although one that brought regrets from the *Times* reviewer:

> The performance was so admirable in spirit and generally in execution that criticisms, in view of its being the end of the season, would be impertinent. There may have been persons in the audience who did not like the performance, but they are of the number of those who do not like the orchestra to have anything to say, regarding it as an accompaniment. (*New York Times*, March 21, 1891, p.4)

The *Tristan* performance was enthusiastically reviewed in the *Tribune* and created an opportunity to attribute guilt to those who had helped to eliminate German opera from the Metropolitan.

> Surely no season of opera in New-York ever closed with such convincing evidences of vital energy in the form of musico-dramatic entertainment heretofore regarded in the light of an exotic. It is doubtful if we are to judge by the rapt attention which even the occupants of the boxes bestowed upon the performance, whether the speeding of the parting guest is looked upon without emotions of sincere regret by a score of those who have voted to return to sweetmeats of the past, to say nothing of the thousands who have been the faithful patrons of the German institution during the last seven years. (*New York Tribune*, March 21, 1891, p.6)

The final matinee of *Die Meistersinger*, on March 21, produced an ovation at the end that resulted in a half-hour of flowers, applause, and finally, demonstrations for Stanton, Seidl, Fischer, Damrosch, Dippel, and several other singers. Fischer made a short speech:

> Ladies and Gentlemen: It is impossible for me to express what I feel for your kindness and love; and I hope it is not the last time that I shall sing for you here, on this stage, in German.

Seidl added a few words of his own:

> Believe me, ladies and gentlemen, I understand the meaning of this great demonstration. For myself, the orchestra, and the other members of the company, I thank you.[45]

Repertoire During the Season of 1890–1891

Because of the final surge in performances of Wagnerian operas, the record of the 1890–1891 season was similar to that of previous seasons. Had Stanton not altered his plans, the preponderance of non-Wagnerian operas would have been startling. As it was, the season was completed with sixty-seven performances, of which thirty-nine were devoted to Wagner. Because of the dismal failure of the three novelties, together they received only eleven performances. Under the policies observed in past Metropolitan seasons, this was a surprisingly small number; in the season of their first presentation (1885–1886) *The Queen of Sheba* was performed fifteen times, *Die Meistersinger* eight times, and *Rienzi* seven times.

No tour followed the season, and the artists presumably returned to Germany to fulfill other engagements and prepare for the next season in Europe.

SUMMARY OF THE GERMAN OPERA PERIOD
AT THE METROPOLITAN

Most of the records of the German opera period were either burned or are inaccessible. All the records in the possession of the Damrosch family were lost in a fire years later; neither Stanton nor Seidl ever made any information available. The Metropolitan Opera archives suffer from a similar lack, since their formal records stem from the beginning of the managerial regime of Gatti-Casazza.[46] Fortunately, newspapers of the period provided a wealth of information that gave a reasonably clear insight into the results of the German opera "experiment." Krehbiel, unquestionably the most influential music journalist of the day, contributed many figures that he acknowledged as "courtesies received at the time from Mr. Stanton, with the sanction of the stockholders"; these data can be assumed to be valid.[47] Reports of a given event frequently appeared in more than one newspaper; figures in these multiple reports generally agreed, indicating that they were released from a reliable source, presumably the Metropolitan Opera management.

Total Performances During the German Opera Period

Thirty-five different operas were produced at the Metropolitan during the seven years of the German opera era. Of these only three, *Lohengrin*, *Tannhäuser*, and *Die Walküre*, were performed every season, whereas *Asrael*, *Un Ballo in Maschera*, *Diana von Solange*, *Euryanthe*, *Fernand Cortez*, *Der Freischütz*, *Das Goldene Kreutz*, *Merlin*, *Norma*, *Rigoletto*, and *Il Vasallo di Szigeth* were performed during one season only. Five of the one-season works were never produced again at the Metropolitan: Goldmark's *Merlin* and the works by Franchetti, the Duke of Coburg, Spontini, and Brüll. *Faust* had up to this time received only sixteen performances, whereas *Tannhäuser* had been repeated forty times, and *Lohengrin* thirty-seven. The seven German opera years provided 438 performances, of which 230 were devoted to Wagner's operas. Operas from the *Ring* totaled 101 performances; of these, *Siegfried* led the list with 40.

Singers and Conductors of Greatest Significance

The only available basis for distinct judgments of the greatest singers of the German opera period were the newspapers reports and, to some degree, attendance figures. Since the audiences were generally large, the newspapers seem a more definitive source.

Female Singers.   Lilli Lehmann achieved a reputation that has survived these many years. Other than an isolated review or two, her acceptance by the press was unanimously strong. Regardless of the opera or role, her performances invariably were attended by capacity audiences. Although she made her debut in *Carmen* and in earlier seasons sang a number of non-Wagnerian roles, the operas of the *Ring* provided the greatest vehicle for her talents. When she appeared in *Norma* at her benefit, she proved her ability to cope with the difficulties of the bel canto style even after many years of portraying Brünnhilde. Both Henderson and Krehbiel reviewed her performance enthusiastically on that occasion. The singers assuming her roles during the final season never achieved any particular stature or lasting reputation in the annals of the Metropolitan.

Amalie Materna was a victim of circumstance. Her short tenure at the Metropolitan was the result of Damrosch's policy of paying her considerably larger fees than her colleagues, resulting in their dissatisfaction. Her own excessive future demands ruled out her reengagement. Although it was generally conceded that her voice was not a great one, her performances in Wagnerian roles, both in New York and Bayreuth, classified her among the greatest interpreters of these parts in the history of opera. Materna's entire conception of these roles was accepted as superior because of her acting and projection, combined with her voice, which although not of the quality of Lehmann's, nevertheless was exciting and dramatic.

Marianne Brandt sang both contralto and dramatic soprano parts and received outstanding reviews throughout her tenure at the Metropolitan. Her greatest triumph and her own choice for her farewell appearance was in *Fidelio*. Here she openly competed with Lehmann and achieved equal success. Her temperament was more difficult than most, as evidenced by her emotional breakdown when exposed to the witless laughter of a spectator during a dramatic moment in *Fidelio*. (It was necessary to stop the performance while she regained her composure.)[48] Henry Finck's description of Brandt refers to Wagner's opinion of the artist:

> In Brandt, Wagner had found a born artist who could do great things of her own
> accord yet derived tremendous benefit from his teaching. Her Ortrud in "Lohen-
> grin" was easily the most thrilling of all the impersonations of that hateful character

Max Alvary as Walther in Die Meistersinger.

the world has seen and heard. Unequaled also was her Fides in Meyerbeer's "Le Prophète"; I can name no actress on the purely theatrical stage that could have surpassed her in emotional grandeur in that part or as the loving wife in Beethoven's "Fidelio."[49]

That her value was great also in terms of utility is shown by the many varied roles she assumed while at the Metropolitan Opera House.

Male Singers.   Among the tenors, the names of Niemann, Alvary, and Dippel were most prominent. Albert Niemann came to the Metropolitan at the final stage in his career, yet he brought a heritage to the great Wagnerian roles that has never been surpassed. The critics hailed his interpretation of Siegmund as definitive and reacted similarly to his other portrayals. Max Alvary, although apparently lacking in vocal brilliance, was an outstanding actor and during his stay in America his singing progressed notably. His most revered performances came as Siegfried, both in *Siegfried* and *Götterdämmerung*, and he was referred to as the "ideal Siegfried."[50] He sang a number of parts in Italian and French operas and was very successful in the more lyrical Wagnerian parts such as Lohengrin and Tannhäuser. Andreas Dippel was included in this list because he came to the Metropolitan during these years; his most significant contributions came later. His first year at the Metropolitan, however, established him as a major artist.

Among baritones, neither Robinson nor Reichmann, although far above average through the years, achieved the renown of their colleagues. Adolph Robinson deserves mention particularly because during his stay at the Metropolitan he sang almost every baritone part in the repertoire. He was extremely versatile and rarely performed any way but creditably. Theodore Reichmann, who replaced Robinson during the last two seasons of this era, was considered an excellent actor, and this capability characterized all of his performances. His reviews were excellent, and like Robinson, he demonstrated considerable versatility.

Emil Fischer stands alone among the basses and ranks with Materna, Lehmann, and Niemann as one of the outstanding singers in the history of the Metropolitan. His definitive interpretation of Hans Sachs remains the ultimate, and his performances as Mephistopheles, Hagen, King Mark, and Ramfis were hailed as superb. Not a single review was found in which Fischer received anything but praise, and his colleagues shared the opinion of the press and public. Although it was not generally known, Fischer also had a successful career as director of the opera at Danzig, where he granted Lehmann many opportunities when she was a young singer.[51]

Much of the artistic success of the performances during this period was due to the remarkable depth of the company. As frequently asserted in the publicity releases, this was a group that of its own volition had disallied itself from the star system. With this policy it had achieved remarkable strength among its secondary singers. The roster included a large number of performers who, although they did not achieve any degree of lasting fame or recognition, contributed in a remarkable degree to the excellence of the performances. Chief among these were such singers as Kemlitz, Staudigl, Goldsticker, Klein, Sonntag-Uhl, and Jahn.

Conductors. The list of conductors who appeared during the German opera period was brief. In order of appearance they were Leopold Damrosch, Walter Damrosch, John Lund, Anton Seidl, Adolf Neuendorff, and Frank Damrosch.[52]

Of the six conductors under consideration, the two of major importance were unquestionably Leopold Damrosch and Anton Seidl. Damrosch promulgated the entire episode and for this alone merits recognition for his foresight and artistic sincerity. In addition, he was highly respected as a ranking conductor and received enthusiastic critical acclaim, as well as the highest regard not only from his artists but also from such men as Liszt and Wagner. Seidl, whose career at the Metropolitan was to continue, achieved an eminence and reverence comparable only with that accorded to Toscanini in later years. The tributes later paid to him at his death give clear indication of his reputation.

Walter Damrosch was at this time a neophyte and received his opportunity to become a major conductor as a result of his father's untimely death. During the seven years of the German opera period he was a factor because of his intimate connection with the Board of Directors and specifically with Stanton. His conducting chores were minimal and did not receive or merit much attention; his influence, however, prefaced the conflict that would later develop when the public brought forth objections to his continuing as a conductor at the Metropolitan. Nepotism is an unkind word, yet throughout the Damrosch career it was apparent that its existence was real. The original inclusion of the completely inexperienced Walter Damrosch in his father's company was open to conjecture, and the engagement of his brother Frank Damrosch for even limited conducting was further suggestion of family influence.

Statistical and Financial Summary of German Opera at the Metropolitan

Other than the receipts for the various individual operas during the first season under Leopold Damrosch, little financial information about the German opera era was available. The *Times* later indicated that the deficit during the first German season amounted to $40,000.[53] The average cost per production has been given as $3,400 and the largest expenditure on a single performance was $4,000.[54] Later reports of financial results during the German opera period begin with the season 1886-1887, omitting the intervening season of 1885-1886. For information on the 1885-1886 season the only figures available were found in Krehbiel's summary of the musical year.

The directors had fixed the assessment on the stockholders in October at $2,000 a box, and their receipts from this source were $136,700; from the general public, $171,463.13; total, $308,163.13. The cost of producing the operas, omitting the charges for new scenery and properties, but including the expenses of the Philadelphia season, was $244,981.96. The fixed charges on the building (taxes, interest,

and rental account) were about $85,000 in the preceding year, and the financial out-
come was so satisfactory to the stockholders that the directors promptly re-engaged
Mr. Seidl, and adopted a resolution empowering the managing director, Edmund
C. Stanton, to make contracts with artists for three years.[55]

The Philadelphia season referred to in the above source involved a two-week period from December 19 to January 4, when the company encountered a disastrous
deficit of approximately $15,000.[56]

In dealing with the final season, the *New York Herald* prepared a report that
allowed a valuable comparison between attendance at Wagner's operas and audience size at other performances; the novelties fared poorly in comparison with any
of the other presentations.* On March 22, 1891, the *Tribune* published a chart showing the average for Wagnerian and non-Wagnerian performances for the final five
seasons of the German opera period. As indicated previously, Wagner outdrew other
productions substantially, especially in the final season and in the season of
1887–1888, when *Siegfried* and *Götterdämmerung* were premiered.[57]

Krehbiel's book presented a variety of financial information that was both valuable and incomplete. Finally, the *Times* published a sketchy resumé of isolated
financial results; the most significant figures reported the expenditures of the fourth
season (1887–1888) as $419,688.33, and those of the fifth season (1888–1889) as
$478,127.12. The deficits were also included; they amounted to $7,808.09 for the
fourth season and $582.13 the following year.[58]

The complete figures will almost surely never be known. The available evidence,
however, confirms that for at least the majority of its years, the German opera period
was as financially successful as unsponsored opera on a grand scale might be expected
to be. Certainly the artistic results were excellent—and in the case of many performances, outstanding and memorable. An impressive list of superior artists appeared,
and an equally great number of *comprimario* singers provided unusually fine support for the major performers. In Leopold Damrosch and in Seidl the Metropolitan
enjoyed two of its finest conductors, devoted and sincere musicians of high caliber.

Stanton must rank high in the list of Metropolitan managers. He provided a comfortable period for the directors and stockholders, during which they could be proud
of the artistic achievements at the Metropolitan Opera House and yet not be overbur-
dened with insurmountable deficits. The end of German opera at the Metropolitan
resulted from a combination of factors, and partial blame had to be placed with the
directors and stockholders. Stanton's errors were to some degree forced upon him by
the pressure of satisfying the directorate while trying to keep the public he had attracted content. Since this public was undoubtedly one of the most selective in the
Metropolitan's history, it was an impossible task. Although the German opera period
terminated on March 21, 1891, the taste for German opera, specifically for Wagnerian opera, survived its demise and remained solidly entrenched among the
patrons of the Metropolitan. The movement that was started with Stanton's and

*Editor's note: The author did not provide a date or page reference for the *Herald* report mentioned.

Damrosch's production policies remained active, eventually emerging as the German wing of a company involved with opera in its native language. Italian opera in German vanished but German opera in Italian had also disappeared, so that gradually the policy of opera in its original language obtained throughout the repertoire. The novelties presented during the German period perished; but whereas Abbey previously had been unwilling to produce new operas, future managements felt impelled to do so in the light of Stanton's willingness to gamble on these ventures.

CHAPTER 5

The Metropolitan Opera House
Under Abbey, Schoeffel, and Grau
(1891–1897)

The change in policy by the directorate of the Metropolitan Opera seemed abrupt; actually, however, the last two years of operation under Stanton had left the directors with many doubts about the wisdom of continuing to perform all opera in German by German-trained singers and conductors. In addition the general attitude of the stockholders had not been favorable toward the heavier Wagnerian operas. Finally, it was apparent that Abbey had regretted his decision to give up the new opera house; he had new ideas, whereby he might return to the operatic scene and take advantage of the satiation with German opera felt by many opera patrons.

Reaction to Termination of German Opera at the Metropolitan

The reaction of the press to the shift away from German opera was something of an anomaly. In view of the generally excellent reviews which had been issued in all the newspapers during the German opera period it was surprising to note the tone in which they commented on the decision to end German opera at the close of the season of 1890–1891. In justification of the return to Italian opera, this time coupled with opera in French, the *New York Herald* suddenly attacked many alleged frailties of the German era. In the light of numerous favorable reviews of performances of non-Wagnerian operas, the *Herald* comments appeared to seize on opportunity more than fact:

> Think of the many broken promises of the three seasons past at the Metropolitan. Think of the lamentable attempts to perform "Carmen," "Faust," and "L'Africaine." Think of "Le Cid," "Le Roi d'Ys," "Gioconda," which we did not hear, and of "Diana de Solange," which, alas we did hear. Think, too, of the shabby little ballets, the discordant baritones, the "dramatic" tenors, the dismal declamation which we have known in these seven years of German opera. (*New York Herald*, March 22, 1891, p.11)

On the same date the *Tribune* published two articles on the same page indicating that the closing of the German season was more than a mundane event. The first article dealt with responsibility for questionable decisions made during what had turned out to be the terminal German season. Stanton was exonerated in this report and the blame was placed on the directors, who had forced him to experiment along lines that hopefully would be more satisfactory to the stockholders and boxholders than to the general public (which had proved its interest and understanding of the Wagnerian repertoire). The change in Stanton's procedure after the *Diana von Solange* debacle was once more explained as his attempt to recoup in some small measure the catastrophic results of the season's first half:

> When Mr. Stanton went to Germany in the spring of 1890 to engage a company he carried with him a definite policy formulated by the directors for the sake of a sentimental passion which some of them felt toward the amiable Italian muse. Feeling that performances by the artists of the Italian stage were unpracticable, they conceived what they thought would be a happy compromise—they would continue the use of the German tongue, but would make marked change in the repertory. Wagner was practically to be shelved except so far as some of his earlier works were concerned, and the season was to be rich in new works of the Italian and French schools. ...For six weeks Mr. Stanton followed the lines of policy which had been adopted, bringing forward within that time three of the novelties which had been promised... however it became manifest that the policy of the directors did not meet with the approbation of the public. One result of the German representations in the preceding six years had been to develop a class of opera patrons with intelligent and fixed tastes. (*New York Tribune*, March 22, 1891, p.7)

The second article mentioned the importance of *Diana von Solange* in the ultimate decision to change to Italian and French performances. The news item also referred to Abbey's opportunism in making his proposal at a time when the directors and stockholders were discontented and receptive to alternative plans. The *Tribune* referred to the opinion held by a large block of opera patrons: that the Metropolitan had taken a severe backward step.

> By a singular coincidence on the night of the first representation of one of the latter day works of Wagner, which, had the directors chosen to read the signs of the times aright and be guided by them, might have ushered in the era of prosperity which they were sighing for yet repelling by their course, the decision was reached to turn over the establishment next season to Mr. Abbey, for performances in "Italian and French" (these words are quoted for future reference). The date was January 14. Since it will be frequently referred to hereafter in...operatic history it deserves to be mentioned with emphasis....So far as the patrons of the opera are concerned the action of the directors was nothing less than the culmination of a conspiracy to set back the clock of musical progress in this community a whole quarter of a century. ...Mr. Abbey seized the right moment to strike, and when he had bagged his game he promptly exhibited it and evoked a loud chorus of cheers from the enemies of the German institution. The directors gleefully continued their course for a little longer, though the handwriting on the wall had begun to blaze forth its warning when all

the canons of art and all the fruits of the culture of years were unsettled by the production of that amorphous creation...entitled, "Diana von Solange." (*New York
Tribune*, March 22, 1891, p.7)

Henry Finck, the eminent critic, had a kindlier opinion of the stockholders,
although his view of their altruistic attitude lacked accuracy to some degree. His reference to the patient patrons who "paid the piper" took more for granted than was
the case. After the experience of the first season, the German opera venture proved
considerably less costly, even in the disastrous final season. Finck's description of the
circumstances, nevertheless, was penetrating.

...grand opera is impossible without the support of society, and a plutocracy willing
to pay lavishly for the most comfortable and conspicuous seats. This applies particularly also to the seven years of German opera given at the Metropolitan. The
wonder is that there were as many as seven. For it was no secret that most of the
wealthy boxholders did not really care for this kind of opera. They would have much
preferred "Lucia" to "Tristan," "Il Trovatore" to "Siegfried." Yet for seven years
they patiently paid the piper and allowed themselves to be bored to death by music
they did not understand.

In truth, these society leaders were in a way heroes and heroines—martyrs in the
cause of highbrow music. Those of us who reveled in the excellent Wagnerian performances which their long purses made possible had reasons to be extremely grateful to them. But the worm turned at last.

Almost as steadily and unexpectedly as German opera had been adopted it was
cast out of the Metropolitan, to be replaced by opera in Italian and French....On
January 15, 1891, it was announced officially that Abbey and Grau had been engaged as managers for the next season.

Great excitement was aroused by this statement among opera-goers. It was generally known that, what the boxholders particularly objected to in German opera
was the predominance of Wagner; but this predominance was due to the fact that
Wagner was just what the *audiences* particularly wanted. Yielding to their clamor,
the management wisely devoted to his operas twenty-five out of the last thirty-five
performances of the seventh and final season of German opera; and the public used
every opportunity of giving tremendous ovations to Seidl and the great singers associated with him, by way of showing its displeasure with the contemplated change.[1]

The cumulative evidence indicates that the attitude of the stockholders was the
cause of the change. As a cause, however, it worked indirectly, since forcing Stanton
to produce less Wagner resulted in a disastrous decline in box-office receipts and increased the deficit. The gradual rise in the stockholder assessment, from $2,000 to
$3,000 through a period of six years, could not be construed as prohibitive; but the
projected future assessment, based on the final season's receipts, provided ample excuse for altering the course of the Metropolitan and turning to the more popular, attractive fare that was suggested.

PERSONNEL OF THE NEW COMPANY

Although seven years had elapsed since Abbey's first season at the Metropolitan, he and his two partners brought back with them a number of singers who had enjoyed a measure of success during that experiment. Among the male singers were included Italo Campanini, Giuseppe Del Puente, and Franco Novara, and one female artist, Sofia Scalchi, also returned. In addition, Abbey's spring season brought Patti to the Metropolitan for three performances, her only appearances with a resident company at that house: *Martha* (April 2), *Lucia di Lammermoor* (April 6), and a matinee of *Il Barbiere di Siviglia* (April 9). In addition to the singers who returned with Abbey, Augusto Vianesi once more assumed the major conducting assignments; however, this time he shared the podium to a limited degree with Seidl and Louis Saar. Seidl conducted *Die Meistersinger* (performed in Italian) and Saar directed all productions of *Aida, Fidelio,* and *Otello.* Saar also conducted the single *Martha* performance during the regular season. In the spring season Luigi Arditi, who had achieved his reputation at the Academy of Music with Patti, directed her three performances, including the only other production of *Martha.*

Abbey, Schoeffel, and Grau headed their roster with Jean and Édouard de Reszke. The tenors, other than Jean de Reszke, included Paul Kalisch from the German company, and two comparatively lesser known singers, Sr. Gianini and Fernando Valero. Sebastian Montariol sang Erik in the only performance of *Der Fliegende Holländer.* Among the baritones, Del Puente had suffered considerable demotion since the season seven years earlier, when he had been a leading artist. He appeared in *Lucia* and *Il Barbiere* with Patti, but these were his only assignments. Édouard de Reszke vacillated between bass and baritone roles, and Victor Capoul, Éduardo Camera, and Jean Lassalle formed a solid group of prominent and experienced baritone singers. At the head of the sopranos was Lilli Lehmann, who had returned after a year's absence. Emma Eames was the most prominent female newcomer. Although born in China, she had moved to Boston in her infancy and was rightfully considered an American artist. Her highly successful career covered a considerable number of years, during which her roles ranged from Marguerite in *Faust* to such Wagnerian parts as Elsa in *Lohengrin* and even Elisabeth in *Tannhäuser.* Beside Eames and Lehmann the Metropolitan was fortunate to have additional strength in Emma Albani and Marie Van Zandt. Scalchi, like Del Puente, suffered a reduction in assignments in comparison with her earlier engagement at the Metropolitan. In her case the difference was not as abrupt, for she still maintained her hold on Siébel in *Faust,* Frédéric in *Mignon,* Maddalena in *Rigoletto,* while sharing the role of Urbain in *Les Huguenots.* The contralto who sang the greatest share of the large roles was Giulia Ravogli, and the remaining parts were given to Jane de Vigne.

In addition to Eames, a major American singer at the Metropolitan was Lillian Nordica. She had been born Lillian Norton and was a native of Farmington, Maine. At age fifteen she had entered the New England Conservatory of Music in Boston. After graduating with honors she sang in various oratorio groups and then departed for Europe, where she eventually made her debut at Brescia, Italy, in *La Traviata*. She continued singing in Europe and finally had successful seasons at St. Petersburg, Genoa, and Paris. After marriage, she continued to enjoy a successful career, and sang in Berlin and at Covent Garden with Jean de Reszke.[2] Her position at the Metropolitan proved unique because of the vast assortment of roles she was able to assume.

Madame Basta-Tavary was involved in one performance during the season, on March 4; it was worthy of note because it was the first of very few bilingual performances in the history of the Metropolitan Opera House. She replaced Giulia Ravogli and sang in German in a performance of *Carmen* that was otherwise sung in French. Although bilingual performances still occur occasionally in Europe, the Metropolitan throughout its history has assiduously avoided this practice except in isolated cases.[3]

THE FIRST SEASON UNDER ABBEY, SCHOEFFEL, AND GRAU (1891–1892)

Abbey, Schoeffel, and Grau's first season opened late—December 14—but after it closed, on March 12, a supplementary season was arranged. This started on March 28 and consisted of ten performances including Patti's three appearances. The final Patti performance closed the spring season on April 9.

Opening Night—Roméo et Juliette *in French with Debut of Emma Eames, Jean de Reszke, and Édouard de Reszke*

By opening with a French opera sung in its original language by a new American soprano, the new management made the shift away from German as dramatic as possible. Eames did not evoke a sensational response; however, the presence in the cast of the two de Reszkes and Victor Capoul was sufficient to provide the opening night performance with more excitement than usual. The *Times* review was particularly interesting in its appraisal of Jean de Reszke's voice, which it likened to tenors of the German and French schools. The new soprano received mildly enthusiastic comments while Édouard de Reszke was judged the outstanding artist of the evening.

> ...Miss Eames is the possessor of a sweet and full soprano voice, of a timbre midway between that of the most plentiful kind of colorature soprano and that of the average dramatic singer. Her style is agreeable. She sang her music last evening in a most painstaking and conscientious manner. Her chromatic scale in the waltz song was one of the cleanest and most finished bits of colorature singing lately heard in this city....
>
> Jean de Reszke, as the chief tenor of the company, was naturally the centre of interest with a great part of the audience. Mr. de Reszke...was once upon a time a

baritone, but he discovered that he had made a mistake and went into training for tenor roles. His voice has something of the baritone qualities in the middle and lower registers, but the upper notes are true tenor tones. His voice has none of the radiant mellowness of the Italian tenors. It resembles the German voices somewhat, but comes nearer to a French voice. It is an agreeable, though not a surprising organ. The tenor is, however, a man of genuine artistic feeling and of high vocal accomplishments. His phrasing is good and his taste is charming. He showed genuine dramatic feeling in his work last night, and will undoubtedly become a favorite with this public.

The hit of the evening, however, was made by the basso, Édouard de Reszke. This singer demonstrated in a single scene that he is a really great artist. His voice is magnificent in power and range and is of noble quality. His phrasing is superb, and his delivery of Friar Laurence's music last night was imposing in its breadth and dignity. The audience was quick to recognize his superlative merit and applauded him with enthusiasm. (*New York Times*, December 15, 1891, p.6)

Vianesi was welcomed back with an orchestral fanfare. The comment about Capoul was that he was "a very old friend, and as everyone knows that he never had a voice, he was not a disappointment." The *Times* noted that the opera "with considerable judgment was presented with the original French text."[4]

The *Tribune* reviewer was less enthusiastic about Eames's voice; the two critics disagreed considerably about her rendition of the waltz song.

...Miss Eames, not a great artist, nor yet a ripe artist, is a singer of good intuitions and fine gifts. Her voice is scarcely large enough for [the] room in which she sang last night, but it has an individuality of color that is agreeable as is the individuality which marks her acting. It is a thoroughly musical voice and its effect is lovely whenever she uses it dramatically and not merely for display. Her most ambitious effort last night was in the arietta in waltz time in the first act, and in that she was a great disappointment. It was heartless singing and technically imperfect. Infinitely better from every point of view was the duet of the second act, where she aimed at truthful declamation and not at vocal display. She is a strikingly beautiful Juliet, moreover. (*New York Tribune*, December 15, 1891, p.7)

The *Tribune* agreed almost completely with the *Times*, however, in its appraisal of the two de Reszkes:

Jean de Reszke, the tenor, is more generously equipped with artistic ability, histrionic and musical, than with voice. The organ itself is sympathetic and lends itself easily to tender accents, but it can scarcely be described as sensuously beautiful. It is more the singer's use of it than the voice itself that charms. That use, however, is prompted by most admirable instincts. His brother, Édouard, a basso with a quality tending toward the baritone...gave greater pleasure than any other male member of the cast, outside of the tenor. To what extent this is great or little praise, we lack time to explain now—other opportunities will come. The audience, after it had overcome the shock of the prologue and opening scenes, was generous in its expressions of grateful approval of the work of Miss Eames and the brothers de Reszke. (*New York Tribune*, December 15, 1891, p.7)

Nordica's Debut in Les Huguenots

Lillian Nordica's initial Metropolitan appearance on December 18 was the result of a last-minute change in plans and was not the auspicious occasion that might have been expected. Possibly for this reason the *Times*, rather than printing an actual review, simply explained the circumstances surrounding her appearance:

> ...Messrs. Abbey and Grau had nominated Mme. Albani for the role of Valentine and Mme. Scalchi for that of the page, but both were sick and unable to appear. Mme. Lillian Nordica was in Cleveland three days ago singing in concert, and the telegram summoned her to this city to take Mme. Albani's place, while Mme. Scalchi's task was undertaken by Mlle. Jane de Vigne. Mme. Nordica's performance of Valentine...was quite up to its usual level last night. (*New York Times*, December 19, 1891, p.4)

Presumably the *Times*' critic had previously heard Nordica in this role, possibly in Louisville on Abbey's independent 1889–1890 tour, which traveled as far as Mexico.[5] The *Tribune*, according her slightly more space, indicated that her performances were expected to be excellent and that this occasion was no particular exception.

> The quality of Mme. Nordica's art as a vocalist, as well as her interpretations of the part of Valentine is familiar to this public; her performance last evening was an exceedingly credible one under the circumstances. She was in excellent voice and acted with great spirit; the audience was prone to forgive one or two disasters of a lesser sort. (*New York Tribune*, December 19, 1891, p.6)

First Metropolitan Cavalleria Rusticana

Abbey, Schoeffel, and Grau produced their first real novelty on December 30, when they introduced Mascagni's one-year-old opera to the Metropolitan patrons. On this occasion it was given in conjunction with Gluck's *Orfeo*. The cast included Eames, Ravogli, Bauermeister, Camera, and Valero; Vianesi conducted. The performance was well received by both the *Times* and *Tribune*, but the opera was not the object of particularly thorough analysis as had been the case in other new productions. The *Times* allotted considerable space to a philosophical discussion of the works of Wagner, Verdi, Gluck, and Mascagni, but also commented briefly on the evening's production.

> ...the presentation of Gluck's "Orfeo," and the young Italian's "Cavalleria Rusticana" in one night was in itself a final evidence of the depth and breadth of Mascagni's artistic sincerity, of the wealth and vigor of his musical equipment...

> ...let us magnify the name of Mascagni. Like Verdi's "Otello," the music of his "Cavalleria Rusticana" is Italian to the core. Like Verdi's "Otello," this opera may be proud of its Teutonism, and that Teutonism is the same kind as Verdi's. It is the best kind of Teutonism, for in this matter Teutonism is, by reason of historical facts,

simply another term for artistic sincerity. (*New York Times*, December 31, 1891, p.4)

The *Tribune* reviewer was disturbed by the treatment given the drama by the Metropolitan's Italian artists; his fondness for the past seasons of the German company was pointedly revealed:

> How utterly foreign the modern dramatic spirit is to the average Italian opera troupe was abundantly illustrated in the performance of Mascagni's hot blooded opera. It makes no difference whether or not the work embodying that spirit be given on German, French, or Italian soil. Verdi's "Otello" was treated with as little respect by Mr. Abbey's last company as Mascagni's "Cavalleria Rusticana" was last night, yet both are Italian products. A single instance may be cited to illustrate what is meant....The instrumental prelude, made up in the familiar overture style out of melodic material drawn from the opera, is interrupted by a Siciliano sung behind the curtain by a tenor. The listener is permitted to imagine that the song is a serenade sung by Turiddu to Lola. The instrumental prelude is then resumed and brought to an impressive close. Last night the music was stopped when the Siciliano was reached, to permit the curtain to be raised on a dark stage. (*New York Tribune*, December 31, 1891, p.7)

First Hamlet *in French*

On January 10, the Metropolitan ventured its second production in French, *Hamlet*, by Ambroise Thomas. The cast was headed by an American singer from Indianapolis, Indiana, Margaret Reid. Lassalle sang the title role and was supported by Ravogli and Édouard de Reszke. The *Times* granted no space to the fact that the performance was in French other than to state so in its description; Reid's origin was also mentioned. The general tone of the review was favorable, though its final sentence suggested a facetious attitude toward the French production, announcing that "Wagner's 'Les Maitres Chanteurs' will be produced with Anton Seidl as conductor."[6] (Actually, the scheduled performance of *Die Meistersinger* was produced in Italian.)

The *Tribune* likewise did not look upon the event as one of importance and failed to comment on the language. The review did, however, refer to Lassalle's closeness to the original conception of the role:

> Time was, in Paris, when "Hamlet" was looked upon as a work of wondrous merit. Mr. Faure created the titular role, and fixed that tremendously potent thing in Paris—which is called tradition. After him came Mr. Lassalle, who won some of his first successes in the part. These successes he duplicated last night. (*New York Tribune*, January 11, 1892, p.6)

(The Faure referred to in the above quotation was Jean Baptiste Faure, who also created the role of Mephistopheles in Gounod's *Faust*.)[7]

Repertoire during the First Season under Abbey, Schoeffel, and Grau

A summary of the season makes evident the remarkable change in Metropolitan policies. Although only sixty-six operatic performances were given, they comprised twenty-six different operas.[8] Ten of the performances were part of the supplementary spring season. The Metropolitan's apparent liking for *Faust* asserted itself strongly under this management, which gave the opera eleven performances, as opposed to four apiece for its leading competitors, *Roméo et Juliette*, *Les Huguenots*, *Lohengrin*, *L'Africaine*, and the double bill of *Orfeo* and *Cavalleria Rusticana*.

Fidelio, *Der Fliegende Holländer*, *Lohengrin*, and *Die Meistersinger* received a combined total of ten performances, all in Italian. *Hamlet* and *Roméo et Juliette* were produced in French, but *Carmen*, *Faust*, and a number of other traditionally French operas were still sung in Italian. Vianesi conducted fifty performances; Saar directed nine, and Seidl four. Arditi conducted at Patti's three spring performances.

Fall and Spring Tours during 1891–1892 Season

Abbey, Schoeffel, and Grau considerably enlarged the touring itinerary of the Metropolitan company. In addition to a fall trip, November 9–December 11, a spring tour carried the company from March 14 through April 26 with interruptions. An innovation was added when the management sent out single-night tour engagements during the regular Metropolitan season. These performances were occasionally simultaneous with productions at the Metropolitan, although this was not usually the case. The 1891–1892 season also marked the beginning of the traditional once-a-week trips to Brooklyn and Philadelphia; these remained part of the Metropolitan procedure until 1937, though with an abbreviated schedule for Philadelphia. Fifty-two stage productions of opera were given, plus one opera concert in Chicago. The bulk of the performances were in Boston, with twelve, and Chicago, with twenty-one. Vianesi and Saar conducted most of Patti's performances. Louisville, Albany, and Troy each received their first visit from an official Metropolitan Opera touring company. The single concert in Chicago, in celebration of the first anniversary of the new auditorium, included excerpts from *Il Trovatore*, *Otello*, *Il Barbiere di Siviglia*, and *Carmen*. Vianesi and Saar conducted, with the "majority of company performing."[9]

1892–1893: STAGE FIRE AND A YEAR'S CLOSING

On August 27, 1892, the Metropolitan suffered the only severe fire in its long history. Front-page headlines dramatically mourned, "A Great Playhouse Gone," but the *Times* article was more realistic about the extent of the blaze:

The damage to the property is not likely to exceed $100,000 if it reaches that figure. The estimate does not include possible loss on the anticipated business of the coming season nor the loss of a great quantity of scenery....

Spontaneous combustion in the paint room is given as the cause of the fire. As Spontaneous Combustion does not seem to be in the least affected by the countless charges of arson preferred against him, it is perhaps just as well to attribute the opera house fire to him. The chances are, however, that some one of the few men who were working about the place during the early morning hours, surrounded by thousands of square yards of heavily-painted canvas, did not obey the rule which makes smoking on the premises a breach of discipline punishable by dismissal.

...William Kline is the night watchman of the building. He leaves at 8 o'clock each morning. He has to make his rounds just before that hour, and his clock shows that he was in the scenery room just at 8 o'clock...he found nothing wrong at that hour....

The stage section of the building had been entirely gutted. Piled in this pit was the ruin of everything which had been above, including the roof girders and a great iron tank which had been suspended from them. The big tank was for use in such an emergency as that of yesterday. It was supposed to hold enough water to supply the entire fire-fighting apparatus of the building. There were automatic sprinklers in the bottom of it plugged with wax which was supposed to melt if there was a fire on the stage and deluge the scenery. They melted all right and the water was released, but its effect was as nothing on the flames....

[Mr.] Stanton, who knows more about the Metropolitan Opera House than any other man, was at the scene of the fire before it was entirely put out....He expressed the opinion that the house could be got in condition for Mr. Abbey on November 21. Secretary McLaren expressed the same opinion....The prevailing opinion seems to be that by exerting every effort the building could be made ready for the opera season...so far as the redecorating and refurnishing of the auditorium is concerned. The rebuilding of the stage and its proper equipment will probably be the stumbling block if the attempt is made....

...Had the asbestos curtain with which the stage is equipped been lowered there is a probability that it would have prevented the forcing of the flames out into the auditorium and so saved all its decorations and furnishings. (*New York Times*, August 28, 1892, p.1)

The *Tribune* also mentioned the insulating curtain, although giving its material as iron, and it described a wooden dance floor that was in the path of the flames:

The iron curtain which should have protected the auditorium from the fire on the stage had not been drawn down....Over the orchestra chairs was a wooden floor which had remained in place since the last ball in the building. Smoke rose from this floor. (*New York Tribune*, August 28, 1892, p.1)

Although it has been claimed that the management had neglected to keep the tank filled with water,[10] no evidence suggests that this was so; the *Times* article (above) noted just the opposite. The cost of the destroyed scenery was estimated as follows:

As to the reports that the burning of the scenery entailed a loss of $250,000, as was generally stated, that figure will serve just about as well as any other, and is just about as accurate as any that can be given now. (*New York Times*, August 29, 1892, p.1)

Stanton's estimate of the time required to repair the opera house was promptly questioned when James A. Roosevelt, president of the Metropolitan Opera-house Company, was interviewed. Asked to comment on the position of Abbey's lease, he replied:

That is broken. Marc Eidlitz, the builder of the house, and Mr. Berg, a member of the firm of J. C. Cady & Co., the architects who drew the plans, went over the building with me today, and they both pronounce it out of the question to restore the place inside of three months, as provided in the fire clause of our lease contract with Abbey, Schoeffel, and Grau. Hence the company is released from its undertaking with the firm. (*New York Times*, August 30, 1892, p.8)

At the same interview Roosevelt admitted that the building had been insured for only $26,000, and the furniture, scenery, and costumes protected for $48,250. The combined insurance on the three-million-dollar enterprise totaled $74,250. Roosevelt gave no credence to the rumor that the opera house would be converted into a hotel.

The new managers of the Metropolitan had not done well financially during their first season and they had obtained a far better arrangement for the next three years. The *Times* reported this on the day after the fire.

After battling through a very unsatisfactory season—from a financial standpoint —Mr. Abbey last year secured the house for the season of 1892–5, three years in all, on the most favorable terms, and he and his partners were reasonably sure of making money under this contract. They practically got the house, and all the costumes, scenery, and properties for something like fifty operas for nothing, and were guaranteed a certainty besides, which assured them against any contingency of loss. (*New York Times*, August 29, 1892, p.2)

The *Tribune* commented with more detail and also suggested Carnegie Hall as a temporary replacement.

In the end Abbey and Grau wished to continue the management of the house provided the conditions would be made somewhat more favorable to them. A few days after the close of the regular season the house was leased to Abbey and Grau for three years, to begin on October 1 next. They were to have full control of it, without rent, and the stockholders were to have the use of their boxes for all performances of the regular season and to pay the managers $2,000 for each of these performances, as was done last season....

...The Carnegie Music Hall could easily be altered into a fine opera house, and probably will be sometime, but there is not time to do it for this season. (*New York Tribune*, August 28, 1892, p.1)

The *Times* entered into a series of editorials expressing thanks for the previous con-tributions of the millionaires in building the opera house and urging these same men to provide for its restoration. The first of these editorials was a long one that ap-peared in the paper four days after the fire:

> We are…compelled to look to our rich and public-spirited citizens for the subven-tion of an opera house. Let us hope that they, who have so often shown generosity in the disposition of their wealth to aid public institutions of other kinds, will perceive the seriousness of the loss with which we are threatened by the disappearance of our annual opera season, and wisely resolve to continue that support which they have given in the past to a form of art at once most attractive and most beneficial. (*New York Times*, August 31, 1892, p.4)

The *Times*, which had so many times attacked these men when the Metropolitan Opera House was being planned and constructed, continued its pleas with a testimonial to their generosity:

> …it is to be hoped that the stockholders will…put their hands into their pockets once more. So long as the Opera House remains an opera house, so long it will remain a conspicuous monument to the generosity and public spirit of the rich men of New-York, and bear testimony in their favor which may at sometime become very useful to them in more serious affairs even than German opera. (*New York Times*, September 4, 1892, p.4)

The barrage continued, and the third editorial apologized for past ungraciousness on the part of the public and press:

> The rebuilding of the opera house, by the same men who built it and have for almost a decade been sustaining it without getting any thanks from anybody, is a shining in-stance of American public spirit, and we ought all to be grateful hereafter, if we have not been grateful before, to the citizens by whom it has been exhibited. (New York Times, September 9, 1892, p.4)

The Metropolitan directors consulted the architectural firm for its recommenda-tion and estimate.

> Mr. Cady and Mr. Eidlitz roughly estimated the cost of restoring the Opera House at between $300,000 and $400,000, but they were careful to state that these figures were largely based on guess work, and might be considerably altered…

> As to the time required for rebuilding the opinions of the experts were equally vague. Messrs. Cady and Eidlitz stated in their reports that they did not think the work could be accomplished before spring. Mr. McElfatrick [the theater architect] …thought that if the work was prosecuted with diligence it could be accomplished in a "few months." (*New York Times*, September 9, 1892, p.9)

The corporation eventually decided to sell the property to satisfy any claims against it, but a group of the stockholders formed a new corporation to purchase the opera-house holdings. This corporation, named the Metropolitan Opera and Real Estate Company, was comprised of thirty-five stockholders who subscribed $30,000 each. A number of them were former stockholders in the original corporation; the balance were wealthy patrons with a sincere interest in preserving the Metropolitan. Gould, Roosevelt, and Field were prominent among those who withdrew from the Metropolitan, while the Belmonts and Juilliards led those who now became stockholders.[11] The history of the Metropolitan Opera has been actively connected with the Belmont family ever since; Mrs. August Belmont was the founder of the Metropolitan Opera Guild which figured so strongly in the saving of the Metropolitan Opera during the depression years.[12]

In the meantime, although it had become too late for Abbey, Schoeffel, and Grau to attempt an opera season, the Metropolitan was repaired and the stage facilities were considerably improved. (One of the *Times* editorials shortly after the fire had mentioned the need for revamping the stage and its equipment, which had presented problems during the first season.)[13]

According to Krehbiel, the new lease consummated with Abbey, Schoeffel, and Grau called for a rental of $52,000, which was then repaid to the managers for the use of the boxes. The term of the agreement was for five years and called for seasons of thirteen weeks of opera with four performances a week. Finally, one clause permitted the stockholders to choose six of the singers each year and to be guaranteed that at least two of those chosen would appear in each subscription performance.[14] The new season was to open on November 27, 1893, and continue with no tour break through February 25. A supplementary spring season would be given after a considerable break, during which the company embarked upon an extended tour.

SECOND SEASON OF OPERA UNDER ABBEY, SCHOEFFEL, AND GRAU (1893–1894)

The roster for the new season showed a number of valuable additions as well as some departures. Among the tenors Kalisch had departed, as had Gianini. Campanini remained, although he appeared at only one performance, a late repetition of *Faust*. Jean de Reszke continued as the first-ranking tenor. Francesco Vignas was brought in to replace Kalisch, and another tenor, Fernando DeLucia, was also added to the roster. Lassalle was still a leading baritone, but Capoul had retired and had been replaced by Eugene Dufriche. Mario Ancona provided additional baritone help. The basso contingent was again headed by Édouard de Reszke, but new singers included Armand Castlemary, an older artist who had been with the Academy of Music, and Pol Plancon, who quickly became recognized as one of the outstanding artists in Metropolitan history.

Nordica and Eames were the most prominent of the remaining female artists. Notable additions included Emma Calvé and Nellie Melba. Two members of Abbey's 1883-1884 company, Emmy Fursch-Madi and Emily Lablache, returned to the list of artists. Another American who had chosen to change her name, Kati Rolla, born Kate Wheate of Wheeling, West Virginia, appeared once as Donna Elvira in *Don Giovanni*.[15]

The staff of conductors showed one major alteration: Vianesi had left and was replaced by two Italian directors, Enrico Bevignani and Luigi Mancinelli, who was an intimate friend and disciple of Puccini.[16] Saar and Seidl continued their association with the Metropolitan.

Debuts of Calvé and Plancon

The second night of the season, November 29, presented a double bill with two debuts, one by Calvé in *Cavalleria Rusticana* and the other by the new basso, Pol Plançon, in Gounod's comic opera *Philémon et Baucis*. Both artists immediately established their value to the company. Calvé brought a great reputation with her, for she had already been acclaimed at the world premiere of Mascagni's *L'Amico Fritz* and, in 1892, as Santuzza in the first Paris performance of *Cavalleria Rusticana*. Plancon had been received with great enthusiasm in his Paris debut as Mephistopheles in *Faust*.[17] The *Times* reviewer praised both singers highly.

> M. Plancon is an admirable basso. His voice is large, full and sonorous, though not of a strikingly warm quality. But he is [a] consummate vocal artist. It is undeniable, that some of his tones last night were not absolutely true, but we are inclined to think this is not an habitual failing. His phrasing was the very essence of elegance, and he invested the role of Jupiter with a most delightful grace of style and gentleness of sentiment. M. Plancon will probably be one of the favorites of the company...

> ...Mme. Calve is a dramatic soprano of the first rank. It is a long time since New York opera goers have had the pleasure of seeing and hearing an artist of such splendid emotional force. Her voice is not a great one, but it is sufficient in power and her ability to delineate character and to express feeling is notable. Her acting is uncommonly fine for the operatic stage. In bearing, gesture, and facial expression, she is at all times eloquent and powerfully influential; and she knows how to put emotional meaning into her singing, never hesitating to sacrifice more sensuous beauty of tone to true dramatic significance. Her success was immediate, pronounced, and thoroughly deserved. (*New York Times*, November 30, 1893, p.4)

The *Tribune* critic, though not pleased with the performance, wrote enthusiastically about both new singers. Apparently he had heard Calvé's portrayal of Santuzza in Paris and already had a high opinion of this artist.

> ...if it had not been for the magnificent talents of Madame Calve the performance would have been flat, stale and unprofitable.

Emma Calvé as Ophelie in Hamlet.

...The pegs must be set high when the merits of Mlle. Calvé were descanted upon. She is a singer of true magnetic instincts, unfailing musical taste and magnetic eloquence in pose, action and vocal utterance. Her "Santuzza" is not one of the Continental marionettes of the operatic stage, but a dramatic creation—a woman with hot blood in her veins, whose voice takes color from the situation, and occasionally sets one's finger-tips to tingling. She blends declamation with singing in a manner which shows complete appreciation of the purposes of music in the modern lyric drama, yet never forgets the rights which music has independent of the drama, in such a hybrid work as Mascagni's. She will be a strong prop of the...Metropolitan throughout the season...M. Plançon won the hearts of the audience with his sonorous bass and suave and finished style. He, too, is destined to be a popular favorite. (*New York Tribune*, November 30, 1893, p.7)

Melba's Debut in Lucia di Lammermoor

Nellie Melba has certainly lived for many years in the memory of those who heard her, and beyond this, she achieved a reputation of the kind reserved for the foremost artists in any field. Her voice is ranked with the outstanding ones in operatic history. Her acting, although never considered a strong feature of her portrayals, did improve during her career and apparently became at least adequate; Dennis Arundell, a major music critic in London at the height of Melba's career, stated, in quoting from a London *Daily Telegraph* review of her performance as Nedda in *Pagliacci* in 1893, presumably at Covent Garden: "As Nedda, the erring wife, Madame Melba showed a marked dramatic advance. That she sang with fine effect needs no assurance."[18] Her December 4 debut at the Metropolitan brought superlative reviews, and the *Times* compared her favorably with Patti:

> Mme. Melba is a soprano whom this public will very speedily learn to admire. If she is not the foremost coloratura soprano of the day, she is certainly in the very front rank. Nature has gifted her with one of the loveliest voices that ever issued from a human throat. It is simply delicious in its fullness, richness, and purity. Some of the notes sound like some of those of Mme. Patti in her prime, but the voice as a whole resembles no other. It has a marked and fine individuality. It is perfectly equalized in all its registers, and its placing is a model of voice production. Indeed, Mme. Melba's whole method is a constant tribute to the veteran teacher, Mme. Marchesi. It so happens that Mmes. Eames and Calvé are also pupils of Marchesi who thus gets a splendid advertisement from the present company. It is only fair to say that Mme. Melba shows the results of more extended vocal training than either of the others. Her voice comes out in that smooth, spontaneous manner that is found only where the "automatism," as the teachers call it, is perfected. If there is anything in the method of singing that Mme. Melba does not know and does not employ without conscious effort she failed to betray it last night. Those who really love good singing will get more pleasure from the beautiful quality of her voice and its exquisite production than from her clean execution of those ornaments which seem to the best taste to be generally out of place in the lyric drama. It should be added that her style is less cold than reports from abroad had led us to expect. (*New York Times*, December 5, 1893, p.4)

For some inexplicable reason the *Tribune* did not actually review the performance. Its report spoke of Melba's debut, compared her to Patti, and discussed the merits of the three prima donnas Melba, Calvé, and Eames.

> ...Mme. Melba effected her entrance last night in "Lucia di Lammermoor" [and] the temptation is strong to say that in vocal equipment, pure and simple, she surpasses all her rivals. If there is to be competition it will be with Mme. Melba only. Comparisons between the three prima donnas will of course continue to be instituted as they bring forward their different roles.
>
> ...Mme. Melba is at the zenith of her powers. Her voice is charmingly fresh, and exquisitely beautiful, and her tone production is more natural and more spontaneous than that of the marvelous woman who so long upheld the standard of the bel canto throughout the world. (*New York Tribune*, December 5, 1893, p.7)

New York Premiere of Carmen in French

Abbey, Schoeffel, and Grau continued to pursue the new policy of bringing French operas into their native language. Calvé's first appearance of the season in *Carmen*, on December 20, featured a cast comprised of the finest artists in the company: Eames sang the role of Micaela, Lassalle was Escamillo, and Jean de Reszke was cast as Don José. Mancinelli conducted the performance, which was viewed by the critics as ideal. The *Times* reviewer indicated previous knowledge of Mancinelli's work, possibly from visits to Covent Garden. Besides touching on various aspects of the performance, the comprehensive article provided a deep insight into Calvé's interpretation.

> ...if any cast offered this season has come near to justifying the epithet "ideal" it was that of last evening. Not that any one person gave a performance which might efface all memories of the past, but because of the admirable evenness of the...individual performances and the fine spirit which underlay the whole representation....As for the orchestra, it is always good, and Signor Mancinelli has not at this late day to prove his knowledge of Bizet's score.
>
> The audience was much moved by Mme. Calve's Carmen, but what will be thought of it in the calmer light of this morning's remembrance it is not easy to tell. ...Her Carmen is a creature of unbridled passion...with a sensuous grace and careless of all consequences...in the second act her impression approached the boundaries of the hazardous. Certainly her dance must have brought up in many minds remembrances of the Midway Plaisance. In her singing she displayed again her remarkable command of vocal color. Some of her tones were almost as expressive as some of her postures, and that is saying a good deal. Altogether it was an uncommon performance, and one that will excite discussion. It was not, however, so forcible in its angrier moods as seemed desirable.
>
> M. Jean de Reszke...achieved a most decided success. His acting was full of eloquence and grace, and his conception of the part was at once manly, poetic, and

Nellie Melba in the title role of Manon.

just. He was in fine voice and sang every measure of his music beautifully....he was one of the very best representatives of the part ever seen on the American stage, and last night added to his already strong hold upon the affections of operagoers.

Mme. Emma Eames...was in good voice and she sang exquisitely. Her phrasing was, as usual, delightful, and her charming demeanor added to the effectiveness of her impersonation. M. Lassalle was the Escamillo, and a most picturesque toreador he was. He sang the popular song of the second act with vigor, and in the remainder of the opera was highly satisfactory. In every way he supplied a fitting complement to the work of the three other artists.

...On the whole, the presentation of "Carmen" was one of the best of the season. The scenery was handsome and the costumes were tasteful. The house was filled... and the enthusiasm was great and well merited. (*New York Times*, December 21, 1893, p.2)

The *Tribune* called attention to Calve's effectiveness, counselling the management that this kind of opera and performance would bring response from the patrons.

Her representation of the operatic character is certainly as frank an exposition of its contents...as the most ardent lover of realism may wish.

...[Carmen] is a most convincing illustration of how dramatic delineation may be consorted with music to the advantage of both elements, and Messrs. Abbey and Grau had occasion to learn last night that works of this character are those which can surely be relied on to win public support. (*New York Tribune*, December 21, 1893, p.6)

Metropolitan Premiere of Mascagni's L'Amico Fritz

Mascagni's *L'Amico Fritz*, when it received its first Metropolitan production on January 10, 1894, proved a pertinent example of the premise that a second opera often falls short of the success enjoyed by its composer's initial work. Although the cast included Calve and Scalchi, the audience, typical for an evening of a new, little-known opera, was not large. As might have been expected, the *Times* compared the work with Mascagni's earlier success, commenting on the difference in effectiveness:

If the performance served no other purpose, it served to correct some false impressions which have been gaining ground. One of these was that Mme. Calve's personal triumph had been so great that people were flocking to the Opera House simply to hear her. Without any desire to detract from the credit due to a great artist, it is only truthful to say that the day has gone by when one star can fill an opera house in this town. It requires a powerful cast in a strong opera to attract the public.

"L'Amico Fritz" is not a strong work. It is pretty and idyllic, but it lacks the throbbing passion that makes "Cavalleria Rusticana" so successful....

...The "cherry duet" and the intermezzo aroused the only enthusiasm of the evening until the last scene, when the tenor and the soprano warmed the audience to prolonged applause. (*New York Times*, January 11, 1894, p.4)

The *Tribune* noted the lack of coordination between story and music, and also remarked that the applause did not necessarily match the artistic merit of the work:

The story itself is a melody, pure, delicate and simple, yet it does not lend itself so readily to musical as to purely dramatic treatment. Its best meaning at many points is lost when the words are sung. When they are spoken just as they should be the hearer can believe that the birds are singing in the trees, and there is the melody. The music...meets the dramatic purpose most truly in such passages as that where Suzel and the old rabbi tell between them the story of Rebecca. It is less pertinent in the love scenes of Fritz and Suzel. There it is vigorous, full rich, warmblooded, but it does not express the...sentiment that could exist between these two persons, the one scarcely daring to love the other, and the other ignorant that he is in love. If the music had been fitted to the thought of the first author of the story perhaps it would have been lost, along with the delicate effects of acting that should accompany it, in the big opera house. As it was, these duets received more applause than anything else, and considered merely as separate songs perhaps they deserved it, but fitness is not always in exact ratio to applause. (*New York Tribune*, January 11, 1894, p.7)

Metropolitan Premiere of Massenet's Werther

The final novelty of the season, Massenet's *Werther*, was produced on April 19, during the spring season, under the direction of Mancinelli. W. J. Henderson, writing in the *Times*, stated bluntly that the opera was included in the repertoire purely for the sake of Jean de Reszke, who had enjoyed success in the role in Paris.[19] His review of the opera bore the subtitle "An Opera For Moonstruck Youth," and the appraisal of the work confirmed this opinion:

A really great composer is seldom or never deceived by mere form. The theatrical symmetry of a story will not satisfy a great musical mind. It will delve beneath the surface, and ascertain whether there is the flame of genuine fire in the motives of the story. M. Massenet has been deceived by the outward appearance of the story of Werther. The only person in the story whose passion is large enough to justify its being taken as one of the chief motives of a tragedy is Werther himself, and the issue of his passion is suicide—a dramatic futility at the best. There have been very few suicides in history whose memory assumed heroic proportions.

...The result...is that the best music of the opera...expresses the passion and despairs of Werther. His solos in the first and second acts and his reading of the poem in the third are good music, the last named being a really fine and moving piece of work. The ensuing duet with Charlotte is theatrically strong, but its impression at a first hearing was one of declamatory bustle, rather than genuine breadth. The role of Charlotte is far from satisfactory. It does not convince the hearer of anything except that Charlotte was particularly unhappy because she did not have the courage of her convictions. As for the other parts, they are mere "feeders" to the two lovers. If

M. Massenet's opera does not have lasting success it will be because it has no genuine depth. Perhaps M. Massenet is not capable of achieving profound depths of tragic passion; but certainly he will never do so in a work like "Werther." (*New York Times*, April 20, 1894, p.5)

The performance of *Werther* was a rare occasion of disagreement between Henderson and Krehbiel, who was fairly complimentary in his appraisal of the opera:

...Massenet's opera proved itself on the first hearing a work of importance, and one that offers much of interest to the...musical student....[It] must not be allowed to pass without setting it down as a work not great, in the sense that "Carmen" and "Aida" are great, though one that must appeal to fine musical sensibilities through its lyric charm, its one dramatic climax and its masterly scoring. (*New York Tribune*, April 20, 1894, p.7)

Repertoire During the Season of 1893–1894

Twenty-two operas were produced during the 1893–1894 winter and spring seasons. The success of *Carmen* was evident: it received fifteen performances, while its closest competitor, *Faust*, was performed ten times. *Cavalleria Rusticana* was presented eight times, in conjunction with *Philémon et Baucis*, *I Pagliacci*, *L'Amico Fritz*, and (once) acts one and four of *La Traviata*. Nine performances of Wagner's operas included five of *Lohengrin* and two each of *Die Meistersinger* and *Tannhäuser*. *Carmen*, *Hamlet*, *Philémon et Baucis*, and *Roméo et Juliette* were all produced in French for a combined total of twenty-seven performances. Considering double bills as one performance, the operatic productions for the season totaled seventy.

The tour included eighteen operas as well as one performance of a single act from *Hamlet*. With a double bill comprising one performance, the total was sixty-nine. *Carmen* was produced fourteen times, *Faust*, eleven. Bevignani and Mancinelli conducted all tour performances. The tour embraced Philadelphia, Brooklyn, Boston, Chicago, and St. Louis; many of the Philadelphia and Brooklyn productions took place as one-night engagements during the Metropolitan season.

1894–1895: THE THIRD SEASON UNDER ABBEY, SCHOEFFEL, AND GRAU

The season of 1894–1895 opened on November 19 with a roster that showed increase, but minimal change. Among the male artists, Campanini, Lassalle, and Vignas were the only major singers who did not return. The new members were Giuseppe Russitano and Francesco Tamagno, tenors, and Giuseppe Campanari and Victor Maurel, baritones. Del Puente returned a third time for his last season at the Metropolitan. Among the women, Calvé and Fursch-Madi were absent, the latter

194THE METROPOLITAN OPERA (1883–1908)

permanently. The new sopranos included Eugenia Mantelli and Libia Drog; Sybil Sanderson, a native of California; and Zelie de Lussan, a lyric soprano who sang such roles as Nedda in *Pagliacci* and Cherubino in *Le Nozze di Figaro*. The same four conductors were associated with the Metropolitan: Bevignani, Mancinelli, Saar, and Seidl. *Falstaff* headed the list of scheduled new productions. Tamagno, said to be the highest-paid tenor of the age,[20] had finally come to the Metropolitan for what would prove to be his only season there. He was scheduled to appear in his most celebrated portrayal, Otello. Sanderson was to be the featured artist in the first French performance of *Manon* in America.

Tamagno's First Metropolitan Performance in Otello

Tamagno's appearance as Otello, although late in his career, was of major import. Perhaps the most pertinent evaluation of the tenor's ability came from Verdi himself. He is credited with these words:

> I have heard all the celebrities from 1837 till now—Rubini, Mario, Roneoni, Malibran, Pasta, Frezzolini, and so on. Do you know whom I consider the most consummate prima donna? Patti! And the most powerfully impressive dramatic tenor? Tamagno!

The *Times* review mentioned that Tamagno had performed locally in *Otello* in 1890. Its description of his characterization of this part at his December 3 Metropolitan debut provides valuable insight into his personality and talent.

> Signor Tamagno's Otello was made known to this public in 1890, as a vivid and powerful interpretation, which justly entitled the tenor to the name of artist....at that time he gave the impression of uncommon intelligence and high ideals. It is a truth and a pity that some of his recent work [in other roles] has done much to destroy that impression and to convince thoughtful persons that his Otello owed more to the training of this Maestro Verdi than to the natural ability of the singer....
>
> ...while Signor Tamagno's Otello has lost some of the dignity that the severe restraint of the master's hand imposed upon it in earlier years, it has lost none of its tremendous power, its sweeping expression of fierce, overmastering passion, and its superb virility of declamation. Some of the very traits of Tamagno's work which calls for condemnation when exhibited in "William Tell" or "Lucia," fit so perfectly into the plan of Verdi's musical embodiment of the Moor that they become virtues. No doubt this is why the master chose him for the role and made him famous. (*New York Times*, December 4, 1894, p.4)

The *Tribune* also regarded Tamagno's performance in this particular role as unique and outstanding. Both newspapers considered the tenor to be more suited for *Otello* than for the less dramatic Italian operas:

> ...if the intentions of the composer are to be fully realized it is necessary that they be interpreted by such artists as performed that beautiful task last night. If Signor

Tamagno's performance be dissociated from that of his colleagues it would be incorrect to say that it surpassed his previous efforts. In fact, he has seldom sung so distressingly and persistently out of tune as he did last·night. But its dramatic forcefulness was brought vividly to the fore by association with M. Maurel. The extent to which these two impersonations supplement each other is altogether worthy of admiring remark. So, too, is the transforming influence of the drama of Boito and Verdi upon Tamagno individually. Between his Otello and his Edgardo, for instance, there is as great a difference as between the ideals of Donizetti and the later Verdi. Wagner substituted singing actors for mere singers in Germany, and with this score Verdi did the same thing in Italy. (*New York Tribune*, December 4, 1894, p.7)

Maurel's performance as Iago was also praised by the *Times*:

Signor Maurel's Iago had not been heard here before last night, nor can it be said that the artist himself was at all known to this public. It is twenty years since he visited America as a young man with only four years' experience on the stage. He returns to us with some of the freshness gone from his voice—never a great one—but with his art at its maturity and backed by an authority of which few operatic idols can boast. (*New York Times*, December 4, 1894, p.4)

First American Production of Elaine *by Herman Bemberg*

The first premiere of the season took place on December 17, a month after the season's opening. The new opera was favorably received by the *Times*; its criticisms did not rule out the possibility that this work might find a place in the permanent repertoire if it could overcome the unwillingness of the public to support opera by a new, unknown composer. The review found one major fault, the lack of heroic feeling at appropriate moments.

...M. Bemberg has followed the modern French method. He has abandoned, almost as a matter of course, any attempt to make use of the old-fashioned formulae of recitative, and has molded his dialogue in that accompanied arioso which is a familiar feature of the modern lyric drama. The passage from this to pure melodic form is...simple, and not abrupt....the facility with which M. Bemberg passes from one form to the other, maintaining always a flowing, melodious accompaniment in the orchestra, is one of the most excellent manifestations of his skill....In addition...we must note that the more salient features of M. Bemberg's music are grace, flexibility, elegance, and tenderness....M. Bemberg's music never assumes heroic proportions, even when it expounds itself in the form of knightly fanfares breathed through trumpets....

...Certainly no one could suspect this composer of ever being anything but amiable. But he has displayed in one part of his work the ability to be serious far beyond what the earlier parts of the opera would lead one to suspect. This is the scene in the hermit's cave. This begins with some dignified measures for the Hermit and Elaine, and at the entrance of Gavain it rises to something like energy. The entire remainder of the scene is beautiful in its warmth and flowing expression of sentiment. This one scene is enough to stamp M. Bemberg as a young man of promise. It gave to M. Jean de Reszke and Mme. Melba their best opportunity last night, and these two singers, but especially the former, made the most of it. It should be added here that M. Bemberg's orchestration is at all times rich, sonorous, and interesting. (*New York Times*, December 18, 1894, p.3)

The *Tribune* praised the same parts of the opera and in essence echoed the words of the *Times*.

M. Bemberg's music...is...of the lyric order, and it was...natural that when he was not called upon to develop a situation, but found one ready...whose emotions he might hymn, he should have been most successful. The ballade of the first act, "L'amour est pur comme la flamme," the scene at the close, "L'air est leger,"...the prayer of the hermit in the third, "Dieu de pitie," and the succeeding duet are all cases in point. They mark the high tide of M. Bemberg's graceful, melodic fancy, and exemplify his good taste and genuineness of feeling. It is not great music, but it is sincere to the extent of its depth....

...The opera was enjoyed and applauded, as it deserved to be, for the good things that were in it, and the Lily Maid had more lilies and roses and holly showered about her than she could easily pick up and carry away. (*New York Tribune*, December 18, 1894, p.7)

The *Tribune*'s reference to *Lohengrin* carefully avoided implying that Bemberg was under any overpowering influence from Wagner:

For the note of chivalry which ought to sound all through the work, M. Bemberg has chosen no less a model than "Lohengrin," but his trumpets are feebler echoes of the original voice than his harmonies on several occasions, as for instance, the entrance of Lancelot in the castle of Astolat. In general, his instrumentation is discreet and effective. He has followed his French teachers in the treatment of the dialogue, which aims to be intensified speech. He has also trodden, though at a distance, in the footsteps of Bizet and Massenet in the device of using typical phrases, but so timidly has this been done that it is doubtful if it was discovered by the audience. (*New York Tribune*, December 18, 1894, p.7)

Sybil Sanderson's Debut in the First French Production of Manon

Besides Sybil Sanderson's debut, the Metropolitan production of *Manon* on January 16, 1895, offered the attraction of being sung in the original French for the first time in America. The cast included three former members of the Academy of Music, who had portrayed the same roles in the Italian performance of the opera during the Academy's 1885–1886 season: Bauermeister, de Vigne, and Rinaldini.

The *Times* commented about the appropriateness of *Manon* to such a large opera house as the Metropolitan—an opinion that has yet to be accepted, for the opera has remained in the repertoire through all these years.

M. Massenet's music is not quite as invertebrate as the story. It is pretty, it is graceful, it is fluent, it is well written....It can be added that the music is full of delicate and poetic significance which was utterly obscured last night by the cast-iron reading of the score by Signor Bevignani....It must be added that the Metropolitan Opera House is altogether too large a place for a work of this kind....works like "Manon"...need the congenial atmosphere of a small auditorium, sympathetic conducting, an orchestra that is like a single, sensitive instrument under the director's hand, and artists who have the refinement of high comedy art. (*New York Times*, January 17, 1895, p.4)

The reaction of the *Times* to the American debutante was not particularly favorable:

And now for Miss Sanderson. In the first place, the American public will not be disappointed in her appearance....Her voice is a very light and colorless soprano of great range. It is known that she sings the high G which the Parisians call her Eiffel Tower note, but it has been remarked frequently that high notes are not her art. Miss Sanderson's voice lacks warmth and emotional character. It is pretty, but it is much too small for the Metropolitan. It frequently runs to the quality called white, and this characteristic is increased by faulty placing at times. Her high notes are thin and strident, but the upper part of her middle register is good. Her staccati are extremely sharp and wooden. Of course, she has a good comprehension of the role of Manon, and at the end of the third scene, in the duet with Des Grieux, she sang with a good deal of feeling. Her acting is graceful, but it is not convincing. (*New York Times*, January 17, 1895, p.4)

The *Tribune* was in some measures more severe, but generally its criticism was in the same vein:

Of Miss Sanderson's performance, it is possible to speak with kindly recognition, if not with enthusiasm. Her voice is not one of the kind to be associated with serious opera. It is pure and true in intonation, which is a virtue that is coming to be more and more highly valued as it grows more and more rare, but it is lacking in volume and in penetrative quality. It is pleasant in timbre and fairly equable throughout its natural register when not forced, but it becomes attenuated as it goes up and its high tones are mere trickles of sound. It is afflicted, moreover, with an almost distressing unsteadiness and is deficient in warmth. These things must be said in view of the rank which the world has been told Miss Sanderson has taken in Paris among the singers of today. That she achieves much pleasure to the eye has already been said, and it may be added that when no stress of feeling is to be portrayed she acts naturally, gracefully, and well. Her debut was witnessed by a superb audience, quickly responsive to every appeal made to its admiration. At the end of the first act, there was a fine demonstration of enthusiasm, which was for her. The second neither invited nor received a repetition of the applause, but the third again called it forth, thanks to the impassioned singing of M. de Reszke. (*New York Tribune*, January 17, 1895, p.7)

North American Premiere of Falstaff

The advent of a new opera by Verdi was as significant as the premiere of a new Wagnerian work. The fact that *Falstaff* was a comedy and had been written since Verdi altered his style unquestionably piqued the interest of the opera patrons. The cast included Eames, Scalchi, de Lussan, Maurel, and Campanari; the conductor was Mancinelli.

In a lengthy review of the February 4 premiere, the *Times* dwelt considerably upon Verdi's position in the music world as well as upon his illustrious career. He was referred to as a "modern Mozart," an epithet that the writer justified by his description of Verdi's graceful handling of the comedy in *Falstaff*.

The advent of a new work by the greatest genius now writing for the stage...is surely an event which dwarfs all other occurrences of an amusement season. It was to be expected that a numerous and brilliant audience would assemble to acclaim Maurel in a new part, for that is the fashion of the public taste, but it would not be surprising to learn that many who went to worship the priest remained to bow before the god of music. Surely none could have left the auditorium without feeling that they had been in the presence of a masterwork, and one, too, little short of miraculous in its superb vitality, coming, as it did, from the pen of a man who had passed the allotted three score and ten by a full decade.

...for many years Verdi had cherished the design of writing a genuine opera buffa, and his Wagnerian studies had served to urge him more and more toward the genre of which "Die Meistersinger" is the foremost type. But Verdi's Wagnerism has never led him to commit the fatal blunder of forgetting his nationality. He has clung through all the changes of his style to Italian methods, and consequently *"Falstaff"* comes before us a purely Italian work, though it is indeed of a new school. The elements of which it is built are old, but they are newly combined and freshly garbed, and the world has to thank the splendid genius of Verdi for giving it in these days of barrenness in art a fine and original work. Perhaps it would have been greater had it been national in character...as "Die Meistersinger" is, but the temptation to go to the source of "Otello" for an equally striking comic figure must have been strong. If Italian literature or legend had offered so excellent a subject for comedy as the fat knight, we may fancy that Boito would have seized upon it. But it may be that both poet and composer saw in *"Falstaff"* a subject known to all the reading nations of the earth, and chose it for that reason.

...But still it is not only easy to believe, but it comes with the force of conviction, that if Mozart had been born, say, thirty-nine years ago, instead of 139, and was still living he might have written "Falstaff." It is impossible to pay a higher tribute to the genius of Verdi than this.

...What will fill every hearer with delight and admiration is the youthful vigor of all this music....It bustles, it glows, it inspires, yet it never transcends the modesty of art. Rich, complex, brilliant, and eloquent as the orchestration is, it never strains for its effects and it never is blatant. Subtle, varied, polished as the recitation is, it has not a measure that cannot be sung, and neither the voice of the singer nor the ear of the hearer, is ever outraged. In short, "Falstaff" is the work of a man whose genius is unexhaustible, whose national fire burns today with the brightness of that dawn when "Ernani" [shone] as the morning star, and whose art has grown with experience and acquisition till he stands forth today a new writer and the father of a new Italian school. (*New York Times*, February 5, 1895, p.5)

The *Tribune* drew an analogy with Mozart and commented on the outstanding use of the orchestra, crediting Verdi with the addition of material to Berlioz's extensive contributions to the art of instrumentation:

> ...how has this play been set to music? It has been plunged into a perfect sea of melodic champagne. All this dialogue, crisp and sparkling; full of humor in itself, is made crisper, more sparkling, and more amusing by the music on which and in which it floats, we are almost tempted to say more bouyantly than comedy dialogue has floated since Mozart wrote "Le Nozze di Figaro." The orchestra is bearer of everything, just as completely as it is in the latter day dramas of Richard Wagner; it supplies phrases for the singers, supports their voices, comments on the utterances, and gives dramatic color to even the most fleeting idea. It is a marvelous delineator of things external as well as internal. It swells the bulk of the fat knight until he sounds as if he weighed a ton, and gives such piquancy to the spirit of the merry women...that one cannot see them come on stage without a throb of delight. In spite of the tremendous stride which the art of instrumentation has made since Berlioz mixed the modern orchestral colors Verdi has in the "Falstaff," added to the variegated palette. Yet all is done so discreetly, with such utter lack of effort-seeking, that it seems as if the art had always been known. The flood upon which the vocal melody floats is not unlike that of Wagner; it is not a development of mixed phrases, though Verdi, too, knows the use of leading motives in a sense, but a current which is ever receiving new waters. The declamation is managed with extraordinary skill, and though it frequently grows out of the instrumental part, it has yet independent melodic value, as the vocal parts of Wagner's "Die Meistersinger" have. Through this Verdi has acquired a comic potentiality for his voice parts which goes hand in hand with that of his instrumental parts. (*New York Tribune*, February 5, 1895, p.7)

First New York Staged Performance of Samson et Dalila

Saint-Saens's *Samson et Dalila* had been heard in New York in oratorio form, and its success led to the Metropolitan's February 8 production. The consensus at this time was that the work was best restricted to the concert hall, and that a stage production did not enhance the value, which was essentially musical.

> The opera is an uneven work, although it contains much that is characteristic of its gifted composer. Some of its scenes are written with immense force and earnestness, and occasionally there are bursts of genuine inspiration. There are other passages which, while they reveal the skill and ingenuity of a man of high musical ability, are after all arid. They betray a want of feeling, and at times even a lack of sympathy with the situation. The style in general has all the fluent, suave, and elegant melody of the French school; but there is a failure to reach the tragic pathos of the story. (*New York Times*, February 9, 1895, p.4)

The *Times* also referred directly to the lack of dramatic content:

> The performance last night suggested one pertinent question, and that was: Why not keep the work on the concert stage? There is so little action in it that it seems

hardly necessary to go to the trouble of dressing and setting scenery. The action is almost wholly confined to the ballet, and even that is not of a superior order. As a costumed concert, "Samson et Dalila" might have considerable attractiveness. It would require singers of a different kind from Signor Tamagno and Mme. Mantelli. The clarion tones of the one do not lend themselves readily to the accents of love, nor does the cold and somewhat forced style of the other suggest the seductiveness of the charming priestess who stole Samson's hair. (*New York Times*, February 9, 1895, p.4)

The *Tribune* review was much the same, and in addition it referred to the sparse attendance at the performance:

It did not require a very shrewd guesser three years ago when Saint-Saen[s]'s "Sampson et D[a]lila" was given by the Oratorio Society to determine that the work had an exclusively musical value, and that a stage performance would add nothing to the public appreciation of it....There was a discouragingly small audience in attendance, and absolutely no enthusiasm. It was a demonstration the meaning of which was too obvious to be overlooked. Whatever else the present regime may have taught, it has not inculcated the idea that the public are more anxious to get acquainted with new works than to hear two or three of their favorite singers. (*New York Tribune*, February 9, 1895, p.7)

Repertoire during Season of 1894–1895

Eighty-two performances of opera were offered during the regular season and supplementary season combined. Twenty-five different operas were produced. Of these, only two were by Wagner, *Lohengrin* and *Die Meistersinger*; together they received seven performances. Obviously Wagner in Italian attracted the management and artists no more than it attracted the public. *Faust*, again, was performed most often, but this season only eight times. *Les Huguenots* was produced seven times. Other than that, no opera received more than five performances; *Falstaff*, *Rigoletto*, and *Roméo et Juliette* had five apiece. Fifteen performances were given in French.

Tour performances for 1894–1895 involved Brooklyn, Philadelphia, Baltimore, Washington, Boston, Chicago, and St. Louis. The Philadelphia and Brooklyn performances were now given either on alternate nights during the regular season or, on rare occasions, simultaneously with Metropolitan productions. Bevignani, Mancinelli, and Saar again shared the conducting duties, although Saar directed only a few performances. Eighty operatic productions were given, three of which were double bills involving *Cavalleria Rusticana*, *Pagliacci*, and portions of *Lucia*. *Faust*, *Otello*, and *Les Huguenots*, in that order, were the operas most often produced on tour. Two concerts were given in Boston, both of Rossini's *Stabat Mater*.

THE FOURTH SEASON UNDER ABBEY, SCHOEFFEL AND GRAU (1895–1896)

The persistent increase in the number of performances every season made necessary a parallel increase in singers in each voice range. Among the artists who did not return, the two most prominent were Eames and Tamagno. Eames embarked on a concert tour after being dissatisfied with her contract, while Tamagno simply retired from the Metropolitan. The tenor section of the roster was enlarged by the addition of Giuseppe Cremonini and Albert Lubert, as well as a Wagnerian artist of little note, Adolf Wallnofer. Although Victor Capoul made only one appearance, he was still listed as a member of the company. Giuseppe Kaschmann, a member of Abbey's company during the initial season of 1883–1884, returned to bolster the baritone forces. A new soprano, Lola Beeth, was added, and Marie Brema strengthened the contralto list.

Mancinelli had departed and Bevignani now became the first Italian conductor. Seidl and Saar returned, and with them came a new Italian director, Armando Seppilli. Donizetti's *La Favorita* was to make its first appearance at the Metropolitan, and the American premiere of Massenet's *La Navarraise* was also promised. These two novelties, combined with *Tristan* in German sung by Jean de Reszke, constituted the only departures from a routine season. The season opened on November 18, continued through February 16, and then, after a tour, reopened for a short post-season from April 13 through April 28.

Tristan und Isolde *in German, with the de Reszkes and Nordica*

It was apparently at the suggestion of Jean de Reszke that the management decided to produce *Tristan* in German. De Reszke portrayed Tristan, his first German-language performance. Nordica appeared as Isolde, Édouard de Reszke as King Mark, and Kaschmann as Kurvenal. The November 27 performance, under Seidl's direction, was a major event of the season and of the era under the managerial triumvirate. The *Times* granted considerable space to the review.

> Standing as he had for some years at the top of the lyric ladder, the favorite tenor of two continents, [Jean de Reszke] has cherished an ambition that beyond all other things demonstrated his worth as an artist. That ambition was to sing Tristan and Siegfried. He will be no more famous with the general public, nor will he be any the greater tenor for having sung Tristan. It is not essential to greatness to be a Wagnerian artist. But M. de Reszke has proved that by adding this role to his repertoire—and in a language new to him—he had the insatiable hunger of the genuine artist to achieve the one grand and noble thing that was left for him to achieve in the whole realm of lyric art....He is one of the very few who have ever undertaken such a task at this time of life, and after such long schooling in the traditions of the French stage. Whether it is to be set forth today that he has succeeded or failed, he himself must feel the boundless satisfaction of the dramatic artist who has breathed a new atmosphere and who has glowed with the spiritual warmth of a fresh inspiration.

Jean de Reszke as Tristan in Tristan und Isolde.

He has carried his brother Edouard along with him into the strange field, and as they stand upon it today they must both realize how immensely they have widened their own artistic experience and deepened their own influence. To the true artist, these secret feelings are far more valuable than the plaudits which tell him merely that he has done well what others have done before. It was Philip Gilbert Hamerton who wisely said: "You cannot put an artist's day into the life of any one but an artist." Yesterday was an artist's day for Jean de Reszke....

M. Edouard de Reszke as King Mark was noble, imposing, and vocally stupendous. His German was quite as good as his brother's and his declamation of the entire speech of Mark at the end of Act II was superb.

Mme. Nordica, by her performance of Isolde, simply amazed those who thought they had measured the full limit of her powers. She has placed herself beside the first dramatic sopranos of her time. Her declamation was broad and forcible, and with the exception of a single false note in the duo, she sang absolutely in tune all the evening. Her conception of the part was correct, and her management of her voice in the difficult recitative was that of a mistress of vocal art. Nothing more beautiful than the close of the "Sink hernieder" passage in the duo between her and M. de Reszke has ever been heard here, and certainly it has never been sung better anywhere. (*New York Times*, November 28, 1895, p.4)

Nordica was praised even more highly in the *Tribune*, the de Reszkes again were highly complimented, and the intonation of all the artists lauded as particularly impressive.

...."Tristan und Isolde" was sung in tune throughout. Never before have we had a Tristan able to sing the declamatory music of the first and last acts with correct intonation, to say nothing of the duet of the second act...Mme. Nordica and M. de Reszke not only sang in tune, they gave the text with a distinctness of enunciation and a truthfulness of expression that enabled those familiar with the German tongue to follow the play and appreciate its dramatic value and even its philosophical purport. It is wonderful how Mme. Nordica rose to the opportunity which Wagner's drama opened to her. The greater the demand the larger her capacity. In the climaxes of the first act, in which Isolde rages like a tempest, her voice rang out with a thrilling clearness, power, and brilliancy....As for M. Jean de Reszke, his voice was warm and every note he sang a heart-throb. And Edouard as King Mark? We have always fared as well with this character, because we have always had Herr Fischer, but Edouard silenced the cavilling of all those whose ignorance touching the higher purposes of the dramatic poet have led [them] to set down Mark and Wotan as gloomy bores addicted to sermonizing. (*New York Tribune*, November 28, 1895, p.7)

Metropolitan Premiere of La Favorita

Both major New York newspapers reacted with minimal enthusiasm for the November 29 production of a work as dated as this opera of Donizetti's. The *Times* called attention to the distinct formula that dictated the composition of operas at the time this work was created. The conclusion was that the considerable progress made in opera since Donizetti's time removed any justification for producing *La Favorita*:

The reason for the decline of the works in public favor are not difficult to discover. They are to be found chiefly in the undramatic conditions which arise from the old-fashioned way of writing operas. The book of "La Favorita" has abundant theatrical strength, and treated in the direct and forceful style of the young Italian school of today, it would reveal its full merit. But Donizetti was a loyal son of the old Ne[a]politan school, which never escaped from the traditions of Handel's day. Each principal singer had to have an aria d'entrata, and the leading male and female singers must have a duo. Concerted pieces and ensembles had to come at the regulation points no matter what the stage of the action or the immediate dramatic situation.

The famous sextet in "Lucia" is an example of this...subservience to musical traditions wholly opposed to truthful dramatic compositions. Of course, the insertion of such numbers gives opportunity for melodious writing, and for the display of the finest vocal graces of the old school. But, since the rise to prominence of the dramatic French school, the rejuvenescence of Verdi, and the development of the young Italians—not to speak of the spread of Wagner's theories—there is little room for such works as "La Favorita." (*New York Times*, November 30, 1895, p.4)

Krehbiel in the *Tribune* accorded to the opera only the value of nostalgic recall:

As for the opera, let it [not] be forgotten that Schumann long ago characterized it more aptly and sententiously than is likely to be ever done again when in his "teater-buchlein" he disposed of it in one German word which can be given in English in three—"Puppet theatre music;" let it be recorded that it is a concert full of pretty tunes, and that it can serve to call up memories of the long ago...when the hearts hardened now to the strains of the late Verdi and the iconoclast Wagner, still throbbed violently to the mellifluous strains of "Ah! Leonora il guarda," "O mio Fernando" and "Spirto gentil." (*New York Tribune*, November 30, 1895, p.7)

American Premiere of La Navarraise

La Navarraise was presented on December 11 in a double bill with *Orfeo ed Euridice*, an indication of its abbreviated length. The *Times* critic considered the opera unsuccessful, and its bloodthirstiness apparently contributed to an unsatisfactorily dissonant, gloomy score. He referred to an isolated scene where Massenet had satisfied him with expressive music:

Perhaps the managers will find in the smallness of this audience another evidence that the public does not desire new works....The new work is certainly brisk and exciting enough in its incidents to satisfy the most jaded; but whether it will take high rank as an opera is another question....

...It is absolutely essential for success in the musical setting of a drama that the salient emotions shall endure long enough to enable the composer to make a musical mood picture, to establish what might be called an emotional tonality. In "La Navarraise" this is possible only at one point—the meeting of the lovers in the first scene—and as an inevitable result that is the only point at which Massenet has given us an expressive and tangible melody.

Most of the remainder of the work is a bustling and incoherent series of ex-
clamatory phrases, without melodic sequence and without even characteristic
homogeneity. The trumpets and the instruments of percussion do yeoman's duty,
and the violas strive vigorously to paint the general darkness of the mood. But it is in
the main formless music, with little or no intrinsic value. It serves as a sort of
melodramatic accompaniment to a rapid and theatrical[ly] effective action. (*New
York Times*, December 12, 1895, p.4)

The horror content of the opera offended the *Tribune* reviewer even more than it
had his colleague and he found no compensating qualities in the work. Calvé's portrayal received complimentary notice in the sense that it was considered sufficiently
frightening:

For twenty minutes last night the opera audience supped on horrors, and if visions
came in the night to the patrons of the opera of a distraught woman pulling open the
eyes of a dead man with her thumbs, they will the better be able to realize the
pleasure and penalties of the tendency given to the lyric drama by the modern
Italian school of "veritism." "La Navarraise" endures twice twenty minutes and the
other half of the time devoted to it was filled with the rattle of musketry, the crash of
big guns, the discordant braying of trumpets, the clanging of bells and the mutter of
orchestral instruments in a register too low for distinctness of utterance.

...Let it go on record, however, that Mme. Calve froze the marrow in the bones of
those who saw and heard her, and more than satisfied the desire for "blugginess" felt
by the grownup Budges and Toddies in the audience. (*New York Tribune*,
December 12, 1895, p.7)

Repertoire During Season of 1895–1896

During the 1895–1896 season twenty-six operas were performed, in addition to the
first two acts of Bizet's *Les Pêcheurs de Perles*. The works most frequently heard were
Carmen, with fourteen performances; *Lohengrin*, with nine; and *Cavalleria*, which
appeared on eight double bills with *Lucia*, *Philémon et Baucis*, and *Pagliacci*, and on
a few occasions with excerpts from longer operas. *Die Walküre* returned to the repertoire for two performances and *Die Meistersinger* was produced once. *Tristan* received seven performances and *Tannhäuser* three, raising Wagner productions to a
total of twenty-two, the highest number since the departure of the Stanton company.
Seidl was now conducting all these operas, whereas in previous seasons under the
management of Abbey, Schoeffel, and Grau, the Italian directors had led more of
the Wagnerian operas.

The tour visited several new cities; the itinerary included Brooklyn, Boston,
Baltimore, Washington, Philadelphia, Buffalo, Detroit, Chicago, and St. Louis.
Mancinelli returned to the company for the tour performances, sharing conducting
duties with Bevignani, Saar, and Seidl. Seventy-one productions were given; these
included eighteen operas.

THE FIFTH SEASON OF OPERA UNDER ABBEY, SCHOEFFEL, AND GRAU (1896–1897)

What was to be the final season for the triple management started on November 16 and closed on April 20 with a benefit concert for Kitty Abbey, the daughter of Henry Abbey, who had died on October 17. The main season ended on February 20 and the post-season opened on April 12 for five opera performances, a concert, and the benefit. Abbey continued to be listed as a manager, and the company carried out the season according to his plans and managerial policies.

The male part of the company's roster showed an overall decrease, while the female section remained about the same size. Changes had ensued, as usual, and some of them were significant. Lubert had not been reengaged, but two new Italian tenors, Antonio Ceppi and Thomas Salignac, had been added to the list. Another Wagnerian tenor, Jules Gogny, was engaged to relieve Jean de Reszke on occasions. A prominent new baritone, David Bispham, came to the Metropolitan to start a five-year stay. An American, born in Philadelphia, and trained in England, he was best known for Wagnerian parts, including Beckmesser, Telramund, Alberich, and Kurvenal. The most distinguished of the departing female artists was Scalchi, who had finally retired. Most of her roles were assumed by Eugenia Mantelli, who had been with the company since 1894, and by Rose Olitzka, who had joined the company in 1895. Félia Litvinne, a new dramatic soprano, had been engaged primarily because Nordica took a year off, feeling personal offense because Melba had been given the exclusive right to sing Brünnhilde. Mancinelli had returned to join Bevignani, Saar, and Seidl as the conducting staff.

The season promised little in new productions. Massenet's *Le Cid* was the only premiere. *Tannhäuser* was sung in French, with several members of the cast using Italian, another rare example of bilingual performance at the Metropolitan.

Siegfried *with Melba and the de Reszkes*

Melba, apparently influenced by the de Reszkes' venture into Wagnerian opera, had mistakenly insisted on the right to appear as Brünnhilde in *Siegfried*. The power of her prestige and influence with the management was obvious, for she was a singer of lyric and coloratura roles such as Lucia, Juliette, and Marguerite in *Faust*. Her December 30 failure in the Wagnerian opera was unavoidable, but the critics were kind to her because of their respect for her artistry in appropriate assignments. The *Times* granted considerable attention to the December 30 performance and obviously considered the event to be of particular importance, in all probability because of Jean de Reszke's first appearance as Siegfried.

> ...[Jean de Reszke's] conception of the part is complete, just, and masterful....there is not a single word of the text or phrase of the music whose meaning he does not understand and reveal. Furthermore, he sets the character of the young Siegfried before us....And it is always entrancing to both eye and ear. Jean de Reszke charms the senses, fascinates the fancy, and fires the imagination....

It is like uttering a truism to say that he sang the music beautifully. It would be perhaps nearer the truth to say that it was never sung before. Jean de Reszke has not now to prove his ability to voice the declamation of Wagner's later style, but it came upon us like a new revelation last night....

...[His] "wander song" was glorious in its verve and rhythmic richness, and the celebration of Nothung at the forge and the anvil was a superb example of all that is noblest in lyric art. The whole of the scene of the forest was...altogether lovely, and in the final duet, warmed to the highest glow of emotional force, the great singer soared into the [regions] of eloquence in song where the hearer could follow him only in that triumphal exultation of spirit which it is the dearest privilege of music to establish...between performer and auditor. M. Jean de Reszke's Siegfried must go into the annals of opera as one of the master creations of the century.

...M. Edouard de Reszke, as Wotan, achieved one of the greatest successes of his career. But he had less to gain than Wagner. It is a pity that the master could not have lived to behold the ideal Wotan in this drama. The massive form and dignified bearing of the great basso, and the sonorous thunder of his organ-like voice rehabilitated Wotan and made of the mysterious Wanderer a genuine father of all the gods, well worthy to hew his spear from the ash-tree Yggdrasil, and with it for his sceptre to rule the world....

Too many considerations for dismissal at this time surrounded the first essay of Mme. Melba in German opera. She appeared, of course, at a late hour, and there were evidences that even her experience and selfconfidence were not proof against the assaults of nervousness. It is undeniable and it may well be said now as later, that the quality of her voice and her style of singing are not suited to a complete embodiment of Brunnhilde, and she can be praised now only for her conscientious effort and for her ambition, which was more potent than wise. (*New York Times*, December 31, 1896, p.5)

In its review the *Tribune* made no reference whatsoever to Édouard de Reszke, a surprising omission in view of the attention the *Times* gave to that artist's performance. The *Tribune* was extremely favorable, but much briefer:

The drama lasted till after midnight, and Mme. Melba could not be seen or heard until its last hour....The accomplishment of M. Jean de Reszke was little short of a miracle. His every word, every tone, every pose, every action, was brimming over with youthful energy, vigor, and enthusiasm. His Siegfried proved to be a worthy companion-piece to his Tristan...but as an artistic creation was even more amazing, more bewildering....Mme. Melba's share in the performance cannot be discussed even in general terms. Her undertaking was more venturesome than M. de Reszke's. (*New York Tribune*, December 31, 1896, p.6)

Subsequent repetitions of *Siegfried*, of which there were four, included Litvinne in the part of Brünnhilde. The performance reviewed above constituted Melba's only venture into the Wagnerian repertoire.

Metropolitan Premiere of Massenet's Le Cid

In his assessment of the February 12 premiere of *Le Cid*, the critic of the *Times* took exception to the opera primarily because of its exceedingly French-schooled composition; clearly, he did not feel it had the expressive power of *Manon*. That *Le Cid* has reappeared in the repertoire only spasmodically substantiates his judgment.

> Massenet's music in "Le Cid" is of imposing front, but it is absolutely superficial, and will not bear analysis. It is full of the insistent vigor of rich sonority and grandiose rhythms, but it never speaks the word of true passion, nor does it ever proclaim the presence of genuine inspiration. It is built on the recognized French model, which is a good one. The French have always aimed at breadth and fluency, and have sought earnestly after dramatic expression. A strong love of elegance in style and an aversion to everything abrupt or harsh have been the most serious obstacles in the way of their attainment of deep dramatic power. With Massenet an exaggerated desire for the purely sensuous beauty of music is coupled with a grave lack of profoundity [*sic*]. In "Le Cid" he is constantly struggling for heroic utterance, but his efforts to be powerful culminate in mere sound and fury. He never once rises to the heroic proportions of his subject, and in the places where his finest opportunities appear he is little better than commonplace. There is delicate, effeminate poetry in many passages of "Le Cid;" as had already been intimated, the brasses are worked like pack horses in the desperate struggle for pompous style, but one gets simply an expression of intolerable clangor...

> Without doubt the best music in the opera is the ballet, which is full of vivacity, sparkle, and character. It is familiar in our concerts, and yet long usage does not prevent it from glowing as a real gem in its setting of pretentious platitudes. (*New York Times*, February 13, 1897, p.6)

In spite of his opinion he gave considerable credit to Massenet as a composer and especially as an orchestrator.

The *Tribune*'s appraisal of the work was not much different from its competitor's. Meyerbeer's influence was noted, as was the presence of three members of the original cast of the opera:

> Its production was due to M. Jean de Reszke, who achieved one of the early great successes of the work when it was first brought forward at the Paris Grand Opera eleven years ago. Three of the members of the original cast took part in last night's representation, appearing in the parts they "created" as the French phrase has it. They were M. Jean de Reszke (Rodrigue), M. Edouard de Reszke (Don Diegue), M. Plancon (Le Comte de Gormas)....

> The ballet music marks the high tide of Massenet's accomplishment in the score. There are woeful stretches of barrenness in the opera. Nearly all the first act is a desert; only once does the music stir the careless listener, and then in an extremely frank imitation of Jean de Leyden's prayer in Meyerbeer's "Prophet," which does the feat. Here it is the Cid's song of triumph which he repeats after he has been cheered by a vision of St. James in the fourth act. Indeed Massenet has never strayed far from the traditions of the grand opera. He has only carried Meyerbeer's liberties a little

further for dramatic effect. What is likely to amaze the musician who hears it for the first time is its want of melodic invention and the copious use of commonplace phrases. (*New York Tribune*, February 13, 1897, p.6)

Repertoire during Season of 1896–1897

Twenty-three operas were produced in seventy-six presentations during the season of 1896–1897. Leading the list were *Faust*, with twelve performances, and *Carmen*, with eight. *Siegfried* was produced seven times and *Roméo et Juliette* six. All the above, with the exception of *Carmen*, included both de Reszkes in major roles— indicating the popularity of the brothers with both the management and the public. *Carmen* numbered Calvé and Salignac in the cast. Twenty performances were given of Wagner's operas; these involved *Lohengrin*, *Die Meistersinger*, *Tannhäuser*, and *Tristan*, again all conducted by Seidl. The sole novelty, *Le Cid*, was performed only twice.

The tour, although it embraced eight cities, included only fifty-three opera performances. The tour conductors were those of the regular season, Bevignani, Mancinelli, Seidl, and Saar; however, Saar was used only sparingly. Again *Carmen* and *Faust* predominated, with twelve and ten performances, respectively. *Lohengrin* and *Siegfried* received five performances each.

RESULTS OF THE REGIME OF ABBEY, SCHOEFFEL, AND GRAU (1891–1897)

The change to opera in French and Italian (although German was eventually included because of public dissatisfacton with Wagner in any other language) brought a far more diversified audience back to the Metropolitan. The star system had returned, although the term was assiduously avoided. The inclusion of various operas at the request of Jean de Reszke and the decision to permit Melba to essay the role of Brünnhilde in *Siegfried* were two obvious indications of this; the way in which attendance figures followed casts that were comprised of the most successful, best-known artists further substantiates the fact.

In the introduction of novelties, this era saw no remarkable change from the German-opera period. Both managements introduced approximately the same number of new works, with similar lack of financial and artistic success. Exceptions, however, existed, and certainly *Falstaff* and *Cavalleria Rusticana* exceeded in popularity any of the offerings of the German period. Conversely, no new opera received fifteen performances in any one year, as had Goldmark's *Queen of Sheba* in 1885–1886. Finally, in Verdi Italian opera was fortunate to have one of its greatest composers still living, a circumstance no longer true for German opera. *Faust*, *Carmen*, and *Roméo et Juliette* dominated the Metropolitan repertoire and at the same time provided excellent vehicles for the talents of Calvé and the de Reszkes. The only Wagner opera continuing to receive regular performances was *Lohengrin*, which actually ranked third in total performances during this six-year period.

Abbey, Schoeffel, and Grau brought a large number of outstanding singers to the Metropolitan. The remarkable caliber of such artists as Calvé, Eames, Melba, Nordica, and the de Reszkes, Capoul, Maurel, and Plançon was beyond question. Among the conductors none but Seidl ever achieved lasting reputation; yet the respect that Mancinelli received from Puccini, as well as from the press, precluded any suspicion that he might have been merely adequate as a conductor. Reviews of performances consistently praised individual artists rather than overall productions, as had been the case during the German opera period. The chorus and orchestra were seldom mentioned, and conductors received far less attention than had been granted to Seidl and Leopold Damrosch during the German-opera years. The slow restoration of German opera brought attention more to the artists than to the operas or the productions thereof.

Complete financial records for the Abbey-Schoeffel-Grau seasons apparently were not made available to the press or to Krehbiel, who was on close friendly terms with all the members of the managerial firm that guided the Metropolitan from 1891 through 1897. At the time of the fire Abbey admitted that the first season of the triple management had been financially unsuccessful. The execution of a new lease at that time gave Abbey, Schoeffel, and Grau a better chance to achieve financial reward, and this was forthcoming. The first season after the conclusion of the new agreement resulted in a profit of about $150,000, but unfortunately the managers lost a considerable amount on other enterprises.[22] The firm found it necessary to seek reorganization, and in 1896 William Steinway headed a group who assumed the debts of the company and issued stock and notes to the creditors. At that time all three managers were placed on a yearly salary of $20,000 each. Ernest Goerlitz was installed as secretary and treasurer, a post he held until Heinrich Conried assumed the management of the Metropolitan in 1908. Abbey died the following October, and Schoeffel became greatly involved with a new major venture, the Tremont Theatre in Boston, which he purchased in the dissolution of the firm of Abbey, Schoeffel, and Grau, Ltd. Grau, in effect, became manager of the company. The season of 1896–1897 resulted in a profit of about $30,000, but this was only after a number of artists had assisted Grau, who was acting in behalf of the deceased Abbey, with a loan of that amount. The de Reszkes and Lassalle were among the group that loaned the money to Grau, who repaid them all before the season ended. Grau and his associates formed a new company to continue the production of opera at the Metropolitan; this company became known as the Maurice Grau Opera Company.[23]

The final tribute to Abbey was the testimonial benefit concert for his daughter Kitty. Calvé, Eames, Litvinne, the de Reszkes, Plançon, and many lesser-known artists contributed to a program that included excerpts from *Roméo et Juliette*, *Carmen*, *Le Cid*, and Boito's *Mefistofele*; Mancinelli, Bevignani, and Seidl shared the conducting. The concert was on the final night of the season, April 20, 1897.

CHAPTER 6

The Metropolitan Opera House
Under the Management of Maurice Grau
(1898–1903)

Since the first season of the Metropolitan, Maurice Grau had established his reputation as an astute administrator. He had been valuable to Abbey during that initial venture, and the last five years had seen him as an active partner in the Metropolitan Opera management. He was described as "a knowledgeable businessman less concerned with his own operatic tastes and most concerned with the financial results of the Metropolitan."[1] He was also acknowledged to be "tactful and diplomatic but strong in dealing with temperamental singers who needed a firm hand; he would put up with no nonsense."[2] Krehbiel, who was viewed as one to whom much confidential information was available, had high regard for Grau and stated that under the triumvirate, although Abbey was "nominally the leader of managing directors...it was Mr. Grau who did the practical work of management."[3] During the season of 1896–1897, the last that was officially under the management of the three men, Grau in essence had been the sole manager, since Abbey had died and Schoeffel had turned his energies elsewhere.

Grau determined not to give any opera at the Metropolitan during the season of 1897–1898; the directors granted him a lease that began the season afterward. The opera house was leased on several occasions to Charles Ellis and Walter Damrosch, both of whom were involved in operatic production during this period. Ellis was the manager of the Boston Symphony Orchestra as well as the personal representative for Melba. Damrosch, still attempting to compete with Seidl, was Ellis's musical director until he decided to enter the symphonic field full-time. His own experiences as an impresario had not been successful, whereas Ellis was in a position to wield both financial and artistic influence. Damrosch did, however, succeed in working out an exchange system with Abbey, Schoeffel, and Grau, whereby they had loaned each other singers during the season of 1896–1897.[4]

During the year 1897–1898 Grau managed Covent Garden, where he introduced many new artists, a need that the English opera house had felt under its previous managerial leadership, that of Augustus Harris.[5] Grau was associated with Covent

Garden until 1901, when he withdrew completely from its operation. When Grau made his decision not to produce opera at the Metropolitan during 1897–1898, he did so partially because Eames and Melba were not available. When Ellis opened his season, Melba, who was under his management, headed his company, which also included Nordica, Fischer, and David Bispham, all previous Metropolitan artists.[6]

Death of Anton Seidl

In March, 1898, Anton Seidl died unexpectedly after a brief illness. His death was a blow to the operatic world and in particular to the Metropolitan Opera, where almost assuredly he would have continued his outstanding career. He had emerged as the choice of both public and press during the earlier competition with Walter Damrosch. Throughout the seasons of German opera Stanton had been willing to continue Damrosch's engagement in spite of violent opposition that asserted itself as early as 1885. At that time a *Musical Courier* article, reflecting the opinion of many who were preparing a petition to the Metropolitan management, assumed that Damrosch would be removed.

> Meanwhile, the address of subscribers to the Metropolitan Opera House season to the directors, requesting the withdrawal of Mr. Walter Damrosch as conductor in favor of Herr Seidl, is *in statu nascenti*, and it will be signed by such an overwhelming number of names that the directors will not be able to turn a deaf ear to the just demand. They will do so all the less when they…compare the financial status of affairs. Figures do not lie, and they will prove conclusively that on the nights when Walter Damrosch vehemently swung the baton the receipts were considerably smaller than on the evenings of Herr Seidl's conducting, and this argument…will weigh more heavily with the directors than the counter plea of debts of gratitude to the memory of the father, certainly not atoned for by the son's bad conducting. We understand that the address of the subscribers is to be handed to the directors [during] the company's fortnightly absence from New York, when they…perform in Philadelphia, and that Mr. Walter Damrosch, after the company's return, will be withdrawn from public sight as a conductor. To some people this will be a serious loss of amusement, for certainly no more amusing sight can be imagined than this youthful Adoni[s] sitting for a quarter of an hour before each rising of the curtain in the conductor's chair and leering at the ladies in the boxes and making the most of his opportunities for demonstrating his personal vanity.[7]

In 1887 Seidl announced his resignation to go to the Royal Opera House in Berlin. At that time he was highly praised and his leaving the Metropolitan was greatly regretted. Ultimately he chose to remain at the Metropolitan, but the following tribute was typical of those paid him when his departure seemed imminent:

> While we are extremely sorry to lose such an eminent man from New York's musical life and from the cause of Wagner and German opera in this city, we heartily congratulate Mr. Seidl on the promotion he has attained, for the position of court-conductor at the principal opera-house of Germany is, after all, a trifle more impor-

tant and satisfactory than the one as first conductor at the New York Metropolitan Opera House.[8]

Seidl was sufficiently enthusiastic about Wagner to obtain the rights to the composer's C-Major Symphony for the season of 1887–1888.[9] He also wrote occasionally on Richard Wagner, and the proof of an undated article by Seidl indicated a vast reverence for the works of the German reformer:

> ...the old style was still firmly established in tradition, and Wagner bravely set himself to the task of destroying tradition. He saw that the passions of mankind offered material for a noble drama fit to be the vehicle of a noble music. So he proceeded to look about for subjects suitable to his purpose. These he found in the Norse legends, which he drew upon extensively and which he developed and almost transformed by his genius.[10]

Seidl received countless letters of praise. One, signed "myself" and bearing no date, compared Seidl, Thomas and Damrosch. The letter was written in Philadelphia, where the writer presumably had heard Seidl and Damrosch conduct opera performances and Thomas lead his symphonic society:

> After...our able devoted "Thomas" and quite interesting "Damrosch"—the magnetism of Seidl's leading is indeed a revelation.[11]

An American composer, Louisa Morrison, wrote to Seidl in 1891, projecting a reverent attitude typical of the many tributes to Seidl's ability and inspiring effect:

> I have often applauded the *great Seidl* at the Metropolitan—sometimes I could not, I was rendered mute by the *great leader* and his Orchestra![12]

Perhaps more important, in 1894 Cosima Wagner requested that Seidl coach Nordica so that the soprano would be ready to sing at Bayreuth the following summer.[13] Three years later Siegfried Wagner stated in a letter to Seidl, "You are destined for awhile longer to represent and advance our cause in foreign lands."[14]

Felix Mottl, who himself was to conduct at the Metropolitan Opera during the first year of Heinrich Conried's stewardship, had been intimately associated with Bayreuth and conducted there for many years. In 1897, when Seidl was due to direct the summer festival, Mottl was apparently involved in preparing some of the works in advance of Seidl's arrival. Mottl was in poor health and obviously had great faith in Seidl's ability to assume many of his obligations at Bayreuth. He wrote to Seidl in May inquiring when the latter would be able to arrive and assume musical responsibilities:

> Dear Friend:
> You would put me in duty of great thanks if you could indicate to me exactly at what time you could be in Bayreuth for rehearsals and performances this summer. I

can only give my free time [for Bayreuth] this year at greatest sacrifice to my health.[15]

After Seidl's death the tributes from major musical personages, friends, and members of the press and public were voluminous.[16] His funeral, held at the Metropolitan Opera House, was an impressive, solemn event attended by a capacity audience of German opera enthusiasts who were deeply moved at the loss of the most celebrated conductor of Wagner's works.

THE FIRST SEASON OF OPERA AT THE METROPOLITAN UNDER MAURICE GRAU (1898–1899)

The first major change that was evident under Grau's management was the large increase in artists on the roster. The initial season of 1883–1884, under Abbey, had listed twenty male and twelve female singers. During the final season of the joint leadership of Abbey, Schoeffel, and Grau, the roster had grown to forty-three, with twenty-seven men and sixteen women. Now, as the Maurice Grau Opera Company announced its prospectus, the list of singers had increased to fifty-two, of which twenty-six were women and twenty-six men; the number of male singers had decreased by one from the previous season.

The new singers of note included a contralto, Ernestine Schumann-Heink; a heroic tenor, Ernest Van Dyck; and a Wagnerian baritone, Anton Van Rooy. A young American singer, Suzanne Adams, also joined the company. Van Dyck's importance was minimized by the return of Dippel, who had been a leading Wagnerian tenor during the season of 1890–1891. Thomas Salignac and Jean de Reszke both returned, and Albert Saléza was added, giving Grau a full complement of leading tenors. Maurel, Campanari, Bispham, and Édouard de Reszke were joined by a new baritone, Henri Albers, as well as by several serviceable second-line singers. Plançon was still the leading basso, but Lampriere Pringle was added to the roster as an alternate in the major roles.

Among the women, both Nordica and Lehmann returned, the latter after an absence of seven years. Marie Brema was reengaged, as was Zelie de Lussan. Melba and Eames still led the lyric sopranos, but Sembrich had returned, and competition was keen. Bevignani and Mancinelli were joined by Frank Schalk, a German conductor whom Grau had brought with him from Covent Garden.

On the whole the roster was remarkable. The presence of Melba, Sembrich, and Eames as lyric sopranos points to the wealth of singers that Grau had brought for his first season. Nordica, Lehmann, Brema, and Schumann-Heink provided an equally impressive roster of Wagnerian artists. With Dippel, de Reszke, Van Dyck, Salignac, and Saléza, a major tenor could be heard at every performance. The list of baritones and basses, including such singers as Maurel, Édouard de Reszke, Van Rooy, Bispham, and Plancon, was no less impressive. Wagner was performed in German, although multilingual casts were still used on occasion. French and Italian operas could be heard in their original languages. Only in the area of novelties was the prospectus unimpressive; one new opera was promised, *Ero e Leandro*, by Mancinelli. The season opened November 29 and lasted through March 26, the longest to that date in the history of the Metropolitan Opera.

Debut of Van Rooy as Wotan in Die Walküre

Die Walküre was produced on December 15, and it was the vehicle for the debut of the new baritone, Anton Van Rooy. The cast included Dippel as Siegmund, Eames as Sieglinde, and Nordica as Brünnhilde. The occasion also marked Franz Schalk's first appearance as a conductor, and he was favorably received. As to the acceptance of Wagner without Jean de Reszke, the *Times* was not optimistic in its prognosis; but it was highly enthusiastic over Van Rooy's debut:

> It is known...that Mr. Grau is not personally a lover of Wagner's dramas. However, he is not in the business of management to gratify his personal taste, but to make money and that is to be done only by giving the public what it likes. Whether the influential box-holders of the Opera House will tolerate the Wagner dramas when they are not used simply as vehicles for the display of M. Jean de Reszke's art is, of course, something yet to be seen. If Wagner has suddenly become fashionable, then "Die Walkure" with Andreas Dippel as Siegmund, will be welcomed again. But we have grave doubts whether "Der Ring des [Nibelungen]" would have been accorded any consideration in Fifth Avenue, if it had not already been patronized by the Mansion House and Belgravia. As for our general public, that, we know, is Wagnerian, and Mr. Grau had a taste of its hearty approval last night....

> ...The most important individual performance was that of Anton von [sic] Rooy as Wotan....He is a man of majestic figure, of splendid bearing, of enormous voice and intense dramatic temperament. He understands the management of his voice much better than bassos of German schooling usually do, and consequently is able to throw a great variety of light and shade into his singing. His conception of Wotan is fine, and he made a deep impression of his audience last night. (*New York Times*, December 15, 1898, p.5)

Van Rooy's immediate success was assured by the complete agreement of the *Tribune* critic.

> ...the most complete illustration was found in Herr van Rooy, in whose case musical and dramatic utterance seem to be so completely merged that there is no desire in the listener to differentiate between them. Moreover, he has a beautiful voice, which he emits without effort, as if it were responsive to feeling alone, as if, indeed, it were the product of that feeling and depended neither on reflection nor will. (*New York Tribune*, December 15, 1898, p.6)

Schumann-Heink's Debut as Ortrud in Lohengrin

On the day following Ernestine Schumann-Heink's January 9 debut, the first press notice to mention the performance was one describing Mrs. Astor's "annual ball." Her residence was on "upper Fifth Avenue," and the opening of the description stated:

> The guests began to arrive at 11 p.m., many coming directly from the opera, which they left before the final curtain fell on "Lohengrin." (*New York Times*, January 10, 1899, p.4)

Notwithstanding this notable event, the press apparently remained to review in its entirety the debut of a woman who, if this is possible, lived to become a legend in opera in America. Of the two major reviewers the critic at the *Times* was less enthusiastic; nevertheless, he accurately predicted a notable future for the artist.

> ...Mme. Schumann-Heink as a debutante claims the place of honor. Her voice is none too easy to describe. It is easy to believe there is more in the voice than was heard last night. It has the contralto quality, especially in its rich and full lower register. The upper notes last night seemed strained and shrill, but this may have been due to temporary causes. It is a voice of sufficient power and fine dramatic character, if not always of sympathetic quality. Mme. Schumann-Heink's style of delivery is essentially German. Her attack is often forced and uncertain in its grasp on the pitch. She often slides to her tones with vicious portamento effect, which is one of the commonest faults of German singers. She declaims superbly and with most eloquent revelation of the meaning of the text, which she enunciates admirably. Her cantilena was not exhibited last night, for she read every measure of Ortrud, even in the duet with Elsa, in what has come to be known as the ultra Wagnerian style. Her conception of the part proved to be perfect and her action was notably good. Her byplay in the first act has not been excelled here. She made a strong impression on the audience and her first appearance may be set down as successful. She will undoubtedly prove, as the season goes on, to be a valuable acquisition to the dramatic force of the company. (*New York Times*, January 10, 1899, p.7)

The *Tribune's* reviewer was obviously impressed, and he placed Schumann-Heink in the tradition of such interpreters of Ortrud as Brandt, Fursch-Madi, and Lehmann (who was a member of the company at this time but did not sing the role). Nordica and de Reszke were in the cast with Schumann-Heink, making the occasion an eventful one.

> The particular interest in the occasion centered in Mme. Schumann-Heink's impersonation of Ortrud, the character which Wagner said he had designed as the type of loveless woman. If that feature of Ortrud's nature has its strongest exemplification in its paganism, then Mme. Schumann-Heink realized it as it has seldom been realized in her invocation of the old Teutonic deities in the second act. Candidates who ask for the admiration of New York in the character of Ortrud do not walk upon a path of roses. To confine the record to the performances at the Metropolitan Opera

House, memories are still alive of Mme. Fursch-Madi, Fraulein Brandt and Mme. Lilli Lehmann in the part, and they are memories which are not easily elbowed out of the way. The excellences of those impersonations need not be either depreciated or ignored in paying tribute to Mme. Schumann-Heink. A reputation calculated to set high the pegs of expectation has preceded her from Germany, and more especially from London, and that expectation was not disappointed; yet we can easily believe she was not either at her best or in her best role last night. (*New York Tribune*, January 10, 1899, p.8)

Krehbiel's review showed his conception of the part of Ortrud as more evil than its usual characterization.

Ortrud is as cruelly difficult a part to sing as it is to act. Wagner gave no heed to the natural limitations of the human voice when he wrote it; it was an extraordinary character in his dramatic scheme, and he demanded that she be an extraordinary one in his musical scheme. Voices capable [of] reaching its depths and its heights and remaining true and beautiful as well as dramatically expressive, are rare. Mme. Schumann-Heink may be said to belong in that category, but [her] high register is by no means as beautiful as her low (which is exquisite in its union of volume and quality), and when she wins admiration in the passages of which Wagner thought neither of contralto or soprano, but only of his Frisian creation, half woman, half witch and all wickedness personified, she compels it by virtue of her thrilling use of tonal color, her giving out of Wagner's ideal, which she has ab-sorbed completely. Her work last night kept the corridors buzzing with enthusiastic ejaculations between the acts. (*New York Tribune*, January 10, 1899, p.8)

First Uncut Ring *Cycle*

Although *Die Walküre* had been performed several times and *Siegfried* once during the season, only on January 12 did the Metropolitan embark on its first group of *uncut* performances of Wagner's *Der Ring des Nibelugen*. The cycle spanned twelve days, all evening performances. *Die Walküre* was produced January 17, *Siegfried* on the 19th and *Götterdämmerung* on the 24th; this was the first Metropolitan performance of *Götterdämmerung* to include the "Norn Scene." Schalk conducted all four performances. Dippel appeared as Froh in *Das Rheingold* and Siegfried in *Siegfried*. Van Dyck sang Loge in *Rheingold* and Siegmund in *Walküre*, while de Reszke appeared as Siegfried in *Götterdämmerung*. Schumann-Heink showed her versatility and the breadth of her repertoire by performing as Erda and Flosshilde in *Das Rheingold*, Fricka and Waltraute in *Die Walküre*, Erda in *Siegfried*, and Waltraute and the third Norn in *Götterdämmerung*. The other female artists to assume major roles were Brema (Fricka in *Das Rheingold* and Brünnhilde in *Die Walküre*), Eames (Sieglinde), Lehmann (Brünnhilde in *Siegfried*), and Nordica (Brünnhilde in *Götterdämmerung*). Bispham appeared in three performances, as did Van Rooy and Pringle.

Reviews of the performances were all favorable toward conductor and singers.

The attendance was excellent and no evidence suggests that any language other than German was used. The cycle was repeated as a matinee series on March 13, 14, 16, and 20. The only significant casting change was that Lehmann portrayed three roles: Sieglinde, and Brünnhilde in both *Siegfried* and *Götterdämmerung*. Since this was her final year at the Metropolitan Opera House, it may be assumed that she was granted this privilege in the sense of a farewell. Her final appearance at the Metropolitan was at the Seidl memorial, when she sang Brünnhilde in an excerpt from the third act of *Götterdämmerung*.

American Premiere of Mancinelli's Ero e Leandro

Luigi Mancinelli's excellent reputation with the Metropolitan patrons failed to bring a large audience to his two-year-old opera at its first American performance on March 10. The *Times* noted considerable influence from Boito, who had written an earlier version of the same story. The impact of Verdi's *Falstaff* on Mancinelli's choral writing in the second act was also mentioned. In general the composer was complimented on his experienced treatment of problems involved in constructing an opera:

> ...Signor Mancinelli's long connection with the Opera House as principal conductor has earned him a large popularity. This ought to have made the audience larger but it is hard to overcome the antipathy of New York operagoers to a novelty....

> Signor Mancinelli's opera was first sung as a cantata at the Norwich festival of 1896, and as an opera the following year. It may be noted here in passing that there is or was another opera of the same name, text by Arrigo Boito and music by Giovanni Bottesini, produced at Turin on January 11, 1879....

> If...any one composer is to be pointed out as Signor Mancinelli's model, it is Boito, for whom in his music he evinces a special partiality. This is to be found in the color of most of the solo parts, in the treatment of the harp, and in the writing of the ensembles. To this, however, one exception must be made. The fugue in chorus at the close of the second act is the result, undoubtedly, of the composer's admiration for the splendid mastership shown in the score of Verdi's "Falstaff," which the music lover will remember ends with a piece of strict polyphonic composition....

> The choral parts and the ensembles are well made, and the orchestration is always rich in eloquent combinations of color, in which the harp provides the most uncommon tints, chiefly through its skillful employment as the foundation of the harmony in unexpected places. The vocal parts are written with the judgment of an experienced conductor, who might be expected to know what would sing well, and there are therefore numerous opportunities for the soloists to win that applause without which existence on the operatic stage would be but an idle waste of time. On the whole, the music, while not remarkable for invention, is pleasing, well-made, and creditable to the composer, and it has the singular merit of being always in keeping with the general character of the scene and the action. (*New York Times*, March 11, 1899, p.6)

Mancinelli had established himself as a conductor with the New York public and apparently he was a favorite with the stockholders. (The *Tribune* review of the premiere of his opera stated that a far greater percentage of subscribers' seats were occupied than seats available at the box office.) The cast seemed interested in the work, and according to the *Tribune*, Mancinelli, if not a brilliant composer, was well enough versed in the necessary fundamentals to compose a more than satisfactory opera:

> ...Signor Mancinelli...is only the last of a number of composers who have yielded to the ambition to sing the love and the fate of the strong swimmer and his love, and it must be set down as admirable how the writer of the book—no less a man than Signor Boito—has succeeded in grouping a number of scenes around the familiar incident, and how Signor Mancinelli has extended the unessentials and sweetened them with music till the sequence of meetings and talkings actually takes on the semblance of a drama. But this is the province and the power of music in the case of stories which come from, and therefore go to, the Roman heart-stories which deal with the musical passion without conventional alloy....[*Ero e Leandro*] is worthy of careful consideration for its text as well as its music...[and] the opera was heard with something more than mere respect...it was sung with genuine enthusiasm by Mme. Eames, M. Saleza, and M. Plancon as the principals...the composer, who conducted it, was made to understand by sincere applause that his work was appreciated highly....(*New York Tribune*, March 11, 1899, p.9)

Testimonial Performance for Anton Seidl

On March 23, two days before the season ended, the Metropolitan presented a testimonial concert in memory of Anton Seidl. In essence the proceeds were to be donated to his widow, with provisions for their disposal after her death. The program was completely composed of Wagnerian excerpts,including Act I of *Lohengrin*, Act III of *Die Walküre*, Act III of *Die Meistersinger,* and Act III, beginning with the funeral music of *Götterdämmerung*. Mancinelli conducted the *Lohengrin* excerpt, and Schalk directed the other three. Participants included almost all the major singers of the company, notably Nordica, Brema, Lehmann, Albers, Jean de Reszke, Van Rooy, Édouard de Reszke, Dippel, and, surprisingly, Sembrich, who managed to penetrate the Wagnerian program by singing the role of Eva in the *Meistersinger* scene. This is not a demanding section for Eva and is sufficiently lyrical so that Sembrich could sing it creditably. Financially, the program was also a success.

> The audience was very large, and it was stated that the receipts amounted to $16,508. This amount is to be invested for the benefit of the conductor's widow, and after her death will go to found a free scholarship in music in Columbia University. Portraits of Mr. Seidl were hung in the foyer and over the stage last night, but otherwise there was no attempt to make the occasion one of especial pictorial effect. (*New York Times*, March 24, 1899, p.7)

Seidl's career both at the Metropolitan Opera and elsewhere was illustrious. He came to the Metropolitan in 1885, when he replaced the deceased Leopold Damrosch, and remained there throughout the era of German opera. During that period he was the central force in six seasons of what has been considered to be the most artistic series of performances in the history of the Metropolitan. He conducted all but a few scattered performances and directed all the premieres of the Wagner operas. He remained at the Metropolitan during the five years following the collapse of German opera and along with Abbey, Schoeffel, and Grau, led the rebuilding of the German wing of the production department at the opera house. The new era of Wagner that included the de Reszkes and Nordica enjoyed the same leadership from Seidl that he had accorded to Lehmann, Brandt, Niemann, and Alvary.

Throughout his tenure at the Metropolitan, Seidl also conducted symphonic concerts in the New York area; he directed the Philharmonic Society from 1891 until his death. He had frequently conducted at Bayreuth, and enjoyed the same spectacular success there that was his at the Metropolitan. Among his personal papers, countless letters reflect the esteem of such persons as Richter, Smareglia, Cosima and Siegfried Wagner, Mottl, Lehmann, and Kalisch, not to mention his teacher, Wagner himself. Unquestionably, no conductor at the Metropolitan ever achieved his reputation, with the possible exception of Toscanini, whose career at that opera house lasted only seven years during which he shared the podium with numerous other conductors, including Alfred Hertz and Gustav Mahler. Seidl's conducting duties during his first six years at the Metropolitan involved practically every performance. They included operas normally in the French and Italian repertoires, as well as the usual German operas, which during later years his reputation brought to him exclusively. He was active at Columbia University where he was listed as a faculty member for a number of years. The most extraordinary aspects of Seidl's career were the unanimity of his excellent reviews by major music critics and the high esteem in which he was held by his fellow artists as well as by the public.

Repertoire during Season of 1898–1899

Grau's first season included the largest total of opera presentations up to that time, one hundred performances, exclusive of concerts, which had also increased considerably to seventeen. (The benefit for Auguste Seidl-Kraus was not included in this total.) A new practice was instituted on January 22, 1899, when Moritz Rosenthal appeared as piano soloist in a Sunday night concert and brought his own conductor, Arthur Friedheim. Friedhiem directed only the Chopin E-minor concerto; the balance of the program was conducted by Schalk.

Lohengrin received nine productions to lead the list, and *Faust* was reduced to eight performances. *Roméo et Juliette*, *Tannhäuser*, and *Die Walküre* were each produced seven times. Wagner was again in the ascendancy, and thirty-six performances of his operas were given. The Wagnerian repertoire for this season included *Götterdämmerung*, *Lohengrin*, *Das Rheingold*, *Siegfried*, *Tannhäuser*, *Tristan und Isolde*, and *Die Walküre*. Mancinelli still conducted *Tannhäuser* but Schalk directed all the other Wagnerian operas. Bevignani and Mancinelli frequently alternated on the same operas, whereas Schalk's conducting was limited to Wagner operas. The concerts were fairly equally divided: Bevignani conducted four, Mancinelli six, and Schalk seven. Melba sang only four performances during the season, two each of *Roméo et Juliette* and *Faust*, many of her roles being assumed by Eames and Sembrich. Twenty-seven different operas were performed; of these, *Cavalleria Rusticana* and *Philémon et Baucis* appeared only once to comprise the sole double bill.

Grau's tour was shorter than might have been expected, totalling sixty-two performances. The gradual resurgence of Wagner was also evident in the tour, which included twenty-two Wagnerian productions. The three conductors of the regular season also accompanied the tour. Mancinelli conducted the first two *Lohengrin* performances; thereafter Schalk, who made his debut on tour in Chicago, conducted all the Wagner operas. Melba sang no tour performances whatsoever this season. The final count on a number of operas was remarkably close to that of the regular season. *Lohengrin* and *Faust* led with nine and eight performances respectively, while *Roméo et Juliette* and *Die Walküre* had seven each. *Il Barbiere de Siviglia*, with six performances, was the only other opera to dominate. The tour traveled to Chicago, Brooklyn, Philadelphia, Boston, Baltimore, Washington, and for the first time, to Pittsburgh.

THE SECOND SEASON OF OPERA AT THE METROPOLITAN UNDER MAURICE GRAU (1899–1900)

The prospectus for Grau's second season showed a conspicuous absence and an equally important addition. Jean de Reszke, who had not been well, took a year off for rest and rehabilitation. He was replaced by the French tenor Albert Alvărez. A major addition to the roster was Antonio Scotti, who embarked on a career that would keep him at the Metropolitan Opera House through 1933, when he finally retired. During this entire period he sang major baritone roles, becoming particularly celebrated for certain parts, especially Scarpia in *Tosca*, and Chim-Fen in *L'Oracolo*, by Franco Leoni. Lehmann had retired from the Metropolitan and Melba was absent for the year. A new lyric-dramatic soprano, Susan Strong, an American, sang many of Lehmann's parts, as did Nordica and Johanna Gadski, who was new to the roster this year. Gadski was destined to create an excellent name for herself and years later, to become involved in one of the few war scandals that the Metropolitan had to deal with. Her husband, Hans Tauscher, was arrested in 1916 by the United States Secret Service for conspiring with agents of the German government to sabotage the Welland Canal, which forms part of the St. Lawrence Seaway in Canada. (The canal was not opened until 1931 but was under construction at the time.) Gadski was dropped from the Metropolitan Opera roster in 1917, although no evidence was found of any disloyalty on her part.[17]

The list of conductors showed changes and an increase. Bevignani and Mancinelli returned, but Schalk did not. Emil Paur became the conductor of German opera. Metropolitan concertmaster Nahan Franko led a few concerts, as did Ernst von Schuch, the highly respected conductor of the Dresden Court Opera. Schuch also conducted the season's last performance of *Lohengrin*. Paur, then conductor of the Philharmonic Society, appeared at the Metropolitan only during this season. His debut with the company took place on November 13, when he conducted *Tannhäuser*.[18] *Fidelio* returned to the repertoire for the first time since 1896, this time with Milka Ternina in the title role. She had created the part of Kundry in *Parsifal* at Bayreuth. The first Metropolitan performance of *Die Zauberflöte* was scheduled with Sembrich, Eames, Dippel, Ternina, Plançon, and de Lussan. Carl Nicolai's comic opera *Die Lustigen Weiber von Windsor* received a single performance, its only one in the history of the Metropolitan Opera. The season opened late, on December 18, Grau having just returned from his longest tour during his tenure at the opera house. The tour had started on October 10 and continued until December 17 in Boston.

Debut of Antonio Scotti in Don Giovanni

Antonio Scotti's debut on December 27 was an event of great importance. The baritone, who became an intimate associate of Caruso, was recognized immediately as an outstanding artist. He was supported in his first appearance by a cast made up of the most prominent artists at the Metropolitan. This cast included Nordica, Adams, Sembrich, Édouard de Reszke, and Salignac, with Mancinelli conducting. The *Times* was highly enthusiastic about Scotti's performance:

> This gentleman, who made his first appearance here as Don Giovanni, was immediately successful. He is a good-looking man, graceful and dignified in bearing and elegant in manner. His voice is fresh, mellow, well schooled and well managed. It has plenty of volume, but was not at any time last night forced. Possibly the quality of the voice is not of the richest, but it was a pleasure to hear such a fresh, unworn organ used with so much freedom. Furthermore, in his treatment of the recitative Signor Scotti showed understanding and at times finesse. He sang the "Champagne Song"...with fine dash and vigor, and won two hearty recalls thereby. The details of his work as Don Giovanni will bear further discussion, but it may be said now that his conception of the part was according to the traditions, and was generally well carried out. (*New York Times*, December 28, 1899, p.7)

The *Tribune* carried an equally favorable review, regarding Scotti as a major addition to the company:

> It was speedily made plain that in Signor Scotti there had been an important acquisition made to the Metropolitan forces. He possesses a beautiful baritone voice, fine and smooth in quality, fluent in execution and managed with admirable skill in most of the matters that pertain to the technical side of the vocal art. But, still further, he is an artist in the highest sense....He sings with intelligence and discrimination, and with the accent of dramatic truthfulness....he showed himself practical in stagecraft, with the added advantage...contributed by a pleasing presence, and his im-

personation of Mozart's graceless hero was marked by courtly grace and cynical insolence. His performance, in a word,...created a distinctly favorable impression, and aroused agreeable anticipations as to his future appearances. (*New York Tribune*, December 28, 1899, p.6)

Gadski's Debut as Senta in Der Fliegende Holländer

Johanna Gadski was considered by many to be one of the foremost Wagnerian artists of all time. Artur Bodanzky, the revered Wagnerian conductor, referred to her as one of the finest Isoldes he had directed, and his experience included performances with Kirsten Flagstad, Gertrude Kappel, Melanie Kurt, Margarete Matzenauer, and Florence Easton, among others.[19] When she made her operatic debut at the Metropolitan on January 6, she had already been heard in New York with the Damrosch and Ellis companies, and in concert at the Metropolitan in December, 1898. The *Times* was favorably inclined but maintained reservations about her pitch:

> Her sincere style and her sympathetic voice gave much pleasure to the audience, but it is a pity that her intonation is not always true. She sings with much tenderness at times, and her personality is pleasing. (*New York Times*, January 7, 1900, p.7)

Gadski's concert accompanist, Paul Eisler, stated privately that her intonation problem was with the notes B and B-flat, but that her high C was most often perfectly on pitch. He described her musically as "outstanding."[20] The *Tribune* was pleased with her performance:

> The newcomer is as welcome an acquisition in the German department as Signor Scotti in the Italian....Very charming musically and pictorially and very convincing dramatically was Mme. Gadski's impersonation of Senta. It was plain that she was happy in her surroundings, for she made her feelings manifest in her work, and her satisfaction was echoed by the public....(*New York Times*, January 7, 1900, p.7)

Metropolitan Premiere of Die Zauberflöte

In its review of the Metropolitan's March 30 premiere of *Die Zauberflöte* in Italian, the *Times* mentioned that the opera was so seldom given because it was so difficult to find sopranos capable of dealing with the technical demands of the Queen of the Night's part. Although Sembrich was apparently not at her best that night, she was not criticized severely; clearly, it was within her power to meet the challenges of the role. The cast, noted in the *Times* review, constituted an impressive list of singers; Eugenia Mantelli, Rose Olitzka, and Suzanne Adams performed in supporting roles, and Mancinelli conducted. Though not completely enthusiastic, the remarks in the *Times* were favorable:

> Last night's performance had been prepared with much care. No doubt those who had not previously heard this remarkable triumph of good music over a poor book

were as much concerned about the opera itself as about its performance. They must indeed have been at a loss to account for the succession of gorgeous scenes and the incomprehensible incidents which passed before them....

Last night's performance will long be remembered for the splendor of its scenic attire and the eager manner in which the public seized at the bait of an array of names. ...But at the end of the first act when twelve of the singers of the company and the conductor, Signor Mancinelli, "lined up," as the football players say, behind the footlights, the great audience well-nigh went wild with enthusiasm.

The merits of the performance are easily and quickly noted. Mme. Eames was a lovely picture and she sang her music well, Mme. Sembrich was unfortunately not in good voice and was unable to do herself justice as the Queen. Mr. Dippel was a respectable Tamino, Mr. Campanari a good Papageno, and Mr. Plancon a grave and sonorous Sarastro. The "three ladies" sang their music charmingly but the "three genii" were only passable. The spectacular features of the entertainment worked fairly well and the audience thoroughly enjoyed the monkeys and reptiles. Signor Mancinelli conducted with authority. (*New York Times*, March 31, 1900, p.9)

Krehbiel, in the *Tribune*, suggested the elimination of the spoken dialogue, a suggestion that was followed many years later.[21]

Mozart's music was beautifully sung at the performance, and it came as a benison, barring the vast amount of recitative, which ought to be [curtailed] for the sake of the movement of the piece, for to those who do not understand Italian and do not wish to follow a libretto when there are such pretty things to see on the stage, this quasi-melodious talk is only a bore....."The Magic Flute" has come to stay as long as time will allow. (*New York Tribune*, March 31, 1900, p.7)

Repertoire for Season 1899–1900

This season offered ninety-six performances; although this number was not the highest to date, when combined with the tour performances, it reached the largest total since the Metropolitan opened. *Carmen, Faust,* and *Lohengrin* were most performed. Remarkably, the repertoire included thirty different operas. With thirty-four performances of his works, Wagner continued to account for more than a third of the performances. Besides the complete *Ring* cycle, *Lohengrin, Der Fliegende Holländer, Tannhäuser, Die Meistersinger,* and *Tristan und Isolde* were performed. *Cavalleria Rusticana* continued to create a double-bill problem. During this season it was combined with *Don Pasquale, Pagliacci, Trovatore,* and *Lucia*; it was still to be some time before the standard bill of *Cavalleria* and *Pagliacci* became established. *Die Zauberflöte* was performed five times, a rather small total for an opera that, though making an appearance as a novelty, had been established as a standard work of high worth in the operatic repertoire. The list of operas was completely traditional, but broad in its coverage. The inclusion of Nicolai's operetta-like work was not explained; it may have been either a submission to an artist's whim or a quiet experiment with this kind of composition.

Grau's tour for the season of 1899–1900 was involved and lengthy, visiting twenty-three cities in Canada and the United States, and staging 112 programs of opera, four of them double bills. *Carmen* was produced twenty-one times; *Faust*, eighteen; and *Il Barbiere di Siviglia*, fifteen. Twenty-four performances of Wagner included *Lohengrin, Tannhäuser, Die Walküre, Der Fliegende Holländer, Die Meistersinger, Das Rheingold, Siegfried, Götterdämmerung*, and *Tristan und Isolde*. The conductors were Mancinelli, Paur, Saar, Bevignani, and Gustav Hinrichs.[22]

THE THIRD SEASON OF OPERA AT THE METROPOLITAN UNDER MAURICE GRAU (1900–1901)

The 1900–1901 season, like the previous one, opened late. It ran from December 18 through March 30, with an extra gala farewell performance on April 29. From the point of view of novelties, the season promised to be interesting. The plans included the first Metropolitan production of Puccini's *La Bohème* as well as the first American production of *Tosca*. One more premiere was offered, *Salammbô* by Ernest Reyer. The roster of conductors changed considerably; only Mancinelli remained from the previous season. Walter Damrosch was engaged for Wagnerian operas, Phillippe Flon for French and Italian opera, and for the bulk of the concert assignments. Flon had conducted successfully at Covent Garden; Grau had brought him to America, as he did many artists during this period when he was managing both opera houses.

The list of singers showed the usual amount of change from the previous season. Among the tenors the most noteworthy alteration appeared in the release of Alvarez and the return of Jean de Reszke. The baritones remained essentially the same. Marcel Journet was a new bass acquisition, Lampriere Pringle having departed. Journet and Plancon jointly accorded considerable wealth of ability to the list. The tenor Giuseppe Cremonini was reengaged after a three-season absence, probably to help relieve de Reszke, who was now approaching fifty-one years of age. Among the women singers, Eames was absent, and so was Sembrich, who had formed a small opera company and gone on a national tour. Melba had conveniently returned to the Metropolitan and filled Sembrich's vacancy with her usual success. Calve had retired temporarily, and Grau had brought in a new American contralto, Louise Homer, who enjoyed notable success for many years; she did not retire until 1930, thus rivaling if not equalling Scotti's record. Fritzi Scheff, later to become leading lady in Victor Herbert's many successful operettas, also joined the company. She was to sing Musetta in the Metropolitan premiere of *La Boheme* but was indisposed for the first performance.

Pol Plançon as St. Bris in Les Huguenots.

Metropolitan Premiere of Puccini's La Bohème

The cast for the Metropolitan's first production of any Puccini opera included Melba, Saléza, Campanari, and Journet, with Mancinelli conducting. The *Times* covered the December 26 premiere in a lengthy story and review, the general tone of which was favorable but not rabidly enthusiastic. The subheadline described *La Bohème* as a "work of the modern realistic school with reminders of Mascagni and Verdi in its tuneful score":

> The introduction of this modern lyric creation to the stage of the representative Opera House of the Western World would call for considerable comment were it not for the fact that the work was long ago made known to New Yorkers, not to those who will not touch with the hem of their garments operas not performed in the holy shrine of fashion, but to all those who go to hear operas for their own sake....
>
> ...The opera belongs to the realistic school. The theory of the members of this school is that they are bringing the opera nearer to the true life of the people. They show us the peasants of Sicily in love and jealousy, a company of mountebanks in the throes of human passion, or a band of Italian cutthroats watching the endeavors of their leader to ruin the daughter of a working woman with a past....
>
> And the music? That, too, is clever, but it is less so than the book....There is an abundance of melody, and their are many twistings of rhythms and harmonic disjointings. But we have learned them all before, Mascagni and Leoncavallo have not labored for naught. The melody of Puccini is fluent and at times he sings the note of human passion. But for the most part he is too fond of making a pretty sound to speak in a convincing accent. The song is too polished, the speech too polite, for the full exposition of the characters of these Bohemians....
>
> ...The chief success of the evening was that of Mr. Saleza, whose Rudolph will assuredly add to the large favor which he already enjoys. His singing is not and never has been satisfactory in respect of voice production, and his tones are too often pinched and strangulated, but he delivers his measures with grace, warmth, sincerity of feeling, and a fine breadth of style....
>
> Mme. Melba was a very competent representative of the light-hearted, fragile Mimi....Her cold silvery voice fitted the music perfectly, and as there was no great acting, she succeeded well enough, save in the last scene, where she was not able to convey the pathos of the situation.
>
> ...The scenery was new and excellent, a feature not always found at the Metropolitan Opera House. The chorus had been carefully rehearsed and the lively action of the second act was carried out with pictorial effect. The orchestra played well and Signor Mancinelli conducted with skill and enthusiasm. (*New York Times*, December 27, 1900, p.6)

The *Tribune* compared some aspects of the opera with Charpentier's *Louise*. The review was far from complimentary to either opera:

The stage of degradation to which dramatic music has been reduced in "La Bo-heme" is that occupied by the art in Massenet's "Navarraise." Sometimes for a mo-ment it is the vehicle of passionate expression, but oftener it is the vehicle of noise and sometimes not the vehicle but the sonorous disturbance itself. Apparently it is the willing slave of the text, but in reality it attempts to be more than the text. Its ten-dency has been carried one step further in the opera "Louise" by Charpentier, which is adored by the sewing girls of Paris because it tells of the noble sentiments with which one of their kind is inspired when she kills a doting father in order to enter the exalted state of harlotry. In "Louise" the street cries of Paris are worked into a sing-ing instrumental fabric over, under and between which the stage folk shriek dis-jointed bits of conversation. The second act of "La Boheme" reaches this phase in which music becomes merely decorative. Silly and inconsequential incidents and dialogues designed to show the devil-may-care life of artistic Bohemia as depicted by Murger in his romance "La Vie de Boheme" (which had a great vogue among addle-pated persons a few decades ago and the spirit of which decadent writers in French have impotently attempted to ape ever since) are daubed over with splotches of in-strumental color without reason and without effect, except the creation of boisterous excitement and confusion. In his proclamation of passion Puccini is more successful as soon as he can become strenuous: but even here the expression is superficial and depends upon strident phrases pounded out by hitting each note a blow on the head as it escapes from the mouths of the singers or accompanying instruments. (*New York Tribune*, December 27, 1900, p.7)

American Premiere of Tosca

Ternina, Cremonini, and Scotti headed the cast for the February 4 premiere of *Tosca*, while Puccini's close personal friend Mancinelli conducted as he had for *La Bohème*. The *Times* appreciated *Tosca* more than *La Bohème* and attributed to the book any blame for weak moments in the opera. The principal singers were splendid-ly praised:

> ...Puccini has written a clever score, one that displays genuine talent and a large command of the materials of opera, especially in the management of thematic ideas. Much of his music has a fascinating quality and his melodies have individuality. One coming into the opera house without knowing who was the composer would have no great difficulty in guessing that the author of "La Boheme" had penned these airs. Grace and sweetness are to be found in abundance and of the usefullness of dis-sonance and abrupt change of rhythm in depicting a tragic situation this composer is well aware. His orchestration is always solid, picturesque, ingenious. He uses voices with the skill of an Italian. In short, he is a gifted and well-trained composer, who has chosen a most unhappy subject, affording little opportunity for a display of the most winning kind of operatic writing, and who has only in the more sentimental episodes of his story risen to the level of that situation. For this we believe the subject is chiefly to blame. The prevailing moods of the story are not inspiring. Puccini will do better work with a better story.

> The performance calls for high praise....Miss Ternina's acting was almost great, and her singing was highly expressive. She dressed the part beautifully and was a commanding figure. Mr. Scotti's Scarpia revealed the combined cunning, cruelty,

and passion of the man fully. His singing was broad and vigorous. Mr. Cremonini was a sympathetic Cavaradossi, and his voice proved to be well suited to the music. The other parts were well done. The chorus was fairly good and the orchestra played very well, indeed. The mounting of the opera was admirable. The new scenes were excellent in design and color. (*New York Times*, February 5, 1901, p.9)

The *Tribune's* critic, again more dissatisfied than his colleague, did not hesitate to dissect Puccini's compositional technique:

Much of it [is] like shreds and patches of many things with which the operatic stage has long been familiar. There are efforts at characterization by means of melodic, harmonic, and rhythmical symbols, of which the most striking and least original is the succession of chords which serves as the introduction to the first scene. This and much else came out of Wagner's logical mind, either in the choice of the material or its development. Phrases of real pith and moment are mixed with phrases of indescribable balderdash, yet these phrases recur with painful reiteration and with all the color tints which Puccini is able to scrape from a marvellously varied and garish orchestral pallette. The most remarkable feature of it all, the one which shows the composer's constructive talent in its highest aspect, is the fluency of it all. Even when reduced to the extremity of a tremolo of empty fifths on the string pianissimo, or a simple sustained tone, Puccini still manages to cling to a thread of his melodramatic fabric, and the mind does not quite let go of his musical intentions. The real melos of the piece from the beginning to end is of that hot blooded passionate type which came in with Mascagni and will probably not go out until composers as well as public have wearied of melodrama and returned either to the lyric drama or opera. (*New York Tribune*, February 5, 1901, p.6)

Metropolitan Premiere of Reyer's Salammbô

Ernest Reyer's *Salammbô*, first performed at the Metropolitan on March 20, was at a distinct disadvantage in having its premiere during the same season as the two Puccini works. If Reyer did not earn lasting success, his opera at least engendered respect in the two major New York reviewers. The work was based on the continuous music drama that Wagner had introduced, and Reyer's use of the orchestra was complimented in the light of its continuity:

...although no one is likely to fall into the error of mistaking "Salammbo" for a work of the first order, the splendor of the scenic plan, the gorgeousness of the attire generously provided for it by Mr. Grau, and the theatrical vivacity of some of its scenes will surely set the audience talking. Such a magnificent production was never before seen on the stage of the Metropolitan, and it has seldom been equaled in the theatres of this country....

His book has the arrangement of scenes for two and ensembles, the alternation of small moving pictures with large tableaus so familiar in the works of Meyerbeer, but it has not the musical distribution of the solos, duets, quartets, and choruses. It contains no set pieces in the old operatic forms, but aims throughout at a consistent dramatic treatment of the text. There are no "numbers" and those who wish to applaud must wait till the end of a scene or else interrupt the music. The voice parts of the music are written in a broad style, often declamatory, occasionally brilliant, but seldom couched in sustained melody. One's mind involuntarily reverts to the score of Massenet's "Le Cid" when listening to this militant, fulminant, strenuous music. ...But Reyer's style is more dignified, more sound, and much less effective, than that of Massenet in "Le Cid."...

But let us note that the composer was a true Wagnerian in so far as he recognized the necessity of a union of the arts of poetry, music, painting, and action in the manufacture of a lyric drama. [In] "Salammbo," the union is perhaps not organic, but it exists; and the effectiveness of the most imposing scenes is wholly due to it. (*New York Times*, March 21, 1901, p.8)

The *Tribune* found more influence deriving from Berlioz, and also alluded to Verdi's oriental sounds in *Aida*. The review was not particularly enthusiastic, although it recognized Reyer's ability in orchestration:

[Reyer's] tastes are modern, his aims far above the frivolity which affects many of his colleagues, but his abilities do not keep pace with his ambition. He clasps hands most warmly with Berlioz, and has some of that Frenchman's peculiarly Gallic reverence for Spontini and Gluck. There are indications in the score that "Les Troyens" occupied much of his attention while he was engaged upon it....Reyer's orchestration is discreet and free from all taint of that instrumental volapük which is so marked in the young Italian School. His subject invites the use of Oriental intervals, and he employs them with the discretion which is noticeable in "Aida," but not with the effectiveness of Verdi. Some of his devices are admirable, but others simply bizarre. ...The chief drawback to the work is its want of spontaneous, varied and expressive melody. (*New York Tribune*, March 21, 1901, p.7)

Farewell of Jean de Reszke in Lohengrin

Concerning Jean de Reszke's final appearance at the Metropolitan Opera House, William H. Seltsam made the following comment:

Announced only as Jean de Reszke's final appearance of the season, this performance was in fact his Metropolitan farewell, for the famous tenor did not return to the company after this year. But many in the audience must have suspected that they were hearing the 51-year-old artist's literal swan song.[23]

Ternina, Bispham, and Édouard de Reszke joined the tenor in this performance, which brought forth startling reviews even without considering Jean de Reszke's age. The audience, according to the *Times*, was wildly enthusiastic.

Mr. Jean de Reszke was in splendid voice and sang Lohengrin as well as he ever did in his life. He was an ideal knight of the grail. Miss Ternina gave a lovely and sympathetic interpretation of Elsa, and sang her music with nice judgement....Mr. Edouard de Reszke was the orotund king of old....

> The audience was out with the intention of being enthusiastic and it had every reason for its demonstrations. There were numerous recalls after each act, and at the close of the opera the procession across the stage was many times repeated. (*New York Times*, March 30, 1901, p.8)

The *Tribune* report was favorable, notwithstanding its evident sarcasm about operatic farewells, final performances, final matinees, last subscription, and the various phrases used to entice large audiences to events that are not as festive as they appear.

> The two Messrs. de Reszke were both in fine voice, and Mme. Ternina as Elsa, added another to the numerous enjoyable impersonations which she has given this winter. Mme. Schumann-Heink was radiant as [Ortrud] (between the acts, when the part permits radiation), and Mr. Bispham died an awful death as Telramund. ...There were flowers for everybody, and joy and peace and good will, and there will be time enough for the last tears of parting when the company comes back from Chicago. (*New York Tribune*, March 30, 1901, p.6)

Repertoire for Season 1900–1901

Performances during the 1900–1901 season totaled eighty-two and included twenty-nine different operas. In number of productions, *Lohengrin* led with nine. The nearest figure to that was five performances, achieved by four operas, *Roméo et Juliette*, *Tannhäuser*, *Die Walküre*, and the new production of *La Bohème*. Wagner's music continued to increase its hold on the repertoire, and this season his works fell only a few short of half, with thirty-four productions of *Die Meistersinger*, *Tannhäuser*, *Lohengrin*, *Der Fliegende Holländer*, *Tristan*, and four *Ring* operas. In spite of its better reviews, *Tosca* only received three performances as compared with the five enjoyed by *La Bohème*. *Salammbô*, the novelty by Reyer, had three performances within a period of a week and then disappeared forever from the repertoire at the Metropolitan Opera House.

The tour repertoire included twenty-six operas and the company journeyed to twelve cities, some as remote as Los Angeles, San Francisco, Denver, Lincoln, and Minneapolis. Ninety-six operatic programs were presented, of which thirty-eight were of Wagner operas, approximately the same ratio as during the regular season. *La Bohème* had ten performances; *Tosca* was produced only four times. Mancinelli, Damrosch, and Flon were the conductors.

During the season a slight flurry was created when Grau entered into negotiations with a vaudeville producer for possible subleasing of the Metropolitan Opera House. When interviewed about the possibility, Grau indicated a far briefer season for the coming year and even questioned whether he would use the Metropolitan Opera House. Although the matter did not come up for further discussion, Grau's remarks indicated that his success on the tours was considerably greater than during the regular season. That Grau eventually retired with a considerable fortune, though his

Metropolitan salary was $20,000 a year, sustained the hypothesis that his tours were rewarding. On being questioned by the *Tribune* reporter about his negotiations with George W. Lederer, a vaudeville producer, Grau stated:

> It is too soon to say anything about such plans, and I do not wish to talk about them. Mr. Lederer has made me a proposition for the house and so have several others. It has been impossible to decide anything as for some time we have not had a quorum of the directors of the Maurice Grau Opera Company. If I give an opera season at all next winter I think that ten weeks will be enough for it. We have had some seasons of fifteen weeks and some of seventeen weeks, but I think that ten weeks will be all that we shall want next year. (*New York Tribune*, March 21, 1901, p.7)

Grau's statement carried an accurate estimate of his plans for the following season, which was reduced not to ten weeks, but to approximately eleven weeks with two extra post-season performances. Nothing further was heard of Lederer or the proposed entry of vaudeville into the Metropolitan Opera House.

THE FOURTH SEASON OF OPERA AT THE METROPOLITAN UNDER MAURICE GRAU (1901–1902)

The season of 1901–1902 at the Metropolitan Opera House offered a greater number of new productions, but these were less significant than the two Puccini premieres of the previous season. Donizetti's *La Fille du Regiment* was scheduled for its first appearance at the Metropolitan, as was Isidore de Lara's *Messaline*. Alvárez had been assigned the role of Otello in a new production, the first since Tamagno's departure. An American premiere of *Manru*, a new opera by Paderewski, created the most excitement, because of the esteem and affection in which the public held the Polish pianist and patriot. Before the season ended, the Metropolitan was prepared for a gala evening of operatic excerpts honoring Prince Henry of Prussia, brother of the Kaiser.

The roster showed few changes; those that took place, however, were significant. Jean de Reszke had retired and Alvárez was back as the leading tenor, along with Dippel. Saléza had not been reengaged, but Grau had brought a new tenor to the Metropolitan. Emilio de Marchi had created the role of Cavaradossi in the world premiere of *Tosca* in Rome, on January 14, 1900; his career at the Metropolitan lasted only a brief two years.[24] Albert Reiss, an unusual tenor who achieved a fine reputation as a singer of secondary roles, had also been engaged; an extremely useful artist at the Metropolitan for many years, he enjoyed the unique distinction of being the first man known to have sung the role of the witch in *Hansel and Gretel*. The list of female artists changed little. Melba was absent again, but Sembrich had returned to complete the exchange that had been going on for several years. Eames and Calve reappeared on the roster, but Nordica was no longer with the company, her roles being assumed by Gadski and Ternina. Damrosch and Flon were reengaged, but Mancinelli was replaced by Armando Seppilli,who had been at the Metropolitan during the season of 1895–1896. Metropolitan concertmaster Nahan Franko conducted one concert. The season opened on December 23 and continued without interruption through March 9. A single benefit performance of *Manru* was presented on March 25, and an operatic farewell concert on April 21 completed the opera season at the Metropolitan.

Metropolitan Premiere of Donizetti's La Fille du Regiment

Marcella Sembrich enjoyed one of her most dazzling successes in Donizetti's *Fille du Regiment*, and the *Times* critic praised her highly while deploring that the opera suffered from the expansive size of the Metropolitan auditorium. The opera can only be produced when a company has an outstanding coloratura; it has been included in the repertoire at the Metropolitan four times, during the eras of Sembrich, Frieda Hempel, Lily Pons, and Joan Sutherland. Discussing the January 6 premiere, the *Times* referred to the work as a "one-man opera," and raised the question of a successor to Sembrich:

> The pretty little opera was certainly new to most of last night's audience. It was received with evidences of the greatest pleasure though it naturally suffered from the loss of much of its effect in the vasty [*sic*] spaces of the Metropolitan auditorium. Like all these comic operas, in which the music is built on slight patterns, the action, facial expression and byplay count for so much. "La Fille du Regiment" should be performed in a small theatre, where the audience and the actors could be close enough together for the stretching of the invisible cord of magnetism between them....
>
> No words except as the reader might take for hyperbole of the most extravagant kind could justly describe the brilliancy of the performance which Mme. Sembrich gave last night....Her every action seems to be spontaneous. Her face is a book. Her gestures are eloquent. And she fills her vocal work with a subtle and infectious humor, when that is called for, and with gentle and touching sentiment when that is required. The climax of her performance was reached in the rehearsal of the song in the second act. Wherein her action, her delightfully humorous and vocally wonderful burlesque of the music, together with her cadenza as she tore up the despised piece of music, carried the audience quite away. It is many a day since such a burst of enthusiasm as followed this has been heard in the Metropolitan Opera House. The audience seemed to realize then that it was present at a marvelously fine performance by the only living woman who could have given it. Whence is her successor to come? Alas! That is the question no one can answer. (*New York Times*, January 7, 1902, p.3)

Krehbiel, writing in the *Tribune*, made a strong case for a new theater for the purpose of housing operas such as this one:

The revival of "La Fille du Regiment" emphasizes a need that often forces itself upon the attention of lovers of the opera in New York—that of a small lyric theatre in which operas of the lighter kind can be heard and seen as they ought...in order to be appreciated. The city needs an Opera Comique as well as the Grand Opera. It is not desirable that interest in lyric comedy shall die; nor is it likely. The strenuous commercial and social life of today demands relaxation more than instruction. Serious music, instrumental and vocal, is tending more and more toward the discussion of psychological and pathological problems. The tendency cannot be checked nor need it be. In the course of time it will discover that idealism for which it is groping through dark and materialistic mazes; but meanwhile music is likely ever and anon to revert to old forms of expression because of the intimate love for sensuous beauty. ...The present generation is not likely to call out for a return to the tragic music of the masters of three quarters of a century more or less ago, but it will not lose the capacity to enjoy "Le Nozze di Figaro," "Il Barbiere di Siviglia," "Don Pasquale," "L'Elisir d'Amore," and "La Fille du Regiment" if it is privileged to hear it under proper conditions. To create and nourish such conditions New York needs an adjunct to the Metropolitan Opera. (*New York Tribune*, January 7, 1902, p.9)

Metropolitan Premiere of Isidore de Lara's Messaline

Isidore de Lara's opera *Messaline* was totally unsuccessful at its January 22 premiere. It was severely criticized by both major newspapers, and serious questions were raised as to de Lara's ability to compose an acceptable opera. The *Times*' review suggested that the opera, in declamatory style, was an attempt to achieve the effect of the "modern school":

> ...de Lara has endeavored to combine melodrama with lyricism. He has accompanied most of the action of his work with illustrative music, while the characters declaim. In certain situations calling for a purely lyrical treatment he has tried to write free melody, not in the set forms, and allied in character to the style of Reyer in "Salammbo" with leanings toward that of Puccini as exemplified in "La Tosca."...

> ...The music...is totally lacking in inspiration and utterly devoid of poetic atmosphere. It is feeble in thematic invention, bald in its want of characterization, and picturesque only in the employment of a few orchestral devices. Perhaps the smartest piece of the orchestration is the use of a xylophone to imitate the rattling of dice by some gamblers in the tavern.

Although the cast included three members of an earlier London production, they were not able to command a successful reaction to the performance, and the *Tribune* concurred with the *Times* in proclaiming the opera a dismal failure:

> Music can chasten and ennoble, but not music like M. de Lara's which, when it strives for anything, strives to give an added atmosphere to the incontinence portrayed in the stage pictures and proclaimed in the text. It is not dangerous music, however, for it is an impotent striving with all its blatant pretense. The composer seeks to fill the opening scene with languor and lassitude; he fills it full of ennui instead....But the composer is not musician enough to invent eloquent melodies or moving harmonies. (*New York Tribune*, January 23, 1902, p.9)

Alvárez in Otello

Albert Alvárez undertook a courageous task on January 31, when he performed in *Otello* in its first revival after Tamagno's departure from the Metropolitan. The *Times* reported that Seppilli "conducted with ability and enthusiasm" and praised Alvárez highly.

> The performance...was admirable. It was filled with the true spirit of the tragedy and was vivified by the whole-souled earnestness of the artists engaged by it....Mr. Alvárez's Otello was a splendid, virile figure, passionate and affecting. He sang the music with brilliant power and eloquence. It was the finest impersonation he has given us. (*New York Times*, February 1, 1902, p.5)

The *Tribune* stressed the importance of Scotti's portrayal of Iago rather than Alvárez's Otello. Both artists, however, were considered outstanding:

> It brought to notice a far more musical Iago than M. Maurel's in Mr. Scotti's impersonation, and a finely conceived and executed Otello in the performance of M. Alvarez. It was a foregone conclusion that the latter gentleman would meet all the musical requirements, and he did it without resorting to the brutality of his prototype, but, with all of Signor Scotti's fine achievements, let us say in "La Tosca," "Pagliacci," "Giovanni," and "Messaline," he never reached the plane he moved on last night. (*New York Tribune*, February 1, 1902, p.9)

First American Production of Paderewski's Manru

The reviews of the American premiere, February 14, of Ignace Paderewski's *Manru* were so startlingly good that the question of the opera's failure to remain in the repertoire, even on an occasional basis, might be raised. The libretto was blamed for certain weaknesses, while Paderewski was lauded for his ability to create an outstanding new work.

> The high favor in which Mr. Paderewski is held by this public aroused deep and widespread interest in his debut here as an opera composer, and every seat in the Metropolitan was sold several days ago....It is seldom that an American audience is as enthusiastic as last night's was at the end of the second act when the composer received fifteen calls.
>
> As a work of art "Manru" commands respectful consideration, and for some of its features frank and hearty admiration. Its promise is great; its achievement not little. Its weaknesses are largely due to its libretto which is unskillful in construction and unpoetic in diction.
>
> ...[Paderewski] has employed...the contemporaneous lyric drama, with more than the usual amount of reliance on Wagner. This does not mean that the composer is a borrower of musical ideas, but that he has utilized the leading motive to some extent, and that he has accorded to the orchestra a leading part in the exposition of the

thoughts of the play. In no opera outside of those of Wagner is the instrumental part raised to such an important position. It is continually painting the picture of the inner life of the personages. It is always an explicator, a vivifier of text and action....That the colors are sometimes too heavy will certainly strike some connoisseurs. As for the general public, it would doubtless willingly sacrifice some of the beauties of the score for a few more elementary tunes in the voice part.

The modern method is carried out faithfully in the treatment of the voices. Declamation of a flexible character, sometimes approaching arioso in its melodic contours, and again returning far toward old-fashioned secco, but also varied and expressive, is employed to carry on the ordinary dialogue. When an emotional state suitable to purely lyric expression is reached, the composer writes in appropriate style, as for example, in the exquisitely beautiful love duet of the second act. (*New York Times*, February 15, 1902, p.5)

The *Tribune* drew an analogy between Paderewski's music and gypsy music, and also spoke of the emotional expressiveness of the score:

Into the music of Manru's songs...Mr. Paderewski has poured such passionate emotional expression as makes them convincing; and he has done more. Music is the language of the emotions and the gypsies are an emotional folk....

...The use of an Oriental interval...characterizes the melos of the first act; the rhythm of a peasant dance inspires the ballet, which is not an idle divertissement, but an integral element of the play; and gypsy fiddle and cymbalon lend color and character to the music which tempts Manru to forget his duty. (*New York Tribune*, February 15, 1902, p.9)

Performance in Honor of Prince Henry of Prussia

The care and enormous effort that went into the preparation for the February 25 visit to the Metropolitan Opera by Henry of Prussia were probably fed by the tradition of opera in Germany and the large complement of German-trained singers at the Metropolitan. The *Times*, speaking of the requirement for evening dress, observed that the speculators were infected with a strange sense of honor on this occasion:

No exceptions were made to the rule requiring evening dress and money was refunded to those who appeared in any other attire. A speculator sold a place in the family circle to one man in a sack coat for $8 and returned the money when the purchaser was not permitted to enter.

The Janitor of the Opera House, even, wore evening dress and silk hat when, as soon as word was received that the Prince had left the club, he appeared before the entrance and spread from the door to the curb a gorgeous red carpet. (*New York Times*, February 26, 1902, p.3)

The program included every notable artist on the Metropolitan roster, and acts and scenes from *Lohengrin, Carmen, Aida, Tannhäuser,* and *Le Cid* were presented. The architect Stanford White had decorated the house, and the programs were made of white satin. Sembrich had been scheduled in a scene from *La Traviata,* which was eliminated when she refused to appear because the Prince had left the opera house.

> The performance was not carried without a hitch. The only trouble of any kind was due to the refusal of Mme. Sembrich to sing her part of Violetta in "La Traviata" because the Prince had left the house just before this act was to commence. The management pleaded with her in vain. She declined, and Max Hirsch, the treasurer of the company, appeared on the stage and announced that, owing to the lateness of the hour, Mme. Sembrich had declined to sing and that this part of the performance would be cut out. (*New York Tribune,* February 26, 1902, p.2)

The only other problem of the evening involved a fire in the wig room. It broke out at a late hour but still during the concert and while the auditorium was packed. The fire was extinguished before it could spread to other parts of the building. The *Times'* description of the fire is cited below:

> Fire occured at 11:30 o'clock last night in a wig room at the Metropolitan Opera House just at the time when Mr. Van Dyck was singing in *Tannhauser* in the second act. Although the fire burned briskly and smoke issued from the room to the dressing rooms where one hundred or more opera singers and the chorus were preparing to go out on the stage, the audience assembled in honor of Prince Henry, who occupied the most prominent box, were unaware of the danger. (*New York Times,* February 26, 1902, p.1)

Among the talent assembled in the program were Gadski, Schumann-Heink, Dippel, Bispham, Édouard de Reszke, Calvé, Alvárez, Scotti, Eames, Homer, Journet, Ternina, Van Dyck, Reiss, and Van Rooy. The *Tribune* estimated their fees:

> If the principals had received their full salaries, it would have amounted to $12,000, but it was whispered that they were all singing at half rates in honor of the occasion. The receipts must have been close to $60,000, for every part of the house was packed and the standing room was all occupied. (*New York Tribune,* February 26, 1902, p.2)

The *Tribune* also carried a set of photographs of eighteen of the most prominent singers, three conductors, and Maurice Grau.[25]

Repertoire during Season of 1901–1902

The 1901–1902 opera season was reduced to sixty-five performances embracing twenty-five operas. *Carmen* led with seven performances; *Aida* and *Faust* followed with five productions. Calvé's return restored *Carmen* to frequent performance and reduced the Wagnerian offering to sixteen, a drop to about half of the previous year's Wagner performances. The novelties received ten performances: four of *Manru*, three of *Messaline*, and three of *La Fille du Regiment*.

Tour performances reached the surprising total of 140 programs of opera, and the company visited twenty-six cities. Several new southern cities were added, and the tour returned to Montreal and Toronto for a week of opera. Twenty-eight operas were performed. Wagnerian operas accounted for forty-one performances, of which *Lohengrin* represented twenty-two. Only seven productions were devoted to operas in the *Ring*. The tour conductors were Damrosch, Flon, and Seppilli. Damrosch had now extended his activities to include *Die Zauberflöte* and *Manru*. Dippel and Van Dyck shared de Reszke's Wagnerian roles, except for one performance of *Götterdämmerung* in Chicago when Alexander van Bandrowski sang Siegfried.

THE FIFTH SEASON OF OPERA AT THE METROPOLITAN UNDER MAURICE GRAU (1902–1903)

Grau's final season at the Metropolitan Opera House opened on November 24, the earlier date being possible because he did not take the company on tour as he had done in the past. The season ended March 21 except for a testimonial farewell concert on April 27.

Plans for new productions were limited to two. The first was to be the Metropolitan premiere of Verdi's *Ernani*; and the second involved the American premiere of *Der Wald* by the British composer Ethel Smyth. The return of Mancinelli brought about a revival of his opera *Ero e Leandro*, which disappeared from the repertoire forever after two performances this season. Grau had reduced the roster in accordance with the abbreviated season and tour. Apparently he had planned cycles of the chief works of Verdi and Mozart, but these were abandoned because Eames became ill.[26] The season was uneventful; in retrospect, Grau's subsequent illness and retirement can be presumed to have affected the overall planning of the Metropolitan's offerings.

Dippel and Van Dyck had both left the Metropolitan; the major replacement for them was Georg Anthes. A secondary German *heldentenor*, Emil Gerhauser, was also added; he only remained one season, however, and left no record of extraordinary achievement. Carlo Dani, the Italian equivalent of Gerhauser, was engaged to spell Alvárez, who was now the principal tenor for French and Italian opera. Robert Blass, Marcel Journet, and Charles Gilibert absorbed the missing Plançon's roles. Édouard de Reszke remained with the company.

Calvé and Melba were absent from the female roster, but Nordica, Eames, and Sembrich, aided by Schumann-Heink, gave Grau sufficient strength to fill his needs in the repertoire. Suzanne Adams and Fritzi Scheff continued to serve as utility singers, occasionally portraying major roles. Gadski and Homer were most involved with the German repertoire, although Homer was a highly effective Amneris in *Aida*.

The first major change in conductors in many years occurred when Grau brought Alfred Hertz to the Metropolitan. Hertz remained as the chief conductor of the German wing through 1915. His tenure at the Metropolitan involved countless revivals and premieres of major works. Hertz, who replaced Damrosch, received consistently favorable reviews and became highly respected. The new conductor was held in great esteem by his colleagues, notwithstanding his explosive temper. Aime Gerber, an administrator with the Metropolitan under every regime from Grau through Edward Johnson (1947), described him as "a magnificent musician...[who] put himself completely into his work."[27] Paul Eisler, who started as his assistant and remained as a conductor under both Hertz and Bodanzky, regarded him as "less dynamic than Bodanzky, but a sounder and more consistent conductor who never turned in a poor performance."[28] Toscanini, however, who castigated most of the conductors who appeared at the Metropolitan when he was a member of the company, reserved some of his most vitriolic words for Hertz.

> "Poor Hertz," he once said in a reminiscent mood. "He had everything going triple forte nearly all the time. I remember one place in Wagner. The clarinet was blowing as if he were going to burst a blood vessel. His face was dark red. But he was not making a sound. Poor Hertz, he didn't know the man was acting."[29]

The newspapers, at that time staffed with notably eminent, respected critics, did not share Toscanini's outlook. Describing the first *Parsifal* performance, Henry Finck said that "under the direction of Alfred Hertz the performance was simply thrilling."[30] Finck also remarked that Hertz's first performance at the Metropolitan was not well received, but that he had defended him, "proclaiming him a conductor of the first rank. He soon became generally recognized as such."[31] Katherine Moran, a singer who had appeared under Hertz's direction, felt that

> he was a magnificent conductor and musician. Singing under his baton, one never had to worry about a cue or the orchestra playing too loud. In fact, his presence in the pit was the most reassuring thing a singer could have.[32]

Hertz's later career as conductor of the San Francisco Symphony (1915–1929) enhanced his reputation even further.

Flon and Mancinelli were the other two conductors. Mancinelli had returned to the Metropolitan for his fourth different engagement. This was to be his final season. Flon would also be replaced under the new management that would follow.

Metropolitan Premiere of Ernani

The rationale behind the Metropolitan's January 28 production of Verdi's early opera *Ernani* was much the same as it had been for previous productions like Massenet's *Werther*. The Massenet opera was staged to provide a vehicle for Jean de Reszke; *Ernani* was resurrected as a further arena of triumph for Sembrich. De Marchi, Scotti, and Édouard de Reszke were also in the cast; Mancinelli conducted. As was to be expected, the *Times* commented on the opera's old-fashioned substance:

> In 1882 "Ernani" was considered an extremely old-fashioned work; and much water has passed under the bridges since then. "Ernani" today is tolerable only because of the opportunities it offers for...display of vocalization....It is full of the luxuriant melody of Verdi's early style...he has lavished throughout it melody with the insistent rhythm and unceasing beat of the orchestra to emphasize it, melody at every opportunity without the remotest connection to the dramatic situation; melody intended to be sung at the gallery from the footlights, and invariably so sung last evening. How dismal and impossible the drama itself is, how crudely... theatrical with its "rabbia" of all sorts. There is never any question of what the characters of the stage are going to do, only what they are going to sing next.
>
> The performance last evening was one that in its manner fulfilled all the traditions of the ancient regime. (*New York Times*, January 29, 1903, p.9)

The *Tribune* admitted that the public was extremely enthusiastic and received the work primarily for Sembrich's magnificent singing. Judging by the *Tribune* review, the opera was produced in the old tradition of melodrama with violent emotions expressed both dramatically and vocally:

> To judge the reception, the work lives pleasantly in the memory of old operagoers; it would be instructive to know the thoughts and emotions of the men who have grown up since the staff of empire was taken out of the hands of Mapleson and the Strakosches....
>
> ...The tenor snarled and whined; the baritone stormed, choked himself with the rage of a dozen Scarpias; the bass labored like a Spanish galleon in the trough of a heavy sea. But Elvira sang with a voice that glorified the music, and a style that all but disproved the old charge of Verdi's tyrannous maltreatment of the voice....The old opera was rapturously greeted, but it was Mme. Sembrich's singing that acted as the first mediator between the almost forgotten strains and the people. Extraordinary interest was displayed by the public, the house being crowded almost to the extreme limit of its capacity and rapturous applause following nearly every scene, with recall after recall after the acts. (*New York Tribune*, January 29, 1903, p.9)

American Premiere of Smyth's Der Wald

Ethel Smyth's opera *Der Wald*, which had been produced in Europe, had not created the sensational reports that would arouse the interest of the Metropolitan audience. The critic Herman Klein wrote of his reaction to the opera, which he heard for the first time at the Metropolitan. He was able to provide some historical background of previous performances of *Der Wald*:

> Dame Ethel Smyth and her opera were comparatively unknown. The woman musician was as much of a novelty in the first years of the new century as the suf-

fragette. It seemed vastly strange that one should be capable of writing a libretto for herself, composing the music, scoring and even conducting it into the bargain. Stranger still that it should have been accepted for the Royal Opera at Berlin and performed there in April before it was done at Covent Garden—a first on record at both places. Alike here and at New York (in March 1903) there was every disposition to welcome *Der Wald* with enthusiasm and place it permanently in the repertory. Unfortunately it excited little beyond a lukewarm interest anywhere. If a genuine success could have been achieved, it surely would have been in London with a phenomenal cast that included Katherine Klafsky, Olive Fremstad, Pennarini, Bispham, and Klopfer, Lohse being the conductor. I did not hear the opera until it was given at the Metropolitan Opera House, when I wrote about it for the *New York Herald*. I sat next to Henry Krehbiel and we both confessed to having been rather bored. What a splendid chance missed![33]

For the American premiere on March 11, the Metropolitan also featured an excellent cast, which included Gadski, Anthes, Bispham, and Blass, with Hertz conducting. Because it was short, the opera was produced on a double bill with *Il Trovatore*. The reviewer for the *Times* was not more impressed than Klein:

> The management of the Metropolitan Opera House at last vouchsafed its patrons the one new opera that was promised at the beginning of the season....

> The audience at the Metropolitan rarely show much avidity for novelties, and when the novelty is one that has made so little stir in the musical world as Miss Smyth's one-act piece, there is hardly to be expected a great public outpouring of eager curiosity to see it....

> "Der Wald" is a music drama, as the title page of the score informs us, and like the [creators] of some other music dramas, Miss Smyth has written her own libretto. ...The treatment is intended to be an allegorical or symbolic treatment of the transitory significance of human conflicts and passions in the tranquility and everlasting calm of nature. To explore this Miss Smyth has unfolded a short and very simple story with all the familiar ear marks of a German folk tale. It is of medieval peasant life brought into contact with the weakness and unholy desires of a ruling landgrave and his mistress....

> Miss Smyth employs the orchestra with great prominence, giving it a continuous and uninterrupted part, and charging it with a large share of the dramatic expression. She has, however, nothing to do with leading motives or recurrent themes except for one or two phrases that reappear occasionally, such as Iolanthe's hunting call, a sinister voicing of the evil principle of the opera. Apart from certain harsh and bizarre passages, it is, on the whole, well scored, with not a little of rich coloring and skillful command of instrumental effect. (*New York Times*, March 12, 1903, p.9)

The *Tribune* also commented favorably on Smyth's orchestration but pointedly compared her opera with *Diana von Solange*, implying a similar catastrophe:

> There was a reminder of the dying moments of German opera at the Metropolitan Opera House last night. In those moments, it may be recalled, a grand ducal opera entitled "Diana von Solange" was brought forward. Last night's opera did not boast a grand ducal composer, but it might as well have done so. In fact it would have

been better for all concerned had the composer of "[D]er Wald" been a royal personage instead of a lady. It would have simplified the task of criticism....She has imbibed modern methods of composition and acquired a pretty skill in orchestration; but her melodic sense does not seem to have shared in her artistic development, and the hour and a quarter devoted to her opera was not richly remunerative to those who heard it. There were many sympathetic friends in the theatre, however, and the composer and the singers involved in the performance (excellent people, all) were recalled over and over again and burdened with flowers at the end....Herr Hertz conducted with superb zeal. (*New York Tribune*, March 12, 1903, p.9)

Farewell Testimonial Performance for Grau

Farewells and testimonials had been established for many years at the Metropolitan when Grau was tendered the honor on April 27. The program included excerpts from *La Fille du Regiment*, *Der Fliegende Holländer*, *La Traviata*, *Faust*, *Les Huguenots*, and *Lohengrin*. The broad coverage among composers, types of opera, and languages made it possible for an enormous number of artists to participate. Gadski was indisposed, but all the other well-known members of the company sang at the performance, which was conducted by Flon and Hertz. Mancinelli was unexplainably absent. The *Times* reported the concert without critical appraisal:

> The enthusiasm was, as it usually is upon such occasions, prodigally expended. There were repeated recalls for everybody—the exact number it would take an expert accountant to reckon. There were flowers lavished upon the prima donnas in great profusion. Mr. Grau himself did not appear, though there was no doubt that if he had, he would have had a special tribute all his own and demands for a speech. As it was, the end of his rule at the Opera House was celebrated with all the manifestations of enthusiastic appreciation that the public could well expend upon his artists. (*New York Times*, April 28, 1903, p.5)

The *Tribune* provided a significant commentary on Grau's background and his connections with Abbey:

> It was truly a gala day at the Metropolitan Opera House yesterday. In the afternoon a silver cup and a book were given to Maurice Grau by the members of his company, from prima donna to office boys, and in the evening a final testimonal performance of opera was given—a hodge podge programme which gave all the singers a chance to appear for the last time under Mr. Grau's management....
>
> His old associate, Henry E. Abbey, went down both financially and physically in the tempest of 1896. But Grau was born to the managerial manner. He was as confirmed a slave to the operatic habit as any of his predecessors in New York or London for two centuries, but differed from them in overcoming misfortune. His advent at the Metropolitan Opera House was in accordance with tradition. He was Mr. Abbey's manager when the house opened, and would perhaps have preferred to be his partner; but the fates were kinder to him than his own desires.
>
> Mr. Abbey wrote his name high among the martyrs in the Italian calendar. In fact, his crown was only a trifle less brillant than that achieved by Mr. Delafield,

who managed to sink half a million dollars in a single London season. For five or six years the lesson that all opera is vanity and vexation of spirit seemed to be deeply impressed upon the minds of both of the genial associates, but when they found that they could conjure with the name of Patti they forgot their vows of objuration and went in again for the laurels or the thorns which are the reward of the operatic manager. Then came the revolution at the Metropolitan. Protesting admiration for German opera as the only safe business proposition, Mr. Abbey turned to Italian and French, and finally polyglot opera. He could not weather the storm of 1896, but Mr. Grau did, and turned failure into unexampled success. Last night he had his reward. (*New York Tribune*, April 28, 1903, p.9)

The loving cup presented to Grau was inscribed:

"To Maurice Grau, our President, associate, and friend on the occasion of his withdrawal from operatic management. A token of devotion, esteem, and affection from the Directors, artists, and staff of the Maurice Grau Opera Company, New York, April 27, 1903." (*New York Times*, April 28, 1903, p.5)

In receiving the souvenir,

Mr. Grau appeared much moved, and spoke a few minutes, telling how hard it was for him to break old associations. He told how unusually kind Mr. Conried had shown himself, he having offered on several occasions, the latest of which was Sunday night, to surrender his place if Mr. Grau wished to return. (*New York Times*, April 28, 1903, p.5)

Repertoire for Season 1902–1903

During the final season under Grau's management, ninety-one performances of opera were presented, encompassing thirty-three different operas. Of twenty-seven performances of Wagner operas, ten were devoted to operas of the *Ring*, with the balance divided among *Meistersinger, Lohengrin, Tannhauser,* and *Tristan. Lohengrin* and *Faust* were each performed seven times, and *Le Prophete* received five productions.

The 1902–1903 tour showed a drastic reduction, both in cities and in total performances. Only six stops were made: Philadelphia, Washington, Boston, Chicago, Cincinnati, and Pittsburgh. Twenty-eight operas were presented, of which eight were by Wagner, including the *Ring* operas. Wagner, with twenty-one performances accounted for slightly under one-third of the total of sixty-four performances. Flon, Hertz, and Mancinelli were the tour conductors.

SUMMARY OF RESULTS UNDER MAURICE GRAU
(1898–1903)

Grau managed the Metropolitan for a shorter period than any of his predecessors (considering the first season as part of Abbey's career at the house). When he inherited the Metropolitan from the triumvirate to which he had belonged, Grau faced an unfortunate situation, although not as chaotic as the one Leopold Damrosch had to contend with. Nevertheless, Abbey, as nominal head of the organization of Abbey, Schoeffel, and Grau, had duplicated many of his mistakes of the initial season, and again, these had to lead to financial collapse. Furthermore, Abbey had repopulated the roster with many of his earlier stars, who by this time were past their prime and for this reason were less attractive to the general public. In addition, after fifteen years of existence the opera house, purporting to be the leader in its field, required constant gradual acquisition of new singers, new operas, new conductors, and new scenery and costumes in order to maintain public interest.

Achievements of the Maurice Grau Opera Company

Grau greatly exceeded the efforts of his predecessors in the quantity of opera presented to the public. In five seasons Abbey, Schoeffel, and Grau had produced 385 programs of opera; in seven seasons the German opera regime had presented 438; while in five seasons Grau had produced 434 programs, eighteen of which had been double bills. These figures average out at 62.6 performances per season in the German opera period; 75 per season under Abbey, Schoeffel, and Grau; and 86.7 programs per season under Grau's solo leadership. In variety Grau's margin over the triple management was only two: he offered forty-seven different operas as opposed to forty-five by the triumvirate. The German opera venture, during its seven-year-tenure at the Metropolitan, had only managed to produce thirty-six different works. Stanton had introduced the Metropolitan company to seven tour cities: Abbey, Schoeffel and Grau traveled to fifteen. Grau with his opera company, however, brought performances to thirty-seven different cities, an accomplishment that certainly helped to build the prestige and reputation of the Metropolitan Opera House.

Stanton had on his staff the outstanding conductor, perhaps, in Metropolitan history, Anton Seidl. The conductors who appeared during the triumvirate were Saar, Seidl, Vianesi, Bevignani, Mancinelli, and Seppilli. Most of the triumvirate's more successful directors were reengaged by Grau, but he added notable conductors during his seasons as manager. They included Bevignani, Mancinelli, Schalk, Franko, Paur, von Schuch, Damrosch, Flon, Seppilli, and Hertz. In Hertz, he brought a major figure to the Metropolitan, one who remained for thirteen years, a prominent figure among conductors of the world's opera houses.

Singers were the strongest feature of Grau's regime. The singers he had under contract simultaneously were remarkable in number and quality. His list of artists was strong in depth and covered all the varieties of opera that attracted the public. Sembrich, Melba, Nordica, Eames, Ternina, Homer, Schumann-Heink, and Gadski were among the women singers, and the male singers included the de Reszkes, Tamagno, Dippel, Alvárez, Van Dyck, Van Rooy, Plancon, Journet, Bispham, and Scotti. These represented only a sample of Grau's offering to the public from year to year. At no other time in the Metropolitan's history have so many celebrated artists been available to the public at one time.

Grau presented many noteworthy premieres during his five-year reign. The list included *La Boheme* and *Tosca* as well as many others that were not to remain in the repertoire. He attempted to bring new operas that would satisfy public demand, but through no fault of his, the available works were not of the desired quality. The first performance of Wagner's uncut *Ring* cycle was a major contribution, both to the New York operatic public and to the public of the tour cities where the cycle was presented.

Unquestionably Grau completed the act of restoring the star system from earlier times. But he was sufficiently astute to be able to manage these temperamental artists and to avoid the conflicts and demands that had destroyed Abbey and Mapleson. If Grau was forced to pay salaries that were considered exorbitant, he was fortunate in promoting opera in such a way that the public would support the performances enough to make the system possible without the bankruptcy of the producer. Henry Finck, of the *Evening Post*, commented many years later on Grau's performance as manager of the Metropolitan:

> He had such a huge company of high-class artists of all nationalities that he could perform every opera in the language it was composed in. No other opera house in the world could do that because none had a sufficient number of singers versed in one or the other of the several styles called for. French and Italian artists *can* sing a German opera, just as German artists *can* sing Italian or French operas; but the results are not altogether delectable. Grau accustomed New York audiences to performances that were idiomatic and had style....
>
> A great manager was Grau. I had often criticized him rather sharply in matters of detail...but I also lauded him as he deserved to be, and when his impending retirement was announced I wrote a regretful editorial which pleased him so much that he came in the evening to seat T 2 to shake my hand warmly and to thank me.[34]

Financial Results under Maurice Grau

No financial results of the Maurice Grau Opera Company have been made available. It is only possible to estimate that it was a highly successful venture by its effect on Grau's personal finances. Grau died in 1907 while living in Paris, and the executor of his estate revealed the following information to Kolodin:

> According to Henry B. Dazian, who was a director of the Maurice Grau Opera Company, and executor for Grau's estate after his death in 1907, Grau left over six hundred thousand dollars—*all* of it acquired, following his earlier bankruptcy, in his final five years of Metropolitan production, from 1898 to 1902–1903. Though a portion of this sum was made by fortunate investments, much of it was made through opera at the Metropolitan. Thus it can hardly be said that the production of opera in the manner espoused by him was uneconomical; or that the public was not cognizant of what was being offered to them.[35]

No evidence indicates that Grau was anything but successful or that his final seasons declined even slightly in quality; his autumn, 1902, announcement that he would retire at the end of the season because of ill health seems to have been truthful. He retired at the zenith of his managerial career, leaving the Metropolitan Opera House with an excellent tradition and on more solid footing than it had ever been. He was an outstanding manager of opera and a strong contributor to the growth of the Metropolitan, both artistically and economically.

CHAPTER 7

The Conried Metropolitan Opera Company (1903-1908)

The circumstances prefacing the entrance of Heinrich Conried into the Metropolitan Opera management were unlike those surrounding any previous changes in administration. Leopold Damrosch had replaced Abbey because of the chaotic financial failure of the initial season, after which Abbey refused to continue under his existing arrangement, and the directors refused to meet his demands. Stanton's appointment started as an interim measure after Damrosch's death, but continued success dictated that he be retained. Abbey, this time in conjunction with Schoeffel and Grau, seized upon the directors' eventual dissatisfaction with German opera, opportunely making an attractive offer to assume the management. After Abbey died, the reorganization of the company and the withdrawal of Schoeffel cleared the way for Grau to assume full control of the Metropolitan. After five seasons Grau retired because of poor health. Considering cumulative artistic and financial effect, Grau's term of management had been the most successful to date. The directors had granted him a lease arrangement that had proved eminently satisfactory to both parties, and his decision to withdraw left them with a highly successful operation but no opera company or prospective manager. From the viewpoint of experience, reputation, and public appeal, three choices seemed to stand out as the most logical. Charles Ellis, Walter Damrosch, and Heinrich Conried each had factors that favored his appointment as impresario of the Metropolitan. Ellis had produced opera in New York and Boston as well as on tours. For his New York performances he had leased the Metropolitan Opera House. Ellis had produced opera most actively during the season of 1897–1898, when no regular Metropolitan company was active. Damrosch entered into a brief partnership with him but withdrew after appearing for a few weeks as Ellis's musical director. Ellis had also pursued other musical enterprises; among them, he was currently managing the Boston Symphony Orchestra and representing Melba in her American business dealings. Damrosch had been involved in various operatic ventures, both local and touring. Although he had not been financially successful, he was well acquainted both with the artists and with the procedures of operatic management.

Conried had considerable experience in areas only remotely associated with opera. He had started his career as an actor and in America had been notably successful in demonstrating for students the different phases of classical drama. He was also well acquainted with performing artists, though with actors and actresses rather than singers.[1] In 1892 he had leased the Irving Place Theatre and presented a German stock company in classics of the German theater. His flair for comedy was well known and he was respected for his theatrical acumen.

Strangely enough, discussions of early candidates omitted the name of Daniel Frohman, mentioned in one *New York Times* report as a possible sucessor to Grau. Frohman was at that time managing the Lyceum Theatre in New York, and his success at that enterprise may have contributed to his unwillingness to consider a Metropolitan offer. The ultimate decision to appoint a man of the theater, as Conried was, made Frohman's consideration logical in retrospect. The same *Times* report also noted that the Royal Opera Company at Covent Garden had offered its services to the Metropolitan:

> While nothing in any way definite has been done yet regarding the opera arrangement for next year, several plans are being formulated by the Board of Directors of the Metropolitan Opera House and Real Estate Company. One of these is to retain the Maurice Grau Opera Company with Daniel Frohman as the successor to Maurice Grau. The Grau company itself is quite willing to remain, provided it can find a suitable head, and as yet it has been unable to do this, but will attempt, however, to do so within a week or more.

> Representatives have gone twice to Daniel Frohman and offered him $25,000 to manage the company next season but he has declined. Considerable pressure, however, is being brought to bear on him, and though he protests that he will not undertake the opera management, it is thought that he may consent finally. That F. G. Latham will take charge of the opera is said to be impossible. Another plan open to the Board of Directors comes in the shape of a proposition made by the Royal Opera Company, which conducts opera at Covent Garden, London. It is stated that this company has offered to furnish opera here next year.

> Neil Forsythe of Covent Garden is said to be willing to come here himself in case the Royal Opera Company obtains the management. (*New York Times*, January 29, 1983, p.7)

Conried's Appointment

For the entire circumstances of Conried's appointment, Henry Finck, the music critic of the *Evening Post*, claimed credit. Other than in Finck's own account, the episode is not mentioned elsewhere in print; if Finck's story is accurate, however, he would have known details unavailable to other observers. In his memoirs Finck related the episode under the heading "How I Made Conried Manager":

> "Good morning, Mr. Conried, would you like to be manager of the Metropolitan Opera House?"

> "Why—I have never thought of such a thing. What makes you ask?"

"Would you accept the position if it were offered to you?"

"I certainly would," he replied, after a brief pause.

"Very well," I continued, "read the *Evening Post* tonight and see what will happen within a few days."

With these words I left Conried's office at the Irving Place Theatre, hurried down to the *Evening Post* and dashed off an editorial in which I pleaded with all my might and main for Heinrich Conried as manager of the Metropolitan.

Grau's death had left a vacancy to be filled. There were several candidates, among whom Walter Damrosch seemed most likely to be the winner. Now I hadn't the slightest doubt that Mr. Damrosch would make an excellent manager; he had the requisite knowledge, experience and business ability; he spoke several languages and was a "good mixer." But—he was a composer and a conductor! The idea that he might produce a new work of his own every season and personally conduct all the most important performances, did not fill my soul with unmitigated joy. So I came out for Conried.

He, like Abbey, had never managed a grand opera company, but he had had experience with operetta companies and was famed as a stage manager....He had repeatedly, at his own expense, given model performances of classical dramas for the students of American universities and been rewarded for his disinterested services with honorary degrees. Into the hands of such a man, I argued in the *Post*, it would be safe to place the interests of our famous Opera.

One of the morning papers—I think it was the *Times*—seconded my motion. The Directors of the Metropolitan met that day (February 14, 1903) and the next morning I got this note:

"My dear Mr. Finck:—
"It gives me great pleasure to inform you that I will be the successor to Mr. Grau, and I sincerely hope that you will lend me, at all times, your most valuable assistance.

"Yours faithfully,
"Heinrich Conried."[2]

Except for Finck's premature burial of Grau, (who did not die until 1907), his statement cannot be disproved. Krehbiel, in reporting Conried's appointment, made no mention of Finck; he did, however, allude to a lengthy conflict between Damrosch and Conried for the position:

On February 14, 1903, the directors of the Metropolitan Opera and Real Estate Company by a vote of seven to six adopted a resolution directing the executive committee "to negotiate with Mr. Heinrich Conried regarding the Metropolitan Opera House, with power to conclude a lease in case satisfactory terms can be arranged." This was the outcome of a long struggle between Mr. Conried and Mr. Walter Damrosch, a few other candidates for the position of director of the institution making feeble and hopeless efforts to gain a position which all the world knew had, after many vicissitudes, brought fortune to Mr. Grau.[3]

Conried's biographer Montrose J. Moses related the episode differently, contending that, on the basis of Conried's theatrical fame, the Metropolitan directors had instituted the negotiations. Moses asserted that Conried adamantly refused the proposition until he was assured of unanimous support from the directors. This description, of course, contradicts Finck's version. Finck, Krehbiel, and Moses all agree, however, that the vote was seven to six. According to Moses's account:

> *Heinrich Conried's* reputation went far beyond the circle of his immediate patronage....When, in the spring of 1903, Mr. Maurice Grau announced his intention of retiring from the directorship of the [Metropolitan Opera House,] Mr. Conried was put forward as a candidate for the vacant place. With his usual independent attitude, when the subject was broached to him, he personally refused to become an applicant...although there is no doubt that...he relished the possible opportunity of struggling with such a big artistic proposition....It was only after he was assured of the unanimous support of the Metropolitan Directors that he consented to have his name put up for consideration.
>
> ...many people...shook their heads with...misgivings, for it is one thing to appoint a man of Conried's experience as the head of a theatre, and...another...that the next Director of the Metropolitan Opera House should be a man with no operatic experience to speak of....
>
> ...Conried's ardent supporters...pointed to his interest in musical affairs...in the past, and emphasized...that he had managed...the American tour of Bronislaw Hubermann, the violinist, and was instrumental in bringing to this country [Ernst] Von Schuch, conductor of the Dresden Opera House.
>
> ...Many preliminary details were entered into between the Metropolitan Opera and Real Estate Company and the regisseur of the Irving Place Theatre. On February 14, the Directors decided, by a vote of seven to six, to instruct the Executive Committee to negotiate with Mr. Conried, and on February 15, 1903, it was announced by the Metropollitan Opera and Real Estate Company that the lease of the Opera House had been given to Heinrich Conried for five years.[4]

Moses also provided information about Conried's financial backing and board of directors.

> At the beginning, Heinrich Conried's financial supporter was Mr. Henry Morgenthau, later strengthened by the support of Messrs. James H. Hyde and Jacob H. Schiff. The latter was invited to join the Directorate, but he was at the time so pressed with other work that he was obliged to decline, requesting however that a member of his firm, Mr. Otto Kahan [sic], be accepted in his stead—a suggestion to which Mr. Conried readily agreed.[5]

The addition of Otto H. Kahn to the Board of Directors of the Metropolitan was significant. Kahn was the most active board member until 1932.

Financial Terms and First-Season Preliminaries

In 1909 the *New York Evening Sun* revealed the details of Conried's financial arrangement with the Metropolitan directors:

> The Impresario's salary of $20,000, and Conried's [annual] benefit, earning $20,000 more, footed up $40,000 a year, or $200,000 for the minimum earnings of Conried's five years in opera. He and his bankers...were to have half of all the Opera Company's profits, which in the first three years, probably netted him $150,000 additional, it was said....He sold to W. K. Vanderbilt, for $90,000, his interest in opera contracts that had three years to run. (*New York Evening Sun*, April 27, 1909, p.4)

Whenever Conried traveled to Europe, which was to be frequently, he received an extra stipend of $150 a week to cover extra expenses.[6] This was the first such arrangement recorded for any Metropolitan Opera manager.[7]

No documents substantiate Grau's statement, at the time the loving cup was presented to him, that Conried had offered to withdraw should Grau change his mind about retiring. Any such offer was more than likely a gesture of kindness with reasonable assurance that it would be rejected, for Conried was already involved in arrangements for the coming season.

Before his first season opened, Conried insisted on certain improvements both in the stage facilities and in the auditorium. Already planning to produce Wagner's *Parsifal*, he needed to revise the scenic equipment substantially. Furthermore, his theatrical sense demanded that the auditorium be redecorated in a richer color scheme. Kolodin described the alterations:

> The manager's training in the theatre and his desire to produce *Parsifal* made necessary a considerable revision of the facilities of the Metropolitan stage, carried out under the direction of Carl Lautenschlager, of Munich. The expense, which was borne by the ownership company, amounted to approximately $150,000. It provided for a mechanical system of counterbalances for flying scenery, to replace the antiquated devices which required several times as much man-power; a new stage floor was installed, with the traps necessary for *Parsifal*; a new proscenium arch, with the front of the stage cut back on a line with it, was constructed; the small doors at either side of the proscenium arch, from which the singers formerly took curtain calls, were eliminated, and ornamental bases were added to the pillars....New seats were provided in the auditorium, in the deep maroon which has since become traditional, and the interior of the house was redecorated, emphasizing the gold background which has remained a characteristic of the Metropolitan's appearance. A smoking-room and foyer were also provided on the grand tier floor. The contractors were Carrere and Hasting, who had built the Empire Theatre.[8]

To a great degree Conried patterned the organization of his opera company after that of Grau's. Although he was under no obligation to fulfill Grau's contractual arrangements, in most cases he entered into new agreements with the same artists, presumably under similar terms. Prominent artists under Grau who sooner or later sang under Conried included Sembrich, Eames, Nordica, Homer, Blass, Schumann-Heink, Alois Burgstaller, Dippel, Journet, Plancon, Reiss, Scotti, and Van Rooy.

Negotiations with Caruso

Conried's acquisition of Caruso's contract is described in conflicting versions by Moses and Krehbiel; other accounts draw upon one or the other. Moses, in his much retold story, claimed that Conried had engaged Caruso "purely by accident."

> Mr. Conried went to the Italian consulate in New York, and inquired of the consul who was the greatest living tenor. The prompt reply was, "Caruso." He next cabled Covent Garden, and across seas came the assurance, "Caruso." Then one day, so the story continues, he was having his shoes shined. "Who is the greatest Italian tenor living?" he asked the bootblack. And the answer came without hesitation, "Caruso." He rushed down to the Italian Savings Bank, in New York City. "Who is the greatest Italian singer?" he asked President Francolini. "Caruso, of course," was the reply. "And what is more," the President continued, "the Secretary of this bank, Signor Simonelli, knows Caruso's agent." In this indirect fashion, Conried got in touch with the great Italian tenor.

> One morning, soon after he arrived in [Berlin], Conried...met Herr Rudolph Christians, who is...Director of the German Theatre in New York. [He] told Conried he was on his way to a certain Italian restaurant for luncheon...because the proprietor had promised to let him hear a phonograph record of...a truly remarkable tenor voice. Everyone, it seemed, was buying these records! The tenor's name was Caruso. The matter dropped from Mr. Conried's mind until he arrived in Paris...on the Boulevard des Italiens...[he] passed a phonograph store, and, the memory of Caruso once more occurring to Mr. Conried, he dropped in and asked to hear the Caruso record played. It was thus that he first heard the great tenor's voice.[9]

Krehbiel passed off this entire narrative as a publicity maneuver. His less dramatic version of the story differed notably:

> I emphasize...that Mr. Conried acquired the contract with Signor Caruso from Mr. Grau because...careless newspapers writers, taking their cues from artful interviews ...by Mr. Conried, have glorified the astuteness of the new manager in starting his enterprise with a discovery of the greatest tenor of his day. Many were the stories... the most picturesque being that Mr. Conried, burdened with the responsibility of recruiting a company, had shrewdly gone among the humble Italians of New York and by questioning them had learned...the name of the greatest singer alive....Confirmed in his decision by his bootblack, he had then gone to Europe and engaged the wonder. Caruso's reputation was made some years before he came to America, and Mr. Grau had negotiated with him at least a year before he got his signature on a contract for New York. Let the story stand as characteristic of many that enlivened the newspapers during the Conried period.[10]

Caruso discussed his Metropolitan contract in an interview with Moses, who suggested that Grau had failed to capitalize on an earlier opportunity to engage Caruso at Covent Garden for less money than the tenor ultimately received at the Metropolitan.

Mr. Caruso...continued the story. "When I heard that Grau had resigned," he declared, "I asked my agent to find out whether my contract would hold good with the new Director, whoever he should be. My friend by correspondence was Simonelli, in New York. Through him we heard of Mr. Conried's appointment. The new Impresario asked if I would come to America for ten performances. 'No,' I cabled, for I was then in negotiations with Monte Carlo, and the opera houses in South America, where I had gained some of my experience, were wanting me back. Finally Mr. Conried said 'Yes,' and I came,—and here I am."

Grau had missed his opportunity at one time, for, while he was at Covent Garden ...he might have engaged Caruso at $700 an evening, but did not do so. The Grau contract [at the Metropolitan] called for $1,000 a night, to be increased if Caruso were a success. We know the result....[Caruso] has proven himself...to be the Opera's greatest financial investment...the gold-mine that came to the rescue of Conried when Hammerstein entered the operatic field.[11]

CONRIED'S INITIAL SEASON (1903–1904)

Before his first season opened, Conried, as noted earlier, had completed contracts with may of Grau's artists as well as with Enrico Caruso. A few previously under contract were not reengaged. Of these, most prominent male singers were Bispham, Dani, Gerhauser, Gilibert, de Marchi, and Édouard de Reszke. The female absentees included Eames, Nordica, Scheff, and Schumann-Heink; Eames and Nordica returned a year later, and Schumann-Heink reappeared as a member of the company in 1906. Scheff, who had departed permanently, was on her way to becoming Victor Herbert's most prominent operetta singer. Of the three conductors during Grau's final season, only Hertz returned.

Ternina had returned to head Conried's Wagnerian forces. She was joined by a singer who had achieved remarkable success in Europe, Olive Fremstad. Fremstad, Gadski, and Ternina combined to provide Conried with a strong group of Wagnerian artists to portray major dramatic roles. Two American-born, European-trained singers joined the company: Edyth Walker, a mezzo-soprano who became a major artist at the Metropolitan, noted for her portrayal of Amneris; and Marion Weed, who alternated with Ternina in the role of Kundry in *Parsifal*. Male additions other than Caruso included Ernst Kraus, a tenor who had occasionally performed with Damrosch, and the baritone Otto Goritz.

Before he retired, Grau had engaged three conductors new to the Metropolitan Opera House. Of the three, the most notable was the noted Wagnerian conductor Felix Mottl. A veteran with much experience at Bayreuth, Mottl had been a close friend of Seidl's and was a product of the same training and background. His revision of Cornelius's *Der Barbier von Bagdad* had been presented at the Metropolitan during the season of 1889–1890. In the prospectus for the 1903–1904 season Mottl was described as *Generalmusikdirektor*, the only man ever listed as such in the Metropolitan's history.

The new Italian conductor, Arturo Vigna, was brought to the Metropolitan from La Scala in Milan; he remained with Conried through the season of 1906–1907. The third new member of the conducting staff was Gustav Hinrichs, who had led Metropolitan performances on tour during the 1899–1900 season. He had considerable experience conducting operas and symphonic works in the Philadelphia area; although not well known in New York, he was respected in Philadelphia by critics and public. His conducting assignments at the Metropolitan during his first season included *Cavalleria Rusticana*, *Faust*, *Mefistofele*, and *La Traviata*. Two other conductors made appearances at the Metropolitan during the season: Henry Hadley was guest conductor at an "American night" concert; and the Metropolitan orchestra's concertmaster, Nahan Franko, directed Delibes's ballet *Coppelia* for three double bills.

Conried's initial season opened November 23 and continued through March 10; the company then began its tour, returning for a post-season group of five opera performances and one concert (April 18–25, ending with a matinee). In addition to several notable debuts, Conried offered three novelties. The first, one of the most important in the history of the Metropolitan Opera, was the first stage performance of *Parsifal* at any theater other than the Festspielhaus at Bayreuth.[12]

Somewhat overshadowed by *Parsifal* were two other novelties: the Metropolitan premieres of Boieldieu's *La Dame Blanche* and Donizetti's *L'Elisir d'Amore*. Although the Donizetti opera was familiar to New York audiences from earlier performances at the Academy of Music, the announced cast, which included Sembrich, Caruso, and Scotti, provided opera patrons with a great attraction. Also of interest was the Metropolitan's first performance of *Die Zauberflöte* in German—not a novelty, but rather a step towards proper presentation of Mozart's *Singspiel*. The cast for this production promised to be as attractive as that for the Donizetti for it included Sembrich, Gadski, Dippel, Reiss, and Goritz.

Caruso's Debut in Rigoletto

Thanks to publicity and widespread knowledge of Caruso's name, the impending debut of the sensational new tenor from Italy created great excitement. In choosing his November 23 opening-night cast, Conried made it obvious that he intended to equal or surpass Grau's casting. Sembrich was scheduled to sing Gilda, with Homer appearing as Maddalena. Scotti was the Rigoletto, and Journet portrayed Sparafucile. Vigna conducted.

Caruso, like Jean de Reszke (and Lauritz Melchior decades later) had started his career as a baritone, and for this reason his voice was largely free of the "white" quality often considered unpleasant in lyric tenors. Strangely enough, however, the critic for the *Times* described precisely such a quality in Caruso's opening night performance, though praising his voice in general:

> He made a highly favorable impression, and he went far to substantiate the reputation that had preceded him to this country. He is an Italian in all his fibre, and his singing and acting are characteristic of what Italy now affords in those arts. His voice is purely a tenor in its quality, of high range, and of large power, but inclined to take on the "white" quality in its upper ranges when he lets it forth. In mezzo voce it has expressiveness and flexibility, and when so used its beauty is most apparent. Mr. Caruso appeared last evening capable of intelligence and of passion in both his

Enrico Caruso as the Duke in Rigoletto.

singing and his acting, and gave reason to believe in his value as an acquisition to the company. (*New York Times*, November 24, 1903, p.1)

The *Tribune*, also complimentary, similarly qualfied its praise. The critic's admission that Caruso was superior to any exponents of the role heard in New York in a generation established Caruso as the best Duke in *Rigoletto* since the founding of the twenty-year-old Metropolitan Opera House. Nevertheless this compliment was guarded, for the list of interpreters of that role at the Metropolitan was comprised of less-than-immortal tenors, including Roberto Stagno, Fernando DeLucia, Giuseppe Russitano, Giuseppe Cremonini, Salignac, and Carlo Dani; in general, the leading tenors of previous seasons did not sing the part during their stay at the Metropolitan Opera House.

> "Rigoletto" is not a tenor's opera, as has been said, but Signor Caruso, the new-comer, did what he could to make it so. He was musically the finest Duke that New York has heard for a generation ....Signor Caruso has many of the tiresome Italian vocal affectations, and when he neglects to cover his tones, as he always does when he becomes strenuous, his voice becomes pallid. But he is generally a manly singer, with a voice that is true, of fine quality and marvellous endurance. That "La Donna e Mobile" was permitted to pass with but a simple repetition was due to the apathy of the audience. He had a gratifying reception in the first act, however, though the honors of the evening went in greatest measure to Mme. Sembrich and Signor Scotti. (*New York Tribune*, November 24, 1903, p.9)

Debuts of Fremstad and Mottl in Die Walküre

The second night of the season, November 25, brought two major artists to the Metropolitan: Olive Fremstad made her debut as Sieglinde in *Die Walküre*, with Mottl conducting. Both newspapers granted considerably more space than usual to reviewing this production, and they received the newcomers with almost boundless enthusiasm. The *Times* made no comment that was not highly complimentary:

> Miss Olive Fremstad, who left this country some years ago as a singer of minor roles, returns as a mature artist of remarkable power—as one, in fact, who is likely to become an important figure in the season now under way....
>
> The performance was in many ways a notable one. It was inspired and stimulated by the potent and masterful sway of Mr. Mottl, who infused the pulsation of life and dramatic energy into the movement of the drama; making the music eloquent and causing the orchestra to speak with an infinitude of expression. His reading of the work was drawn on large and broad lines, and yet was filled with significant detail. Enough was seen and heard of his work last night to realize the foundation that bases his great repute....
>
> Mme. Fremstad's performance was a delight with small alloy. Her accomplishment as both a singer and an actress, the power and depth of her art, were such as to fill the lovers of the German works in which she is to appear with present satisfaction and jubilant expectation. Her voice is of extraordinarily beautiful quality and large range, in the lower notes, particularly, of the richest contralto coloring, and its

freedom and flexibility, the volume with which she poured it out, the nobility and broad sweep of her phrasing, showed in her the true artist—the artist who comprehends the essence and the significance of Wagner's musical style. (*New York Times*, November 26, 1983, p.4)

The critic for the *Tribune*, while not quite so overwhelmed, reacted most favorably to the performances of both new artists. Fremstad's stride and her somewhat overpowering attitude was criticized as incongruent with Sieglinde's character; Sieglinde, however, proved to be the most frequently featured role of Fremstad's career. Mottl's tempi were considered to be slower than average throughout his career, although on rare occasions he was accused of rushing. Here, as invariably, the critic qualified his observations on tempo by admitting that Mottl achieved some special effect by his variance of traditional speeds. Neither Mottl nor Fremstad could have derived anything but satisfaction from the *Tribune* review of the performance:

Miss Fremstad has everything appertaining to voice and appearance in her favor, and though a tendency toward the Teutonic stride and pose which Bayreuth has encouraged militated against the sweet naturalness of which the character of Sieglinde is an index, she took rank with most of her predecessors in the part; and New-York has seen and heard the finest representatives imginable in it....Herr Mottl is a conductor who, without the least apparent effort, impresses his individuality upon every portion of the performance. His tempi are slower than ordinary, especially in what may be called the orchestral monologues, but he has a vast variety of expressive nuances at his command, and he brings them out infallibly and convincingly. (*New York Tribune*, November 26, 1903, p.9)

Edyth Walker's debut as Amneris in Aida

The list of prominent American singers at the Metropolitan had slowly grown. Edyth Walker was to add considerable prestige to the ranks of native artists who have appeared in the course of Metropolitan history. She made her debut on November 30 as Amneris in a performance of *Aida*, in company with a memorable cast that included Gadski in the title role, Caruso as Radames, Scotti as Amonasro, Plançon as Ramfis, and Adolph Muhlmann as the King. Vigna conducted a performance that the reviewers considered excellent. Walker's outstanding success in Vienna and in other German and Austrian opera houses had earned her a considerable reputation. The review in the *Times* was at once complimentary and puzzlingly apathetic:

Miss [Edyth] Walker comes with a reputation that the favor of the Viennese public...at the Imperial Opera House...causes to loom large there and in the opera houses of Germany. She was received with favor; but it did not seem at first as if she showed quite enough of either vocal endowment or the skill of an actress to justify all that has been said of her operatic performances.

She made no very deep impression in her first scenes, nor did her voice show in them all of which she is capable. In the later ones, however, and particularly the last act, she rose to a pitch of dramatic fervor and disclosed vocal capacities that are likely to go far in giving her a place in the esteem of this public. Her voice is a mezzo-soprano of power, clear and penetrating, of undimmed freshness, and of remarkable evenness of quality throughout its range, yet of no great warmth of color. Her style is finished and artistic without showing distinction, so far as was made manifest last evening, and while she gave an adept and thoroughly intelligent interpretation of good power and quality, but without exceptional distinction in either respect, and while she gave a sincere interpretation of the part of Amneris, it was far from over-topping some that have previously been heard here. Miss Walker is an artist of experience and familiarity with the requirements of the operatic stage, and is likely to be a valuable member of Mr. Conried's company. (*New York Times*, December 1, 1903, p.5)

The *Tribune* was considerably more enthusiastic, with no qualification of its praise. Walker's performance was compared with Gadski's performance as Aida, and both artists were praised for their contribution to the success of the production:

> Miss Walker is comely, familiar with the conventions of stage deportment and the possessor of a voice of lovely quality, though not of great volume. There is a decided charm in her singing, the most marked artistic grace of which is the perfect evenness of its quality up to the point where the pitch puts a strain upon her. Her voice is also a capital vehicle for feeling, an extremely essential attribute to the dramatic singer. Miss Walker left her hearers in doubt as to her gift in this respect until the scene with the priest in the last act, but then she made a most moving manifestation of it. Indeed her performance of this feat was probably the finest that the patrons of the Metropolitan Opera House can recall, and was only equalled in the evening's representation by Mme. Gadski's superb singing and acting in the Nile scene. (*New York Tribune*, December 1, 1903, p.9)

On the day of Walker's Metropolitan debut the Brooklyn Academy of Music was totally destroyed by fire; the *Times* headline read "Brooklyn Academy of Music In Ruins."[13]

First Stage Performance of Parsifal Outside Bayreuth

Conried determined early in his career as Metropolitan impresario that he would be the first to produce *Parsifal* at a place other than Bayreuth; his Metropolitan Opera House affiliation assumed a dramatic turn when this fact became known. Various problems arose, not the least of which concerned the question of whether it was proper to produce this work in a purely theatrical atmosphere. The opinion that Parsifal and Kundry personified Christ and Mary Magdalene was common; however, Wagner's designation of the opera as *ein Buhnenweihfestspiel* (a festival play for the dedication of a stage) did not mark the work as a religious composition. In the final analysis, the protests of those who considered the opera religious were for the most part ignored. A protest less easily cast aside was that launched by Wagner's heirs. They objected to Conried's "pirating" of the opera on two counts: first, that he was not respecting the sanctity of the work as Wagner had planned it (they insisted that he wished it produced only at Bayreuth); and second, that they owned the rights and that he might produce it only upon paying them an enormous royalty.

Conried's position was that Wagner's agreement with B. Schott's Sons, the publishers of the score, prevented the Wagner family from exercising any rights whatsoever. Apparently Wagner had granted the company exclusive rights to publication for a fee of 75,000 marks. After Wagner's death a second contract was made, by which the heirs were restored the right to determine productions of the work but in turn relinquished publication rights in Germany and abroad. B. Schott's Sons then sent scores to Schirmer's in New York for sale in this country. These scores carried what appeared to be a protective statement, but the judge who ruled on the case decided that while this phrase provided protection under German law, in the United States such a phrase was ineffective if the score was complete. His decision was that neither the publisher nor Wagner's heirs could prevent the performances. The case and the judge's views were cited in the *New York Tribune* on the front page:

> It is unnecessary to inquire what were Richard Wagner's intentions on entering into this contract. Its language is clear, precise and unambiguous, and it must be assumed that the parties who thus express themselves in written contracts intend what they express. This contract did not make B. Schott's Sons merely the agents of Richard Wagner to introduce his "musical-dramatic work" to the world, reserving to him the power to regulate the time, place, manner and content of each introduction; for a valuable consideration he transferred to them the exclusive right of publication for all countries, and all that such publication implies. He did reserve the acting right in regard to theatres, and it is understood that under the law of Germany a publication of the entire work coupled with the notice to the effect that acting rights are reserved secures such rights to the composer's family for a certain number of years after his death....

> Subsequent to Richard Wagner's death, possibly before there had been any publications, even in Germany, of the entire work, this original contract of September 16, 1881, was modified by a contract between his heirs and the firm of B. Schott's Sons. This second contract is dated October 29, 1884. It recites that by the first contract "Herr Richard Wagner has formally resigned in favor of the firm of B. Schott's Sons, the acting right of 'Parsifal' as to concerts." The heirs relinquish 15,000 marks of the consideration named in the first contract. (*New York Tribune*, November 25, 1903, p.1)

The court's decision about the phrase carried by the score was stated by Judge Lacombe as follows:

> ...it is the well settled law of this country that, if the publication is complete, such notice is ineffective to reserve the very right which such publication dedicates to the public....The three volumes contain the score of "Parsifal" completely and fully. In view of such publication, neither the composer nor his heirs can insist that performance be enjoined. (*New York Tribune*, November 25, 1903, p.1)

With all the attendant publicity, Wagner's heirs had created the impression that every music lover in Germany was violently opposed to Conried's planned production of *Parsifal*. Milka Ternina, who had created the role of Kundry at Bayreuth, was interviewed by the *Times* at once upon her arrival in New York:

> [Mme. Ternina] has come direct from Germany, and according to her, the musical population there has no objection at all to Mr. Conried giving "Parsifal" to New York. It is only the kinsmen and very intimate friends of Frau Wagner that think it ought to be kept in [Bayreuth] forever.
>
> Over Mme. Ternina's part, Kundry, there [exist] as much debating and controversy as over the deepest of Browning's poetry or the most complex of Ibsen's heroines. Students have sat up nights trying to fathom Wagner's innermost thought when he wrote such and such a line, the result being, as might be expected, that they have come to many different conclusions....To [Mme. Ternina] Kundry is the symbolization of sin—fascinating, seductive sin, in direct opposition to Parsifal, who is the personification of innocence and purity....
>
> "...As to Parsifal being sacred," continued Ternina, "I think it is certainly not what you would call religious. I am sure that when he wrote it Wagner never intended the hero and Kundry to represent Christ and Mary Magdalen." (*New York Times*, November 26, 1903, p.4)

An editorial in the same issue of the *Times* took Wagner's heirs to task for their greediness and supported Conried, contending that his performances would equal or excel in artistry the performances seen at Bayreuth:

> No one...in this city can fail to be gratified that Judge *Lacombe* has found himself constrained by his judicial duty to frustrate that attempt...of a monopolist to continue a monopoly...though the copyright laws of all countries fix a term beyond which monopoly...shall no longer be lawful. But the attempt to base a monopoly on moral and quasi-religious grounds and to assume "sacred" motives for squeezing the last pfenning (*sic*] out of it is really disgusting....
>
> The heirs of Wagner in their characters of managers of the Bayreuth Opera House are notified that they must henceforth rely upon the merits of their production...in competition with that given by Mr. *Conried* in the Metropolitan Opera House of New York....the performance at Bayreuth will be improved accordingly in direct proportion to the importance there attached to American patronage. And, though Mr. Conried does not pretend to be actuated by any other than a business motive in the work...in which he has already given earnest of a brilliant success, it is quite safe to say that the atmosphere of the box office of the Metropolitan during the production of "Parsifal" will be quite as "sacred" as that of the box office at Bayreuth on the like occasion. (*New York Times*, November 26, 1903, p.6)

The day after the December 24 performance, New York papers carried two-column spreads with huge headlines proclaiming the event as an epochal achievement in the city's cultural development. The *Times* contained the most conclusive description:

Parsifal, A Triumph

Production Unrivaled in History of Opera in New York—Immense Audience, Deeply Impressed with Wagner's Festival-Play Listens Breathlessly Throughout the Performance...

A Splendid Production

"Parsifal" was presented in a manner wholly befitting its distinctive character as a work of art—a manner that recognized and gave a full exposition of the solemnity and dignity of its theme, the lofty eloquence of its treatment, the overpowering impressiveness of the drama. This must be clearly made known, to serve as it may and as far as it can to answer the sneers that have been leveled at the artistic appreciation, understanding and standard of achievement of the New York public.

The artistic value of the "Parsifal" production was of the very highest. It was in many respects equal to anything that has ever been done at Baireuth, and in some much superior. It was without doubt the most perfect production ever made on the American lyric stage. Those who wish to quarrel with the performance on aesthetic, moral or religious grounds have still as much upon which to stand as before; artistically it was nothing less than triumphant.

The spirit that filled the representation in most of its elements and that animated all that participated in it was one of reverence and devotion to the ideals of the master, of zealous eagerness in carrying out his intentions in all things great and small, in the score. The interpreters of the chief personages of the drama were singers who have drawn knowledge and understanding of its requirements from the fountain head at Baireuth, and who have been among the most distinguished participants in the festival performances there—Mme. Ternina, Mr. Burgstaller, and Mr. Van Rooy.

The chief masters of stage craft and of scenic manipulation had been summoned from Germany to superintend and coordinate the material factors. Scenery and costumes had likewise been brought from German ateliers, the work of artists and of artisans intimate with the necessities of the drama, instructed by the exposition of them made at Baireuth, willing to improve upon these models, and actually doing so.

The musical direction was in the hands of a master-conductor thoroughly imbued with the style and significance of Wagner's music, and of authority to compel a realization of his wishes—Mr. Alfred Hertz.

All that money, thought, care, and incessant and intelligent labor could do had been lavished upon the production of "Parsifal." The results as shown in last evening's performance nobly crowned the work of many months. (*New York Times*, December 25, 1903, p.1)

The interest in the opera was so intense that the *Times* printed a half page of themes from the work in actual music notation. Ten themes were included: The Last Supper; The Holy Grail; Belief; Amfortas Suffering; Promise; The Wild Kundry; Kundry, the Helpful; Parsifal; The Lament; and *Herzeleide*.[14]

The first two and a half pages of the *Times* and *Tribune* were devoted to pictures, attire of the audience, carriage regulations, prominent people in attendance, and tributes such as "Conried's great achievement." The remaining item of particular interest revolved around a resolution adopted by the directors of the Conried Metropolitan Opera Company at a special meeting. The resolution read:

> Resolved, that the board of directors takes this occasion to put on record its appreciation of Mr. Heinrich Conried's untiring efforts during the last year of preparation, and its admiration for his splendid executive and artistic ability in the presentation of grand opera in New-York. It also wishes to express its entire sympathy and hearty support in his production of "Parsifal," which puts before the music lovers of this country so worthy a presentation of Wagner's great work. (*New York Times*, December 25, 1903, p.1)

Metropolitan Premiere of Donizetti's L'Elisir d'Amore

Once more the New York critics referred to the practice of staging an opera explicitly for the purpose of gratifying a leading singer, whether at the request of the singer or as a managerial decision to present a noted artist in a role well suited to that singer's voice and personality. The production of Donizetti's *L'Elisir d'Amore* was predictably criticized on this ground; the fact that the work has survived these many years, of course, weakens the validity of the criticism. The Metropolitan premiere of the opera at the January 23 matinee, under the direction of Vigna, included Caruso, Sembrich, and Scotti. A substitution, unheard of in today's performances of the opera, was made by Sembrich in the light of some "almost unsingable music" for Adina. The performance was well received by the *Times* and, according to the review, also by the audience:

> The presence of Mme. Sembrich in the company of the Metropolitan Opera House was obviously the chief instrument to a revival of this, as it has been in recent years of Donizetti's other comic operas, "La Fille du Regiment" and "Don Pasquale."...The opera has all the conventionalities of what has aptly been designated the "palaeo-technic Italian style," both in the libretto and in the music. Yet there is real humor in the former which such accomplished comedians as those concerned in the representation have the most of....

> It is very slight in texture, a trifle light as air, and requires much facility and lightness of touch to carry it off successfully. But in this way it was treated by Mme. Sembrich and all her companions in the cast....In the last act she substituted the allegro of the air "Prendi per me sei libero," the air from "Lucrezia Borgia," "Il mio riguardo," as being a more tuneful and effective piece than the almost unsingable music that Donizetti has written there, and not likely to disturb the equanimity of any sticklers for the unities....

> ...The score, indeed, is full of melody of the sort in which Donizetti was so facile and though it becomes rather monotonous to modern ears, with its phrases turned on the same model and its everlasting similarity of cadence, its grace and fluency are unceasing, and its vivacity is most dexterously consorted with the rippling of the comic spirit. The appeal it made to the audience yesterday afternoon was evident. (*New York Times*, January 24, 1904, p.5)

The singers were all praised for their contributions to the performance, particularly Caruso for his singing of the popular aria "Un furtiva lagrima." The *Times* review included coverage of the evening performance, *Aida*, as well, and remarked on Vigna's chore of conducting two operas the same day. The *Tribune* was much less enthusiastic about the opera, obviously considering it an unnecessary revival, but was pleased with the singers.

> ...Mme. Sembrich has done the service for Donizetti's opera that Mme. Gerster did for it twenty years ago, and we should be grateful. We have drifted far from the old moorings in the interim, but they loom up invitingly when singers like Mme. Sembrich, Signor Caruso, Signor Scotti and Signor Rossi point them out so graciously as they did yesterday. The story of the opera is tenuous and flimsy. Its feelings lie in the surface, and the humor of the quack Dulcamara is not calculated to entertain us long. But there is a winning grace and a pretty sparkle in Donizetti's music which fits the simple scene, and it really seems yesterday to have taken on freshness with the stage pictures and the dresses of the characters. (*New York Tribune*, January 24, 1904, p.11)

Metropolitan Premiere of La Dame Blanche

The primary result of the performance of Adrien Boieldieu's *La Dame Blanche* was to reaffirm the need for a smaller theater devoted to the production of *opera-comique*. At its February 13 premiere the opera was performed in German, as *Die Weisse Dame*. The city's two major newspapers disagreed on the merits of the work. The *Times* regarded it as dated and as having lost most of its favorable attraction.

> The necessity of "Die Weisse Dame" came from Mr. Conried's new tenor, Mr. Franz Naval, for whose debut it was expressly agreed upon....
>
> [The opera] presented a somewhat wrinkled visage at its emergence upon the Metropolitan's stage yesterday afternoon. It shows its years more than some of the other operas of an earlier time that have recently been revived on that stage. It abounds in melody of an old-fashioned sort; there are few solo airs for the chief personages, but a number of duets and trios effective after their kind; and there is much for the chorus to do of the most conventional character. But "Die Weisse Dame" has not much sparkle or buoyancy left in its music to-day. "L'Elisir d'Amore" and "La Fille du Regiment" are old-fashioned enough, but there is an effervescent spirit in them which keeps their vitality. (*New York Times*, February 14, 1904, p.9)

The *Times* review carried a subheadline referring to the opera as "Boieldieu's Opera Comique." This implication was carried further by the *Tribune*, which found the opera far more rewarding, even in the vast Metropolitan auditorium:

> ...Boieldieu's music is charmingly melodious, and Mr. Mottl read it with obviously sincere sympathy and affection. Care had been bestowed upon the preparation of the work on its musical side, and it made quite as excellent an impression as could have been expected. That it is wholly out of place in the Metropolitan Opera House need scarcely be said. That its music and comedy could give us as much pleasure as

they did emphasizes again the need several times discussed in this place...of an adjunct to one large operatic institution adapted to the requirements of polite opera comique. (*New York Tribune*, February 14, 1904, p.9)

Repertoire during the First Season under Conried

The season of 1903–1904, Conried's first at the helm of the Metropolitan, produced results somewhat different from those of Grau's policies. Only twenty-six operas were performed, but productions totaled ninety-four. *Parsifal*, produced twelve times, was the most sensational offering in many years, if not since the opening of the Metropolitan Opera House. *Cavalleria Rusticana* appeared eight times, coupled with *Pagliacci*, *Mefistofele*, or *Coppelia*. *Aida* received six performances. The remaining works were fairly evenly distributed, and *Carmen* and *Faust* no longer dominated. No Wagnerian opera, other than *Parsifal*, received any concentrated degree of attention. The Wagnerian offering consisted of twenty-six productions divided among six operas, including two complete *Ring* cycles.

The first tour under Conried's auspices traveled to eleven cities, presenting sixty-one operatic performances. *Carmen* and *Faust* enjoyed their usual lead, with eight and seven performances, respectively; *La Traviata* ranked third with five productions. The trend toward equalizing the number of productions of the tour operas continued, and the disparities were small. Five conductors were engaged in the tour, Franko, Hertz, Hinrichs, Mottl, and Vigna.

THE SECOND SEASON UNDER CONRIED'S MANAGEMENT (1904–1905)

Conried's second season failed to meet the challenge of the sensational first effort. The *Parsifal* premiere and Caruso's debut, by themselves, had provided the new manager with all that was necessary to inject an air of flamboyancy into his first season. The second year produced only two novelties, neither of them as significant. The first novelty was the Metropolitan premiere of Donizetti's *Lucrezia Borgia*—the Metropolitan's only performance of that opera to this date. The second novelty, and Conried's second benefit for himself (the first had been the premiere of *Parsifal*) was to be the Viennese light opera *Die Fledermaus*, by the younger Johann Strauss. Conried added sufficient talent to the operetta's party scene to insure a capacity audience.

The roster stimulated more interest than did the list of operas. Eames and Nordica had returned, but Calvé had retired permanently from the Metropolitan after the previous season. Campanari and Gadski had absented themselves temporarily, and Ternina had joined Calvé on the retirement list. Saléza, who had been a leading tenor during Grau's regime, returned for one more season at the Metropolitan. No major male artists were added, and the most significant change in the female roster, other than those already mentioned, involved the return of Melba and Katti Bettaque, now Katherine Senger-Bettaque, who had been with the German company during the season of 1888–1889. The list of conductors had been narrowed to three. Mottl had left, dissatisfied with Metropolitan performances, and Hinrichs had not been reengaged. Hertz and Vigna were joined by Franko, who had again been elevated to the status of a regular conductor. The season opened on November 21 and closed on March 5, with no supplementary season.

Metropolitan Premiere and Only Performance of Donizetti's Lucrezia Borgia

The production of *Lucrezia Borgia*, one of the only two novelties of the season of 1905–1906, met with practically no favorable response. The *Times* was impressed neither by the opera nor by the quality of the singing at the December 5 premiere. Its criticism of the lack of correspondence between music and libretto probably pinpoints the reason for the opera's failure, then and since. The subhead for the review read: "Reason for this opera's revival not apparent."

> Whatever plausibility of excuse may have been found for the resuscitation in recent years of half a dozen other neglected operas of the old Italian list there is very little for this. "Lucrezia Borgia" has lain on the shelf in New York for twenty-two years; and it has deserved the neglect into which it has lapsed....
>
> Donizetti filled it full of his prettiest and most inconsequential melodies, which flow unctuously through the score, with no imaginable relation to anything that goes on upon the stage, and whose only object is plainly to give the singers something to sing. They certainly give no kind of expression to the dark deeds and flatterings of wickedness that constitute the texture of the opera. It is a repetition of empty formulas and passages and is absolutely without a trace of dramatic characterization. Modern historians have done a good deal to rehabilitate the name and fame of the wicked Borgia; but there is not much but blame for her doings as they were represented by Donizetti's librettist, who followed Hugo's deep-dyed tragedy. Nobody would suspect it, however, from the music that is sung by her or about her.
>
> "Lucrezia Borgia," to be tolerable, must be sung with all the beauty and distinction of "bel canto"; but there was very little of that in last evening's performance....
>
> ...Mr. Vigna conducted with his usual energy....But neither he nor any of the others concerned...could give any good reason...why "Lucrezia Borgia" should be galvanized again into a semblance of life in this day and generation, and set before the public of this day and generation. (*New York Times*, December 6, 1904, p.6)

The *Tribune* was even less encouraging of Conried's attempt at an attractive novelty.

> There was an Italian revival at the Metropolitan Opera House last night, happily also a burial. After a gracious silence of twenty-two years had enwrapped all of Donizetti's "Lucrezia Borgia," except the brindisi, which was hauled forth and vulgarized at Sunday night concerts for years, the opera was brought forward again last night. If it did not receive its quietus there is much misery still to be endured by Mr. Conried's subscribers. Perhaps he will be compassionate and save it for a Lenten season.

There has been a reason for nearly all of the Italian operas of the Rossini, Bellini, Donizetti period which have been kept on or restored to the repertory of the Metropolitan during the last score of years. In the case of some like the "Barber of Seville," the perennial freshness and beauty of the music and the sprightliness of the comedy have pleaded their own cause. In the case of others like "La Fille du Regiment" and "L'Elisir d'Amore," there were irresistable pleaders like Mme. Sembrich, and latterly Signor Caruso. Why the [cerements] of "Lucrezia Borgia" were ripped open and the mouldering corpse dragged forth is a mystery. A great vogue the opera never had, even when Donizetti stood for what was thought to be old and good as contradistinguished from the rude forcefullness of Signor Verdi. Yet with Grisi, Alboni, Mario and Tamburini or Lablanche singing the music, there must have been something reasonable in its appeal to the popular heart. (*New York Tribune*, December 6, 1904, p.7)

Metropolitan Premiere of Die Fledermaus

The annual benefit for the manager was still a contractual obligation of singers at this time. For his February 16 benefit, Conried chose to produce *Die Fledermaus*, a vehicle in which he could bring before the audience as many of his leading singers as possible, assuring himself of a full auditorium at advance prices.[15] The singers scheduled to appear in the second-act ballroom scene of the Strauss opus comprised a nearly endless list. The program of the concert in Act 2 was reproduced in newspapers on the following day:

Cavatina from *Semiramide*...Rossini
　by Mme. Maria de Macchi
Tyrolean Quartet...Koschat
　by Robert Blass, Alois Burgstaller,
　　Frank Pollock, and Anton Van Rooy
Norwegian Song, "God Morgan"...Grieg
　by Mme. Aino Ackte
Air "Quand'ero paggio," from *Falstaff*.....................................Verdi
　by Antonio Scotti
Quartet from *Rigoletto*...Verdi
　by Mmes. Louise Homer and Lillian Nordica;
　　Enrico Caruso and Eugene Giraldoni
Song "Les Filles de Cadiz"...Delibes
　by Miss Olive Fremstad
Trio from *Faust*...Gounod
　by Mme. Emma Eames, Pol Plançon and
　　Francesco Nuibo
Conductor: Nahan Franko[16]

The final chorus, "Bruderlein und Schwesterlein," received a remarkable performance by the Metropolitan Opera chorus augmented by the voices of all the company's leading singers. The cast included Sembrich, Walker, Bella Alten, Dippel, Reiss, and Goritz. A guest artist was present: Max Hänseler of the Irving Place Theatre, another of Conried's theatrical ventures, played Frosch, the jailer.

The *Times* again commented on the loss of effectiveness of this type of production at the Metropolitan Opera House:

> Soberly speaking, "Die Fledermaus" loses much in being presented on so big a stage and in so big an auditorium as those of the Metropolitan Opera House. There is much spoken dialogue and the quick touches of fun do not carry through its whole extent. The finer and more delicate portions of the music, as in many operas of a more intimate quality than the one given in that house, evaporate. But these were considerations that did not count for much last evening. Everybody was in the gala spirit; the operetta sparkled and flashed. (*New York Times*, February 17, 1905, p.5)

Writing in the *Tribune*, Krehbiel was less generous toward Conried's choice of *Die Fledermaus*, comparing Strauss to Offenbach and to Gilbert and Sullivan. The review was titled "Operetta and Vaudeville."

> The generation of to-day, whose recollections of [Strauss's] waltzes are the recollections of youth, remember him also as the creator of a dozen operettas, which are as characteristic of Vienna as Offenbach's were of Paris under the Second Empire and Gilbert and Sullivan of the England of our time. Of these…"Die Fledermaus" is the best. But that fact does not fit it for the repertory of the Metropolitan Opera House. There its music, with all its piquancy and grace, sounds thin, and there its comedy is wasted. The humor of the dialogue is dissipated in the yawning spaces…and the vulgarity of the farce in the third act, with its scenes of drunkenness and its horseplay, is out of place….The most irresistible representation of the vis comica was Mr. Haenseler, of the Irving Place Theatre, as the drunken jailor. (*New York Tribune*, February 17, 1905, p.9)

Krehbiel's comments about the operetta's vulgarity reflect the conservative nature always evident in his reviews, later to be so obvious when Richard Strauss's *Salome* was introduced.

Repertoire during the Season of 1904–1905

Ninety-three operatic presentations were given during 1904–1905, Conried's second season. Wagner dominated; the number of productions of his operas had grown back to thirty-six, better than one-third of the total. All the best-known Wagner operas except *Der Fliegende Holländer* were performed. *Parsifal* was staged eight times, *Die Meistersinger* seven, and *Lohengrin* six. The *Ring* received two complete productions. *Aida* had five performances; Conried's offering tended to favor large spectacle operas.

The second tour by the Conried Metropolitan Opera Company was far more extensive than its initial venture. Sixteen cities were included on a tour that went as far west as California, as well as into the deep South. *Parsifal* received nineteen performances, many of them in cities not visited the previous year. *Cavalleria Rusticana* and *I Pagliacci*, as a double bill, were produced seven times; they shared this frequency of performance with *La Gioconda*, *Les Huguenots*, and *Lucia di Lammermoor*. Sixty-five programs were the total effort of the tour.

THE THIRD SEASON UNDER CONRIED'S MANAGEMENT
(1905–1906)

As in the preceding season, the third year of Conried's management produced minimal change in the roster of artists. Melba had once again left the Metropolitan but Sembrich remained, so there was no problem with the roles that they had shared. Of the new artists the most prominent was to be Heinrich Knote, a heroic Wagnerian tenor. With Dippel and Alois Burgstaller, his addition brought Conried's total in this category to three. Among the women the new acquisitions included Bessie Abott, an American, and Marie Rappold, a lyric soprano fitted for the lighter Wagnerian heroines. The conductors remained the same, Franko, Hertz, and Vigna, but Engelbert Humperdinck, the composer of *Hänsel und Gretel*, appeared as a guest conductor at a Sunday night concert.

The season promised an improvement over the previous year's offerings as far as new productions were concerned. *Hänsel und Gretel* was to be the first new opera produced and Conried had selected Johann Strauss's *Der Zigeunerbaron* as the performance for his benefit. As with *Die Fledermaus*, the benefit would serve the dual purpose of benefit and premiere performance. The season opened on November 20 and ran until March 18 with no supplementary season.

Metropolitan Premiere of Humperdinck's Hänsel und Gretel

The Metropolitan's singers in the November 25 matinee premiere of Humperdinck's *Hänsel und Gretel* were joined by Lina Abarbanell, who was a member of Conried's Irving Place Theater Company, as had been the case with Max Hänseler the previous year. Abarbanell portrayed Hänsel. The rest of the cast consisted of Bella Alton as Gretel; Marion Wood as the Mother, Gertrude; Otto Goritz as the father; and Louise Homer as the Witch. Hertz conducted, and Humperdinck, who had achieved extra renown as Siegfried Wagner's teacher, was in the audience. New York had heard *Hänsel und Gretel* ten years earlier when Augustus Harris, the English opera producer, had brought it to Daly's Theatre for a performance in English under Seidl's direction. The *Times* gave high compliments both to the opera and to its composer, finding Humperdinck's ability evident in the orchestration, brilliancy of thematic usage, and remarkable knowledge of counterpoint, with which the score abounded:

> Mr. Humperdinck has used certain familiar folk tunes; he has devised others of his own in their spirit. His more pretentious themes have charm, expressiveness, and fine feeling. His writing for the orchestra is subtle and full of the most delicate color effects, brilliancy and warmth, yet always delightfully transparent. In thematic treatment he commands all the art and learning that the modern contrapuntist has learned from Wagner's latest methods.

> And the composer, it must be said, is deeply indebted to Wagner, especially to the Wagner of "Die Meistersinger." There are many pages in the first act whose relation

to that score are too obvious to be overlooked. There is much of the "Meistersinger" color and feeling throughout the work, and there are suggestions from "The Ring" and even a strain from "Tannhäuser." But the disposal of such borrowing from such a source, in such a manner, is the work of a man of remarkable cleverness. It is not given to all to bend the bow of Ulysses as he has. (*New York Times*, November 26, 1905, p.9)

The *Tribune* was equally lavish in its praise and also took the opportunity to cast further aspersions on Conried's choice of operettas for his benefits. *Hänsel und Gretel* was referred to as an artistic achievement of significance:

"Hänsel und Gretel" still maintains its dewy freshness, keeping young the physically aging hearts of those who knew it in its youth, and showing how supreme art can be used to preserve the ingenuousness of appreciation which lies at the bottom of all sense of the truly beautiful. It is doubtful if Mr. Conried will do anything more artistic this season than this production of Herr Humperdinck's opera [and] when he lowers a noble institution to produce another operetta, to take advantage of popular curiosity and the idly careless spirit of the times for the sake of his private exchequer, the ghosts of Hansel and Gretel ought to rise up to shame him. Meanwhile it is to be hoped that the fairy opera will have many representations. (*New York Tribune*, November 26, 1905, p.7)

Debut of Bessie Abott in La Bohème

Bessie Abott was another in the constantly increasing list of American singers who became respected members of the Metropolitan Opera Company. Her career was limited because the size of her voice was insufficient for the auditorium of the Metropolitan. Prior to her operatic debut she "plunked a banjo and sang 'coon' songs with her sisters on the vaudeville stage."[17] She came to the Metropolitan, however, as a pupil of Jean de Reszke, who had by this time established a remarkable reputation as a singing teacher in his home city of Paris. Reviewing her January 20 debut, the *Times* found her most promising in spite of the limitations in the volume of her voice:

The idea she gave of her powers last evening was considerably higher than she gave at her previous appearance on the concert stage. She took the part of Mimi, in which this public is accustomed to artists of the highest rank, and took it very acceptably. Her voice in the Opera House sounded small, except when she made her greatest demand upon it, like a delicate thread; but it carried well, and while it is penetrating, it is yet agreeable in quality, and she knows how to use it with some skill in giving utterance to varied emotional expression, within a certain range. (*New York Times*, January 21, 1906, p.7)

The *New York Tribune* review, signed by Krehbiel, granted Abott credit for her pure, sweet voice but called attention to her lack of ability to portray the pathos and drama necessary to satisfactory performance in a role such as that of Mimi. Nevertheless, the reviewer recognized her promise and achievement:

It is a voice of lovely timbre, especially in its medium register, of impeccable purity, of considerable sweetness, and because of its purity it has a carrying power out of all proportion to its quantity, its size, as some would say. It is a sympathetic, a winning voice, and is the medium of an ingratiating if not a large artistic intelligence. It is in exquisite harmony with a charming personality. It is not assertive enough to escape effacement in ensemble, nor does she yet know how to hold attention to herself by distinctive dramatic work, as last night's second act disclosed; therefore she cannot sound the tragic note which even so frail a work as Puccini's opera makes possible. But there was nice achievement and better promise in all she did. (*New York Tribune*, January 21, 1906, p.7)

Metropolitan Premiere of Der Zigeunerbaron

Conried's third benefit took place on February 15, 1906, with a performance of Johann Strauss's *Der Zigeunerbaron*. Again he had arranged for an array of artists to head a bill that would attract a capacity audience. The cast itself included Dippel, Goritz, Blass, Alten, Rappold, and Homer. Some of the extra artists to take part were Mmes. Abott, Eames, Fremstad, Sembrich, Walker, and Weed; MM. Burgstaller, Caruso, Campanari, Dufriche, Journet, Knote, Plançon, Reiss, Scotti, and Van Rooy; pupils of the Opera school; members of the ballet.[18] Nordica was to appear but was "indisposed." Conried had first produced *Der Zigeunerbaron* twenty years earlier at the Casino Theatre. On the present occasion the *Times* again offered the opinion that an operetta was "ill adapted to the Metropolitan Opera House." The newspaper did not actually review the performance but instead commented sarcastically on the method of inserting the additional artists into the story and estimated Conried's return from the proceeds as $22,000:

> The plea that the operetta is worthy of a place in the repertory of the Metropolitan Opera House because it has been in the lists of German houses is specious and maladroit. It was not produced at the Court Opera in Vienna, but at the Teater-an-der-Wien.

> "Der Zigeunerbaron" has never been admitted to the repertory of the Court Opera. Only one of Strauss' operettas has received this honor, and that was only for a brief space and under unusual circumstances. Mr. Mahler desiring to do something handsome financially for the pension fund of the members of the opera house, gave three or four gala performances of "Die Fledermaus," with the principal singers of the opera in the cast. The performances were all out of the regular course, however, and no other operetta of Strauss's has thus been signalized, though, we believe one of Offenbach's has.

> ...Moreover, if the great works of the masters are to be sacrificed for the sake of such fly-by-nights as "Fledermaus" and "Zigeunerbaron" the mission of the Metropolitan Opera House is at an end. (*New York Tribune*, February 16, 1906, p.7)

The program inserted into the third act was as follows, omitting the Nordica selection due to her failure to appear:

Comin' Thro' the Rye...Abott
Couplets de Vulcain (*Philémon et Baucis*)..............................Journet
Brindisi (*Lucrezia Borgia*)...Walker
Parla Waltz (Arditi)...Sembrich
Der Verlaubte Bua (Koschat).............................Knote, Burgstaller,
                                               Van Rooy, Blass
Les Filles de Cadiz (Delibes)...Fremstad
Aria (Hunyadi Laszlos) (Erkel)...Nordica
Serenade (*La Damnation de Faust*) (Berlioz).........................Plançon
Habanera "Tu" (Fuentes)...Eames
Duo (*La Forza del Destino*).................................Caruso and Scotti[19]

Caruso Performs Carmen *in French for the First Time*

The first performance in a new language by an artist of the stature of Caruso created considerable anticipation among the opera patrons of New York. That Fremstad was to appear as Carmen and Journet as Escamillo further intensified public interest. Abott was chosen to portray Micaela, and Vigna was the conductor. The performance drew a capacity audience. The *Times* review of the March 5 performance showed mixed emotions; the critic appreciated Caruso's singing, found his acting out of character with the role, and called attention to the tenor's addiction to the affectations of Italian opera:

> It is true that in the highest pitch of the emotional tension at the close of the opera [Caruso] cannot refrain from some of the lachrymose manifestations that usually accompany his denotements of great passion. But in this and the third act as well he showed some powerfully temperamental traits in his acting. He sings the music, of course, with much beauty of tone. The purely lyric portions he delivered delightfully, as the duet in the first act, and the song about Carmen's flower in the second. It was strange that in neither of his entrances in the first two acts was a hand given to welcome him. In the second act, after his flower song, his ingrained Italian impulse to acknowledcge applause even in the most affecting situations brought him the tribute of a burst of laughter from the audience. (*New York Times*, March 6, 1906, p.9)

Krehbiel, writing in the *Tribune*, provided greater detail and indicated that Caruso had appeared in a ridiculous light. Caruso, generally considered to be sensitive in his feelings, must have been upset by the frivolity, even if his actions had generated it.

> Some of the dramatic blood which courses hotly through the opera seemed for a moment to have got into the brains of Signor Caruso in the second act. He had sung the romance with impelling fervor and fallen on his knees behind Carmen, sulking at a table. Then came the applause. It sprang up, swelled like a tornado, then died away as if a sudden intellectual awakening had brought the thought that the dramatic situation had reached a point where Don Jose should get up and fill himself again with the emotion of which he had just rid himself. Even Signor Caruso seemed to have come to a realization of the obviously proper thing. But the devotees of his voice began the plaudits again. Now there were hisses. Again the applause, and,

though the hisses were redoubled, the strain was too much for the tenor. He put aside his attitude of piteous, desolate supplication, rose, acknowledged the applause, and returned to weep on Carmen's right shoulder blade. The humor of the new situation seized upon the audience, then spread to the stage, the dramatic illusion had taken wings. (*New York Tribune*, March 6, 1906, p.7)

Repertoire during Conried's Third Season at the Metropolitan (1905–1906)

The third season under Conried's management had resulted in one highly successful premiere, *Hänsel und Gretel*, and the manager's second attempt to produce light Viennese opera, exemplified by *Die Fledermaus* and the latest choice, *Der Zigeunerbaron*. Caruso's first appearance singing in French and Abott's debut completed the major efforts of the season. Conried had occasion to demonstrate his admirable desire to avoid changing operas at the last minute. On January 19, 1906, Nordica, who was to sing Leonora in *Il Trovatore*, was indisposed. Previous Metropolitan impresarios would certainly have changed the opera, but Conried availed himself of the services of a prima donna from Mexico who was in New York for a brief period. Helene Noldi sang the role and made her only Metropolitan appearance, resulting in the performance of the scheduled opera.

The season's production consisted of 103 performances of thirty-one operas. Krehbiel's express desire to see frequent productions of *Hänsel und Gretel* was realized; that opera led the list with eleven performances. The nearest total to this was five performances, a distinction shared by six operas: *La Bohème, Faust, The Queen of Sheba, Lohengrin, Lucia di Lammermoor,* and *Rigoletto*. Wagner's operas accounted for twenty-nine productions, including two complete *Ring* cycles. *The Queen of Sheba*, which had previously been produced for three seasons during the German opera period, made its only reappearance in the history of the Metropolitan. During its best season, 1885–1886, it had been immensely successful, playing to capacity audiences and leading the repertoire with fifteen performances. Its record during 1905–1906 was mediocre; it had obviously lost its appeal. Marie Rappold's assumption of the role of Sulamith, sung by Lehmann in the earlier period, may have been a factor in the failure of the work to appeal to the public this season.

The third tour by the Conried Metropolitan Opera Company was abbreviated by the San Francisco earthquake. After two performances in that city, the disaster destroyed buildings, scenery, equipment, and instruments. San Francisco was the eighth city visited on that tour; forty-six productions had been given up to the time of the tragedy. Twenty-six works were performed. Of these, four operas shared the most repetitions at five performances apiece. These were *Faust, Hänsel und Gretel, The Queen of Sheba* and *Lohengrin*. Franko, Hertz, and Vigna were the conductors. Eleven productions of Wagner operas were included in the total.

THE FOURTH SEASON OF OPERA
UNDER CONRIED'S MANAGEMENT (1906–1907)

The fourth season under Conried was one of the most sensational in Metropolitan history. Premieres of new works included Richard Strauss's controversial *Salome*, as well as Giordano's *Fedora*, Berlioz's *La Damnation de Faust*, and two Puccini works, *Manon Lescaut* and *Madama Butterfly*. Coupled with these events came the debut of the Metropolitan's most celebrated American singer, Geraldine Farrar, and a guest conducting appearance by Camille Saint-Saëns. Emil Fischer returned for a benefit testimonial concert, during which he appeared as Hans Sachs in excerpts from *Die Meistersinger*, most artistically interpreted, according to the critics. His age was given as sixty-nine or seventy.

Knote had absented himself for the year, but the Metropolitan had acquired a new baritone, Riccardo Stracciari, who would remain for two seasons and sing major roles. He was overshadowed by Scotti but well received by public and press. A French tenor, Charles Rousselière, sang a few performances and appeared with Farrar in her debut on opening night in *Roméo et Juliette*. This was the only opening night during Conried's leadership when Caruso was not included in the cast. Presumably Farrar was already sufficiently celebrated to choose her own debut vehicle and Caruso's French was not yet at a level that permitted him to attempt the role of Roméo.

The major change in the female roster, other than the addition of Farrar, involved the return of Gadski and Nordica's final departure from the Conried forces. She later returned for a brief period under Gatti-Casazza. Krehbiel contended that Farrar was actually a protegée of Grau's, whom the former manager had been guarding until she was ready for her Metropolitan debut. In speaking of the transition period between Grau's and Conried's leadership, Krehbiel stated, "Mr. Grau had also negotiated with Felix Mottl, had 'signed' Miss Fremstad, and was holding Miss Farrar, in a sense his protegée, in reserve till she should 'ripen' for América."[20] A native of Melrose, Massachusetts, she was at this time twenty-four years of age.

For the first time Conried engaged a conductor for French operas, Samuel Bovy, who directed the opening-night performance with Farrar. *Lakme* was restored to the repertoire, conducted by the new director.

Farrar's Debut in Roméo et Juliette

Farrar had been hailed as a star in Europe and came back to the United States with a reputation far beyond her years. Her debut was sensational and the newspapers accorded her high praise both as a singer and as an actress. Her charm and personality received much comment and were to be predominant throughout her long career at the Metropolitan. Some of the more startling aspects of her portrayals did not unveil themselves in her initial seasons under Conried's management. The *Times* commented on the fact that she had sufficient youthful charm to portray Juliette and that it was coupled with the necessary vocal attributes:

Miss Farrar comes back to her native land as one of the American singers who have made fame and name for themselves abroad. It is not always easy to establish the same success in this country, and it may be that all she does will not meet with quite so unqualified acceptance as it has abroad. But she went far upon that road in what she accomplished last evening. She made a most agreeable impression in her impersonation of Juliette; for she is full of excellent instincts making for the best things as a lyric actress. She has a charming personality, a graceful and a winning one, and her stage presence is alluring and one with much of the girlishness of Juliette.

It has been said that by the time an actress has learned the art of denoting the passion and the ecstatic emotion of Juliette she could rarely still be in possession of the juvenile charm that the part needs. But Miss Farrar has it and has at the same time skill and resource in stage craft. She is a singer of remarkable gifts. Her voice is a full and rich soprano, lyric in its nature and flexibility, yet rather darkly colored and with not a little of the dramatic quality and with a power of dramatic nuance that she uses in the main skillfully. Her singing is generally full and spontaneous in delivery, well phrased and well enunciated, yet she is not a wholly finished vocalist, and there are matters in her singing that could not meet with entire approbation, as in the duet in the fourth act, where she sang with a certain constraint.

There will be more interesting and more important music for the exhibition of her artistic powers before the season is much further advanced. But there was ample cause in her [Juliette] of last evening for the high expectations that have been raised for her in the musical public of New York. (*New York Times*, November 27, 1906, p.9)

The *Tribune* was equally enthusiastic in its review and was particularly impressed by Farrar's voice. The comment directed at her overacting revealed more of an element of the prima donna than was generally found by critics of the early days of Farrar's Metropolitan career. Although this subject appeared in the review cited below, there was never any record of major conflicts between her and her colleagues:

Miss Farrar was most graciously received, and was then permitted with kind encouragement to win her way to popular approval. She won that approval, and she won more: she achieved her place among those whom a metropolitan [*sic*] audience recognizes as in the foremost of the world's operatic artists. She appeared as a beautiful version; youthful, charming in face, figure, movement and attitude. She sang with a voice of exquisite quality in the middle register, and one that was vibrant with feeling almost always. She acted like one whose instincts for the stage were full and eager, but also like one who, not needing to learn what to do, had neglected to learn that it is possible to do too much. Had she been one-half less consciously demonstrative, whenever she stepped out of the dramatic picture, one-half less sweeping in her movements and gestures when she was in the picture, she would have been twice as admirable to her compatriots who were rejoicing in her success, and twice as convincing to those who were sitting in judgment upon an artist for whom the trumps [*sic*] of acclaim have been so loudly sounded that their din will make calm listening difficult for some time to come. But she has won a welcome that must have emphatic expression. The few crudities in her vocalization are pushed into notice by the very excellence of her merits. Red and warm blood flows in her voice and pulses in harmony with the emotions of the play. She is eloquently truthful in declamation, and correct taste dictates her choice of nuance and vocal color. It is only when she forces her upper tones that sensuous charm leaves her voice in a measure and one deplores the departure all the more because the voice is of a carrying power that makes strenuousness unnecessary. (*New York Tribune*, November 26, 1906, p.7)

American Premiere of Giordano's Fedora

Umberto Giordano's *Fedora* represented Conried's second American premiere at the Metropolitan, *Parsifal* having been the first. The immense success of the Wagner work was rivaled only by the dismal failure of Giordano's opera. The primary objection was to the lack of material for an opera in the book; Giordano was criticized mainly for his choice of libretto. Reviewing the December 5 premiere, the *Times* made no derogatory comment about the composer's music for the new work:

> ...much dialogue...goes rapidly to the points when spoken, but is retarded by music. There are scenes like that in the first act—the greater part of the act—in which there is a police inquiry as to the murder of Fedora's fiance. In this, as in a number of others throughout the opera, music has little to do, little to say, because the scenes are prosaic or essentially not lyric; or they have not the emotional prompting that finds its right expression in music. What Giordano has done, and rightly done, as Puccini has done in "Tosca" in a very similar predicament, is to make most of his music an excited and fragmentary accompaniment to the action, and to seize moments of special emotional or dramatic significance and enforce them by musical elaboration. (*New York Times*, December 6, 1906, p.9)

The *Tribune*, likewise, found the work equally unfitted for an opera, but it also doubted that Giordano had the necessary equipment to be a successful opera composer. The critic commented favorably, however, on certain musical elements that were rather independent of the opera and its movement:

> Sensuous beauty is no longer sought; the tones have become only a condiment, a hot spice, which occasionally give raised expression to a shriek, but for the rest retard the action and disturb attention which might possess the power of characterization, and can color his melody as well as his harmony and orchestral judgment. Nothing approaching his skill could be found in Giordano's "Fedora." A more sluggish and intolerable first act than the legal inquest can scarcely be imagined. Fragments of inconsequential tunes float along in a turgid stream, while above it the people of the play chatter and scream, and become intelligible and interesting only when they lapse into ordinary speech. Ordinary speech is the only speech that an expeditious drama can tolerate, and it is not raised to a higher power by the blowing of brass or the beating of drums. The frankest confession of the futility of Giordano's effort to make a lyric drama out of "Fedora" is...that only those moments in this score are musical in the accepted sense when the play stops, as in...the intermezzo which cuts the second act in two, or when the old operatic principles wake again into life as in Loris's confession of love. Here, in the first instance, a mood receives musical delineation, and in the second a passion which is naturally lyrical receives utterance. One device new to the operatic stage in its externals, at least, in ingeniously employed by the composer. The conversation in which Fedora exhorts a confession from Loris is carried on while a pianist entertains the princess's guests

with a solo upon his instrument. But the fact that singing tones are used and not
spoken adds nothing to the value of the scene. (*New York Tribune*, December 6,
1906, p.7)

American Premiere of La Damnation de Faust

The December 7 production of Berlioz's *Damnation de Faust* as an opera was as
interesting to the public in 1906 as it might be today. The work had been heard in
concert form but not as an opera. The music was full of the interesting sounds for
which Berlioz even then was known. The eminent musicologist Paul Henry Lang has
described it as:

> ...sonority for its own sake; sonority which engenders ideas. The violence of
> [Berlioz's] mental experiences was such in these compositions that he was able to in-
> vest significant melodic invention with breath-taking intensity. His orchestra seizes
> one with a color[ing] that is never static but always dynamic, bent on moving the
> listener and carrying him away. Hence the great variety of contrasts in his orchestral
> writing, from brutal mass effects to the most delicate whispers.[21]

The critic for the *Times* considered that the operatic version added considerable
impact to Berlioz's music. He maintained that the composer wrote from a pictorial
viewpoint and that the visual representation therefore added to and was demanded
by the suggestions in the music:

> The result of last evening's performance goes to show that the music undoubtedly
> gains by a pictorial setting. Whatever Berlioz's musical inventiveness may have
> been, he had a riotous pictorial imagination. His score is full of scenic suggestions
> and indications that are addressed to the listener's mental vision. The thoughts lay
> near to carry those out by the resources of the stage setting and stage illusion, and the
> vividness of Berlioz's imagination is repeatedly attested by the success of the stage
> pictures. The passing of the soldiers to the strains of the Rakoczy march is a fine stage
> pagent. The [scene] of the Auerbach cellar has all the richness and variety of a pic-
> ture by Tesiers. (*New York Times*, December 8, 1906, p.11)

Krehbiel, writing for the *Tribune*, found the staging "only effective in spots." On
the other hand, he described the production and spectacle in laudatory terms, judging it as worthwhile:

> Not an opera, but a series of detached scenes, a beautiful spectacle wedded to
> some of the best music that came from the fantastic and glowing imagination of Ber-
> lioz. Mr. Conried's production is worthy of the best traditions of the Metropolitan
> Opera House....The piece has been provided with gorgeous raiment and the dance
> of the sylphs is performed by the Ballet Aerien-Heidenreich. (*New York Tribune*,
> December 8, 1906, p.7)

Christmas Concert by Saint Saëns

Camille Saint-Saëns had been on tour in the United States and made his final appearance at a Christmas concert at the Metropolitan. Nahan Franko shared the podium with Saint-Saëns, who conducted the latter portion of the program, which featured only compositions by the guests. The composer's part of the program, with the soloists who performed, was as follows:

Overture (*Les Barbares*)
Le Deluge..Nahan Franko
Trio, from Oratorio *Noel*.............................Rappold, Dippel, Simard
Danse Macabre
Marche du Couronnement[22]

The earlier part of the program, directed by Franko, had included a song, a selection from *Le Jongleur de Notre Dame*, an aria from *Samson et Dalila* and the "Fantaisie pour Piano," played by the composer. Although Saint-Saëns's conducting did not impress the critic on the *Times*, the dignity of the composer and his manner of carrying out his tour brought the highest praise.

Saint-Saëns' conducting exhibits many of the same qualities that are shown in his piano playing. It is smooth and even and graceful, seldom dynamic. He held his baton rather stiffly, and contented himself with pointing out nuances and effects with the least possible effort....

The dignity which has been one of the features of the Saint-Saëns tour was maintained during this concert, and the French composer can leave America knowing that he has resorted to none of the cheap tricks often used to advertise foreign celebrities. (*New York Times*, December 26, 1906, p.7)

The *Tribune* reviewer was completely unimpressed by the entire episode and showed no hesitation in stating so:

M. Saint-Saëns beat time for his music undemonstratively and accurately, but disclosed no other qualities as a conductor. Kind friends tried to infuse warmth into the affair, but in vain; it was neither inspiring nor edifying. (*New York Tribune*, December 26, 1906, p.7)

Metropolitan Premiere of Puccini's Manon Lescaut

The January 18 Metropolitan premiere of this early Puccini opera was an artistic triumph. Critical response was excellent, both to the work and to the artists involved in the premiere. The cast included Caruso, Scotti, and Lina Cavalieri; the conductor was Vigna. The *Times* granted the performance high praise:

The music has a remarkable flow of melody and the score has the transparency and unfailing charm by which Puccini is raised above his fellows of the contemporaneous Italian School. His style in "Manon Lescaut" is considerably more naive and spontaneous than it is, for instance, in "Madame Butterfly." He indulges more freely in definite and outspoken melody; he has not yet attained all the orchestral finesse, still less the extremely modern harmonic sense of the later work, and he relies less on effects of instrumental and harmonic color for getting his ends....The orchestra is consistently melodious, constantly expressive, rarely a merely accompanying medium. There is much variety and piquancy in its treatment, and there are many passages of dramatic warmth. (*New York Times*, January 19, 1907, p.7)

The *Tribune* critic, Krehbiel, was highly receptive to the opera, questioning why it had not been produced earlier at the Metropolitan. He reminded his readers that it had been performed at Wallack's Theatre in 1898 by a "vagrant Italian Company." He compared the opera favorably with other works by Puccini and commented on the excellent performance by Caruso:

Why it should have waited till now, and for the stimulus of the composer's coming before reaching the Metropolitan Opera House will not easily be explained by those admirers of the composer who have long known, or at least felt, that in spite of the high opinion in which "La Boheme," "La Tosca," and "Madame Butterfly," are held here, "Manon Lescaut" is...fresher, more spontaneous, more unaffected and more passionate in its climaxes, as well as more ingratiatingly charming in its comedy element than any of the works from his pen that have succeeded it. The unmistakable voice of Puccini rings through all of its measures, but it is freer from the formularies which have since become more or less stereotyped, and there are a greater number of echoes of the tunefulness which belongs to the older period, between which and the present time the work marks a transition. After last night's performance there is little likelihood that "Manon Lescaut" will again be permitted to fall into a desuetude, at least so long as Signor Caruso remains associated with the opera in New York, for in the character of the Chevalier des Grieux that artist has one of the finest mediums that he has yet disclosed for the exploitation of his phenomenal gifts of voice and manner. (*New York Tribune*, January 19, 1907, p.7)

American Premiere of Richard Strauss's Salome

The controversy created by the proposed production of *Salome* was as sensational as the opera itself. For weeks preceding the January 22 performance, which was a benefit for Conried, the question of its propriety was raised in the pulpit as well as in operatic circles. No evidence indicates that the Board of Directors took any stand whatsoever prior to the actual performance, although many stockholders absented themselves from their boxes on the night of the premiere. Alfred Hertz was the hero of the occasion; what little space was granted to critical writing rather than to philosophical dispute awarded full credit for the excellence of the production to Hertz. The *Times* review praised him in the following terms:

Above all and through all in this performance was the commanding influence of Alfred Hertz, the conductor whose unflagging zeal and contagious enthusiasm, whose complete mastery of the score and authoritative exposition of it brought forth last night's remarkable performance after months of the most exacting preparation. The orchestra, upon whom falls perhaps the most arduous burden of all this task, accomplished wonders. It played with immense power and color, with all the shades of dramatic nuance demanded of it. Everyone connected with this production earned praise. (*New York Times*, January 23, 1907, p.9)

The *Tribune* review by Krehbiel likewise held Hertz in high esteem for his part in the performance:

> As for the praise deserved by Mr. Hertz for preparing the work and guiding his 130 artists through its labyrinths, it can scarcely be pitched in too high or eloquent a key. It was the accomplishment of something near a miracle. (*New York Tribune,* January 23, 1907, p.7)

The cast included Fremstad in the title role, Van Rooy as Jokanaan, Burrian and Weed as Herod and Herodias, and Dippel as Narraboth. The opera was preceded by a concert in which Caruso, Farrar, Scotti, Sembrich, Burgstaller, and Journet led the list of singers. The financial results were estimated at $23,000 for Conried, from a capacity audience. All three conductors appeared at the gala evening, Bovy and Vigna directing the concert and Hertz the opera. The Dance of the Seven Veils was performed by Bianca Froelich, the prima ballerina of the Metropolitan.

Both newspapers carried more information on the behavior and reaction of the audience than on the performance itself. The *Times* described the scene in these words:

> After the curtain went up on "Salome" there was no sensation until the dance began. It was the dance that women turned away from, and many of the women in the Metropolitan Opera House last night turned away from it. Very few men in the audience seemed comfortable. They twisted in their chairs, and before it was over there were numbers of them who decided to go to the corridors and smoke.

> But when...Mme. Fremstad began to sing to the head before her, the horror of the thing started a party of men and women from the front row, and from the Boxes 27 and 29...two parties tumbled precipatately into the corridors and called...to get their carriages.

> But in the galleries men and women left their seats to stand so that they might look down upon the prima donna as she kissed the dead lips of the head of John, the Baptist. Then they sank back in their chairs and shuddered. (*New York Times,* January 23, 1907, p.9)

The *Tribune* revealed the fact that Conried was home, ill. An impressive article on the music admitted that there were "beautiful spots" and alluded to Strauss's ability to perform amazing feats of coloring by the use of six horns. Krehbiel, in his book *Chapters of Opera*, attributed the following unsigned article to W. P. Eaton , who he asserted spoke for him:[23]

> ...the opera moved to its appointed end, sinister, compelling, disgusting.

> ...It remains to record that in the audience at the performance, as at the dress rehearsal on Sunday, the effect of horror was pronounced, many voices were hushed as the crowd passed out into the night, many faces were white almost as those at the rail of a ship, many women were silent, and men spoke as if a bad dream were on them. The preceding concert was forgotten; ordinary emotions following an opera were banished. The grip of a strange horror or disgust was on the majority. It was significant that the usual applause was lacking. It was scattered and brief. (*New York Tribune,* January 23, 1907, p.7)

On January 26 the Board of Directors released the following communication to the press, having communicated it to Conried earlier:

> The Directors of the Metropolitan Opera and Real Estate Company consider that the performance of "Salome" is objectionable and detrimental to the best interests of the Metropolitan Opera House. They therefore protest against any repetition of this opera. (*New York Tribune*, January 27, 1907, p.1)

The *Tribune* continued the article in which the above was quoted with the following comments:

> To say that this letter was a bomb in the Conried camp is putting it mildly. The house is almost sold out for next Thursday's performance already; the work is the climax of the season from Mr. Conried's point of view, and he has rehearsed for six months, and spent much money on the production. Finally, Mr. Conried is under contract to Richard Strauss to play the opera ten times this season in America. Not to do so means to forfeit many thousand dollars to the composer...and to give back all the money taken in for next Thursday alone would hurt. (*New York Tribune*, January 27, 1907, p.1)

Conried had issued a defense for his position and this appeared in the same issue of the newspaper in a separate article:

> Mr. Conried holds that the production of "Salome" is a great artistic achievement. Inasmuch as this music drama has been acknowledged by the musical world as one of the most important, if not the most important musical production since Wagner, and has been produced in many of the most important opera houses in Europe, including the Royal opera houses of Dresden and Berlin, as well as La Scala in Milan, and in Turin, in Italy, and is now in preparation for production at the Imperial Opera House in Vienna and the Grand Opera House in Paris, Mr. Conried said that it was his duty to the musical public of New York to produce this work. He had spared no effort or expense to make the production in all respects a worthy one. There have been numberless acknowledgements of the greatness of the work, and the success of the production, and but few hostile criticisms. The only religious personage in the work, John the Baptist, is treated with the utmost dignity and reverence. Mr. Conried hopes that the directors of the Metropolitan Opera and Real Estate Company, upon full consideration of the subject, will withdraw their objections and will share his view that the musical public is entitled to an opportunity to hear this masterwork adequately produced. (*New York Tribune*, January 27, 1907, p.1)

History records the fact that the directors did not alter their view, and Conried was prevented from further productions of *Salome*. Krehbiel, in an emotional statement years later, remarked that "the sale of tickets amounted to next to nothing, and Mr. Conried yielded with as much grace as possible."[24] The newspapers quoted here, however, indicated that the demand for tickets was great and that the performance scheduled for the following Thursday was already sold out. It was never revealed whether the directors reimbursed Conried for his huge expenditure; it is certain, however, that *Salome* did not reappear at the Metropolitan Opera House until January 13, 1934, when it was performed with Gota Ljungberg, Friedrich Schorr, Max Lorenz, Dorothee Manski, and Hans Clemens; Artur Bodanzky was the conductor.[25]

Metropolitan Premiere of Madama Butterfly

The earlier newspaper report remarking that the season had reached its climax with the *Salome* production did not allow for the importance of the Puccini premiere yet to come. On February 11, 1907, Conried produced *Madama Butterfly* with a cast that included at least four of the Metropolitan's foremost singers—Caruso, Farrar, Homer, and Scotti. Vigna was the conductor. The *Times* review was highly laudatory to Farrar while complimenting Caruso's singing, if not his acting. Scotti's performance as Sharpless was considered excellent. The report also gave a significant account of the critic's opinion of the opera:

> Puccini has wrought his music into the very substance and spirit of the drama. It is his subtlest and most highly finished orchestral score, and denotes an advance on his previous operas in the matter of fine detail as well as orchestration and the manipulation and development of his themes....His use of local color compels admiration for its skill and sincerity, as well as for its restraint; for an excess would soon weary and offend. The several Japanese tunes he employs are unmistakable in their character, but they bring no ugly and jarring element into the score....So [also] with the strain of "The Star Spangled Banner," which he brings in from time to time... and which is by no means the uncouth intrusion that it might be.
>
> He has heard new harmonies, and has adventured further afield in the use of augmented intervals and chords of the higher dissonances in strange sequences than he has done before, even in "Tosca." Nor has he forgotten the flowing and mellifluous melody that sparks eloquently in "La Boheme" and "Tosca," as in his love duet between Butterfly and Pinkerton at the end of the first act. (*New York Times,* February 12, 1907, p.9)

The *Tribune* gave a detailed account of the performance of the major singers. Farrar received the greatest praise, but the other artists were also lauded for various aspects of their performances. The review, on the whole, was one of the most outstanding of the Conried period at the Metropolitan.

> "Madama Butterfly" has brought to Miss Farrar another opportunity to disclose her splendid gifts of dramatic representation. Freed from occasional extravagance of action, which robs it of repose, which is as essential in tragic moments of the second and third scenes as in the comedy of the first, her impersonation would be almost ideal. In pose, gesture, vocal interpretation, facial expression, movement, it is full of eloquence and grace. She sounds the note of deep pathos in both action and song convincingly, and last night won the tribute of tears from many eyes. Her growth into womanhood and from womanhood to tragic stature is beautifully presented without abruptness and with real power. As she is a beautiful vision, her triumph was complete. Of Signor Caruso no one would expect an impersonation with even a little dramatic illusion; but the music is a perfect vehicle for his voice, or his voice for the music. Signor Scotti, besides singing well, has filled a needed plea for America by making a manly man out of the Consul Sharpless. Madame Homer

looks, sings, and acts the part of Suzuki with lovely devotion to every detail, and Mr. Reiss makes an amusing busybody out of Goro, the matchmaker. (*New York Tribune*, February 12, 1907, p.7)

Testimonial Concert for Emil Fischer

On March 15, the Metropolitan presented a benefit in the form of a testimonial concert for the aged and revered Emil Fischer. Of the artists who participated, only Dippel had been a member of the Metropolitan when Fischer left there in 1891. The program, a strenuous one, included the first act of *Die Walküre* with Fremstad, Burgstaller, and Blass; the first and second scenes of Act II of *Lohengrin* were given with Gadski, Schumann-Heink, and Goritz. The final excerpt was Act III, Scene 1, of *Die Meistersinger* with Gadski, Schumann-Heink, Dippel, Goritz, Reiss, and Emil Fischer himself, now approximately seventy years old. This was one of the few occasions in the history of testimonial performances when the recipient of the honor performed on the program. In spite of his advanced age, the critics, kindness aside, found considerable merit in his performance. Both major reviewers commented on his artistry, which had not left him and which made it worthwhile to hear him at his farewell. The critic of the *Times* spoke in these terms:

> [Fischer] gave the part with much of his old spirit of geniality, humor, and tenderness that roused many memories. Time has made its inroads upon his voice, but the old finish of style and excellence of diction, the old declamatory expressiveness were there, and the fact that Mr. Fischer sang with so much voice and beauty of tone as he did in this, his sixty-ninth year, bespoke the art of the singer....
>
> It was stated that the benefit had realized for Mr. Fischer a sum between $7,000 and $7,500. (*New York Times*, March 16, 1907, p.9)

The *Tribune* found equally favorable words for Fischer's performance:

> Mr. Fischer, in spite of his seventy years, disclosed in his middle register much warmth of tone. Above and below the old voice was gone. But the old grace and charm and authority were not. It was good to look upon him.
>
> ...Mr. Conried donated the opera house and the services of every attendant and paid for his own box. (*New York Tribune*, March 16, 1907, p.7)

Repertoire During Season 1906–1907

The season's total was ninety-five productions of opera. The number of performances was fairly evenly distributed, with *Hänsel und Gretel* and *La Bohème* each produced seven times. *Tosca* ranked third with six performances. Twenty-four Wagnerian productions were given, but included only one complete *Ring* cycle. Puccini had started to rival Wagner in total performances; *Tosca*, *La Bohème*, *Manon Lescaut*, and *Madama Butterfly* totaled twenty-one productions during the season.

The tour comprised fifty-nine productions and traveled to twelve cities. The west coast was excluded from this tour, possibly because of the destruction of the auditoriums in San Francisco, or understandably, because the artists had too recently lived through the 1906 earthquake. *I Pagliacci* and *La Bohème* led the list with eight performances each. *Aida, Hansel und Gretel*, and *Tannhäuser* were produced seven times apiece. Only six performances of Wagner were given. The four Puccini operas were presented at twenty-one performances. The popularity of these operas was mounting steadily, and Conried was sufficiently astute and perceptive to take advantage of this trend.

THE FIFTH AND FINAL SEASON UNDER CONRIED
(1907–1908)

The management of the Metropolitan Opera House was to work the same effect on Conried that it had on his predecessor. Illness had started to affect him during the fourth season and he died in 1909, a single year after his retirement from activity at the Metropolitan Opera.

The roster for the fifth season showed little change except in conductors. Two major male artists were added, Alessandro Bonci, a tenor, and Feodor Chaliapin, the noted Russian basso, an extraordinary actor among opera singers. Bonci was overshadowed by Caruso, as were all tenors during this period. His reviews indicated that he possessed an excellent voice, but he left the Metropolitan after three years. Heinrich Knote had returned to bolster the heroic tenors. Among the female singers the only significant absence was that of Schumann-Heink, who had left for a two-year period.

Among the conductors only Bovy and Hertz were retained. Vigna did not return. Franko was missing from the list of conductors until the season of 1912–1913, when he carried out his final season in that capacity. The new conductors were Rudolfo Ferrari and Gustav Mahler. Ferrari was a member of the company for only one season and was released with the arrival of Toscanini the following year. Mahler remained for three years, and in addition to being a major composer, proved to be an outstanding conductor who injected new life into performances at the Metropolitan Opera House.

The season opened on November 18 and continued through April 18 with the exception of a week's tour to Boston early in April. In addition to Chaliapin's debut in *Mefistofele* and Mahler's debut conducting *Tristan und Isolde*, two novelties were scheduled: Francesco Cilea's *Adriana Lecouvreur* and Pietro Mascagni's *Iris* both received their Metropolitan premieres. Operatic competition with the Metropolitan was mounting, because Oscar Hammerstein was in his second season at the Manhattan Opera House, where he was specializing in French opera with Mary Garden, conducted by Cleofonte Campanini. Hammerstein's repertoire included such works as *Pelléas et Melisande, Thaïs, Louise*, and *La Navarraise*. Ultimately the Metropolitan Opera was forced to buy Hammerstein out in order to destroy him as a competitor.[26]

Chaliapin's Debut in Boito's Mefistofele

In his November 20 portrayal of Mefistofele in Boito's opera, Feodor Chaliapin was sufficiently extreme in his make-up and acting to startle the critics and the public. His thoroughly demoniacal conception of the part was in contrast to that of his predecessors. The *Times* found the Russian basso to be in poor voice, an opinion not shared by the *Tribune* reviewer. The former willingly admitted, however, that the new artist was a worthwhile addition to the company:

> Mr. Chaliapine was a striking and singular Mefistofele seeking apparently to emphasize all the disagreeable traits that could be attributed to the Prince of the Powers of Darkness. He is of herculean size and an actor of resource and skill. His voice is a ponderous bass, but it was plainly not in good condition last evening. There were evidences of his hoarseness; and, indeed, it was at one time doubtful whether he would be able to make his appearance at all last night. He made a deep impression, nevertheless, if not always a wholly agreeable one, and gave promise of doing much that will prove interesting in the course of the season. (*New York Times*, November 20, 1907, p.9)

Strangely enough, the *Tribune* commented most favorably on his voice, mentioning neither the hoarseness nor the possibility that he might not have appeared. Apparently Chaliapin's reputation as an actor had preceded him, but the critic had not expected a voice of fine caliber. The review was excellent.

> M. Chaliapine is undoubtedly an artist, even if his ideals are not praiseworthy. His physical appearance ought not to create greater admiration than his splendidly rotund voice and his eloquent declamation. It may be a pleasure, instead of a mere excitement, to see and hear him in other parts. At least it would be a pity if the chief result of his coming would be only the transformation of Boito's opera into something like a Christmas pantomime or a raree [*sic*] show. (*New York Tribune*, November 21, 1907, p.7)

Metropolitan Premiere of Mascagni's Iris

Mascagni's *Iris* proved to be a disappointment, even though the critics found its technique smoother and subtler than that of the composer's earlier *Cavalleria Rusticana*. Lacking, apparently, was the dramatic quality he had successfully achieved in *Cavalleria Rusticana*, which continued to enjoy numerous performances each season. The *Times* description of the December 6 premiere was enlightening:

> In "Iris" he has got miles away from the blatant musical style of "Cavalleria Rusticana," by which alone he is still known to most American music lovers. There can be no doubt that the later opera is the product of a more refined and sensitive feeling than the earlier; a more delicate feeling for orchestration, a subtler harmonic sense—and also of a deliberate aiming at the bizarre, with far less of that turbulent [directness], tunefulness, and hot-blooded expressiveness that has kept the vitality in "Cavalleria Rusticana" in spite of all its egregious faults, for so many years. There is little passion in "Iris" and little heart....The musical texture is made up of short

strands, semi-melodious phrases, declamatory passages, with now and again a longer development in the orchestra. A good deal of the melodic material is banal and there are echoes of Mascagni's predecessors and contemporaries to be heard at times. There is also a certain striving after harmonic originality...that takes the form of strained and inconsequent discordance that seems often at variance with the prevailing tone of the picture. (*New York Times*, December 7, 1907, p.9)

The *Tribune* noted that the composer had directed the opera in New York about five years before. At the time Mascagni had been on a brief American tour directing four of his operas, *Iris*, *Zanetto*, *Ratcliff*, and *Cavalleria Rusticana*. After a catastrophic attempt in New York he had gone to Boston. Following that episode the composer became involved in an unpleasant struggle with his managers, the Mittenthal brothers. Krehbiel gave a pathetic story of the outcome:

After his New York fiasco Signor Mascagni went to Boston, where troubles continued to pile upon him till he was overwhelmed. He fell out with his managers, or they with him, and in a fortnight he was under arrest for breach of contract in failing to produce the four operas agreed upon. He retorted with a countersuit for damages and attached theatrical properties in Worcester which the Mittenthals said did not belong to them, but to their brother. The scandal grew until it threatened to become a subject of international diplomacy, but in the end compromises were made and the composer departed to his own country in bodily if not spiritual peace. One achievement remained: the Musical Protective Union of New York had asked the federal authorities to deport the Italian instrumentalists under the Alien Labor Contract Laws, and the Treasury Department at Washington decided in its wisdom that no matter how poor a musician might be, he was not a laboring man, but an artist, and not subject to the law. Exit Mascagni.[27]

The previous year had brought *Madama Butterfly* to the Metropolitan and *Iris*, with a Japanese plot, suffered by comparison. The *Tribune* critic liked neither the play nor the music but approved the performance as produced by Conried's forces:

This Japanese opera loses much in being brought into contrast with "Madama Butterfly." The play is diffuse and ill constructed. No one can possibly want to follow its symbolism, and without that symbolism there is no cogency in the plot, but much weariness of the flesh for those who follow the music....Mr. Conried has provided an admirable representation. (*New York Tribune*, December 7, 1907, p.7)

Mahler's Debut in Tristan und Isolde *with Fremstad*

There was no question of Gustav Mahler's prestige when Conried brought him to the Metropolitan. The interest in his debut was intense, and Fremstad's appearance as Isolde added to the anticipation. The performance on New Year's Day, 1908, featured a cast that included Fremstad, Homer, Knote, Van Rooy, and Blass, supported by Muhlmann and Reiss. Both Mahler and Fremstad received excellent critiques, and Mahler's new interpretation was accepted with enthusiasm as well as surprise:

The influence of the new conductor was felt and heard in the whole spirit of the performance. He is clearly not one of the modern conductors, upon whom the ban of [Bayreuth] of the present day rests, with the result of dragging the tempo and weighting the performance of Wagner's works with lead. His tempos were frequently somewhat more rapid than we have been lately accustomed to; and they were always such as to fill the music with dramatic fire.

Most striking was the firm hand with which he kept the volume of orchestral sound controlled and subordinated to the voices. These were never overwhelmed; the balance was never lost, and they were allowed to keep their place above the orchestra and to blend with it always in their rightful place. And yet the score was revealed in all its complex beauty, with its strands of interwoven melody always clearly disposed and united with an exquisite sense of proportion and an unerring sense of the larger values. Delicacy and clearness were the characteristics of many passages, yet the climaxes were made superbly effectual. Through it all went the pulse of dramatic passion and the sense of fine musical beauty....

Mme. Fremstad's voice is of indescribable beauty in this music, in its richness and power, its infinite modulation in all the shades and extremes of dramatic significance. It never sounded finer in quality and never seemed more perfectly under her control. And her singing was a revelation in the fact that the music was in very few places higher than she could easily compass with her voice. The voice seems, in truth, to have reached a higher altitude; and to move in it without strain and without effort. (*New York Times*, January 2, 1908, p.9)

The *Tribune* critic also noted the speedier tempi that Mahler brought to the opera, and like his colleague, commented favorably on the result. Fremstad's performance failed to evoke the unqualified praise that the *Times* reviewer had accorded it:

It was easy to recognize in Herr Mahler's work last night that he is a master of his art whom New Yorkers will take particular delight to honor....Mr. Mahler did honor to himself, Wagner's music and the New York public. It was a strikingly vital reading which he gave to Wagner's familiar score; livelier in tempo in many portions than we are used to, and, inasmuch as the acceleration of tempo in nearly every instance [was] to the benefit of the dramatic effect, to that extent admirable—eloquent in phrasing, rich in color, elastic in movement and always sympathetic with the singers....
   Mme. Fremstad delighted her admirers by her singing of the music of Isolde, which was found, quite unexpectedly, to lie well within the range of her profoundest depths by the power of her action. Her conception of the character of Isolde is imaginative and beautifully expressed in many respects, but it is far from finished, except in some of its smaller details. It is weakened, for instance, by her failure to realize the significance of the ironical and scornful speeches to Tristan in the first act but it is vocally opulent and frequently eloquent. (*New York Tribune*, January 2, 1908, p.7)

Fidelio *Conducted by Mahler*

Mahler instituted many changes in *Fidelio* at his first performance of this work at the Metropolitan Opera House on March 20. In addition to certain scenic alterations, he transposed clarinet parts in isolated sections of the opera in order to achieve greater effect in the orchestra. Apparently he had done similarly in *Don Giovanni*, which he had conducted on January 23. The *Times* reviewer recognized these changes and raised—but did not answer—the question of whether Mahler was within his rights as a conductor.

> Mr. Mahler is a man of strong original ideas of his own, and his treatment of the Wagnerian dramas and "Don Giovanni" has shown that he makes no fetish of great masterpieces, and refuses to be bound by tradition, or even by the letter of the text. How far such an attitude is justified on the part of the conductor aiming to set an operatic performance in what he deems the most effective manner before the public, may be open to question. It is certain that in "Fidelio" Mr. Mahler makes a number of changes from accepted traditions and even in certain passages from the orchestration as set down by Beethoven. (*New York Times*, March 21, 1908, p.9)

The *Tribune* commented on the restraint in the orchestra and its resulting effect on the singers. The critic mentioned the division of the strings into smaller sections to achieve the necessary balance. The tone of the excerpt below indicated at least summary approval of Mahler's reduced string sections. Although all of his changes may not have met with the reviewer's approval, there was no question of Mahler's having overstepped the bounds of propriety:

> He has subordinated the orchestra to the singers so that every word and note can be heard, understood and felt. He has proceeded with freedom in the matter of nuance and has used his string voices in whole or detachments as he thought best from time to time....One effect was to enforce so much care upon the singers that they frequently appeared to be laboring under restraint and displayed little of the spontaneity which is essential to complete success. That the audience felt the power of the music was proved by the rapt attention with which it was heard, the applause after the first act, when Mr. Mahler was called before the curtain, as well as at the close, and the delight manifested after the overture. (*New York Tribune*, March 21, 1908, p.7)

Final Performance under Conried's Management—Götterdämmerung

The final performance of Conried's regime on April 18, 1908, involved a cast of major artists and was under the direction of Alfred Hertz, who had been with the manager throughout the latter's entire tenure at the Metropolitan Opera House. Martha Leffler-Burkhard sang Brünnhilde and Louise Homer was the Waltraute. The male singers included Burgstaller, Blass, and Muhlmann. The *Times* commended the performance but made reference to a number of inferior presentations earlier in the season:

> There was the same large attendance that had marked the three previous performances in the cycle, and there was every evidence that a profound impression was made upon the hearers by this performance.
>
> It was, in truth, one of the best performances of "Götterdämmerung" heard here in several years, one that cheered the hearts of the admirers of Wagner's colossal

masterpiece; one that was fitted to efface unhappy memories of bungling, incompe-
tent striving, and failure that have marred too many of the recent attempts at
Wagnerian music drama at the Metropolitan Opera House. (*New York Times*, April
19, 1908, p.9)

The *Tribune* made mention of Burgstaller's recent illness and commented that
Leffler-Burkhard had improved over her earlier performances. She had been heard
as Brünnhilde in *Die Walküre* four nights earlier. As had been the case in the past, at
the end of Conried's regime both newspapers had brought forth criticism for past
performances and the general result of the manager's administration:

> Record can be made, and it is made with a great deal of pleasure, of a thrillingly
> effective representation of "Götterdämmerung" at the Metropolitan Opera House
> last night. It was the close of the supplemental season of opera under the administra-
> tion of Mr. Conried, and what little feeling crept in which was not in harmony with
> joyous elation was that inspired by the theory that the dramas of Wagner had not
> received equally reverential and eloquent treatment all of the season. If they had
> there would have been less talk then there has been of the decline of popular interest
> in them, and less dispraise of Mr. Conried's management. (*New York Tribune*, April
> 19, 1908, p.7)

Repertoire during Conried's Fifth Season

Conried's final year saw more performances than any other season during the
twenty-five years of the Metropolitan's existance. One hundred twenty-five programs of opera were presented in a well-balanced repertoire. With three exceptions,
all operas received from three to seven performances each; *Adriana Lecouvreur, Das
Rheingold,* and *Götterdämmerung* received two, one, and one, respectively. *Aida,
La Bohème* and *Mefistofele* led the list with seven productions of each opera.
Twenty-four Wagnerian performances were given, with one complete *Ring* cycle included. The four Puccini operas received twenty-four performances collectively.
The French repertoire continued to decline, with a total of eleven performances, six
of *Faust* and five of *Mignon*.

Conried's final tour was drastically curtailed and totalled only forty-four performances of opera. *La Bohème* and *Il Trovatore* were performed five times each, *Die
Walküre* on four occasions, and the rest of the operas each had from one to three productions. Other than eight presentations of opera in Chicago, the tour confined itself
to the eastern states.

CONRIED METROPOLITAN OPERA SCHOOL

During Conried's tenure at the Metropolitan Opera House he instituted an "opera
school" for the training of young singers. Little if anything has ever been known
about this organization. A number of performances at the Metropolitan during the
Conried period numbered opera school students in their casts. In addition to the

small roles in which these young singers appeared there were ensembles that were made up either partially or entirely from their ranks. The Flower Maiden's chorus in *Parsifal* provided an example of this procedure. Almost no reference to the opera school was found in the periodicals of the period although a large photograph of an Italian class was found in the rotogravure section of the *New York Times*[28]

Two sources were found in persons who had actually been involved with the opera school, one as a student and one as a teacher. Katherine Moran Douglas, who had been a member of the Conried Metropolitan Opera Company from 1903 through 1908, had also been a student in the opera school. Paul Eisler was at that time an assistant conductor; a duty assigned to him was coaching the singers in the opera school. He ultimately married one of these students, Edith (later Edythe) Vail Ross, who was also a member of the company and a student at the school for a number of years (1905–1908). In answer to specific questions, Katherine Moran Douglas, who when interviewed was a retired singer but an active teacher, replied as indicated below:

Question: When was the opera school founded?
Answer: In 1903 when Conried took over the opera house.
Question: By whom was it founded?
Answer: By Conried himself.
Question: For what specific purpose was it founded?
Answer: Theoretically for "cultural purposes" but this was only what Conried persuaded the directors of the opera to believe. Actually the venture was the laughing stock of New York. In it with Conried was Aurelia Jaeger, who had lived on the grounds at "Wahnfried" [Wagner's home] while her husband, Ferdinand, was studying with Wagner. I believe he created either Siegmund or Siegfried at Bayreuth.
Question: Who provided the financial backing for the school?
Answer: The Conried Metropolitan Company footed the bills. Mrs. Jaeger received about $5,000 a year salary. She had an assistant, a Mrs. Collins, who received about $1,000. The pianist-accompanist was Melanie Rice who got about the same salary.
Question: Who were the teachers?
Answer: Besides Jaeger, there were several. Luyster taught the only regularly scheduled class; this was sight-singing. Edouardo Petri taught Italian. There were no dancing or acting lessons. Every once in a while Paul Eisler or Kurt Schindler came to us and we really learned something. They were outstanding musicians as time showed and we learned more from them in a few minutes than in anything else we did in the opera school. Both were assistant conductors at that time. Eisler stayed on to become a regular conductor but Schindler became discouraged and left to make his career elsewhere.
Question: How many students were there and did they pay tuition?
Answer: There were usually about thirty students and they paid a high price although I only remember that it seemed high, I don't recall the amount. Lucy Lee Call was one of them and she was the daughter of a senator from Florida. She later became a voice teacher in Rochester at the Eastman School. Lucille Lawrence was another, whose voice was one with an incurable "break" in it but they never told her so. Your mother was there and also Blanche Yurka who, as you know, became a celebrated actress.

Question: In what operas did students participate in the chorus?

Answer: I specifically remember two, Boito's *Mefistofele*, and, of course, *Parsifal*. The students were useful to the opera for small parts as well as chorus.

Question: What students do you specifically remember participating in performances at the Metropolitan?

Answer: Lucy Call in *Die Walküre*, myself in *Hänsel und Gretel*, your mother, Edythe Vail [Ross] in *Hänsel und Gretel* and *Rigoletto*, Lucille Lawrence as the Shepherd in *Tosca*, Roberta Glanville in *Hänsel und Gretel*, Estelle Sherman also in *Hänsel* and of course a number of us in *Parsifal*. Alfred Piccaver later became a truly famous tenor in Vienna but never had a chance when he was a student. There just were no parts for a young tenor.

Question: What brought an end to the opera school?

Answer: There was no further interest; the thing was a fiasco and a farce.

Question: To what do you attribute its lack of success?

Answer: No boss, no scheduling, no formula, no organization, no curriculum—it was all freedom which really meant disorganization. With no one truly to head it, it never amounted to anything.

Question: What years were you there?

Answer: I was really the veteran; I stayed with it till the end, I was there from 1903 through 1908.

Question: Would you recommend revival of the school?

Answer: Years ago, I would have said, "yes," if it were properly run, but now, no, there are too many established competitors that are well organized such as the Mannes School, Juilliard, and the Manhattan School of Music. I believe they have Schorr and Brownlee there, for example, two truly qualified teachers.

Question: What percentage of students of the opera school continued in singing in your opinion?

Answer: Not more than two or three percent.

Question: You had both male and female students?

Answer: Yes, a few men, but they were nothing and amounted to nothing.

Question: What can you say about Conried as a manager?

Answer: The opera was poorly managed but it went on its own impetus because great singers like Caruso, Eames, Nordica, and Schumann-Heink made sure things were properly taken care of. They constantly reminded Conried of details which he then assigned to Goerlitz to carry out.

Question: Is there anything else you have that you would like to contribute?

Answer: Yes, I just had to smile as I remembered that your mother had her name changed at the suggestion of Alfred Hertz. We were taken to dinner one night by your father and Hertz. In the course of the conversation Hertz said to your mother, "You can't sing under the name of Ross, it means horse in German. You are delicate, why not use the name of Vail, your middle name—and spell Edith with a 'y'—it is more theatrical!" Your father then said he would take care of changing your mother's name, and he did.[29]

Eisler, when questioned regarding the opera school, had a similar opinion of its worth:

Actually, it was a publicity stunt that Conried devised when he first took over from Grau. He was looking for new things to do to impress the directors and this sounded very educational and altruistic. I taught there about once or twice every month and there were talented students. Conried used them frequently in performances and saved money that way. Schindler and I both were assured that we would be able to build a nucleus of future stars there but we realized the talent was not available. The best ones were Moran, Vail, and Call and they proved to be worthwhile artists. On the whole, the school was really worthless but the girls were charming and eager to learn so we did what we could.[30]

The interviews revealed that Mrs. Douglas's and Mr. Eisler's memories were excellent. The details that could be checked proved to be accurate. On this basis it was assumed that their opinions and enlightening information could be termed valid. Under the conditions described above it was not surprising that Conried failed to release considerable publicity concerning his opera school. The only singers ever to achieve any measure of success resulting from membership were those few mentioned by Mrs. Douglas or Mr. Eisler. Their talent was undoubtedly sufficient to have brought them some recognition without the aid of the opera school.

THE SAN FRANCISCO EARTHQUAKE

The earthquake which all but destroyed San Francisco in April, 1906, came two days after the Metropolitan Opera had opened its tour season there. Many stories have been told concerning the heroism of the artists and many amusing anecdotes have been related describing the occurrences that plagued the operatic refugees. Quaintance Eaton spent a number of years assembling details of the various tours and compiled numberless programs from old newspapers. The resulting book has been a valuable asset, and her description of the earthquake's effect on the Metropolitan Company is more complete than any other.[31] Of particular interest here are the figures provided by that author:

As soon as Conried learned that his flock had suffered no fatality, he turned his mind to figures. He would lose $210,000 on his properties, for which insurance would recompense him only $50,000. He would be obliged to refund $118,000 to San Francisco ticket-buyers—if they could be found. The artists must be paid to the end of their contracts. Conried determined further to give each male chorister a new suit and $5, each woman a $15 bonus.[32]

This excerpt was revealing in that it indicated that contracts in those days apparently carried no clause excusing the employer in the case of an "act of God," as is customary today.

Reports of the earthquake were included in the interviews with Moran and Eisler, who were both present during the catastrophe. The former described the event in her own words, as follows:

I was sharing a suite with your mother [Edythe Vail]. We got up immediately and ran out of the room in our nightgowns. After a few moments we went back in and dressed quickly. Of course all of the scenery, costumes, props and the theatre were burned. We were invited by the wife of the theatre owner to come to their house which was on Clay Street out beyond the devastated area. Caruso came in a taxi and stayed with us while they were getting water; there were no toilet facilities of any kind in running order. Scotti arrived a few minutes later with an empty cattle truck and he and I and your mother and Caruso toured the broken streets in that truck on our way to meet everyone at Golden Gate Park. This was only a few hours after the shock and yet I distinctly remember counting twenty-two coffins in the streets in the Chinese section and seeing the women, who had never been out of their houses because of tradition, running up and down the sidewalks weeping. After we met everyone we agreed to take the ferry to Berkeley the next morning. Caruso and Scotti took us back to the house on Clay Street and they went to the Family Club, a branch of the Bohemians in New York. We, your mother and I, first saw Caruso and Scotti in front of the hotel about fifteen minutes after the quake, both dressed in pajamas. The stories you read about them being immaculately attired in ascots and stickpins are pure baloney![33]

Eisler's story told of different people but essentially the same type of situation. He described his actions as follows:

Hertz and I were living in a suite. When the quake came, Hertz's bureau pinned him against the wall and he couldn't get out of bed. I heard him yell and rushed in and between us we got it loose. We both dressed quickly in the minimum attire and rushed down the back stairs to the street. There we found Goerlitz, Blass, Burgstaller, and Louise Homer. We stayed in the park in front of the hotel and watched until a horse and wagon came by. We rented them from the man for $100 and told him we would return them the next day. We all piled in, Homer included, and started looking for a restaurant. We finally found a little tavern on a side street and, although it was closing, we convinced the man to let us in for an extra $20 and we drank beer and ate cheese and crackers for an hour or so. Eventually we started for the Family Club and when we arrived there we met Dippel and Journet. Later Caruso and Scotti arrived and we all slept a few hours on chairs, sofas, and the floor. We later took the horse and wagon to the police station and left them, explaining where we had gotten them. The name was on the wagon and I am sure it was returned. We finally found a cab driver who agreed to take us to the ferry where we met the others.[34]

The consensus of the evidence indicated that the opera singers remained amazingly cool and good-humored during the tragedy. No mention was made in the Eaton book, or in the two interviews cited here, of any uncontrolled hysteria on the part of the Metropolitan Opera people.

SUMMARY OF RESULTS UNDER HEINRICH CONRIED

Conried, unlike his predecessors, had inherited a fairly stable and established company from Grau. He had his choice of a considerable number of reputable artists who had enjoyed an enthusiastic reception from the Metropolitan Opera patrons.

Grau, when he assumed the management of the opera house after Abbey's death, had found that the roster was populated with artists who had long passed their peak of efficiency. This was not the case with Conried, for many of the singers of the previous regime were either still developing or had reached the apex of their productive period and showed no signs of any decline. Gadski and Homer were typical of the former group, while artists who were in their most productive years included Eames, Nordica, Sembrich, Dippel, and Plancon. There were many others in both categories and Conried had no trouble casting his operas while he continued the quest for gradual replacements.

The scenery, costumes, and general *accoutrement* which Grau had used had been the recipient of favorable comment and was not to be compared with much of the equipment that Abbey had owned for many years; ultimately this had become the property of the Maurice Grau Opera Company after the triple management was dissolved by Abbey's death.

In the matter of conductors Conried was less fortunate. Hertz was the only major director to continue with Conried. Mancinelli had been at the Metropolitan almost continually for ten years and, although always considered a foremost conductor, he no longer appealed to the public as an exciting interpreter of opera. Hertz by contrast, had only conducted at the Metropolitan for one year previous to Conried's directorate and had enjoyed an enthusiastic reception after a somewhat dubious first few weeks.

Artistic Achievements of the Conried Metropolitan Opera Company

Conried's output at the Metropolitan exceeded that of any of his predecessors by a considerable number. During the five years when he headed the Metropolitan Opera, 510 programs of opera were presented as opposed to 434 by Grau's company in the same length of time. Conried's variety of opera exceeded that of the previous leader in this area, Grau, by five operas. The former had presented fifty-two different operas to the Metropolitan audiences during his five years at the head of the company.

From the point of view of tours, Conried had spent more time on the west coast than Grau but had not opened the new channels for opera that his predecessor had. Grau was far more interested in travelling than Conried and had taken the opera company to Canada and many areas with which Conried did not concern himself. Nevertheless, Conried's tour efforts were highly successful and did involve extensive travel. His policy was inclined to take him to a major city for an extended engagement rather than the short stops for which Grau contracted.

The engagement of prominent conductors was an outstanding feature of Conried's tenure as manager of the Metropolitan. Where previous impresarios had been content to have one major conductor on their roster, Conried often brought two men in the same area to the Metropolitan simultaneously. Two prime examples of this technique were provided by the engagement of both Mottl and Mahler during the period when Hertz was on the staff of conductors. During Conried's period as manager of the Metropolitan, his list of conductors included Bovy, Ferrari, Franko, Hertz, Hinrichs, Mahler, Mottl, and Vigna. In addition to this his policy was to engage occasional guest conductors as an attraction; most frequently these were composers rather than conductors, but they were sufficiently noted to attract an audience eager to see them perform in a new area. Henry Hadley, Engelbert Humperdinck, and Camille Saint-Saëns were examples in point. The concerts performed during Conried's leadership featured remarkable artists performing in the capacity of guests. Eugene Ysaye, the Belgian violinist, and Josef Hofmann and Moritz Rosenthal, world renowned pianists, led the list of guests during these years.

Singers were outstanding under Conried, but their roster represented a combination of Grau's and Conried's acquisitions. Caruso, the greatest attraction in the history of opera both at the Metropolitan and elsewhere, was signed by Grau but made his debut under Conried. Geraldine Farrar, the beloved American soprano, was a Conried addition to the list, as were Fremstad, Walker, Abott, and Chaliapin. Eames, Gadski, Nordica, Dippel, Scotti, Plançon, Journet, Blass, Burgstaller, Calve, Melba, and Sembrich were all the result of Grau's administration, but served to make many of the performances under Conried of the highest artistic level.

New productions were frequently sensational during Conried's career at the Metropolitan. The *Parsifal* premiere achieved the ultimate in both artistry and public appeal. The opera was repeated twenty-six times within a period of five years. In addition to this it frequently led the tour offerings. *Salomé*, although it only received the one performance as a result of the controversy, was a major artistic effort and was the result of Conried's courage as well as his desire for sensation. Metropolitan premieres of *Manon Lescaut* and *Madama Butterfly* contributed to the rise of Puccini to leadership of the repertoire. Numerous less successful works were presented for the first time during the five years in question, but the premieres of *Hansel und Gretel* and *L'Elisir d'Amore* were of more than passing importance. The most performed operas during this period were *Aida, Parsifal*, and *La Bohème*, with 27, 26, and 25 performances, respectively. Wagner was produced on 157 occasions, with ten operas represented. Puccini's four works at the Metropolitan accounted for 67 performances, while Verdi, with five operas, received 75 productions. Donizetti ranked fourth with 33 productions of five operas.

The opera school could not be considered as a serious effort from any available evidence. Moses in his biography of Conried avoided any detailed account of its operation. He described what was probably its primary function in one sentence when he commented on the problems of a chorus strike that had beset Conried:

> The orchestra, under Nahan Franko, remained loyal, and as far as the chorus was concerned, Mr. Conried reaped the benefit resulting from his establishing an opera school. He called upon the pupils in the different classes for aid. [35]

Financial Results under Conried

As in the case of all the previous managers, financial results were neither publicly revealed nor turned over to the Metropolitan Opera House. In the matter of

Conried's management the closest sources to the actual figures were probably Kreh-biel and Moses. Krehbiel was entrusted with considerable confidential information by all the impresarios when he was writing his book, *Chapters of Opera*. Moses who was a close friend of Richard Conried, the manager's only son, was granted access to the impresario's papers both before and after the manager's death.

Isolated reports of receipts and expenses provide a degree of insight into Conried's operation. From information revealed by Moses it was deduced that the box office receipts during the season of 1906–1907 totalled $1,312,068; approximately $1,209,000 was the gross for 1905–1906; box office receipts for 1904–1905 were $1,285,000; $1,107,000 was the comparable figure for 1903–1904.[36] Krehbiel's figure for 1906–1907, the only year for which he reports, was considerably lower, at $1,005,770.[37] For the receipts from *Parsifal*, Krehbiel and Moses provided identical results, $186,308 for eleven performances, averaging $16,947.[38]

Information on singers' salaries provided valuable figures for comparison. Caruso's salary was given at $2,000 per night; Nordica's was $1,250 each perform-ance; Sembrich's salary was given at $1,000 each appearance; and Eames received $1,500 per performance. Although these salaries were not necessarily for the same year, they are indicative of the general trend.[39]

Conried, who had assumed management for all of Caruso's ventures, managed a tour for him in 1908. In seven concerts the gross receipts amounted to $42,656; after expenses the profit to the manager was $2,000 per concert;[40] The manager's personal income received assistance each year from the benefit performance. The operatic evenings netted him about $20,000 and the final benefit concert during his last season resulted in financial aid amounting to $18,819[41] The cost to Conried of staging the ill-fated *Salome* was given at $25,000, which it was assumed he took as a personal loss.[42] A final testimonial concert, voluntarily presented by members of the company on March 24, 1903, added $19,119 to Conried's income.[43]

Perhaps one of the greatest contributions that Conried made was to further the ac-ceptance of American-born singers. He brought Weed, Walker, Abott, Farrar, and other natives to the principal roles, while his ill-advised opera school did result in chances for such as Vail, Moran, Sherman, Call, Lawrence, and Glanville. Henry Hadley, the eminent American conductor-composer, made his first major ap-pearance as a guest conductor at a Metropolitan Sunday night concert. Conried, an Austrian-born, European-trained man of the theater, evidenced a deep interest in American artists. Whether this was the result of a superior business sense or a purely altruistic motive may not be determined, but the effort was made and the result, to a notable degree, was successful.

CHAPTER 8

The First Twenty-Five Years: Summary and Conclusions

Five administrations operated the Metropolitan Opera during the first twenty-five years. (This figure is the result of considering the German opera period as one, although Leopold Damrosch's death resulted in a change of management to Edmund C. Stanton. Since Stanton in essence carried out Damrosch's original ideas, the period was considered to be one administration.) Because the organization was so new, the success or failure of each administration determined a new policy. There was no past history to provide a tradition from which to digress; startling shifts in policy became the history of the Metropolitan simultaneously with their existence. However, each period of management produced certain outstanding performances, premieres, singers, and conductors. Varying degrees of quality and financial success pervaded the twenty-five years under consideration here, but during this era each season contributed in some degree to the impressive history of the organization.

FACTORS INVOLVED IN SUCCESS OR FAILURE

Henry E. Abbey Management

The failure that quickly overtook this opening regime could be attributed to any of three factors involved in the first season of opera at the Metropolitan: the public, the stockholders, and Abbey himself. The audiences demanded expensive prima donnas and quickly indicated a preference for performances that featured an idol in the cast at the expense of an efficient, well-rounded production. These boxholders and ticket purchasers cared little for the quality of the work or the obvious plethora of old favorites that took the place of promised novelties.

Abbey's efforts in regard to new productions were also limited by the need to contend with all the problems of a new building, as well as a new organization. As a result, *La Gioconda* was his only contribution toward increasing and enhancing a repertoire consisting of established and frequently heard operas.

In the matter of singers Abbey's record was better. Nilsson, although a leading prima donna of the time, never returned to the Metropolitan and therefore did not become a significant artist in its history. The same might be said of Italo Campanini, although he appeared briefly during two seasons when Abbey once more became involved in the administration of the Metropolitan. However, Abbey brought two female singers to the opera house who returned after the German opera period and achieved outstanding records. Sembrich has been regarded as among the very finest lyric-coloratura sopranos, as Scalchi has occupied a similar position among contraltos. Among conductors, Vianesi enjoyed a sound reputation, while Cleofonte Campanini was later to have a distinguished career with Hammerstein, rather than at the Metropolitan.

Abbey's initial effort was complicated by the enormity of the struggle for survival between the newly-constructed Metropolitan Opera House and the older, established Academy of Music. The competition resulted in exorbitant salaries for the singers and conductors and the division of a single audience between two houses for opera. Famed prima donnas were featured at both theaters, but the general quality of performances was highly irregular because the chorus, orchestra, and supporting singers were of considerably less degrees of excellence, due to the high cost of star salaries.

Abbey failed to show the courage to operate the new venture along lines any different from those that Mapleson and the other managers had pursued for years. Had he been willing to gamble on a new procedure and produce operas other than the humdrum works that had been repeated in New York for a generation or more, and had he likewise been willing to defect from the star system with which he was competing, he might slowly have overcome the habits of a complacent public and provided the impetus for change that was needed. His first year might have been less sensational, but a second would have occurred, and the deficit would certainly have been less than he suffered with the extravagant salaries he was paying to Nilsson and Campanini, notwithstanding the adjustment period during which public support would have been curtailed.

The directors had to share the blame for their pressure on Abbey to produce familiar operas with stars and to make the costumes and decor of the new opera house supersede the performances in importance. Their refusal to invest more money after they had sunk a huge amount into the actual construction of the building was inconsistent with their professions of sincerity and public service as reasons for the original venture.

The German Opera Period

In a comparative analysis of the five administrations that operated the Metropolitan Opera during its first twenty-five years, this regime would have to be considered eminently successful. The factors involved in its success were not complicated; in fact, the simplicity of the operation contributed in a great degree to its success. From the viewpoint of the directors and consequently the stockholders, this period was one in which they were not burdened with any extraordinary assessments for supporting the opera house. The rent they paid for the use of their boxes was the total that they needed to donate.

The management during the German opera period was to be congratulated for its maintenance of a superior and balanced staff of outstanding performers. While there were few or no stars, there were numerous exceptional singers, even in minor roles, and conductors of extraordinary ability and reputation. The orchestra and chorus achieved a level of perfection that was not equaled in any period within the scope of this study. The only obvious criticism that might have been directed toward the management was the policy of frequently repeating an opera four or five times within a two-week period. The caliber of performances, when the operas were of the traditional German repertoire, was consistently high. The public, certainly not the same public that patronized Abbey's initial season, was superior in its appreciation of artistry. It applauded the productions and supported them at the box office.

Although many artists brought credit to this period, two conductors and three singers stand out above the rest. Leopold Damrosch and Anton Seidl both ranked with the conductors of highest repute. The former, unfortunately, enjoyed only one season at the Metropolitan before his untimely death. Seidl had a distinguished career that lasted eleven years and included two great eras of Wagnerian performances, those during the period referred to in this paragraph and later performances with the de Reszkes under the management of Abbey, Schoeffel, and Grau. The singers during the German opera period were all fine, but it was possible to select three, Lilli Lehmann, Marianne Brandt, and Emil Fischer, as the most significant artists of that era.

The artistic achievements of the German opera period have been recounted in other chapters of this study. Besides the introduction of almost the complete Wagnerian repertoire to the Metropolitan, this management experimented with a number of new and lesser-known operas. Almost all of these ventures resulted in failure, but two operas of superior quality were introduced to the Metropolitan, Goldmark's *The Queen of Sheba* and Cornelius' *Der Barbier von Bagdad* (as revised by Mottl).

Mapleson survived only one more year and offered only token competition to the Metropolitan. The stockholders, however, although enjoying a financial respite, ultimately refused to tolerate the heavier music dramas by Wagner. This attitude resulted in unsuccessful productions of non-German operas in German. The general public, which was now a Wagner-oriented group, refused to support exceptions to the repertoire they had learned to expect.

The final decision to desert German opera was made by the Board of Directors when Abbey, this time with Schoeffel and Grau, offered to reestablish Italian opera at the Metropolitan. Financially, the venture into German opera had resulted in comparative economic success; even in its final years the deficits were astoundingly small compared to the initial season's loss.

Abbey, Schoeffel, and Grau Management

This portion of the first years of the Metropolitan was unique in that it enjoyed failure and success simultaneously. The return to Italian opera was an exaggerated one that brought back not only what had been performed during the first season but a host of archaic works that had previously been discarded. This management also produced a number of new operas, but as in the previous period, significant and successful novelties were at a minimum. Notable exceptions were Massenet's *Manon* and Verdi's *Falstaff*, certainly the most outstanding of the new works.

Important singers were abundant during this era. Melba, Eames, Nordica, and Calvé have come to be regarded as the most eminent among the women, while the male performers were headed by the two de Reszkes, Plançon, and Tamagno. The latter was in the last days of an important career, but his interpretation of Otello was regarded as a landmark at the Metropolitan. Sembrich and Scalchi, mentioned under the resume of Abbey's first season, achieved even more success during this period. The Wagnerian performances were remarkable, with casts including the de Reszkes and Nordica. Seidl remained the only virtuoso conductor of the period.

The roster was comprised of many of the same artists who had sung originally either with Abbey or with Mapleson during the final years of the Academy's existence. The quality of both instrumental and choral ensembles suffered, especially by comparison with the German opera period. Surprisingly strong box-office support, at least in the beginning, came from that section of the public which had ignored the seven years of German opera. By the time this public was becoming saturated with the same fare, Abbey, Schoeffel, and Grau had succeeded in bringing new artists of merit to the company, and this counterbalanced the repertoire's lack of variety.

The star system was back, but performances now featured casts that included a number of celebrated artists rather than one who exceeded his colleagues by a wide margin, both in fame and virtuosity. In spite of these casts, the management succeeded in showing an occasional profit because the audiences were large. Magnificent voices sparked the performances, but other features such as scenery, stage direction, costumes, and the auxiliary forces were inferior. The directors had no problems; they simply leased the opera house in exchange for their boxes and enjoyed the selection of operas best suited to their tastes, with casts that delighted them. The public, for a time, enjoyed the same features of the productions that appealed to their wealthy colleagues in the boxes, great voices and attractive people singing familiar operas in the manner to which they had become accustomed.

The three managers lost sufficient money in outside enterprises to destroy any profit they made at the Metropolitan. Abbey's untimely death resulted in the dissolution of the partnership.

The Maurice Grau Opera Company

The successor to the triumvirate, Maurice Grau, was the most successful of all the impresarios. He brought great singers like Schumann-Heink and Scotti to the Metropolitan and surrounded them with excellent costumes, newer scenery, competent conductors, and consistently large audiences. He gave increased prominence to gifted American singers like Eames and Nordica, and instituted a return to German opera in German, combined with Italian and French works in their original languages. The rosters were vastly increased, and slowly an entire new group of younger and more talented vocalists were brought to the Metropolitan. Mancinelli was Grau's first conductor and kept the performances generally at a higher artistic level than the previous management had succeeded in doing. Alfred Hertz, who went on to become one of the most eminent conductors in Metropolitan history, came to the opera house in Grau's final year and further raised the quality of the Wagnerian performances. Grau also made the Metropolitan tours into monumental journeys across the United States, where huge audiences greeted the company with enthusiasm.

Grau was fortunate in finding operas of merit to introduce to the public, and Puccini aided his cause enormously. The *verismo* sensation was at its peak, and Grau was sufficiently wise to capitalize on it. His premieres included *La Boheme* and *Tosca*, as well as the first American production of Paderewski's *Manru*. (The latter received excellent reviews, even superior, in fact, to those accorded to the two Puccini works.) Grau also produced a number of novelties that were unsuccessful at the time, among which the best known were *La Fille du Regiment* and *Ernani*.

During this period society made the opera house the nucleus for its gatherings. The singers were accepted socially and became adornments for the large balls and receptions of the elite.

Grau succeeded in converting the Metropolitan into an opera house noted for authentic performances of opera in any of three languages and, above all, in the tradition and manner associated with each nationality. This resulted in a cosmopolitan audience, representing all of the elements that had from time to time granted their support to the Metropolitan. In establishing this practice, Grau placed the Metropolitan in a unique and leading position in the world of opera.

Grau received a salary and a share of the profits. His retirement was prompted by ill health rather than any dissatisfaction on his own part or that of the Board of Directors. The end of his tenure as manager found the Metropolitan Opera on solid footing and provided Grau with security that would have lasted far longer than his life did. A permanent audience support was established, the stockholders were content, and the Metropolitan had secured the enormous prestige that, in varying degrees, would always remain part of its tradition.

The Conried Metropolitan Opera Company

Conried's regime was the most sensational in the Metropolitan's history, partly because of Caruso, and primarily because of Conried's successful introduction of *Parsifal* and the collapse of the *Salomé* experiment. Conried's tenure as manager was also marked by controversial light-opera performances, the earthquake catastrophe, Mottl's and Mahler's periods of leadership, Farrar's debut, and the height of the Puccini period.

It was difficult to assess the relative success or failure of the period under Conried's management. The question of its quality was couched in terms of unusual values which were emphasized by his tendency toward sensationalism for its own sake and for his personal gratification, both financial and emotional. Those who were prone to criticize Conried attacked his production of light-opera evenings for his own benefit, into which he contrived to fit star-laden extra attractions. His technique in these cases was regarded as more allied to that of Phineas T. Barnum than appropriate to the manager of the Metropolitan Opera House. Another criticism revolved about his choices of novelties and revivals during the five seasons he managed the Metropolitan. The neglect of French operas opened Conried to criticism and undoubtedly was the determining factor in Hammerstein's successful beginning at the Manhattan Opera House. Hammerstein's productions of works such as *Pelleás et Melisande, Louise,* and *Thaïs* made him a successful competitor to the Metropolitan and ultimately forced the Metropolitan Board of Directors to buy him out of the operatic field. Had it not been for Conried's omissions in the Metropolitan repertoire, the opera patrons of New York would have found Hammerstein's efforts less appealing.

The most questionable criticism of Conried as a manager stemmed from the moral issue involved in the production of *Salomé*. Here the mores of the time had a large effect; from a present-day standpoint, the halting of performances of the new Richard Strauss work could not be justified. Evidence indicated that Conried's defeat in this matter was the result of the Board's willingness to submit to pressure from overly concerned women, particularly Mrs. Herbert Satterlee, J. Pierpont Morgan's daughter.[1] Krehbiel's attacks on the moral propriety of the production also served to influence the directors, a tribute to Krehbiel's prestige more than to his judgment. The fact that the next announced performance of the opera had been quickly sold out spoke highly of the appreciation for the work among the general public. Regardless of the outcome, the controversial premiere of *Salomé* was an achievement that demanded a vital effort from all the participants as well as courage on the part of the impresario. Hertz was hailed as the motivating force in an artistic triumph, and Fremstad, van Rooy, Dippel, Burrian, and Weed received only praise for their contributions to the performance.

The outstanding production of Conried's five years was unquestionably *Parsifal*. In this instance Conried demonstrated his skill, dedication, and high standards of production in such a manner that they superseded the charge of sensationalism which constantly recurred during his period of management. Reviews were unanimously excellent and public response to the opera was most enthusiastic.

Conried's flamboyant leadership brought some outstanding artists to the Metropolitan. He added Mahler to the list of distinguished conductors. (Mottl was only at the Metropolitan for one season and did not make a lasting impression.) Perhaps the best-known of all Metropolitan singers were Caruso and Farrar, both of whom launched spectacular careers under Conried, although the former was actually discovered by Grau. Chaliapin and Fremstad were Conried's other leading contributions to the overall record of excellence at the Metropolitan.

Conried's financial success, discussed earlier, was obvious. At the same time, the Metropolitan Opera Board of Directors found no reason to complain about their share in the rewards. Conried never found it necessary to come to them for aid, notwithstanding the impressive list of artists and conductors to whom he paid eminently large fees, nor the great cost of mounting new productions in the most luxurious manner. The relative success or failure of Conried's management was arguable, but the evidence in his favor seemed preponderant. The artistic results were good, if not as great as during the Grau period, and the opera house was generally filled to capacity. Conried, like Grau, retired because of ill health, and his retirement marked the end of the period outlined for this study.

CRITICAL RESPONSE FROM MAJOR REVIEWERS

Examination of critical reviews and analyses of the period revealed serious and valuable material. The critics were remarkable in the attention which they paid to operatic productions. Whereas in recent decades reviewers deal only with the first production of an opera each year, during the period covered in this study the correspondents assiduously made an effort to attend all performances and to write at least a brief report each time on the caliber of the artists and the overall production.

Considerable space was dedicated to such items as libretto, thematic analysis, compositional techniques, and background of the work itself, facets which receive far less attention today. In the reviews written by Krehbiel concerning Wagnerian premieres, he often divided his report into a two or three-day period, covering the points listed above in a precise, orderly, and above all thorough, fashion. Comments show that the critics stayed until the end of the performances, since they frequently made reference to the fact that they could not complete their reviews in time for the morning editions. Today's reviewers frequently indicate that they have departed at an early hour for precisely this purpose.

It was remarkable to note the unanimity of the critics in reviewing the performances of new singers, the ability and interpretation of conductors, the performance of established artists, and the quality and characteristics of unfamiliar operas. However, Krehbiel tended to favor Wagner and to make derisive comments about Italian opera and its clichés. Henderson, on the other hand, was not convinced that Wagner's reforms had been completely beneficial to the form of opera. He frequently made reference to this opinion and expressed audible relief at the periods of respite provided by Italian and French performances. Finck was inclined to idolize certain artists and managers beyond the limits of good judgment. Richard Aldrich, who joined the staff of the *New York Times* during the season of 1902–1903, was extremely objective in his reviews, and his comments were valuable since they showed no preconceptions. By the same token, like any new correspondent, he lacked the basis for comparison that can be provided only by experience.

The prose contributed by Krehbiel, particularly, was colorful and of literary merit, if frequently archaic by today's standards. His language provided a certain element of drama and charm which his colleagues lacked. Whether this was beneficial from a purely objective viewpoint was questionable, but his careful, sometimes labored, descriptions of events made his feelings appear more candid than in the case of most reviewers. Henderson inclined strongly toward sarcasm which, however, he frequently tempered with an effort to find something praiseworthy in any program he reviewed.

Space placed inordinate limitations on the length of excerpts cited in this study, but the complete reviews served to grant an insight into many features of the performances, from which it was possible to derive a qualified opinion of the general trend and quality of the productions under each managerial regime. An attempt was made to quote excerpts that as a combined group provided insight into contrasting features of the performance in question. On occasion, where the content was significant, similar portions of two or more reviews were presented for contrast, but more often an attempt was made to investigate more facets of a performance by including material on the production from one newspaper and critical analysis of the artists' performances from another. Krehbiel and Henderson were selected for most examples because of their reputation and the importance of the newspapers they represented.

CONCLUSIONS

The first 25 years of existence of the Metropolitan Opera involved 23 resident seasons, since 1892-1893 and 1897-1898 saw the house closed to regular operatic performances. During the entire period 93 operas were produced under five different managements. It was difficult to determine what might be referred to as Metropolitan premieres, since every opera performed during the first season could be considered as such. Therefore, performances were considered as premieres only when they were specifically billed as such. This usually occurred when the opera was of major importance, or conversely, when the opera was not one normally found in the repertoire of leading opera houses at that time. Particular versions of operas were treated as premieres; examples of this technique were provided by the "Paris" version of *Tannhäuser*, the Mottl revision of *Der Barbier von Bagdad*, and the operatic performance of *Samson et Dalila*, formerly heard in this country on the concert stage. Special events, such as the performance in honor of Prince Henry of Prussia, received attention because of their significance in the particular season under consideration.

Based on this list, the accusation frequently voiced against the Metropolitan Opera, that it has consistently refused to perform new works, operas by obscure composers, or even lesser-known works by major composers, has not been justified, at least not with regard to the period under consideration. It would be more accurate to state that the managements have been prone to neglect a new work after a year, or possibly two, even if it received favorable reviews. Examples of this failing included Paderewski's *Manru* and Bemberg's *Elaine*. Evidence indicated, however, that this attitude of the impresarios was frequently influenced by the public, which notwithstanding favorable reviews regularly refused to support these new works at the box office.

It was found that criticism of the Metropolitan for refusing to give American singers and conductors an opportunity was only partially accurate. American conductors were not acceptable to the Metropolitan because of their lack of experience and routine in the operatic repertoire. There were no instances in which students of conducting went for training under European directors or at one of the many small European opera houses. Certainly there was a lack of opportunities for an embryonic conductor to gain any experience in the United States. European singers, however, often stayed in America and opened studios where they passed on their technique and valuable experience to young vocalists. The first issue of *Musical America* carried twenty-six advertisements for vocal instruction on one page.[2] Other instrument instruction was offered, and music schools and conservatories were listed; even two conductors were included, but they advertised for piano and vocal students. No notices were found offering instruction in conducting.

American singers found their way to the Metropolitan if their ability merited this opportunity. A number of these changed their names after studying in Europe, but several did not find this necessary. The list of native-born singers who performed at the Metropolitan Opera during its first twenty-five years included many notable artists such as Nordica (Lillian Norton), Eames, Bispham, Hauk, Valleria, Homer, Blass, Abott, Walker, Weed, and de Lussan. Considering that America was not a country with an operatic tradition, this was quite a remarkable record and certainly did not show any hesitation in engaging American singers on the part of the various managers. The reputation earned by most members of the list cited above destroyed the misconception that native-born singers were not capable of succeeding in a European art involving several foreign languages.

The safety record of the original Metropolitan Opera House was remarkable, particularly when considered over the life-span of the building rather than merely for the first twenty-five years. It was noted that the absence of fire and panic included not only the periods when the resident company was at the Metropolitan, but also the many occasions when the house was rented. The only major fire was the stage fire, recorded earlier, which because of its occurrence late in August necessitated the closing of the house for the season of 1892–1893. A minor fire in the wig room in 1902, on the night of the performance in honor of Prince Henry of Prussia, was quickly brought under control.

One accident of importance occurred on stage during a performance. On January 7, 1905, a bridge collapsed in the first act of *Carmen* and injured several members of the chorus, who were hospitalized. The performance was resumed and there were no fatalities. Other than this, only minor and amusing incidents have marred the record. The usual series of anecdotes involved with trap-doors, locked churches, lost trousers, anvils which refused to split, and swords that could not be removed from trees were as numerous in the earlier days at the Metropolitan as they probably are in current performances.

APPENDIX

1

Metropolitan Opera
and Real Estate Company
New York

April 30, 1919.

Mr. Marvyn Scudder,
    43 Exchange Place,
        New York City.

Dear Mr. Scudder:

I have your letter of yesterday relative to valuation of stock of this Company owned in the Luther Kountze Estate. You will perhaps remember having made inquiry similar to this with respect to a number of estates in which you have acted as expert appraiser and you are quite familiar with the circumstance of this Company, that as it gives the Opera managing Company the use of its property practically rent free, but has its insurance, repairs and City taxes to meet at its own cost, it looses [sic] a substantial sum of money, which is defrayed by annual assessment on its Stockholders. The only books we keep are a cash book, which makes no showing of liabilities or assets from which a balance sheet such as you suggest could be prepared.

The Transfer Tax Department, I think, has aloted [sic] a conventional figure at which they appraise the ownership of an entire box, equivalent to 300 shares of stock of the Company, and my impression is that that valuation was placed at $100,000.00. Among the recent estates in which such holders have been appraised are, —

Estate of J. Pierpont Morgan,	300 shares	
" " George S. Bowdoin,	200 "	(2/3 of a box)
" " Wm. C. Whitney,	300 "	
" " George G. Haven,	150 "	(1/2 of a box)
" " D. O. Mills,	300 "	
" " Elizabeth C. Bryce,	150 "	(1/2 of a box)
" " Thomas Hitchcock,	300 "	
" " James B. Haggin,	300 "	
" " William D. Sloane,	150 "	(1/2 of a box)

"	"	H. McK. Twombly,	150	"	(1/2 of a box)
"	"	John Jacob Astor,	300	"	
"	"	R. T. Wilson,	300	"	

I think that you will find in connection with all these estates there was, at any rate the most recent of them, a uniform valuation on basis of $100,000 was adopted.

The assessed valuation of our Real Estate totals $3,985,000.: outside of this, we have no assets except the unexpended balance of the season's assessment with which we meet taxes, etc. for the ensuing year. The total stock is 10,500 shares. (35 boxes, each @ 300 shares.)

I understand that when the arbitrary basis was adopted, Mr. Yearanco went into the matter thoroughly on behalf of the Transfer Tax Department, and some weight was given to the fact that the stock represented a position of art patronage rather than a commercial investment.

If I can be of further assistance, please command me.

> Very truly yours,
> Frank Dodd
> Secretary.

(handwritten note)
This question will also soon arise again in connection with Estate of Augustus D. Juilliard, (300 shares), who has just died—He was our President for many years.

2

A COPY OF THE CERTIFICATE OF INCORPORATION OF THE METROPOLITAN OPERA-HOUSE COMPANY LIMITED

We the undersigned, George Peabody Wetmore, of Newport, R. I.; George Henry Warren, of the City of Troy, N. Y.; George G. Haven, Robert Goelet, James A. Roosevelt, and William K. Vanderbilt of the City of New York, do hereby certify that we propose to form a company of the class of limited liability companies, pursuant to the provisions of an act to provide for the organization and regulating of certain business corporations, passed June 21, 1875, and do hereby set forth:

First—the name of the said corporation is to be the Metropolitan Opera-house Company of New York Limited.

Second—the object and nature of the business for which said corporation is to be formed is for the business of encouraging and cultivating a taste for music, literature and the arts, and for erecting and maintaining and renting a building, or buildings, for that purpose, and that the locality of the said business is to be in the City of New York.

Third—the amount of the capital stock of the said corporation is to be $600,000.

Fourth—the number of shares which the capital stock shall consist of is to be 6000 and the par value of each share is to be $100.

Fifth—the location of the principal business office of the said corporation is to be in the City of New York.

Sixth—the duration of the said corporation is to be for the term of 50 years.

3

IN RE ESTATE OF EDWARD B. SMITH
DECEASED JANUARY 7th, 1918
METROPOLITAN OPERA HOUSE

VALUE OF STOCK—

This company was organized under the laws of the State of New York some time ago. It forfeited its right to do business for failure to comply with the laws governing it. It went out of existence in 1888. Since that time its stock has been reported as worthless and we submit it as such at January 7, 1918.

APPROVED BY,
Marvyn Scudder

Report to—

Managing Clerk
Controller's Office
233 Broadway
New York City

4

State of New York
COMPTROLLER'S OFFICE
New York City Branch
233 Broadway

October 11, 1916.

RE ESTATE OF MARY VAN NEST JACKSON.

Marvyn Scudder,
55 Wall St.,
New York City.

Dear Sir:

We wrote you under date of October 4th, 1916, asking you to appraise the stock of the Metropolitan Opera & Real Estate Co. I would state for your information that our card index shows that this stock has been valued in the following estates.

Mathew D.C. Borden,	May 27, 1912,	at 333 1/3,
John Jacob Astor,	April 15, 1912,	at 333 1/3,
George S. Bowdoin,	Dec. 16, 1913,	at 333 1/3,
J. P. Morgan,	Mar. 31, 1913,	at 333 1/3,
James B. Haggin,	Sept. 12, 1914,	at 333 1/3,
John E. Parsons,	Jan. 16, 1915,	at 333 1/3,

Yours very truly,
Edward R. Rayher
Managing Clerk.

5

ESTATE OF GEORGE S. BOWDOIN, DECEASED DECEMBER 16TH, 1913. (Cont.)

METROPOLITAN OPERA & REAL ESTATE COMPANY.

INCORPORATED —	under the Laws of the State of New York.
CAPITAL STOCK —	$1,050,000.
PAR —	$100.
DIVIDENDS —	None.
FUNDED DEBT —	$1,000,000. 4 1/2% Bonds.
OFFICERS 1914.	President: Augustus D. Guillard,
	Secretary: Frank N. Dodd,
	Treasurer: George G. Haven,
OFFICE —	150 West 40th Street, New York City.
VALUE OF STOCK —	December 16th, 1913. (*Feb. 19, 1916*)

This stock is closely held and no sales have been made public for many years. We understand that the Company is not operating at a profit and that to cover expenses the stockholders are assessed yearly 10% of their holdings (, *and last year to the amount of 50%*).

The property owned by this Company is very valuable and in case of liquidation in 1910, we were given to understand (*are advised*) there would be realized for the stockholders about 300% per share. This stock was then held by a number of large estates including the Samuel D. Babcock Estate and the William C. Whitney Estate, (*and others*) but those Estates did not appraise the shares yearly at correct value and informed us that although it was held on the books at par it was (*is*) really worth considerably more and that its value in 1907 (*as of date above*) was about $300. per share.

Since that year the value of the property, which is the Company's only asset, has increased greatly in value and the stock should be worth at a conservative figure $300. However, we have not succeeded in obtaining sufficient data in regard to the value of the property held, and as we believe $300. per share to be very conservative (*under the circumstances*), we hesitate to make affidavit to this valuation, (*as of Feb. 19, 1916.*)

The Secretary of the Corporation under date of June 18th, 1915 wrote the following: —

"I would say that this Company does not prepare an annual Balance Sheet or Income Account; nor does it keep any record of prices at which sales of stock are made. Such transactions, as you can readily imagine, are usually kept quite private between the interested parties, so as to avoid the newspaper notoriety, as far as possible, which usually depicts the purchaser as a plutocrat with social "aspirations," in thoroughly unwelcome fashion.

This office received a number of similar inquiries from the executors of stockholders' estates, and I would name the following as among the Estates in which stock of this Company has recently been appraised by your Department:

Estate of William C. Whitney,
George C. Haven,
H. McKay Twombly,
Richard T. Wilson,
Darius O. Mills,
John Jacob Astor,
Wm. Bayard Cutting,
Cornelius N. Bliss,

Matthew C. D. Borden,
J. Pierpont Morgan.

I have an indistinct idea that the State Comptroller has in all cases in the past six or seven years, adopted a uniform valuation for the appraisal of such stock; and I might further say, that in a period of about seven years past, I figured recently for our Treasurer, that the Company, after assessing its Stockholders $105,000 a year to supplement its otherwise trifling income, and to meet its payments for City, State and Federal Taxes; Insurance; Bond Interest; Office Expenses; and its contribution toward subsidy of the opera conducted by the Metropolitan Opera Company, has run behind in cash from year to year and also increased its bonded debt; so that it is now confronted with the need of appealing to its stockholders for their consent to an increase in the annual assessment made on them; a similar effort about eight years ago was unsuccessful, because the trustees of some trust estates owning stock, felt that on account of the trust relation they couldn't join in the plan;—Hence the increase in Mortgage debt.

Personally I should think the J. Pierpont Morgan appraisal would be the best guide. Mr. George S. Bowdoin was a (retired) partner of Mr. Morgan's, and did not survive him very long."

We communicated with Mr. Joyce and asked for permission to peruse the statements mentioned but he expressed his doubt as to his having these documents in accessible location.

Mr. Joyce referred us to the Attorney for the Estate who advises he has valued the stock at 250% or $250. per share. He was unable to furnish statements or values of the properties, and we therefore are not in position to state an accurate opinion but consider $250. to be an extremely conservative figure.

Editor's note: Italicized material in parentheses above is handwritten by an unknown author in the original.

6

October
Twenty-second
1915

PERSONAL

Dear Sir:—

We beg to acknowledge receipt of your communication of October nineteenth relative to the stock of the Metropolitan Opera Company.

In answer thereto [we] would say that our Profit and Loss account to date shows net loss of Three Hundred and Ninety-three Thousand, Eight Hundred and sixty-four Dollars and ninety-eight ($393,864.98) cents, which is more than the entire capital stock.

I understand that Mr. Gregory's three shares of stock were sold for One Hundred ($100) Dollars. I know of no other sales of this stock that have taken place in recent years.

Very truly yours,
METROPOLITAN OPERA COMPANY
(Signed "J. Brown")
Business Comptroller

Mr. Marvin L. Scudder
c/o Investors' Agency, Inc.
No. Fifty-five Wall St.
Manhattan

7

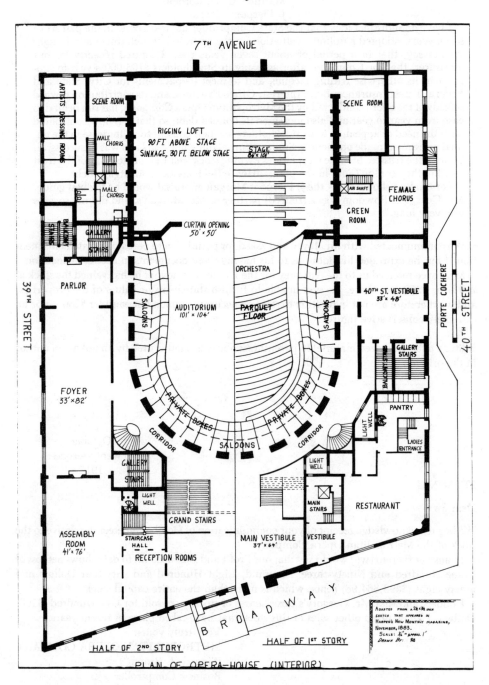

Plan of the Metropolitan Opera House. Drawing above was adapted from a 2-1/2-inch × 3-1/2-inch sketch appearing in Harper's New Monthly Magazine, Vol. 67, No. 402 *(November, 1883), p. 879.*

8

RESOLUTION PASSED BY THE
METROPOLITAN OPERA-HOUSE COMPANY
AT THE TIME OF THE DEATH OF DR. LEOPOLD DAMROSCH

The Directors of the Metropolitan Opera House Company in expressing their sympathy and regret at the death of Dr. Leopold Damrosch, desire to make official recognition of the great loss they have suffered.

Dr. Damrosch assumed the responsibility of the present opera season under circumstances most discouraging and with little promise of success.

Activated by devotion to his art, he was led to undertake what seemed almost impossible.

He imparted this enthusiasm, first to the Directors of the Opera House, then to all those whose aid he enlisted, and, finally, by his charming presence and indomitable spirit brought about the success which has received such general public recognition.

A new musical era has been inaugurated by him in New-York, and we look upon his loss as a great misfortune, irreparable to the public, as it is to his family and friends.

His fine qualities endeared him to us all, and the purity and sincrity of his character have left with us a deep impression. The Board of Directors will attend his funeral in a body.
(*New York Times*, February 18, 1885, p.5)

Notes

CHAPTER 1

1. Mary Ellis Peltz, *Metropolitan Opera Milestones* (New York: The Metropolitan Opera Guild, Inc., 1944), p. 11. During the first season the house was leased to Henry E. Abbey, who directed the company known as Abbey's Italian Opera Company. This company functioned at the Metropolitan for one year and then gave way to a seven-year period during which only opera in German was produced. Abbey then reappeared, this time in association with John B. Schoeffel and Maurice Grau. Even at the time of his first season at the Metropolitan, Abbey had been associated with Schoeffel and Grau in other enterprises. Sources that include the latter two in the managerial structure of the first season at the new opera house are in error. After Abbey's death in 1896 still another managerial regime, that of Grau alone, preceded the appearance of Heinrich Conried as manager.

2. Ruth Adams Knight, *Opera Cavalcade* (New York: Metropolitan Opera Guild, Inc., 1938), p.48; verified by examination of old programs.

3. Allan Nevins, *The Emergence of Modern America 1865–1878*, in *A History of American Life*, Arthur Meier Schlesinger and Dixon Ryan Fox, eds., vol. 8 (New York: The Macmillan Company, 1933), pp.90–91.

4. *Art Journal for 1875*, n.s., no. 1 (New York: D. Appleton and Company, January, 1875), p. 26.

5. *Ibid.*, p. 27.

6. Henry Collins Brown, *New York in the Elegant Eighties*, in *Valentine's Manual of Old New York* (Hastings-on-Hudson, N.Y.: Valentine's Manual, Inc., 1927), p. 120.

7. *Grove's Dictionary of Music and Musicians* (1902), 1:10.

8. Peltz, *Metropolitan Opera Milestones*, p. 1.

9. Ruth Adams Knight, Irving Kolodin, Mary Ellis Peltz.

10. Irving Kolodin, *The Metropolitan Opera, 1883–1935* (New York: Oxford University Press, 1936), p. 2; the source for Kolodin's figure is not given.

11. Frank N. Dodd, Secretary of the Metropolitan Opera Company, to Marvyn Scudder, a prominent New York attorney, April 30, 1919, Marvyn Scudder Collection, Columbia University, no. 3009.03. (See Appendix for text.)

12. Peltz, *Metropolitan Opera Milestones*, p. 1.

13. *Harper's New Monthly Magazine*, vol. 67, no. 402 (November 1883), pp. 878–880.

14. This is the meeting dated as April 3, 1880, in Kolodin, *Metropolitan Opera*, p. 1.

15. *Ibid.*, p. 3.

16. *New York Times*, April 8, 1880, p. 5. This appears to be a more accurate count than the seventy stockholders mentioned in Knight, *Opera Cavalcade*, p. 48.

17. *New York Times*, April 11, 1880, p. 5; *New York Tribune*, April 11, 1880, p. 2. (See Appendix for text of certificate of incorporation.)

18. *New York Times*, April 29, 1880, p. 8.

19. Scudder Collection, no. 2589. (See Appendix for text of material cited in notes 19–24.)

20. *Ibid.*

21. *Ibid.*

22. *Ibid.*

23. *Ibid.*

24. *Ibid.*

25. Cleveland Amory, *Who Killed Society?* (New York: Harper and Brothers, 1980), p. 119.

26. *Ibid.*, p. 120.

27. *Social Register* (New York: Social Register Association, 1898); *Society List*, 1894–1895.

28. *Dictionary of American Biography* (1928), 7:454–455.

29. *Social Register* (New York: Social Register Association), vol. 13, no. 1 (1898).

30. Interview with Finley Jay Shepard, August 17, 1959, Wallingford, Vt.

31. *Dictionary of American Biography* (1928), 1:399–400; 2:169–170; 13:6–7, 175–182; 19:169–176.

32. *Ibid.*, 11:411–412.

33. Kolodin, *The Metropolitan Opera*, p. 9.

34. *New York Times*, March 15, 1881, p. 8.

35. *Ibid.*, February 20, 1884, p. 5.

36. *Ibid.*, May 24, 1883, p. 1.

37. *Harper's New Monthly Magazine*, vol. 67, no. 402 (November 1883), p. 882.

38. *Ibid.*, p. 889.

39. Henry Edward Krehbiel, *Chapters of Opera* (New York: Henry Holt and Company, 1911), p. 86.

40. *New York Times*, October 14, 1883, p. 5.

41. Francis Robinson, "Adieu," *High Fidelity Magazine*, November 1958, p. 38.

42. *Ibid.*, p. 39.

43. Robinson to the author, Sept. 29, 1964, "Anything I got on Bergh would have been from Kolodin's book, Mrs. Peltz's *Behind the Gold Curtain*, or an article on him some years ago in *Opera News*." Robinson's source proved to be the *Opera News* article (vol. 5, no. 21, March 10, 1941), which provided more insight into Bergh's connection with Cady's architectural firm and the building of the Metropolitan Opera House. Bergh's sister, Miss Lillie d'Angelo Bergh, however, was the primary source for the information in the following account of Bergh's role.

44. *Opera News*, vol. 5, no. 21 (March 10, 1941), pp. 4–9.

45. *New York Tribune*, November 12, 1883, p. 5.

46. *The Diary of Philip Hone, 1828–1851*, 2 vols., Allan Nevins, ed. (New York: Dodd, Mead and Company, 1927), p. 103.

47. *New York Times*, January 20, 1884, p. 4.

48. *Ibid.*, February 20, 1884, p. 5.

49. Arthur Meier Schlesinger, *The Rise of the City*, in *History of American Life*, Schlesinger and Fox, eds., vol. 10, p. 158.

CHAPTER 2

1. *New York Times*, February 27, 1880, p. 5.

2. *Ibid.*, February 28, 1881, p. 2.

3. William H. Seltsam, comp., *Metropolitan Opera Annals* (New York: The H. W. Wilson Company in association with The Metropolitan Opera Guild, Inc., 1947), p. 105; Quaintance Eaton, *Opera Caravan* (New York: Farrar, Straus and Cudahy, 1957), pp. 188–190.

4. Henry C. Lahee, *Famous Singers of Today and Yesterday* (Boston: L. C. Page and Company, 1890), p. 269.

5. *New York Times*, October 9, 1883, p. 5.

6. *Ibid.*, October 14, 1883, p. 5. Although not indicated in many secondary sources, this article was unquestionably the main source for the descriptions they provided.

7. Henry Edward Krehbiel, *Chapters of Opera* (New York: Henry Holt and Company, 1911), p. 90.

8. *New York Times*, October 20, 1883, p. 8.

9. *Dictionary of American Biography* (1928), 1:89.

10. *National Cyclopedia of American Biography* (1897), 7:141.

11. Lahee, *Famous Singers*, p. 269.

12. Herman Klein, *The Golden Age of Opera* (New York: E. P. Dutton & Company, 1933), pp. 63–69.

13. Seltsam, *Metropolitan Opera Annals*, p. 4; Eaton, *Opera Caravan*, pp. 14, 189.

14. Lahee, *Famous Singers*, p. 163.

15. *Ibid.*, pp. 212–214.

16. Klein, *Golden Age*, p. 244.

17. Lahee, *Famous Singers*, p. 301.

18. W. J. Henderson in the *New York Times*, December 27, 1894, p. 4.

19. Eaton, *Opera Caravan*, p. 12.

20. Krehbiel, *Chapters of Opera*, p. 90.

21. Klein, *Golden Age*, p. 36.

22. *Ibid.*, p. 14.

23. *New York Times*, April 16, 1884, p. 7.

24. *Ibid.*, October 27, 1883, p. 5; Irving Kolodin, *The Metropolitan Opera, 1883-1935* (New York: Oxford University Press, 1936), p. 15.

25. Kolodin, *Metropolitan Opera*, p. 14.

26. *New York Dramatic Mirror*, October 27, 1883, p. 1.

27. Dixon Webster, *The Saga of American Society* (New York: Charles Scribner's Sons, 1937), p. 332.

28. Krehbiel, *Chapters of Opera*, p. 102.

29. Lahee, *Famous Singers*, pp. 301-302.

30. *New York Times*, January 21, 1884, p. 4.

31. Seltsam, *Annals*, p. 5.

32. Kolodin, *Metropolitan Opera*, p. 18.

33. John B. Schoeffel to Henry Edward Krehbiel, quoted in Krehbiel's *Chapters of Opera*, p. 91.

34. A deficit of $600,000, when applied only to performances at the Metropolitan Opera House, represents an average loss per performance of over $10,000. The same figure applied to the 118 performances given in total by the company sets the loss at approximately $5,000 per performance. The second calculation seems more reasonable in view of Abbey's expenses of $35,000 per week at the Metropolitan Opera House.

35. *New York Times*, February 14, 1884, p. 5.

36. *Ibid.*, January 15, 1884, p. 8.

37. *Ibid.*, January 31, 1884, p. 2.

38. Lilli Lehmann, *My Path Through Life* (New York: G. P. Putnam's Sons, 1914), p. 340.

CHAPTER 3

1. *New York Times*, October 21, 1883, p. 8.

2. *Ibid.*, February 14, 1884, p. 5.

3. *Ibid.*, April 20, 1884, p. 14.

4. *Ibid.*, April 22, 1884, p. 4.

5. *Ibid.*, April 29, 1884, p. 5.

6. *Ibid.*, May 8, 1884, p. 5.

7. *Ibid.*, July 3, 1884, p. 4.

8. *Ibid.*, July 8, 1884, p. 8.

9. *Ibid.*, July 12, 1884, p. 4.

10. *Ibid.*, July 13, 1884, p. 1. That any prima donna in this era would openly admit she was only "second best" may have brought this remark's front-page location.

11. *Ibid.*, July 15, 1884, p. 4.

12. *Ibid.*, July 24, 1884, p. 4.

13. *Ibid.*, August 2, 1884, p. 4.

14. *Ibid.*, September 6, 1884, p. 5.

15. Arthur Meier Schlesinger, *The Rise of the City*, in *A History of American Life*, Arthur Meier Schlesinger and Dixon Ryan Fox, eds., vol. 10 (New York: The Macmillan Company, 1933), p. 153.

16. *New York Times*, April 23, 1884, p. 4.

17. Article by Henry T. Finck in *Anton Seidl, A Memorial By His Friends* (New York: Charles Scribner's Sons, 1899), p. 30.

18. Maurice R. Davis, *World Immigration* (New York: The Macmillan Company, 1936), p. 71.

19. *Ibid.*, pp. 69-70.

20. Walter Damrosch, *My Musical Life* (New York: Charles Scribner's Sons, 1926), p. 51. According to Walter Damrosch, his father's ambition was "to carry out the dream of his life, introduction of the Wagner music-dramas to America, and to sweep away forever the artificial and shallow opera of the old Italian school with which Mapleson, Max Strakosch, and others had until then principally fed our public" (p. 53). This was a strong statement, given that such operas included works by Donizetti, Mozart, Rossini, Verdi, and Meyerbeer.

Walter Damrosch also commented on his father's attitude towards the dubious results of Abbey's first season at the Metropolitan. The elder Damrosch had much to offer in the way of criticism, partly valid, a great amount inaccurate. In Walter Damrosch's autobiography it was impossible to make a sharp separation between Leopold Damrosch's remarks and his son's, since in essence Walter reflected his father's attitude and training. One of the criticisms concerned the selection of a church architect whose plans, it was claimed, made no provision for shifting scenery—a flaw never mentioned before or since. The orchestra, according to

Damrosch's book, was so deep in the pit that the singers could not hear it (p. 51). Actually, the pit had been raised before the house was opened, and Leopold Damrosch himself had it lowered a number of years later. Damrosch's statements about the first year's endeavors constituted a remarkably confused analysis of the Academy of Music and the Metropolitan Opera combined into one paragraph:

> For their season Abbey, Schoeffel and Grau engaged a large number of operatic stars, including Nilsson, Patti, Sembrich, Trebelli and many others of distinction, but there was absolutely no artistic head of the enterprise nor any one who had any real managerial experience with grand opera, and in consequence all these stars stepped on each other's feet and trains and the confusion was incredible....the season ended in failure and the bankruptcy of Abbey, Schoeffel and Grau (page 52).

This statement contained a number of inaccuracies: Abbey was in fact the responsible administrator and Grau was only his business manager, while Schoeffel was in no way connected with the company at this time. Patti, whom Damrosch credited with being a member of Abbey's company, was indeed his fiercest artistic competitor as the leading prima donna of Mapleson's company. No press reviews of the first season's performances indicated any of the confusion referred to by Damrosch. The statement that Abbey, Schoeffel and Grau went bankrupt had no basis whatsoever.

21. *New York Times*, September 7, 1884, p. 2.
22. *Ibid.*, September 19, 1884, p. 4.
23. *Ibid.*, September 25, 1884, p. 4.
24. *Ibid.*, September 18, 1884, p. 4.
25. *Ibid.*, September 25, 1884, p. 4.
26. *Ibid.*, November 11, 1884, p. 2.
27. *Ibid.*, April 13, 1884, p. 2.
28. *Ibid.*, April 21, 1884, p. 8.
29. *Ibid.*, April 29, 1884, p. 8. The judge ruled that "Col. Mapleson's company had not been...caused... any appreciable loss."
30. *Ibid.*, July 3, 1884, p. 4.
31. *Ibid.*, September 5, 1884, p. 1.
32. *Ibid.*, September 9, 1884, p. 1.
33. Tamagno sang at the Metropolitan during the 1894–1895 season.
34. *New York Times*, October 2, 1884, p. 4.
35. *Ibid.*, October 7, 1884, p. 8.
36. *Ibid.*, October 12, 1884, p. 9.
37. *Ibid.*, October 23, 1884, p. 4.
38. *Ibid.*, October 27, 1884, p. 4.
39. *Ibid.*, November 1, 1884, p. 4.
40. *Ibid.*, November 2, 1884, p. 8.
41. *Ibid.*, November 3, 1884, p. 1.
42. *Ibid.*, November 13, 1884, p. 8.
43. *Ibid.*, November 15, 1884, p. 2.
44. *Ibid.*, November 16, 1884, p. 9.
45. Personal interviews with many former members, covering many years of participation.
46. According to his son Walter, his salary was $10,000 (Walter Damrosch, *My Musical Life*, p. 53).
47. Henry Edward Krehbiel, *More Chapters of Opera* (New York: Henry Holt and Company, 1919), p.289.

CHAPTER 4

1. *New York Times*, September 17, 1884, p. 4.
2. *Ibid.*
3. *Ibid.*
4. Henry E. Krehbiel, *Chapters of Opera* (New York: Henry Holt and Company, 1911), p. 131.
5. William H. Seltsam, comp., *Metropolitan Opera Annals* (New York: The H. W. Wilson Company in association with the Metropolitan Opera Guild, Inc., 1947), p. 8.

6. *New York Times*, January 3, 1885, p. 4.

7. Henry C. Lahee, *Famous Singers of Today and Yesterday* (Boston: L. C. Page & Co., 1908), p. 172.

8. *New York Times*, January 31, 1885, p. 5. Materna also assumed the role of Gerhilde in the same performance.

9. *Ibid.*, February 18, 1885, p. 5.

10. *Ibid.*, February 16, 1885, p. 1.

11. Walter Damrosch, *My Musical Life* (New York: Charles Scribner's Sons, 1926), p. 57.

12. *New York Times*, February 17, 1885, p. 2.

13. *Ibid.*

14. *Ibid.*, February 21, 1885, p. 4.

15. Collection of Seidl manuscripts and papers, Columbia University, Box 3 (English translation by the author).

16. Lilli Lehmann, *My Path Through Life* (New York: G. P. Putnam's Sons, 1914).

17. The closing section of the February 20 *New York Times* report announced that at a meeting of the Oratorio Society Board of Directors, Walter Damrosch was "unanimously elected to succeed his father."

18. *New York Times*, February 20, 1885, p. 5.

19. Quaintance Eaton, *Opera Caravan* (New York: Farrar, Straus and Cudahy, 1957), p. 24.

20. Damrosch, *My Musical Life*, p. 63.

21. *New York Times*, April 22, 1885, p. 4.

22. *Ibid.*, September 13, 1885, p. 14.

23. *Ibid.*, September 19, 1885, p. 5.

24. *Ibid.*, October 14, 1885, p. 5.

25. *Ibid.*, October 11, 1885, p. 9.

26. *Ibid.*, November 3, 1885, p. 5.

27. Seidl Collection, Box 4 (English translation by the author).

28. *Ibid.*, Box 2.

29. *Ibid.* "Aussicht schlage zwölf Auffuhrungen des Tannhäusers November in Trieste zu dirigieren, telegraphen Sie mir" (English translation by the author).

30. *Ibid.* "Wagner wollte nicht erlauben aber war dann über den Erfolg selig" (English translation by the author).

31. *Ibid.*

32. Krehbiel, *Chapters of Opera*, p. 156.

33. *New York Times*, December 5, 1885, p. 4.

34. *Ibid.*, January 29, 1886, p. 4.

35. *New York Tribune*, March 5, 1878, p. 5.

36. *New York Times*, February 4, 1886, p. 5.

37. Seidl Collection, Box 2, Section E.

38. Seltsam, *Metropolitan Opera Annals*, p. 28.

39. Lehmann, *My Path Through Life*, p. 375.

40. *Ibid.*, pp. 375-376.

41. Herman Klein, *The Golden Age of Opera* (New York: E. P. Dutton & Company, 1933), p. 115.

42. Duke Ernest II of Saxe-Coburg-Gotha was the older brother of Queen Victoria's consort, Albert of Saxe-Coburg-Gotha.

43. Krehbiel, *Chapters of Opera*, p. 203.

44. On March 15, 1907, a testimonial concert was given for Fischer's benefit. On this occasion he sang Hans Sachs in the final excerpt from Act III, Scene 1, of *Die Meistersinger*.

45. Krehbiel, *Chapters of Opera*, pp. 206-207.

46. Interview with Mary Ellis Peltz, March, 1960.

47. Krehbiel, *Chapters of Opera*, p. 166.

48. Krehbiel, *Chapters of Opera*, p. 174.

49. Henry T. Finck, *My Adventures in the Golden Age of Music* (New York: Funk and Wagnalls Company, 1926), p. 213.

50. *Ibid.*, p. 216.

51. Lehmann, *My Path Through Life*, pp. 86, 100.

52. Neuendorff was Grau's conductor on the spring tour of 1885-1886. Frank Damrosch, although not listed on the roster of the Metropolitan Opera, conducted the ballet *Die Puppenfee* during the 1889-1890 season.

53. *New York Times*, March 22, 1891, p. 12.

54. Krehbiel, *Chapters of Opera*, p. 138.

55. *Ibid.*, pp. 153–154.

56. *Ibid.*, pp. 152–153.

57. *New York Tribune*, March 22, 1891, p. 7.

58. *New York Times*, March 22, 1891, p. 12.

CHAPTER 5

1. Henry T. Finck, *My Adventures in the Golden Age of Music* (New York: Funk & Wagnalls Company, 1926), pp. 202–203.

2. Henry C. Lahee, *Famous Singers of Today and Yesterday* (Boston: L. C. Page & Co., 1908), pp. 220–230.

3. Chaliapin sang Boris Godunov in Russian at performances otherwise in Italian.

4. *New York Times*, December 15, 1891, p. 6.

5. Quaintance Eaton, *Opera Caravan* (New York: Farrar, Straus and Cudahy, 1957), p. 197.

6. *New York Times*, January 11, 1892, p. 4.

7. Lahee, *Famous Singers*, p. 285.

8. Gluck's *Orfeo ed Euridice* and Mascagni's *Cavalleria Rusticana* were produced as a double bill and are therefore tallied as one performance, but as two operas.

9. Eaton, *Opera Caravan*, p. 200.

10. Henry E. Krehbiel, *Chapters of Opera* (New York: Henry Holt and Company, 1911), p. 226.

11. Irving Kolodin, *The Metropolitan Opera, 1883–1935* (New York: Oxford University Press, 1936), pp. 52–53.

12. At that time the Juilliard Foundation also came forward with a substantial sum for the aid of the organization. According to Edward Ziegler (later an assistant manager of the Metropolitan), the installation of Herbert Witherspoon as manager was the price demanded by the Juilliard Foundation for this aid.

13. *New York Times*, August 28, 1892, p. 2.

14. Krehbiel, *Chapters of Opera*, pp. 228–229.

15. William H. Seltsam, comp., *Metropolitan Opera Annals* (New York: The H. W. Wilson Company in association with the Metropolitan Opera Guild, Inc., 1947), pp. 54, 56.

16. Herman Klein, *The Golden Age of Opera* (New York: E. P. Dutton & Company, 1933), p. 221.

17. Lahee, *Famous Singers*, pp. 236–242, 317–318.

18. Dennis Arundell, *The Critic at the Opera* (London: Ernest Benn, Limited, 1957), p. 376.

19. *New York Times*, April 20, 1894, p. 5.

20. Lahee, *Famous Singers*, p. 282.

21. Giulio Gatti-Casazza, *Memories of Opera* (New York: Charles Scribner's Sons, 1941), p. 195.

22. Krehbiel, *Chapters of Opera*, p. 229.

23. *Ibid.*, pp. 229–231.

CHAPTER 6

1. Interview with Paul Eisler the elder (father of the author), formerly of the Metropolitan Opera Company, August 15, 1951.

2. Interview with Hermann Weil, formerly of the Metropolitan Opera Company, November 2, 1948.

3. Henry E. Krehbiel, *Chapters of Opera* (New York: Henry Holt & Co., 1911), p. 272.

4. *Ibid.*, p. 259.

5. P. G. Hurst, *The Operatic Age of Jean de Reszke* (New York: Robert M. McBride Company, 1959), pp. 166, 167.

6. Krehbiel, *Chapters of Opera*, pp. 279–286.

7. *Musical Courier*, December 16, 1885.

8. *Ibid.*, February 16, 1887.

9. Collection of Anton Seidl manuscripts and papers, Columbia University, Box 4.

10. *Ibid.*, Box 3.

11. *Ibid.*, Box 2.

12. *Ibid.*

13. *Ibid.*, January 10, 1894.

14. *Ibid.*, January, 1897 (English translation by the author).

15. *Ibid.*, ' Lieber Freund: Du würdest mich zu grossen Dank verpflichten, wenn Du mir genau angeben wolltest, welche Zeit Du in diesem Sommer in Bayreuth für Proben und Aufführungen zu bringen kannst. Ich kann mir mit meine freie Zeit für meine Gesundheit...erkaufen!" (English translation by the author).

16. These tributes included the memorial volume *Anton Seidl, A Memorial by His Friends* (New York: Charles Scribner's Sons, 1899), published in a limited edition.

17. Rose Heylbut and Aime Gerber, *Backstage At the Opera*(New York: Thomas Y. Crowell Company, 1937), p. 80; Krehbiel, *More Chapters of Opera* (New York: Henry Holt and Company, 1919), pp. 382–383.

18. *Opera News*, vol. 4, no. 22 (March 16, 1942), p. 31.

19. Interview with Artur Bodanzky, July, 1938.

20. Interview with Paul Eisler, July, 1938.

21. Krehbiel made many new translations of Mozart with dialogue for the William Wade Hinshaw opera company, which toured in 1920–1921, many years later (personal communication from Paul Eisler, who was Hinshaw's musical director, though not permitted to conduct performances because of his contract with the Metropolitan).

22. Gustav Hinrichs did not appear at the Metropolitan Opera House until the season of 1903–1904.

23. William H. Seltsam, comp., *Metropolitan Opera Annals* (New York: The H. W. Wilson Company in association with the Metropolitan Opera Guild, Inc., 1947), p. 118. Jean de Reszke's last appearance in a full-length opera at the Metropolitan was followed by one post-season appearance there on April 29, 1901, in a gala evening that included Act 2 of *Tristan*.

24. *Ibid.*, p. 121.

25. *New York Tribune*, February 26, 1902, p. 7.

26. Krehbiel, *Chapters of Opera*, p. 317.

27. Heylbut and Gerber, *Backstage*, p. 156.

28. Interview with Paul Eisler, August, 1951.

29. Howard Taubman, *The Maestro* (New York: Simon and Schuster, 1951), p. 119.

30. Henry T. Finck, *My Adventures in the Golden Age of Music* (New York: Funk & Wagnalls Company, 1926), pp. 323.

31. *Ibid.*

32. Interview with Katherine Moran Douglas, member of the Conried Metropolitan Opera Company (1903–1908), April, 1960.

33. Herman Klein, *The Golden Age of Opera* (New York: E. P. Dutton & Company, 1933), pp. 240–241.

34. Finck, *My Adventures in the Golden Age of Music*, pp. 245–246.

35. Irving Kolodin, *The Metropolitan Opera, 1883–1935* (New York: Oxford University Press, 1936).

CHAPTER 7

1. Montrose J. Moses, *Heinrich Conried* (New York: Thomas Y. Crowell and Company, 1916).

2. Henry T. Finck, *My Adventures in the Golden Age of Music* (New York: Funk and Wagnalls Company, 1926), pp. 318–319.

3. Henry E. Krehbiel, *Chapters of Opera* (New York: Henry Holt and Company, 1911), p. 326.

4. Moses, *Heinrich Conried*, pp. 172–174.

5. *Ibid.*, p. 174.

6. *Ibid.*, p. 175.

7. Interview with Paul Eisler the elder, August 16, 1951. Eisler noted that in later years conductors received expense accounts when they traveled to Europe to audition singers or attend operatic festivals to search for prospective artists.

8. Irving Kolodin, *The Metropolitan Opera, 1883–1935* (New York: Oxford University Press, 1936), pp. 92–93.

9. Moses, *Heinrich Conried*, pp. 192–193.

10. Krehbiel, *Chapters of Opera*, pp. 327–328.

11. Moses, *Heinrich Conried*, pp. 193–195.

12. Music from Parsifal had been heard in concert at least twice in the New York area. Anton Seidl directed the Seidl Society in a concert version of *Parsifal* in Brooklyn on March 31, 1890 (collection of Anton Seidl manuscripts and papers, Columbia University, Box 2, concert program). Excerpts from *Parsifal* were performed at a Sunday night concert at the Metropolitan Opera House during the season of 1890–1891.

13. *New York Times*, December 1, 1903, p. 3.

14. *Ibid.*, December 25, 1903.

15. *New York Tribune*, December 6, 1904, p. 7.

16. *New York Times*, February 17, 1905, p. 5; *New York Tribune*, February 17, 1905, p. 9; William H. Seltsam, comp., *Metropolitan Opera Annals* (New York: The H. W. Wilson Company in association with the Metropolitan Opera Guild, Inc., 1947), p. 152.

17. *New York Times*, January 21, 1906, p. 7.

18. Seltsam, *Metropolitan Opera Annals*, p. 160.

19. *Ibid.*

20. Krehbiel, *Chapters of Opera*, p. 327.

21. Paul Henry Lang, *Music in Western Civilization* (New York: W. W. Norton & Company, Inc., 1941), p. 861.

22. Seltsam, *Metropolitan Opera Annals*, p. 165.

23. Krehbiel, *Chapters of Opera*, p. 344.

24. *Ibid.*, pp. 345–346.

25. Seltsam, *Metropolitan Opera Annals*, p. 568.

26. April 26, 1910.

27. Krehbiel, *Chapters of Opera*, p. 325.

28. *New York Times*, November 26, 1905, p. 2 (Pictorial Section).

29. Interview with Katherine Moran Douglas, April 12, 1960.

30. Interview with Paul Eisler, August 15, 1951.

31. Quaintance Eaton, *Opera Caravan* (New York: Farrar, Straus and Cudahy, 1957), pp. 113–124.

32. *Ibid.*, p. 123.

33. Interview with Katherine Moran Douglas, April 12, 1960.

34. Interview with Paul Eisler, August 15, 1951.

35. Moses, *Heinrich Conried*, p. 265.

36. *Ibid.*, p. 219.

37. Krehbiel, *Chapters of Opera*, p. 357.

38. *Ibid.*, p. 334; Moses, *Heinrich Conried*, p. 250; five of the *Parsifal* performances were at doubled prices.

39. Moses, *Heinrich Conried*, pp. 220–221.

40. *Ibid.*, p. 223.

41. *Ibid.*, p. 225.

42. *Ibid.*, p. 295.

43. *Ibid.*, p. 328.

CHAPTER 8

1. Montrose J. Moses, *Heinrich Conried* (New York: Thomas Y. Crowell and Company, 1916).

2. *Musical America*, October 8, 1898, p. 2.

Bibliography

BOOKS

Alda, Frances. *Men, Women, and Tenors*. Boston: Houghton, Mifflin Company, 1937.

Amory, Cleveland. *Who Killed Society?* New York: Harper and Brothers, 1960.

Anton Seidl, A Memorial By His Friends. New York: Charles Scribner's Sons, 1899.

Arundell, Dennis. *The Critic At The Opera*. London: Ernest Benn Limited, 1957.

Barzun, Jacques. *Pleasures of Music*. New York: W. W. Norton and Company, Inc., 1935.

Bentley, Eric. *Shaw on Music*. Garden City, N.Y.: Doubleday and Company, Inc., 1955.

Blum, Daniel. *A Pictorial Treasury of Opera in America*. New York: Grosset and Dunlap, 1954.

Brockway, Wallace and Herbert Weinstock, *The Opera: A History of its Creation and Performance (1600–1941)*. New York: Simon and Schuster, Inc., 1941.

Caruso, Dorothy. *Enrico Caruso*. New York: Simon and Schuster, Inc., 1945.

Chase, Gilbert. *America's Music; from the Pilgrims to the Present*. New York: McGraw-Hill Book Company, Inc., 1955.

Cross, Milton. *Stories of the Great Operas*. New York: Washington Square Press, Inc., 1961.

Curti, Merle. *The Growth of American Thought*. New York and London: Harper and Brothers, 1943.

Damrosch, Walter. *My Musical Life*. New York: Charles Scribner's Sons, 1926.

Davenport, Marcia. *Of Lena Geyer*. New York: Grosset and Dunlap, 1936.

Davie, Maurice R. *World Immigration*. New York: The Macmillan Company, 1936.

Dent, Edward, J. *Opera*. London: Penguin Books Limited, 1940.

Dillon, Dorothy. *The New York Triumvirate*. New York: Columbia University Press, 1949.

Eaton, Quaintance. *Opera Caravan*. New York: Farrar, Straus and Cudahy, 1957.

Elson, Arthur. *A Critical History of Opera*. Boston: L. C. Page and Company, 1901.

Finck, Henry T. *My Adventures in the Golden Age of Music*. New York: Funk and Wagnalls Company, 1926.

Gatti-Casazza, Giulio. *Memories of Opera*. New York: Charles Scribner's Sons, 1941.

Graf, Max. *Legend of a Musical City*. New York: Philosophical Library, 1945.

Grout, Donald Jay. *A Short History of Opera*. New York: Columbia University Press, 1947.

Haggin, B. H. *Conversations with Toscanini*. Garden City, New York: Doubleday and Company, Inc., 1959.

Henderson, W. J. *What Is Good Music?* New York: Charles Scribner's Sons, 1898.

Heylbut, Rose and Aime Gerber. *Backstage At The Opera*. New York: Thomas Y. Crowell Company, 1937.

Howard, John Tasker. *Our American Music*. New York: Thomas Y. Crowell Company, 1939.

Hurst, P. G. *The Operatic Age of Jean de Reszke*. New York: Robert M. McBride Co., 1959.

Jacob, H. E. *Johann Strauss*. Garden City, New York: Halcyon House, 1948.

Klein, Herman. *The Golden Age of Opera*. New York: E. P. Dutton & Company, 1933.

Knight, Ruth Adams. *Opera Cavalcade*. New York: Metropolitan Opera Guild, Inc., 1938.

Kobbe's Complete Book of Opera. London and New York: Putnam, 1922.

Kolodin, Irving. *The Metropolitan Opera, 1883-1935*. New York: Oxford University Press, 1936.

Krehbiel, Henry Edward. *A Book of Operas*. Garden City, New York: Garden City Publishing Company, Inc., 1909.

_____. *Chapters of Opera*. New York: Henry Holt and Company, 1911.

_____. *More Chapters of Opera*. New York: Henry Holt and Company, 1919.

_____. *More Stories of Famous Operas*. New York: Alfred A. Knopf, 1955.

Lahee, Henry C. *Famous Singers of Today and Yesterday*. Boston: L. C. Page and Company, 1908.

Lavignac, Albert. *The Music Dramas of Richard Wagner and his Festival Theatre in Bayreuth*. New York: Dodd Mead, 1898.

Lehmann, Lilli. *My Path Through Life*. New York and London: G. P. Putnam's Sons, 1914.

Marek, George. *Puccini, a Biography*. New York: Simon and Schuster, Inc., 1951.

Maretzek, Max. *Crotchets and Quavers*. New York: S. French, 1885.

Moore, Frank Leslie. *The Handbook of World Opera*. London: Arthur Barker Limited, 1961.

Moses, Montrose J. *Heinrich Conried*. New York: Thomas Y. Crowell and Company, 1916.

Nevins, Allan (ed.). *The Diary of Philip Hone, 1828-1851*. 2 vols. New York: Dodd, Mead and Company, 1927.

Newman, Ernest. *Stories of the Great Operas*. Garden City, New York: Garden City Publishing Company, Inc., 1928.

Peltz, Mary Ellis. *Introduction to Opera*. New York: Barnes and Noble, Inc., 1956.

_____. *The Magic of the Opera*. New York: Frederick A. Praeger, Inc., in cooperation with the Metropolitan Opera Association, 1960.

_____. *Metropolitan Opera Milestones*. New York: The Metropolitan Opera Guild, Inc., 1944.

Puccini, Giacomo. *Letters*. Philadelphia: J. L. Lippincott Company, 1931.

Rourke, Constance. *The Roots of American Culture*. New York: Harcourt, Brace and Company, 1942.

Salazar, Adolfo. *Music In Our Times*. New York: W. W. Norton and Company, Inc., 1946.

Scholes, Percy A. *The Oxford Companion to Music*. London: Oxford University Press, 1938.

Seltsam, William H. (comp.). *Metropolitan Opera Annals*. New York: The H. W. Wilson Company in association with the Metropolitan Opera Guild, Inc., 1947.

Sheean, Vincent. *First and Last Love*. New York: Random House, 1956.

Slezak, Walter. *What Time's The Next Swan?* Garden City, New York: Doubleday and Company, Inc., 1962.

Social Register. New York: Social Register Association, 1898.

Society List. 1894-1895.

Strauss, Richard. *Correspondence Between Richard Strauss and Hugo von Hofmannsthal, 1907-1918*. New York: Alfred A. Knopf, Inc., 1927.

Taubman, Howard. *The Maestro*. New York: Simon and Schuster, 1951.

Thomas, Theodore. *A Musical Autobiography*. Chicago: The Lakeside Press, 1905.

Victrola Book of the Opera. Camden, New Jersey: RCA Manufacturing Company, Inc., 1929.

Wagner, Alan. *Prima Donnas and Other Wild Beasts*. Larchmont, New York: Argonauts Books, 1961.

Wagner, Richard. *My Life*. New York: Dodd, Mead and Company, 1911.

Webster, Dixon. *The Saga of American Society*. New York: Charles Scribner's Sons, 1937.

Weinstock, Herbert and Wallace Brockway. *The Opera: A History of its Creation and Performance (1600-1941)*. New York: Simon and Schuster, Inc., 1941.

Wilkinson, G. T. *French Operatic Reading*. New York: Oxford University Press, Inc., 1938.

BOOKS: PART OF SERIES

Brown, Henry Collins. *New York in the Elegant Eighties* (*Valentine's Manual of Old New York*, 2 vols.) Hastings on Hudson,

New York: Valentine's Manual, Inc., 1927.

Coad, Oral Sumner and Edwin Mims, Jr. *The American Stage. The Pageant of America,* edited by Ralph Henry Gabriel, Vol. XIV. New Haven: Yale University Press, 1929.

Gabriel, Ralph Henry (ed.). *The Pageant of America.* 14 vols. New Haven: Yale University Press, 1929.

Nevins, Allan. *The Emergence of Modern America 1865–1878.* (A History of American Life, edited by Arthur Meier Schlesinger and Dixon Ryan Fox, Vol VIII.) New York: The Macmillan Company, 1933.

Schlesinger, Arthur Meier. *The Rise of The City.* (A History of American Life, edited by Arthur Meier Schlesinger and Dixon Ryan Fox, Vol. X) New York: The Macmillan Company, 1933.

PERIODICALS

Art Journal for 1875, new series, no. 1. New York: D. Appleton and Company.

Bartlett, Robert. "A Voice From America. The Hope of Literature," *Heraud's New Monthly Magazine,* III (n.d.).

Harper's New Monthly Magazine, vol. 67, no. 402 (November 1883).

High Fidelity (November, 1958).

Musical America (October 8, 1898).

Musical Courier (December 16, 1885).

Musical Courier (February 16, 1887).

Opera News V, No. 21 (March 10, 1941).

Opera News VI, No. 22 (March 16, 1942).

ARTICLES IN COLLECTIONS

Finck, Henry T. Article in *Anton Seidl, A Memorial By His Friends.* New York: Charles Scribner's Sons, 1899.

ENCYCLOPEDIC WORKS

Grove, Sir George, D. C. L. (ed.). *A Dictionary of Music and Musicians.* London: Macmillan and Company, Limited, 1902.

Johnson, Allen (ed.). *Dictionary of American Biography.* New York: Charles Scribner's Sons, 1928.

National Cyclopedia of American Biography. New York: James T. White and Company, 1897.

Neilson, William Allan (ed.). *Webster's Biographical Dictionary.* Springfield, Mass.: G. & C. Merriam Company, 1961.

COLLECTIONS OF PRIVATE PAPERS

Scudder, Marvyn. Collection of manuscripts and papers. New York: Columbia University.

Seidl, Anton. Collection of manuscripts and papers. New York: Columbia University.

NEWSPAPERS

New York Dramatic Mirror, October 27, 1883.

New York Evening Sun, April 27, 1909.

New York Herald, March 22, 1891.

New York Times, 1880–1908.

New York Tribune, 1880–1908.

Index